VARIORUM COLLECTED STUDIES SERIES

Rights, Laws and Infallibility in Medieval Thought

Brian Tierney

Rights, Laws and Infallibility
in Medieval Thought

VARIORUM
1997

This edition copyright © 1997 by Brian Tierney.

Published by VARIORUM
Ashgate Publishing Limited
Gower House, Croft Road,
Aldershot, Hampshire GU11 3HR
Great Britain

Ashgate Publishing Company
Old Post Road,
Brookfield, Vermont 05036–9704
USA

ISBN 0–86078–648–X

British Library CIP Data
Tierney, Brian.
Rights, Laws and Infallibility in Medieval Thought.— (Variorum Collected
Studies Series: 578). 1.Natural Law. 2. Law, medieval. 3. Philosophy,
medieval. I. Title. II. Series: Variorum Collected Studies Series: CS578.
323'.01

US Library of Congress CIP Data
Tierney, Brian.
Rights, Laws and Infallibility in Medieval Thought / Brian Tierney.
  p. cm. — (Variorum Collected Studies Series: CS578.) Includes index.
1. Natural Law—History. 2. Canon Law—History. 3. Popes —Infallibility
—History. I. Title. II. Series: Collected Studies: CS578.
K415.T54   1997   97–2265
387.5'09182'2—dc21   CIP

The paper used in this publication meets the minimum requirements of the
    American National Standard for Information Sciences - Permanence
    of Paper for Printed Library Materials, ANSI Z39.48-1984. ∞ ™

Printed by Galliard (Printers) Ltd
    Great Yarmouth, Norfolk, Great Britain

VARIORUM COLLECTED STUDIES SERIES CS578

CONTENTS

This volume contains x + 340 pages

PREFACE

The papers presented in this collection fall into three main groups. The articles in the first group are concerned with the origins and early development of the idea of natural rights. My interest in this theme grew out of a growing dissatisfaction with the existing state of scholarship in the area. Many modern historians assume that the idea of natural rights was a seventeenth-century innovation, though they do not agree about which particular aspect of seventeenth-century life or thought was of decisive importance. Another widespread school of thought finds an earlier origin for natural rights thinking in the nominalist and voluntarist philosophy of William of Ockham. But none of the current accounts deals adequately (if at all) with the substructure of medieval juridical thought, within which a language of natural rights first grew into existence. The studies printed below were written in the course of my work on a book that attempts to trace the development of natural rights theories from twelfth-century jurisprudence to seventeenth-century political theory, from Gratian to Grotius.[1]

A middle group of miscellaneous articles is concerned with various aspects of medieval law and political thought. They include an overview of some of the modern work on medieval canon law. Also included are studies on the structure of the church, the theory of the state, and the relationship between church and state.

The papers in the last group deal with the history of the doctrine of papal infallibility. The article entitled 'From Thomas of York to William of Ockham' may help to explain how I became engaged with this topic. The paper was originally prepared for a conference in Rome on the general theme of the pope's *sollicitudo omnium ecclesiarum*. I had earlier been interested in Ockham's role in the development of conciliar theory, but in reading his works again, I became aware of another dimension to his thought. In defending earlier papal pronouncements favoring the Franciscan teaching on evangelical poverty, Ockham insisted on the irreformability of papal doctrinal definitions, with implications of papal infallibility. Yet he also believed that Pope John XXII and his immediate successors were all heretics. My awareness of this paradox led to the research that eventually resulted in a book called *Origins of Papal Infallibility, 1150–1350*. The paper included in

---

[1] *The Idea of Natural Rights. Studies on Natural Rights. Natural Law and Church Law. 1150–1625* (Atlanta: Scholars Press, 1997).

this collection with the title 'Origins of Papal Infallibility', presents a summary of the argument of the book. The book itself evoked both praise and criticism. A response to one of the critics is given below in the paper on John Peter Olivi.[2]

Cornell University
December 1996

BRIAN TIERNEY

---

[2] Various other critical approaches to my book are discussed in a *Postscript* added to the second impression of the work. See *Origins of Papal Infallibility, 1150–1350. A Study on the Concepts of Infallibility, Sovereignty and Tradition in the Middle Ages*, 2nd Impression with a postscript (Leiden: E.J. Brill, 1988), 298–327.

ACKNOWLEDGEMENTS

The author and publisher would like to acknowledge copyright and express their appreciation for permission to reproduce the articles in this volume to the following: Hamline University School of Law (I); Imprint Academic (II); Libreria Ateneo Salesiano (III, XV); John Witte, Jr. (IV); Professor Giuseppe Alberigo, *Cristianesimo nella storia* (V); Cambridge University Press (VI); Professor Leonard Boyle, the Vatican Library (VII, X); Medieval Academy of America (VIII); Fordham University Press (IX); The editor, *Concilium* (XI); Sage Publications, Inc. (XII); Augustinian Historical Institute (XIII); University of Toronto Press (XIV); Professor Leonard Swidler, Temple University (XVI); Georgetown University (XVII, XVIII).

PUBLISHER'S NOTE

The articles in this volume, as in all others in the Collected Studies Series, have not been given a new, continuous pagination. In order to avoid confusion, and to facilitate their use where these same studies have been referred to elsewhere, the original pagination has been maintained wherever possible.

Each article has been given a Roman number in order of appearance, as listed in the Contents. This number is repeated on each page and quoted in the index entries.

I

RELIGION AND RIGHTS: A MEDIEVAL PERSPECTIVE*

In this paper I want to present some background material about the interplay of religious concepts and rights theories during the Christian middle ages. We may note at the outset that there always were elements in the Judeo-Christian tradition that could be conducive to the growth of a doctrine of rights, especially the fundamental command to respect the person and property of our neighbor. Ronald Dworkin pointed out that the necessary basis of all other rights is an "abstract right to concern and respect taken to be fundamental and axiomatic."[1] The axiom entered the mainstream of medieval jurisprudence in the first words of Gratian's Decretum, the foundation of the whole subsequent structure of Western canon law. "The human race is ruled by two means, namely by natural law and usages. The law of nature is what is contained in the Law and the Gospel, by which each is ordered to do to another what he wants done to himself and is forbidden to do to another what he does not want done to himself."[2] Or in modern language, one might say, "Show concern and respect."

But if the notion of individual rights is implicit in Christian tradition, it has not always been explicit. Developed in one way, Christian thought can lead to intolerance and persecution, to a denial of the rights that we should consider most basic.[3] Developed in another way, Christianity can lead to an ideal of self-abnegation that implies an abandonment of all personal rights. Consider St. Benedict's instructions for his monks. "They should have absolutely nothing, not anything . . . indeed it is not allowed to them to have their own bodies or wills in their own power."[4] This seems to leave no room for any assertion of individual rights. So I don't want to suggest that in the Christian tradition there is some ineluctable development that leads inevitably from Luke to Locke—not with St. Benedict standing in the way. My argument is a more limited one, that in a specific, contin-

* © 1988 The Catholic University of America

1. R. Dworkin, Taking Rights Seriously XV (1977).
2. Gratian, Concordance of Discordant Canons (Decretum) 1140, Dist 1.
3. This theme is explored in Professor Noonan's paper in the present volume: Noonan, *Principled or Pragmatic Foundations for the Freedom of Conscience*, 5 J. L. and Relig. 203 (1987).
4. Rule of St. Benedict Ch. 33.

gent historical context, Western Europe in the twelfth century, the interactions of religion and society did in fact form a new kind of Christian culture, a sort of seedbed in which theories of human rights and civil rights could take root and flourish.

There are three aspects of medieval religion that I want to consider. First, and fundamental, is the concept of each human being as a person, entitled to consideration as a person, capable of moral discernment and self-determination. I shall suggest that the specific development of this concept of personality in the jurisprudence of the twelfth century contributed significantly to the whole future Western tradition of individual natural rights.

Second, we have to consider the church not just as a collection of separate individuals but as a corporate community, sustaining a life of its own, apart from the secular power, sometimes opposed to secular government, sometimes limiting the power of the state. This role of the medieval church in impeding the rise of royal absolutism is perhaps its most obvious contribution to the growth of Western rights concepts.

But there is still a third, more subtle yet significant aspect of Christian thought—the relation between the individual Christian and the church conceived of as a united whole, a mystical body. The point here is that the twelfth-century theology of the mystical body influenced twelfth century law on the structure of corporate communities in general, including corporate political communities. So, in considering individual rights within a medieval community, one can pursue a chain of argument that begins with abstract theological concepts and finishes with a consideration of very practical, down to earth documents like Magna Carta. It seemed appropriate to include some brief discussion of Magna Carta at the end of this paper, because, although it is only one of many such charters of liberties that were issued in many parts of medieval Europe, it has acquired a symbolic significance in our legal tradition; and if one is concerned specifically with the interplay of religion and rights, it is fitting to remember that the first clause of Magna Carta declares, "The English church shall be free and shall have its rights entire. . . ."

But let us begin with my first main theme, individual personality and the concept of natural rights. There exists now a substantial modern literature exploring the new individualism or personalism or humanism of twelfth-century religious culture. (One good work of synthesis, is called precisely *The Discovery of the Individual.*)[5] Most recently Harold Berman has shown how a new concern with individual intention and individual will helped to shape the whole content of twelfth-century canon law, which he properly describes as the first Western legal system.[6] Yet there has been almost no consideration of how twelfth-century jurisprudence contributed to the concept of individual natural rights. One can read through a standard work like Leo Strauss's on the history of natural right without ever being made aware that there was a twelfth century at all.[7]

The origin of natural rights theories is usually dated much later, often in the seventeenth century. About 1610, for instance, Suarez defined the word *ius* not as objective law but as subjective right, a kind of power or faculty (*facultas*) inhering in a person;[8] and such definitions become common among later authors. In an influential work of twenty years ago, C. B. MacPherson associated these seventeenth-century rights theories with the rise of early modern capitalism. He described such theories as a form of "possessive individualism," the ideology of a property-owning class that wanted only to legitimize its own power.[9]

Other scholars have found an earlier origin for rights theories in late medieval nominalism. Some emphasize the contribution of Jean Gerson who defined *ius* as "a faculty or power (*facultas seu potestas*) . . . in accordance with right reason" Gerson, in turn, is usually seen as dependent on the great fourteenth-century nominalist philosopher, William of Ockham. A philosophy that attributed reality only to individuals, and that emphasized will rather than reason, naturally led to a doctrine of individual rights, it is suggested. Michel Villey, in particular, has argued that, before the fourteenth century, the expression *ius naturale* was always associated with a concept of cosmic harmony and that Ockham instituted a "semantic revolution" when he applied the term to a power of the individual person. Villey regarded this as a lamentable departure from a sounder earlier tradition, a result of "egoism" and "distorted Christian morality."[10]

5. C. MORRIS, THE DISCOVERY OF THE INDIVIDUAL, 1060-1200 (1972).
6. H. BERMAN, LAW AND REVOLUTION: THE FORMATION OF THE WESTERN LEGAL TRADITION (1983).
7. L. STRAUSS, NATURAL RIGHT AND HISTORY (1950). Strauss leaps from Plato and Aristotle to Hooker and Hobbes with only the briefest glance at Thomas Aquinas on the way. He does not consider medieval jurisprudence at all.
8. I DE LEGIBUS, § 2.5.
9. C.B. MACPHERSON, THE POLITICAL THEORY OF POSSESSIVE INDIVIDUALISM: HOBBES TO LOCKE (1962).
10. M. VILLEY, LA FORMATION DE LA PENSEÉ JURIDIQUE MODERNE (1968). *Idem, La*

But Villey could reach this conclusion only by ignoring all the canonistic jurisprudence of the preceding centuries. Gratian, we saw, defined *ius naturale* as the Golden Rule; "Do unto others as you would have them do unto you." This might imply that others have rights, but Gratian was still using the old language of precept, of *mitzvah* that Professor Cover explained in his paper. Gratian, however, went on to quote texts that gave other definitions of *ius naturale*, and his early commentators undertook to classify and explore all the possible significances of the term. Among their definitions we often encounter the language that modern historians have seen as a fourteenth-century innovation—*ius naturale* defined as a faculty, power, force (*facultas, potestas, vis*) of the human personality.[11] The greatest of the Decretists, Huguccio (c. 1190), distinguished carefully between *ius naturale* as a rule of objective law and as a subjective power of the soul, and he insisted that the latter meaning was the proper one. Huguccio was concerned precisely with the concept of human personality as moral and self-determining that I emphasized at the outset.[12] It was this already formed canonistic language that Ockham inherited. Ockham deployed this language for his own purposes in the Franciscan poverty disputes of the fourteenth century and Gerson in turn transmitted it to the first early modern rights theorists. The subject requires much more investigation, but I believe such an investigation would establish that the first theories of individual natural rights were formed in the matrix of twelfth-century juridicial humanism.

Let us turn now to my second major topic, the church considered not just as a collection of individuals, but as an ordered community, sustaining its own corporate life, independent of the secular power. Our First Amendment reminds us of this salutary arrangement and continually gives rise to new problems about civil rights, but the principle involved is no eighteenth-century invention. It goes back to the beginnings of Christianity when Jesus said "Render to Caesar the things that are Caesar's and to God the things that are God's." At first the Church grew up as an alien society within the Roman state, with its own separate institutions apart from the state. When the em-

---

genègese du droit subjectif chez Guillaume d'Occam, ARCHIVES DE PHILOSOPHIE DE DROIT 97 (1964).

11. For some examples of such usages *see* R. WEIGAND, DIE NATURRECHTSLEHRE DER LEGISTEN UND DEKRETISTEN VON IRNERIUS BIS ACCURSIUS 145, 197, 209, 314 (1967).

12. *Id.* at 215. A more detailed appraisal of Villey's views is presented in my paper, Tierney, *Ockham, Villey, and the Origin of Rights Theories*, to appear in the forthcoming FESTSCHRIFT for Harold Berman.

perors became Christian in the fourth century, and subsequently the whole Empire, there was indeed a possibility for a time that the Church might become just a sort of Department of Religion in an imperial bureaucratic theocracy. But instead, the old tradition of autonomy was vigorously reasserted—for instance in the striking phrases of St. Ambrose (c. 380), "Palaces belong to the emperor, churches to the priesthood," and again, "Where matters of faith are concerned bishops judge Christian emperors, not emperors bishops." A century later Pope Gelasius declared, in a famous phrase, "There are *two* means by which the world is chiefly governed, the sacred authority of the priesthood and the royal power." In between, St. Augustine had launched his haunting image of the two cities, a symbolic way of affirming that the Christian's ultimate allegiance could never be to the powers of this world.[13]

These early texts were not forgotten. On the contrary, they exploded into life again in the papal reform movement at the end of the eleventh century—the papal revolution as Professor Berman rightly calls it—when the church was threatened by a new kind of imperial theocracy, based this time on the German monarchy. Against this threat Pope Gregory VII proclaimed as a sort of warcry his call for the freedom of the church—*libertas ecclesiae*—the phrase echoes again and again in his letters. In the ensuing struggle, neither side could completely dominate the other. And so a kind of duality was permanently built into Western society. The church remained autonomous, claiming specific rights for itself and its members, always insisting that there was a whole sphere of human thought and action which was in principle outside the legitimate power of the temporal government. When this tradition was challenged by new forms of divine right monarchy in the sixteenth and seventeenth centuries, the challenge evoked new forms of protest—one of them eventually crystallized in our First Amendment.

To understand the importance of all this we must bear in mind that the medieval situation was highly unusual. Theocratic absolutism—the rule of a divine emperor, a sacred monarch—is a very common form of human government. Karl Wittfogel described dozens of examples from all around the world in his book *Oriental Despotism*— ancient China, Japan, India, Egypt, Peru, Iran. But, in medieval Christendom, the resistance of the church always prevented national

---

13. For a brief introduction to these texts and the whole problem of medieval church-state relations see B. TIERNEY, CRISIS OF CHURCH AND STATE 1050-1300 (1964) [hereinafter Tierney].

monarchies from congealing into theocratic despotisms in which all individual rights would have been extinguished. The other side of the coin is that medieval kings were always strong enough to prevent the rise of an absolute, theocratic papacy when the popes were tempted to assert such a role for themselves.

The situation had many consequences both in theory and in practice. In theory, it was virtually impossible within this tradition to construct a doctrine of pure absolutism. The tradition shaped the thought even of those who tried to escape from it. I thought of this recently while re-reading Thomas Hobbes, perhaps the pre-eminent theorist of absolutism in the western tradition. Hobbes of course attacked the autonomy of the church as destructive of sovereignty. An absolute state, he wrote, could not tolerate alongside the temporal sovereign another "ghostly authority," "another kingdom, as it were a kingdom of fairies," to which men also owed allegiance. The reason was plain. If any independent spiritual power could claim the right to determine what was sin it would soon challenge the right to declare what was law.[14] It is so true of course. That is why Americans of various religious persuasions are constantly challenging laws that they perceive as legalizing sin.

Hobbes was trying to be as absolute as he could. Subjects had no rights, he said, except in areas that the sovereign chose not to control, that he "pretermitted." Hobbes mentioned as obvious examples the subjects' rights freely to contract with one another, to choose their own abodes, to bring up their children as they saw fit.[15] Apparently he could not conceive of a sovereign who would meddle with such things. But these are the very sinews of a modern totalitarian regime—economic regulation, internal passports to control freedom of movement, indoctrination of the young through state control of all education. Hobbes went on to explain that the power of his sovereign was unlimited, but then added "otherwise than as he himself is the subject of God and bound thereby to observe the laws of nature." Later he observed that the laws of nature could be summed up in one sentence, "Do unto others as you would have them do unto you."[16] So our basic axiom from Scripture and canon law has crept in by a back door. It may be that Hobbes was really an atheist and that such phrases are mere rhetoric. The point is, Hobbes was using the only rhetoric available to him and the only one likely to persuade the audi-

---

14. T. Hobbes, LEVIATHAN, 29.
15. 2 *Id.* at 21.
16. 2 *Id.* at 21, 26.

ence he wanted to persuade. Whatever his own religion, he was saturated with the preconceptions of a Christian society. And in that world of thought, the author of *Leviathan* could not even imagine our modern post-Christian monster, the totalitarian state.

But I must get back to the Middle Ages. The persistent tension between church and state in that epoch not only impeded the growth of absolutist doctrine. It stimulated new thinking about constitutional rights. The most obvious one that came to be affirmed as a direct result of the medieval conflicts between popes and kings was the right of consent to government. When Pope Gregory VII tried to depose King Henry IV in 1076, Henry declared that he was "King, by the grace of God." A papal supporter, Manegold of Lautenbach, contesting this assertion, offered one of the first theories of government based on consent and contract. At one point he inelegantly compared the king to a hired swineherd who was removable by his master, the people, if he failed to attend to his duties. More formally, Manegold wrote, "If (the king) breaks the contract by which he was elected . . . he has absolved the people from their duty of submission to him."[17] It was not only papal supporters who used the argument from consent. When, later on, the popes grew over-ambitious and began to claim that the power of all kings was derived from them royalists found it expedient to use the same argument. John of Paris wrote (c. 1300) that a king did not derive his power from the pope but from God "and the people who elect or consent."[18] A little later Marsilius of Padua, a more bitter anti-papalist, framed a pure doctrine of government by consent without any element of divine right.

Marsilius' populist, anti-papalist, political theory was probably influenced in part by the practice of Italian city-state republics. But there is an element of irony here. It was as allies of the papacy in the church-state conflicts of the twelfth century that the communes of Northern Italy, which would grow into the great city-states of the Renaissance, first won their freedom from imperial control. And it was in those cities that the concept of civic rights—rights of citizenship—was first elaborately formulated.

This mention of communes and cities leads to my third major topic, the relationship of individual and community in medieval religious thought and in actual practice. The standard Marxist criticism of Western rights theories is that they have always been based on self-

---

17. Manegold of Lauterbach, in TIERNEY, *supra* note 13 at 78-80.
18. TIERNEY *supra* note 13, at 78-80, 206-210.

ish individualism, "not on the association of man with man but on their separation." But medieval thought about rights was not based on any such notion. It involved an awareness of the balance between individual and community, one might say, of a creative tension between them.

This tension goes back to the beginnings of Christianity. Consider two texts from Paul's epistle to the Romans. In *Romans* 15 we read, "Each one of us will render an account of himself before Christ. . . ." There is no vision of human destiny more starkly individualistic than that of the last judgment that haunted medieval minds, when each soul would stand alone, naked, trembling before the divine judge. But now consider *Romans* 12, "We, although many, are one body in Christ," and again, "We are members one of another." Christian individualism was balanced by this vision of the church as one body, united to Christ as head, a body in which the members could help and sustain one another, spiritually through their prayers, and corporally through works of charity.

This tension in Christian thought was mirrored by a tension in twelfth century social reality. So far, I have referred mainly to the individualism or humanism of that age. But this is a rather new understanding of twelfth century culture. Fifty years ago it was commonly held that medieval people hardly had any sense of individuality, little awareness of themselves, except as members of corporate groups. We are now beginning to see that there is truth in both points of view. The twelfth century produced both brilliant self-aware individuals and an extraordinary, vigorous growth of new forms of corporate life—monasteries, cathedral chapters, collegiate churches, communes, boroughs, guilds, confraternities. Moreover, the very persons we most readily think of as vividly self-aware individuals were often associated with the growth of new kinds of communities—Bernard of Clairvaux and the Cistercians, Peter Abelard and the schools of Paris that grew into the University, Francis of Assisi and the vast Franciscan Order.

The combination of intense individualism and intense corporatism may seem paradoxical but perhaps it is not really so. Human beings become fully persons in intimate social intercourse with one another, not in desert-island isolation. Trying to explain the phenomenon, I wrote recently, "Perhaps it is only when persons become more sharply aware of themselves as individuals that they need to reflect consciously on the rules by which they form themselves into organized groups."[19] My point was that the actual growth of corporate life in the twelfth century was accompanied by a great new body of juridical thought about the nature of corporations, especially from the canonists. Here again, as so often, medieval canon law was an area of interaction between abstract theology and day to day social life; for the new law of corporations, which affected the actual conduct of medieval groups, was itself influenced by the theology of the mystical body. This was pointed out long ago by Maitland, the greatest of legal historians.[20] More recently Ernst Kantorowicz has explored in detail the interplay of theological and juridical concepts in medieval thought about the structure of corporate groups.[21] One result of this interplay was that the medieval corporation was often conceived of in a new way, not simply as an association of members but as an organic union of a head and members. Like Christ and the church, so too bishop and cathedral chapter, abbot and monks, mayor and corporation, eventually king and parliament. The same pattern of thought and practice keeps recurring. Moreover medieval corporation law as developed by the canonists was intensely concerned with the rights of individuals within corporate communities. A cathedral canon, for instance, by virtue of his membership in the corporate cathedral chapter, held some rights in common with the other members, but his rights also included an individual right in his own prebend—a *ius in re*—which he could defend at law if necessary. As Maitland put it, with his usual epigrammatic force, "The corporation aggregate was almost resolved into a mere collection of corporations sole."[22]

Again there was a link between these legal doctrines—which in turn are related to Christian theological concepts—and the growth of civil liberties in day to day life. For the vast extension of civil liberties that occurred in the twelfth century came through the grant of charters of rights to corporate communities, churches, boroughs and cities for instance; but often the rights were of a kind that could actually be exercised only by individuals, e.g. the right of a merchant to come and go freely. Earlier medieval society had certainly recognized individual rights, especially feudal rights, but there was nothing liberal or egalitarian about them. A baron's right was typically an exemption

19. B. TIERNEY, RELIGION, LAW AND THE GROWTH OF CONSTITUTIONAL THOUGHT 37 (1982).
20. POLLOCK AND MAITLAND. THE HISTORY OF ENGLISH LAW 495 (2d ed. 1898). "Now the idea of the Church as the mystical body of Christ has had an important influence on the growth of the law of corporations. . . ."
21. E. KANTOROWICZ, THE KING'S TWO BODIES (1957).
22. POLLOCK & MAITLAND, *supra* note 20, at 507.

from royal jurisdiction, a right to dominate others. One of the most cherished of feudal rights was the right to have a gallows. But when rights or liberties, exemptions from official meddling in certain areas of life, began to be granted to corporate communities, they took on a new tone and quality and became diffused through much broader classes of the population. From the twelfth century onward thousands of urban communities acquired such rights through purchase or negotiation or sometimes outright rebellion—rights like freedom from arbitrary taxation and arbitrary arrest, freedom from servile dues, the right to be tried by one's own townfolk in a local town court, and the right to elect a mayor and other city officials. This was rich soil where later more generalized theories of civil rights would take root and grow. As Alan Harding observed, "Urban liberties gave content to the idea of individual liberty."[23]

Perhaps we can even fit Magna Carta into this context of broadening civic liberties. There have been many interpretations of that enigmatic document. Some historians have seen it as a noble charter of national liberty; others' at the opposite extreme, interpret it as a selfish contrivance of reactionary feudal barons. Many clauses of Magna Carta do deal explicitly with the barons' feudal claims, selfish claims if you will. But others contain the great broad principles that have echoed down the centuries in our common law. "No free man shall be taken or imprisoned . . . save by the lawful judgment of his peers and by the law of the land." "To no one will we sell, to no one will we deny or delay right or justice." The interpretations that dwell on the Charter's more generous provisions often emphasize the role of Stephen Langton, the great theologian and Archbishop of Canterbury, who negotiated on behalf of the barons. But recently J. C. Holt, while acknowledging Langton's influence, suggested a new way of looking at the Charter. He sees it as a vast communal privilege, inspired in part by the privileges already granted to various other corporate communities like boroughs and cities. "Just as communal liberties had been won by a sworn association whereby citizens pledged themselves to fight for their liberties, so the barons pledged themselves to fight for the liberties of the realm." Holt adds that the barons "envisaged the establishment of one great 'commune of all the land'."[24] He suggests that if we look at Magna Carta in this way—with reference to earlier communal charters of liberties—we can ex-

---

23. Harding, *Political Liberty in the Middle Ages*, SPECULUM 442 (July 1980).
24. J.C. HOLT, MAGNA CARTA 48-49 (1965).

plain without anachronism how the apparently "progressive" ideas of the Charter could naturally have found expression in a primarily feudal document of the earlier thirteenth century.

But a problem remains. Could anyone's mind, around 1200, have made the conceptual leap involved in considering the whole people of a realm as a corporate entity comparable to the members of a city commune? Holt mentions in this connection the Annals of Dunstable Priory which refer to Magna Carta as a charter "concerning the liberties of the realm." But this is still vague. The Annals do not assert that the whole realm could be conceived of as analogous to a single incorporated city. It is difficult to say anything fresh about Magna Carta at this date, but perhaps I can add another shred of information here. We now know a good deal about Richard de Mores, the Prior of Dunstable at the time of Magna Carta. In his earlier days he had been a famous canonist, known to the law schools of Bologna as Ricardus Anglicus; and in one of his canonistic commentaries, discussing the origin of royal authority, Ricardus wrote, "The corporate body of a city can confer jurisdiction . . . how much more the corporate body of a whole realm." It is precisely the comparison that Holt suggests might have been present in people's minds.[25]

Still Ricardus is only a witness to the *mentalité* of the times. If we are looking for an intersection of religious ideas and rights concepts in Magna Carta the most important figure is still Stephen Langton who was actually there at Runnymede helping to negotiate the terms of the Charter. We are learning more about Langton too. His role in the drafting of Magna Carta was first strongly emphasized, perhaps exaggerated, by Kate Norgate. She wrote, ". . . the terms were drawn up by Stephen Langton with the concurrence of the other bishops who were at hand, and of the few lay barons, on either side, who were statesmen. . . ."[26] This view has been contested. But most contemporary scholarly work attributes a substantial, though not exclusive, role to Langton in shaping the final version of Magna Carta. Much of Langton's earlier theological work remains unedited, but we do know something about the views on law and political thought that

---

25. On the text of Ricardus see B. TIERNEY, RELIGION 22 (1982). The phrase *communia totius terrae* actually occurs in MAGNA CARTA Clause 61. Holt renders this as "the commune of the whole land" in accordance with his own understanding of the Charter (p. 335). But *communia* is usually translated more neutrally as "community." *See, e.g.,* STEPHENSON AND MARCHAM, SOURCES OF ENGLISH CONSTITUTIONAL HISTORY 125 (1937), ". . . the community of the entire country . . ."

26. K. NORGATE, JOHN LACKLAND 234 (1922).

he expressed in them.[27] Like Richard de Mores, Langton referred to the people of a realm as forming one corporate community, though he envisaged them not as an enlarged city but rather as a miniature church, a *congregatio fidelium*—as behooved an archbishop after all. Langton maintained that the duty of a king was to defend the rights of layfolk and the peace of the church.[28] He wrote that the clergy should always espouse the cause of the poor "because the blood of the poor is the blood of Christ."[29] Some parts of Magna Carta are easier to understand if we try to see them through the eyes of a Stephen Langton and not just through those of a resentful feudal baron.

It remains true obviously, that the grant to free men excluded a whole population of serfs; but the point is that the whole existing political order was now being defined as a structure of rights, and the principle was capable of indefinite extension. Moreover the process did not take so very long. Already by the fourteenth century, Parliament redefined Magna Carta's "free man" as any person "of whatever estate or condition." And Parliament also redefined the vague "law of the land" as meaning "due process of law"—already the classic phrase that has become so familiar to us.[30] No doubt Magna Carta came to mean many things that its framers had never intended. No doubt a myth of Magna Carta grew up. But, as Holt again has observed, "The myth . . . was part of the document's potential." And it was so because Magna Carta emerged from an exceptionally rich and fertile medieval Christian culture. To understand documents like Magna Carta in all their complexity we need to know something about the structure of medieval communities in general, and about the rights of individuals within those communities, and even about the all-embracing vision of the church as a Christian community within which particular medieval institutions took shape.

We have considered some complicated aspects of medieval thought. But the points I have made can be summed up in a few simple sentences. In the twelfth century a concern for the moral integrity of human personality led to the first stirrings of natural rights theories. An autonomous church asserted its own rights and limited the

---

27. The best introduction is still F.M. POWICKE, STEPHEN LANGTON (1928).
28. Quoted in J.W. BALDWIN, MASTERS, PRINCES AND MERCHANTS: THE SOCIAL VIEWS OF PETER THE CHANTER AND HIS CIRCLE 111 (1970). "Just as it is for the clergy to elect a bishop, as it is for all the faithful of the realm . . . to establish for themselves a ruler who may guard the rights of layfolk and the peace of the church."
29. G. DUBY, THE THREE ORDERS: FEUDAL SOCIETY IMAGINED 320 (1978).
30. F. THOMPSON, MAGNA CARTA: ITS ROLE IN THE MAKING OF THE ENGLISH CONSTITUTION 69 (1948).

power of the state so that it never became truly absolute. Individual civic rights grew up within a context of communal institutions that were shaped in part by the growing law of the church. These points have broader implications. They suggest that Western rights theories did not have their origin either in early modern capitalism or in late medieval nominalism; rather they are rooted more deeply in the tradition of Christian humanism that has shaped much of our political culture.

II

ORIGINS OF NATURAL RIGHTS LANGUAGE: TEXTS AND CONTEXTS, 1150–1250

Modern histories of natural rights theories usually place the origin of such doctrines in the late medieval or early modern periods; rights theories are commonly associated with the rise of nominalist philosophy or the beginnings of an entrepreneurial economy. In this paper I want to suggest that the humanistic jurisprudence of the twelfth century, especially the writings of the medieval Decretists, may provide a better starting point for investigating the origins of natural rights theories than either fourteenth-century nominalism or the nascent capitalism of the seventeenth century.[1] To write a full history of natural rights theories, even for the modern period, would be a formidable task. Ever since the days of Hobbes and Locke (at least) the concept of individual rights has been of central importance in Western thought. But also, from the seventeenth century to the present day, rights theories have been persistently attacked, and from many different points of view. The result is paradoxical. On the level of international politics a professed regard for 'human rights' is mandatory; we argue mainly about which regimes are most cynical in purporting to defend them. But, on the level of philosophical discourse, the existence of natural or human rights is often dismissed altogether. According to Alisdair MacIntyre, for instance, 'there are no such rights and belief in them is one with belief in witches and in unicorns'.[2]

A historian cannot hope to solve all the problems that are raised in this area by modern jurists and moral philosophers.[3] But modern discourse about rights is often associated with an implicit or sometimes quite explicit set of assumptions about the history of rights theories. So perhaps a historical approach can contribute something, at least peripherally, to the ongoing arguments. MacIntyre himself asserts,

---

[1] The present paper is an attempt to develop further an approach to natural rights theories that I suggested in two recent critical articles: Brian Tierney, 'Tuck on Rights: Some Medieval Problems', *History of Political Thought*, IV (1983), pp. 429–41 and Brian Tierney, 'Villey, Ockham, and the Origin of Individual Rights', in *The Weightier Matters of the Law. A Tribute to Harold J. Berman*, ed. T. Witte and F.S. Alexander (Atlanta, 1988), pp. 1–31.

[2] A. MacIntyre, *After Virtue* (Notre Dame, 2nd edn., 1984), p. 69.

[3] For an extensive bibliography see R. Martin and J.W. Nickel, 'Bibliography on the Nature and Foundations of Rights, 1947–1977', *Political Theory*, VI (1978), pp. 395–413. Anthologies on rights which have appeared since 1977 often include some historical material. Among them are *Rights*, ed. D. Lyons (Belmont, 1978); *Human Rights*, ed. E. Kamenka and A.E. Tay (New York, 1978); *Bioethics and Human Rights*, ed. E.L. Bandman (Boston, 1979); *The Human Rights Reader*, ed. W. Laqueur and B. Rubin (New York, 1979); *Philosophy of Human Rights*, ed. A.S. Rosenbaum (Westport, 1980); *Human Rights: Nomos XXII*, ed. J.R. Pennock and J.W. Chapman (New York, 1981). R. Martin and J.W. Nickel, 'Recent Work on the Concept of Rights', *American Philosophical Quarterly*, XVII (1980), pp. 165–80 provides an overview of some main trends of modern thought.

Reprinted from *History of Political Thought*, vol. no. 10 (1989), pp. 615–46. © Imprint Academic, Exeter, UK.

mistakenly, that no language existed in which the concept of a right could be expressed before about 1400. Leo Strauss and C.B. Macpherson and Ian Shapiro, in different ways, all base criticisms of modern rights theories in part on their understanding, or misunderstanding, of a supposed seventeenth-century origin of those theories.[4] Often natural rights theories are treated as a modern aberration from an older, perhaps sounder, tradition of natural law. Jürgen Habermas, for instance, has written of a 'positivization' (*Positivierung*) of classical natural law in the modern era. The older tradition, he explains, laid down norms for virtuous living; the new doctrine of natural rights allowed 'a neutral sphere of personal choice' in which each individual could egotistically pursue his own advantage.[5] In this new way of thinking, a right was a freedom to act in any way that was not explicitly prohibited. Habermas refers here specifically to Hobbes. Earlier, Georges de Lagarde had made a similar point in discussing Ockham's rights theories; he found in Ockham's philosophy of natural law 'a zone of human autonomy' where, because nothing was prohibited, all was licit, and where human freedom could be exercised without restraint. 'Là, òu elle ne défend rien, tout est licite.'[6] This notion that *ius naturale*, 'natural right', could define an area of human liberty as well as a body of restrictive law was of central importance in the emergence of modern rights language.

Habermas and de Lagarde both drew a contrast between the modern doctrine of natural rights and the thought of Thomas Aquinas, in whose work the older tradition of natural law found a classical expression. This observation, a commonplace in much recent writing on natural law theories, is true enough so far as it goes; but it has led to a radical error of periodization in most modern writing on the history of natural rights. John Finnis observed that, since there is no doctrine of subjective rights in Aquinas and there is such a doctrine in Suarez, a 'watershed' must be situated somewhere between the thirteenth century and the seventeenth.[7] But this view rests on the fallacy, widespread among modern jurists and philosophers who are not medieval specialists, that if an idea is not to be found in Aquinas it is not really a medieval idea at all. Another explanation is possible. It may be that a juristic, distinctively non-Aristotelian language of natural rights had grown up before Aquinas, that Aquinas did not choose to assimilate such language into his Christian–Aristotelian synthesis, but that it did enter the mainstream of Western political thought through other channels. This is the thesis I want to explore.

---

[4] Leo Strauss, *Natural Right and History* (Chicago, 1950); C.B. Macpherson, *The Political Theory of Possessive Individualism: Hobbes to Locke* (Oxford, 1964); I. Shapiro, *The Evolution of Rights in Liberal Theory* (Cambridge, 1986). In a methodological article, 'Realism in the Study of the History of Ideas', *History of Political Thought*, III (1982), pp. 535–78, Shapiro comments, 'If we want to understand our own beliefs as fully and critically as possible it is essential . . . to see where our beliefs come from and what functions they serve in the contemporary world' (p. 577). I agree with this approach; but it only emphasizes the need to get our history straight. Shapiro writes as though the world began in the seventeenth century.

[5] J. Habermas, *Theory and Practice*, trans. J. Viertel (Boston, 1974), p. 84.

[6] G. de Lagarde, *Naissance de l'esprit laique au déclin du Moyen Age*, VI (Paris, 1946), pp. 122, 157.

[7] J. Finnis, *Natural Law and Natural Rights* (Oxford, 1980), pp. 206–7.

The Question of Origins

Natural rights theories seem to be a distinctively Western invention. (It would be hard to imagine a Confucian Hobbes or Locke.) But such theories have not been characteristic even of Western culture at all times and places.

Whether the ancient Greeks had any concept of subjective rights at all is debated; certainly they had no doctrine of natural rights.[8] (Sophocles' Antigone did not assert a God-given right; she found herself bound by an inexorable law.) Stoic thinkers conceived of a divine reason pervading and ordering the whole cosmos, and they envisioned a natural law inherent in humankind as one aspect of this pantheistic world-view. Diogenes Laertius held that 'our undivided natures are parts of the nature of the whole universe', and Cicero wrote of a *vis innata*, an innate force in humans through which they could discern the law of nature, *ius naturae*, that they were bound to observe.[9] But all this is far from a doctrine of individual natural rights.

It is the same with classical Roman law. Julius Paulus gave an objective definition of *ius* as 'what is right and good' — or, as a modern author puts it, 'the what's fair' — and similar language was used to explain the primary meaning of *ius* by Aquinas a thousand years later.[10] Classical jurists, like Stoic philosophers, knew of an objective natural law, accessible to human reason, but they did not derive from it a doctrine of subjective natural rights. In early Christian thought too, Paul wrote of a law written on the hearts of men; but he did not assert that 'all men are endowed by their Creator with certain inalienable rights'.[11]

---

[8] For differing views on the ancient Greeks' concept of rights see J.W. Jones, *The Law and Legal Theory of the Greeks* (Aalen, 1977), p. 191; M. Ostwald, *Nomos and the Beginnings of Athenian Democracy* (Oxford, 1969), p. 113; K.J. Dover, *Greek Popular Morality in the Time of Plato and Aristotle* (Berkeley and Los Angeles, 1974), p. 157.

[9] Diogenes Laertius, *Lives*, VII, 88; Cicero, *De Inventione*, II.22.65. On Stoic concepts of natural law in humans see M.C. Horowitz, 'The Stoic Synthesis of the Idea of Natural Law in Man: Four Themes', *Journal of the History of Ideas*, XXXV (1974), pp. 3–16. For Stoic influence in the Middle Ages see G. Verbeke, *The Presence of Stoicism in Medieval Thought* (Washington, DC, 1983). Some Stoic thinkers, especially the later ones, found a place for conscience and choice in their systems, but choice meant only a capacity to accept or reject a fate that was already predetermined. Seneca wrote 'fata volentem ducunt nolentem trahunt' (*Ep.* 107. 11).

[10] *Digest*, 1.1.11. Other definitions followed, but they did not include the idea of *ius* as subjective right. For Aquinas see *Summa Theologiae*, 2.2ae.57.1. Ulpian gave a definition of *ius naturale* (often quoted in medieval sources) as 'what nature has taught all animals' (*Digest*, 1.1.1.3).

[11] Perhaps the crispest statement denying the existence of any ancient classical or Christian doctrine of human rights is that of Kenneth Minogue, 'The idea of human rights is as modern as the internal combustion engine', in Laqueur and Rubin, *Human Rights Reader*, p. 3. See also H.L.A. Hart, 'Bentham on Legal Rights', reprinted in *Rights*, ed. Lyons, p. 126, 'The concept of a right, legal or moral, is not to be found in the work of the Greek philosophers . . . Jurists of stature have even held that . . . Roman law never achieved a clear concept of a legal right. Thus Maine wrote . . . "the clear conception of a legal right . . . belongs distinctively to the modern world." ' The most systematic argument asserting a lack of any concept of subjective rights among the ancient Greeks, the classical Roman lawyers and Aquinas is presented in the numerous works of M. Villey. His views are summed up in *Le droit et les droits de l' homme*

Many scholars have suggested that a doctrine of natural rights was always implicit in Judeo-Christian teaching on the dignity and moral autonomy of each individual human person. Such a concept of human personality can indeed provide a fitting basis for a theory of natural rights; and, of course, it does not nowadays have to be expressed in terms of Jewish or Christian theology (though religious cultures that regard individuation as illusory are not likely to develop rights theories spontaneously). But, if a doctrine of rights has always been implicit in Judeo-Christian thought, it has certainly not always been explicit.[12] Merely calling attention to Judeo-Christian values does not solve the problem of origins. The historian's task remains — to understand the particular situation in which an old ideal of human dignity could first find expression in a new theory of natural rights. There are two basic questions to be answered. When did the phrase *ius naturale*, which traditionally meant cosmic harmony or objective justice or natural moral law, begin to acquire also the sense of a subjective natural right? and what cultural context, what set of contingent historical circumstances, made the shift of meaning possible and acceptable?

The two questions are really inseparable. Nowadays we are often reminded that, when we purport to study the history of political ideas, we are really concerned — or should be — with political language, with the history of political discourse. Hence our first task is to understand the context that sustains a particular style of discourse and renders it intelligible. Different modern authors dwell on different kinds of context.[13] Some metahistorians write as though the study of language itself is enough, as though language constitutes a magic kingdom of its own, a context sufficient to itself. Other critics, more sensibly I think, insist that we can and should situate language in a real world of life and action. In any case, a characteristic, recurring problem for historians is that patterns of discourse persist in contexts different from the one that first gave rise to them. So perhaps we need to be reminded that 'the performance of speech acts not merely modifies language, but leads to the creation and diffusion of new languages', that 'any text may be an actor in an indefinite series

---

(Paris, 1983). (Villey's work is discussed in more detail below, p. 623–4.) For a contrary position see A. Gewirth, *Reason and Morality* (Chicago, 1978), pp. 98–102 and, for a different view of Aquinas, R.P. Hering, 'De jure subjectivo sumpto apud sanctum Thomam', *Angelicum*, XVI (1939), pp. 295–7. I think that Villey is too intransigent. In Aristotle or Gaius or Aquinas we can find a vague notion of rights, though the concept remains peripheral and unelucidated in their thought. The main point for us is that they have no idea of subjective rights as human or natural rights, rights inherent in the human person as such.

[12] John A. Henley, 'Theology and the Basis of Human Rights', *Scottish Journal of Theology*, XXXIX (1986), pp. 361–78 discusses recent literature on Christianity as a basis for rights theories. He refers to 'the silence of much of the Christian tradition on the subject' (p. 367). R.M. Cover recently pointed out that Jewish law has always emphasized a concept of *mitzvah* (obligation, duty) rather than one of rights, R.M. Cover, 'Obligation: A Jewish Jurisprudence of Social Order', *Journal of Law and Religion*, V (1987), pp. 65–74.

[13] For a recent critical discussion of some current approaches see A. Pagden, 'Rethinking the Linguistic Turn: Current Anxieties in Intellectual History', *Journal of the History of Ideas*, XLIX (1988), pp. 519–29.

of linguistic processes',[14] that '*all* linguistic interpretation involves interpretation by *an* audience'.[15]

Sometimes the currently favoured hermeneutical approaches to intellectual history may seem merely portentous ways of stating platitudes that old-fashioned historians used to take for granted. After all, we have understood for a long time, without benefit of advanced literary theory, that the words of Magna Carta did not mean the same thing to a seventeenth-century parliamentarian as to the barons of 1215; and to tell a historian of ideas that what he has been reading and writing all the time is really language may seem merely like telling M. Jourdain that what he has been speaking every day is really prose. But not all the points raised by recent intellectual historians are trivial and sometimes they are relevant for our inquiry. Dominick LaCapra defined our problem precisely, if unintentionally, when he discussed 'noncanonical readings of canonical texts' and emphasized the need 'to pose as an explicit problem the way in which texts are related to contexts'.[16] Our texts are 'canonical' in a stricter sense than LaCapra intended and our purpose is precisely to understand how canonistic texts inherited from classical and early Christian sources were reinterpreted in the context of a new age.

There was plenty of room for reinterpretation. The simple-looking little phrase, *ius naturale*, is a semantic minefield. Erik Wolf once observed that the word 'natural' has seventeen meanings and the word *ius* fifteen; so, he concluded, there could be two hundred and fifty-five possible meanings for *ius naturale*. But this was too modest a count. Arthur Lovejoy more enterprisingly found sixty-six meanings for 'natural', and the canonist Johannes Monachus gave over twenty definitions of *ius*.[17] The number of possible combinations becomes mind-boggling. Fortunately we do not need to consider all of them. We will be concerned mainly with *ius* as meaning either objective law or subjective right, and with 'natural' as meaning either a primeval state of affairs or the intrinsic permanent character of any being, as when we speak of 'the nature of man'. It is the latter meaning that is more important in investigating the origins of natural rights theories.

---

[14] J.G.A. Pocock, 'The Concept of Language and the *métier d'historien*: Some Considerations on Practice', in *The Languages of Political Theory in Early-Modern Europe*, ed. A. Pagden (Cambridge, 1987), pp. 19–38, pp. 29, 31. Balzac put it more simply at the beginning of *Louis Lambert*, 'Quel beau livre ne composerait-on pas en racontant la vie et les aventures d'un mot? Sans doute il a reçu diverses impressions des évènements auxquels il a servi; selon les lieux, il a réveillé des idées différentes'. The passage is quoted in S. Ullman, *Semantics* (New York, 1962), p. 14.

[15] Shapiro, 'Realism', p. 546.

[16] D. LaCapra, 'Intellectual History and Defining the Present as "Postmodern" ', in *Innovation/ Renovation. New Perspectives on the Humanities*, ed. I. Hassan and S. Hassan (Madison, 1983), pp. 47–63 at p. 54.

[17] E. Wolf, *Das Problem der Naturrechtslehre* (Karlsruhe, 3rd edn., 1964). A.O. Lovejoy and G. Boas, *A Documentary History of Primitivism and Related Ideas*, I (Baltimore, 1935), p. 448; Johannes Monachus, *Glosa Aurea* (Paris, 1535) *ad Sext.* 1.6.16, fol. xliv. The text of Johannes Monachus is discussed in Tierney, 'Villey'.

Sources of Modern Rights Language

Let us begin with some examples of the language used by modern rights theorists. (I do not want to be anachronistic but if we are to explore origins we need to know first what we are seeking the origins of.) Seventy years ago, W.N. Hohfeld gave an influential taxonomy of rights as claims, liberties, powers, or immunities.[18] Modern jurists and philosophers who 'take rights seriously' continue to emphasize such words as 'freedom', 'claims', 'power', 'choice'. When specifically natural rights are discussed the patterns of language include words like 'moral', 'licit', 'rational'. Natural rights are also often related to the basic needs of humans as moral agents. Alan Gewirth has argued that, to function as a rational purposive agent at all, every person must assert a right to freedom and a right to well-being and that, logically, he must acknowledge such rights in others. Gewirth distinguishes between two classes of rights in the phrase, 'rightful claims or powers'; other authors use the terms 'passive rights' and 'active rights' or 'benefit rights' and 'choice rights' to make the same distinction. Some modern rights theories emphasize more the powers, others more the claims. Plamenatz, in an early formulation, declared that, 'A right is a *power* which a creature ought to possess'.[19] Joel Feinberg defined a right rather as a 'valid claim' justified by 'some set of governing rules or moral principles'. He distinguished sharply between favours, 'motivated by love or piety or mercy', and rights that could be 'demanded, claimed, insisted upon'.[20] For him a real right was a claim that could actually be asserted against society as a whole or against some specific person.[21]

A common theme in modern discourse on rights is the relationship between rights and free choice. Human free will is a basic presupposition of the argument. Feinberg points out that the holder of a right can 'choose whether or not to exercise it'.[22] H.L.A. Hart also emphasizes freedom of action. The right-holder has autonomy or 'sovereignty' in the relevant sphere. In the case of a promise, for instance, 'If he chooses to release the promisor no one else can complain'.[23] According to this

[18] W.N. Hohfeld, *Fundamental Legal Conceptions* (New Haven, 1919).

[19] J.P. Plamenatz, *Consent, Freedom and Political Obligation* (Oxford, 1938), p. 82. Cf. T.H. Green, *Lectures on the Principles of Political Obligation* (London, 1941), p. 207. 'A right is a *power* of acting . . . secured to an individual by the community.' Similarly F.C. von Savigny, *System des heutigen Römischen Rechts*, I (Berlin, 1840), p. 7, 'die der einzeln Person zustehende Macht: ein Gebiet worin ihr Wille herrscht'. For discussion of rights theories in Germany, see A. Vonlanthen, *Zum rechtsphilosophischen Streit über das Wesen der subjectiven Rechts* (Zurich, 1964).

[20] J. Feinberg, 'The Nature and Value of Rights', *Journal of Value Inquiry*, IV (1970), pp. 243–57, p. 257; J. Feinberg, 'Duties, Rights, and Claims', *American Philosophical Quarterly*, III (1966), pp. 137–44, p. 143.

[21] This led to difficulties when Feinberg considered natural rights. A starving child in a third-world country has an obvious claim to be fed, but in an impoverished society there may be no one to whom the claim can be meaningfully addressed: Feinberg, 'Duties, Rights, and Claims', p. 142. Feinberg concluded that such claims, arising from basic human needs, can and should give rise to rights but that they can be called actual rights only through an exercise of 'rhetorical licence'. Feinberg, 'Nature and Value', p. 255.

[22] Feinberg, 'Nature and Value', p. 250.

[23] H.L.A. Hart, 'Are There Any Natural Rights?', *Philosophical Review*, LXIV (1955), pp. 175–91, p. 184.

understanding of the term, a right defines a sphere of licit action within which a person is free to exercise a power or make a claim, free to act as he chooses. Robert Louden, inveighing against an alleged modern 'infatuation' with rights, explains that 'rights are permissions rather than requirements. Rights tell us what the right bearer is at liberty to do, not what he *must* or must not do'.[24] In the language of Habermas, rights define 'a neutral sphere of personal choice'.

Many modern rights theorists, including Feinberg and Hart, have made the further point that to be the beneficiary of a duty is not necessarily the same thing as having a right, even though this is often the case. Feinberg referred to a general 'duty of charity' which does not necessarily give rise to a right in any particular recipient. Hart gave an example of third-party beneficiaries. If *a* promises *b* to confer a benefit on *c*, then *c* has no right against *a* (though *b* does).[25] We shall find these arguments recurring in medieval discourse. The underlying point is that, in using the language of subjective rights, we can make moral assertions that are not always identical with those of moral systems concerned only with duties or objective justice. The distinction is significant because moral codes do not have to be expressed in terms of rights, and indeed they usually have not been so expressed. Hart pointed out that we should not normally regard the Ten Commandments as conferring rights. He also observed that natural law thinkers down to the end of the sixteenth century usually conceived of natural duties but not of natural rights.

This takes us back to the historian's problem of origins. If adequate moral systems can be articulated without any appeal to subjective rights, and normally were so articulated until quite recently, how did rights language emerge in the first place? What is its source? Back to a certain point in time the answer seems clear enough. The language of twentieth-century writers echoes that of the classical natural rights theorists of early modern Europe. At the beginning of the seventeenth century Suarez defined *ius* specifically in terms of the powers and claims of an individual. In a complex discussion of all the meanings of the word he wrote:

According to its strict signification *ius* is called a kind of moral power (*facultas*) which anyone has concerning his own property or something due to him. So the owner of a thing is said to have a right in the thing and a workman is said to have a right to his wages . . . [26]

A little later (*c*.1625) Grotius gave three meanings of *ius*. The word could mean 'what is just' (the preferred definition of Aquinas), or it could mean a kind of law, and in that sense *ius naturale* was a 'dictate of reason'. But between these two definitions

---

[24] R.L. Louden, 'Rights Infatuation and the Impoverishment of Moral Theory', *Journal of Value Inquiry*, XVII (1983), pp. 87–102, p. 95.

[25] Feinberg, 'Nature and Value', p. 244. Hart, 'Natural Rights', p. 180. For medieval discussion of this question see below p. 640.

[26] Suarez, *De Legibus ac Deo Legislatore*, Vol. I, ed. L. Pereña (Madrid, 1971), I.2.5, p. 24, 'Et iuxta . . . strictam iuris significationem solet proprie ius vocari facultas quaedam moralis, quam unusquisque habet vel circa rem suam vel ad rem sibi debitam; sic enim dominus rei dicitur habere ius in re et operarius dicitur habere ius ad stipendium . . .'.

Grotius introduced another, subjective, sense of *ius* and this he explored in most detail: '*Ius* is a moral quality of a person enabling one to have or do something justly.'[27] This 'moral quality' could also be called a faculty; it could include power over oneself, meaning liberty, and powers or claims in relation to other persons or things.

Suarez and Grotius distinguished a subjective meaning of *ius* from other connotations of the word. It was left for Hobbes to insist that the subjective meaning was the only proper one:

> The RIGHT OF NATURE which writers commonly call *jus naturale*, is the liberty each man hath, to use his own power, as he will himself, for the preservation of his own nature . . . A LAW OF NATURE, *lex naturalis*, is a precept or general rule found out by reason, by which a man is forbidden to do that which is destructive of his life . . . law, and right, differ as much, as obligation and liberty . . . [28]

Later he explained that the sphere of liberty was defined by 'the silence of the law'; where laws did not command or forbid, a person was free to act as he wished. Hobbes deviated from the preceding tradition in giving an exclusively subjective definition of *ius*, and also in excluding the idea of moral rightness from his definition. This was indeed an aberration. (For Suarez and Grotius *ius* was a *moral* power, a *moral* quality.) But later authors developed Hobbes's distinction between natural rights and natural law in ways that restored the moral content of a natural right.

Perhaps the most clear and coherent account of natural laws and natural rights in a fully developed, eighteenth-century Enlightenment form of the doctrine is that given by Christian Wolff. For Wolff, law (*lex*) is a rule that obliges us. Natural law, law inherent in the rational nature of man, obliges each person to seek self-perfection. But the fulfilment of moral obligation requires a certain freedom of action; and, Wolff declared, 'This faculty or moral power of acting is called a right (*ius*)'. Carrying the argument further, Wolff explained that 'What the law of nature obliges to as an end, *ius* gives as a means'.[29] He gave as an obvious example the right to food as a means of self-preservation. Wolff also held that, besides commanding and prohibiting, natural law could be merely permissive, indicating behaviour that was licit but not obligatory; natural rights existed in this area of permissive natural law.[30] One is

---

[27] Grotius, *De Iure Belli et Pacis* (Amsterdam, 1646) (reprinted Washington, DC, 1913), I, 1.4, p. 2, '. . . quo sensu jus est, Qualitas moralis personae, competens ad aliquid juste habendum vel agendum'.

[28] T. Hobbes, *Leviathan*, ed. M. Oakeshott (Oxford, 1946), I. 14, p. 84. Hobbes, however, was practising a sort of linguistic legislation here. In normal seventeenth-century discourse the word *ius* did not have the exclusive sense he attributed to it, as one can gather from the texts of Suarez and Grotius; rather the word could be used in one sense as equivalent to *lex*, a kind of law, or it could be used in a different sense to mean a subjective right. We shall find the same situation in medieval discourse.

[29] C. Wolff, *Institutiones Juris Naturae et Gentium*, ed. M. Thomann, in *Gesammelte Werke*, Vol. XXVI (Halle, 1750) (reprinted Hildesheim, 1964), I. 1.46, p. 24, 'Facultas ista, seu potentia moralis agendi dicitur Jus . . . Quodsi ergo lex naturae obliget ad finem, jus quoque dat ad media . . .

[30] See below, note 88. Among modern authors, Villey has especially emphasized the idea of permissive law as a source of subjective rights. See Villey, *Le droit et les droits*, p. 123, 'Ainsi nâit le droit subjectif'.

reminded again of Habermas' 'neutral sphere of personal choice' or of de Lagarde's 'zone of human autonomy'.

By the seventeenth century, then, complex rights theories existed in which words like 'nature', 'reason', 'licit', 'right', were interwoven with words like 'power', 'freedom', 'faculty'. We still need to ask: Where does this cluster of ideas come from? How did these patterns of language arise? There have been many explanations, most of them concerned with the context of seventeenth-century life itself. Some scholars have argued that the English Levellers' claim to religious freedom was the first adaptation of the old natural law tradition to defend a new doctrine of subjective natural rights.[31] C.B. Macpherson discerned, behind the religious rhetoric of the age, the presuppositions of a free market economy; and he argued that these presumptions engendered a doctrine of 'possessive individualism' in which freedom was identified with property, and natural rights theories served the narrow interests of the propertied classes.[32] Leo Strauss called attention to the shift from final causes to efficient causes associated with the Scientific Revolution. The old tradition of natural law had been concerned with human ends; in the new world of thought one had to start from man's motives, his innate desires, which Hobbes presented as rights. So rights replaced duties as the starting point for political reflection. Strauss did not regard it as a change for the better.[33]

Such views are typical of those that find the origin of modern rights theories in some aspect of the religious, economic or intellectual life of the seventeenth century. Michael Oakeshott, in a seminal essay on Hobbes, suggested that we need to consider the problem in a broader context; seventeenth-century thinkers, he suggested, were influenced not only by the circumstances of their own age but also by an earlier tradition of thought that they had inherited. Specifically, the scepticism and individualism of Hobbes were 'gifts of late medieval nominalism'.[34]

This point of view has been worked out in most detail by Michel Villey in a long series of books and articles written over the past forty years. According to Villey, the modern doctrine of subjective rights emerged quite suddenly in the fourteenth century. Its creator was the nominalist philosopher, William of Ockham, who defined *ius* as 'a licit power'. As Villey explains things, Ockham's voluntarism emphasized power rather than reason and his nominalism attributed reality to individuals rather than universals; so his political philosophy was inevitably concerned with the powers

---

[31] M. Roshwald argued that an ancient doctrine of natural law and a medieval emphasis on concrete individual rights first came together to form a theory of natural rights in the works of the Levellers: 'The Concept of Human Rights', *Philosophy and Phenomenological Research*, XIX (1958–59), pp. 354–79. More recently W. Garrett has suggested that medieval natural law served to defend the autonomy of secular government against the church; in developing natural rights theories, the Levellers aimed rather to defend the religious freedom of individuals against the state: 'Religion, Law, and the Human Condition', *Sociological Analysis*, XLVII (1987), pp. 1–34.

[32] Macpherson, *Possessive Individualism*, pp. 1–4, 220–38.

[33] Strauss, *Natural Right and History*, pp. 166, 180–1.

[34] Introduction to *Leviathan*, ed. Oakeshott, p. liii.

of individuals, which Ockham called rights.[35] Villey regards this as destructive of the whole preceding natural law tradition. He points out that, in classical Roman law, and still for Aquinas, *ius* meant 'what is just' in an objective sense. But Ockham persistently twisted the sense of *ius* (right) to give it the meaning of *potestas* (power),[36] and so combined two ideas that had formerly been quite distinct. For Villey this was a 'Copernican moment' in the history of law. Ockham had inaugurated a 'semantic revolution'.[37] He had created 'a hybrid monster, a doctrine of natural right based on nominalism, a right which one no longer claims to extract from cosmic nature, but from the asserted nature of man as an individual'.[38]

Villey's views have been widely and often uncritically accepted. Ockham remains by far the favourite choice as innovator among those who seek a pre-seventeenth-century origin for natural rights theories. But recently the contribution of another late medieval theologian, Jean Gerson has also been emphasized. Reinhold Schwartz has maintained that the subjective concept of *ius* suggested by Ockham was first clearly enunciated by Gerson.[39] Gerson did in fact give an explicit definition of *ius* as 'an immediate faculty or power pertaining to anyone according to right reason' and of *lex* as 'a rule in conformity with right reason'.[40] So, as Richard Tuck pointed out, he had already made the distinction that we encounter later in seventeenth-century works between subjective right and objective law. In Tuck's view, Gerson 'really created the theory' of natural rights.[41] We should add that Gerson also associated *ius* with the idea of *synderesis*, which he called a 'superior' kind of reason, a capacity for moral discernment akin to our conscience.[42] So, for him, *ius* was primarily an innate power to act rightly according to reason and conscience. This is not quite what we mean by a natural right in modern discourse. But Gerson further declared that from *ius* so defined it was possible to deduce, by a sort of mathematical reasoning,

---

[35] M. Villey, *La formation de la pensée juridique moderne* (Paris, 4th edn., 1975), pp. 199–272. For detailed criticism see Tierney, 'Villey'.

[36] Villey, *La formation*, p. 248.

[37] *Ibid.*, p. 261.

[38] *Ibid.*, p. 270.

[39] R. Schwartz, 'Circa naturam iuris subiectivi', *Periodica de re morali canonica liturgica*, LXIX (1980), pp. 191–200, p. 191, 'Quod apud Gulielmum Occam (ca. 1290–1349) adhuc minus clare apparet, iam 1402 a Ioanne Gerson (1363–1424) primarius pronuntiatur conceptus iuris: "Ius est facultas seu potestas ..." '. See also A. Folgado, *Evolucion historica del derecho subjetivo* (Madrid, 1960), pp. 147–60.

[40] J. Gerson, *De vita spirituali anime*, in *Jean Gerson. Oeuvres complètes*, III, ed. P. Glorieux (Paris, 1962), p. 141, 'Jus est facultas seu potestas propinqua conveniens alicui secundum dictamen rectae rationis.' The definition of *lex*, with a slightly different definition of *ius*, is in J. Gerson, *De potestate ecclesiastica, Oeuvres*, VI (Paris, 1965), p. 242, 'Jus est facultas seu potestas propinqua conveniens alicui secundum dictamen primae justitiae ... lex est regula conformitatem habens ad dictamen rectae rationis.'

[41] R. Tuck, *Natural Rights Theories. Their Origin and Development* (Cambridge, 1979), pp. 25–6.

[42] Gerson, *De Vita*, p. 142. According to Gerson, man could know the universal principles of good through *synderesis* and from them deduce particular rules of action. On *synderesis* in medieval natural law theories see M.B. Crowe, *The Changing Profile of the Natural Law* (The Hague, 1977), pp. 123–35.

a whole theory of government and property.[43] He held that there were God-given rights which included liberty, understood as freedom of the will, 'a faculty of acting or not acting', and dominion, 'a right of taking inferior things for one's use and preservation'.[44] Gerson further associated his idea of *ius* with the Pauline doctrine of evangelical liberty (here perhaps following Ockham). He thought the people of his own age were hemmed in by a mass of stifling ecclesiastical regulations more oppressive than those of the Old Law;[45] they needed liberty, a sphere of free choice, Gerson held, because liberty was essential for spiritual renewal.

Gerson was widely quoted by later Parisian conciliarists and by the Spanish scholastics of the sixteenth century. Christopher St. Germain used his work in England, and Suarez listed the specific chapters in which Gerson discussed the meaning of *ius* as among the major sources of his own treatise, *De legibus*. Clearly, then, Gerson was very influential. It is not so clear though that his views on rights — or those of Ockham — were also highly innovative.

If we are to find an earlier origin for natural rights theories we need to look for patterns of language in which *ius naturale* meant not only natural law or cosmic harmony, but also a faculty or ability or power of individual persons, associated with reason and moral discernment, defining an area of liberty where the individual was free to act as he pleased, leading on to specific claims and powers of humans qua humans. I want finally to argue that this whole complex of associated ideas, this lattice-work of language, first grew into existence in the works of the medieval Decretists. The authors we will need to discuss — Rufinus and Ricardus and Huguccio and Alanus and others whose names have been forgotten — are not much read nowadays except by specialists in this field. None of them wrote an accessible, explicit little treatise on natural rights, which perhaps helps to explain why they are not much noticed in modern histories of the concept. Their patterns of thought have to be reconstructed from scattered, sometimes laconic glosses on a variety of topics. There is no one text that could find a place in the canon of 'great works' on Western political theory. But the Decretists' views were widely diffused in the law schools of Europe by the end of the twelfth century and, transmitted in eclectic works like the Ordinary Gloss to the Decretum and Guido de Baysio's *Rosarium*, they continued to influence late medieval writers, not least Ockham and Gerson. Gerson himself mentioned the opening chapters of the Decretum in introducing his discussion of rights. He proposed to follow a different methodology, he wrote, but added, 'We shall not say things different from others, though perhaps differently'.[46]

---

[43] Gerson, *De vita*, p. 143.

[44] *Ibid.*, p. 145.

[45] *Ibid.*, p. 129.

[46] *Ibid.*, p. 143, '. . . non quidem alia dicturus quam alii, quamquam forte aliter'. Gerson did not overtly quote canonistic texts as frequently as his master in theology, Pierre d'Ailly. But he was intensely interested in canon law, partly indeed because of his dissatisfaction with the state of the discipline at the beginning of the fifteenth century. See L.B. Pascoe, 'Law and Evangelical Liberty in the Thought of Jean Gerson', in *Monumenta Iuris Canonici, Series C: Subsidia*, VII (Vatican City, 1985), pp. 351–61, and F. Oakley, 'Gerson and d'Ailly: An Admonition', *Speculum*, XL (1965), pp. 74–83, p. 81.

Let us begin with the twelfth-century world in which the canonists lived and taught.

Canonistic Rights Language — Contexts

Medieval society was saturated with a concern for rights. At the very highest level popes asserted rights against emperors and emperors against popes. The papal claim to 'rights of heavenly and earthly empire' (*terreni simul et celestis imperii iura*), included in Gratian's Decretum at *Dist.* 22 c.1, gave rise to extensive theoretical argument among the canonists and to endless conflict in the sphere of real-life politics. (The text also provided the starting point for one of Gerson's most detailed discussions on the rights of rulers.)[47] Since neither the spiritual nor temporal power could wholly dominate the other, medieval government never congealed into a rigid theocratic absolutism in which rights theories could never have taken root. Instead, in the vigorous, fluid, expanding society of the twelfth century, old rights were persistently asserted and new ones insistently demanded. A great feudal lord could enjoy simultaneously all the rights enumerated in Hohfeld's modern classification — a claim to rents and services, a power to do justice, an immunity from external jurisdiction, a liberty to, say, hunt over his own land. Cathedral canons asserted their rights against bishops. Bishops and barons defended their rights against kings. Newly-founded communes sometimes bought their rights and sometimes fought for them. (In the twelfth century grants of rights were often made to corporate groups, but as A.L. Harding has pointed out, they were commonly rights of a kind that could be actually exercised only by individual persons.[48]) Even peasants, emigrating to found new villages in the still vast expanses of forest and wasteland, could claim enhanced liberties from lords who needed fresh supplies of labour.[49] Medieval people first struggled for survival; then they struggled for rights.

Of course all these rights were rights of particular persons or classes; they provide only a background for our inquiry into the origins of natural rights theories. But, before turning to that theme, we need to consider some other aspects of medieval individualism. It is unprofitable, perhaps, to ask whether the twelfth century 'discovered' the individual. I suspect that in all cultures some persons are more self-aware than others, more given to reflection on individual experience. But twelfth-century civilization was certainly marked by a new emphasis on personalism or humanism, and it found expression on many levels of thought and feeling. Courtly love literature explored the joys and pains of human lovers. Religious piety cultivated an intense emotional relationship between the individual Christian and the person of Jesus. Peter Abelard taught that the moral value of an act was determined entirely by individual intention. Private scrutiny of conscience, followed by private confession, became a common practice. Such concern for human persons could easily lead on to reflection about human rights; and, if the development of a natural rights theory

[47] Gerson, *De potestate*, p. 236.

[48] A.L. Harding, 'Political Liberty in the Middle Ages', *Speculum*, LV (1980), pp. 423–43.

[49] On peasant 'individualism' see A. MacFarlane, *The Origins of English Individualism* (Cambridge, 1979). I doubt whether the English experience was so exceptional as the author supposes.

really required a formal philosophical basis, as Villey insists, a perfectly adequate one was provided by the moderate realism (or moderate nominalism) of the twelfth-century schools, which attributed reality primarily to individuals, and to universal qualities only insofar as they inhered in individuals. We have learned too to understand that the corporatism of the age was not antithetical to its individualism but complementary. Medieval individuals flourished best in corporate communities.[50]

Among all the 'renaissances' of the twelfth century the one most significant for us was the revival of legal studies, first the recovery of the whole corpus of Roman law, then the reordering of the confused mass of church law that had accumulated over many centuries, in the Decretum of Gratian (c.1140), 'the first comprehensive and systematic legal treatise in the history of the West', according to Harold Berman. The concern with individual intention, individual consent, individual will that characterized twelfth-century culture spilled over into many areas of canon law. In marriage law, by the end of the twelfth century, the simple consent of two individuals, without any other formalities, could constitute a valid, sacramental marriage. In contract law, a bare promise of one person to another could create a binding obligation — it was the intention of the promisor that counted. In criminal law, the degree of guilt and punishment was again related to the intention of the individual defendant, and this led on, as in modern legal systems, to complex considerations about negligence and diminished responsibility, areas of law that we nowadays think of as mediating between the rights of individuals and the maintenance of public order.[51]

Given this whole background, one might expect to find an emphasis also on individual rights in the works of twelfth-century academic lawyers. Villey was reluctant to admit this. He acknowledged that, in vulgar medieval discourse, the word *ius* might be used carelessly to mean an individual right, but he argued that this usage could not infect academic jurisprudence until Ockham had provided a new philosophy to justify it.[52] But the evidence against his position is overwhelming. Indeed Villey himself, and Tuck too, following Villey, saw that a doctrine of subjective rights was implicit in the civilian glossators' treatment of dominion — ownership, rulership, mastery — as a kind of right. Neither of the two modern authors, however, seemed interested in following up the implication of his own argument. Villey wrote dismissively that the writings of the civilian glossators were full of 'contradictions

[50] The best overview of twelfth-century culture is *Renaissance and Renewal in the Twelfth Century*, ed. R.L. Benson and G. Constable (Cambridge, Mass., 1982). See especially the contribution of J.F. Benton to this volume, 'Consciousness of Self and Perceptions of Individuality' (pp. 263–95). For an introduction to various aspects of twelfth-century individualism see C. Morris, *The Discovery of the Individual, 1050–1200* (London, 1972) and the further literature cited in the discussion between Caroline Bynum and Morris in *Journal of Ecclesiastical History*, XXXI (1980), pp. 1–17 and pp. 195–206. The question of corporatism and individualism is also considered here.

[51] The most recent full-scale treatment of these themes is H. Berman, *Law and Revolution. The Formation of the Western Legal Tradition* (Cambridge, Mass., 1983).

[52] Villey, *La formation*, p. 239.

and hesitations and frustrated endeavors'.[53] Tuck found in the twelfth-century glosses only an inadequate theory of passive rights, apparently because the glossators of Roman law referred to *dominium* as a right that could be claimed or asserted against all other persons (but Tuck's argument grows very fuzzy at this point in his work).[54]

Neither Villey nor Tuck paid much attention to the treatment of *ius* in the canonists' writings. Tuck found in their work only a collection of claim rights again, and Villey an assertion of legal or moral precepts. Both authors were interested mainly in investigating the origin of active rights, *ius* conceived of as liberty or power, and they seem to have found little to interest them in the work of the Decretists. Tuck, for instance, suggested that Gerson was the first to treat liberty as a *ius*. But in fact Gratian himself wrote of the *iura libertatis*, rights of liberty, that could never be lost however long a man was held in bondage;[55] and the association of right and power, *ius* and *potestas* (Ockham's 'semantic revolution' according to Villey), was commonplace in twelfth-century canonistic discourse. The papal election decree incorporated into the Decretum at *Dist.* 23 c.1 referred to 'the right of the power to elect' (*ius potestatis eligere*). In discussing the status of bishops-elect, Huguccio wrote simply, 'They have the power of administering that is the right of administering'.[56] Gratian attributed to the pope a right (*ius*) of establishing laws (surely an active right), and Huguccio observed that since the pope had been given the right, therefore he had full power in this matter.[57] Innocent III referred to the right of electing as a *facultas* and a glossator paraphrased his words by describing the right (*ius*) as a 'free power'.[58]

Such examples could be multiplied. Individual rights were important to the canonists. They had to be protected. In the Ordinary Glosses to both the Decretum and the Decretals we can read that no one was to be deprived of his right except for grave cause.[59] The canonists also understood clearly the difference between claim rights and active rights; and around 1200 they developed a technical vocabulary to

---

[53] M. Villey, 'Le "jus in re" du droit romain classique au droit moderne', in *Conférences faites à l'Institut de Droit Romain* (Paris, 1950), pp. 187–225, p. 190.

[54] At the outset of his *Natural Rights Theories* (p. 5) Tuck distinguishes sharply between *ius* as meaning *dominium*, an active right with 'implications of control and mastery', and *ius* as 'simply a claim on other people'. But at p. 15, where he discusses the work of the early glossators, *dominium* becomes a passive right because it was 'a claim to total control against all the world'. Then at p. 17 *dominium* turns back into an active right again; but here claim rights are also treated as active rights. It is hard to discern any coherent argument running through these pages.

[55] *Decretum Gratiani . . . una cum glossis* (Venice, 1600), C. 16 q.3 *dictum post* c.15.

[56] Huguccio, *Summa ad Dist.* 23.c.1, MS Admont 7, fol. 29rb, '. . . habent potestatem administrandi id est ius administrandi sed non habent executionem illius iuris in actu'.

[57] C.25 q.1 *dictum post* c.16; Huguccio *ad Dist.* 4 *dictum post* c.3, MS Admont 7, fol. 6vb.

[58] *Decretales D. Gregorii Papae IX cum glossis* (Lyons, 1614), 1.4.8 '. . . ius eligendi abbatem adiudicare curetis, ut sic de caetero liberam habeant facultatem . . . eligendi . . .'. The *casus* of the *glossa ordinaria* has '. . . adiudicent monachis . . . ius eligendi abbatem, ut liberam habeant potestatem . . . eligendi . . .'.

[59] Gloss *ad Dist.* 56 c.7; Gloss *ad* X.4.13.11.

distinguish between them — the terms *ius ad rem* and *ius in re* that were still being used by Suarez in his seventeenth-century rights theory. All this is reasonably straightforward. In a world where rights were constantly being asserted and demanded, the language of the jurists reflected the realities of their age. The context serves to explain the texts.[60] The point would hardly be worth making except that it has been disputed. But we have still not reached the heart of the problem. We have not yet addressed the question of when and how a doctrine of *natural* rights came to be asserted. To understand this we have to turn from the social and cultural context of the canonists to the fundamental, tangled text that they laboured to expound, Gratian's *Concordantia discordantium canonum*, commonly known as the Decretum. This text itself forms part of the context that we need to understand if we are to interpret adequately the discourse of twelfth-century canonists.

Canonistic Rights Language — Texts

The canonists could not avoid detailed scrutiny of the term *ius naturale* because Gratian chose to base his whole structure of jurisprudence on an initial distinction between natural law and human usages, set out in the first words of the Decretum:

> The human race is ruled by two (means) namely by natural law and by usages. Natural law (*ius*) is what is contained in the Law and the Gospel by which each is commanded to do to another what he wants done to himself and forbidden to do to another what he does not want done to himself.[61]

To distinguish thus between universal natural law and varying human practices may seem a typical medieval tactic. The difficulties arose because, when Gratian sought to buttress his initial definition with canonical authorities and to pursue their implications, his argument led to a morass of internal contradictions, or apparent contradictions. After giving his opening definition, Gratian quoted in support of it some words of Isidore of Seville: 'All laws are either divine or human. Divine laws stand by nature, human by usage . . . *Fas* is divine law, *ius* is human law. To pass through another's field is *fas*, it is not *ius*.'[62] We shall have to return to *fas* and *ius*. But to continue with Gratian's argument — he went on to present another text of Isidore which included multiple descriptions of the content of natural law:

---

[60] In emphasizing contexts, I am not suggesting any kind of historical determinism. Of course different persons respond differently to the same situation. Among the twelfth-century canonists, for instance, Huguccio and Alanus held sharply opposed views on the rights of popes and emperors. But to understand either Huguccio or Alanus we have to know something about the context of papal-imperial relations at the end of the twelfth century and about the context of Decretist thought within which both authors worked.

[61] *Dist.* 1, *dictum ante* c.1, 'Humanum genus duobus regitur, naturale videlicet iure et moribus. Ius naturale est, quod in lege et Evangelio continetur: quo quisque iubetur alii facere quod sibi vult fieri et prohibetur alii inferre quod sibi nolet fieri.'

[62] *Dist.* 1 c.1, 'Omnes leges aut divinae sunt, aut humanae. Divinae natura, humanae moribus constant . . . Fas lex divina est, ius lex humana. Transire per agrum alienum fas est, ius non est.'

Natural law (*ius*) is the law common to all peoples, in that it is everywhere held by instinct of nature, not by any enactment: as, for instance, the union of man and woman, the generation and rearing of children, the common possession of all things and the one liberty of all, the acquisition of those things which are taken from air and land and sea; also the return of a thing deposited or money entrusted, the repulsion of force by force.[63]

Some difficulties may already be apparent. The texts cited in support of Gratian's opening definition did not contain the Golden Rule that constituted natural law for Gratian himself. Moreover Isidore's natural law was not a rule enjoined by Scripture, like Gratian's, but a product of instinctual behaviour. Again, Isidore's natural law included principles not evidently compatible with Scripture. Isidore, for instance, wrote of common property as an aspect of natural law, but Scripture recognized private possessions.

There are various other anomalies in the first chapters of the Decretum but it will be enough for our purpose to pursue the argument about property. Apparently unaware of any difficulties, Gratian forged serenely ahead. Natural law, he wrote, held primacy over all others in time and dignity for it began with the origin of rational creatures and remained always immutable. It differed from human law because, by natural law, 'all things are common to all', whereas human law had established private property.[64] Finally, Gratian declared that any human law contrary to natural law was to be held null and void.[65] The conclusion seems obvious. The human law instituting private property was null and void. But Gratian really had no intention of asserting any such doctrine. In his own day both canon and civil law recognized the licitness of individual property and Gratian simply took the fact for granted throughout the whole subsequent argument of the Decretum. In Causa 12, for instance, he wrote that even a bishop could have private property.

The implicit contradiction was never discussed by Gratian himself. But the canonists who commented on the texts of the Decretum from about 1150 onwards could see the difficulties inherent in them at least as clearly as any modern reader can; and almost at once they realized that the apparent incoherence in Gratian's thought and language arose from the fact that the texts he presented used the term *ius naturale* in several different senses.[66] If one could discriminate between them,

---

[63] *Dist.* 1 c.7, 'Ius naturale est commune omnium nationum eo quod ubique instinctu naturae non constitutione aliqua habetur, ut viri et feminae coniunctio, liberorum successio et educatio, communis omnium possessio, et omnium una libertas, acquisitio eorum quae caelo, terra, marique capiuntur, item depositae rei vel commendatae pecuniae restitutio, violentiae per vim repulsio.'

[64] *Dist.* 8 *dictum ante* c.1, 'Nam iure naturali omnia sunt communia omnibus . . . Iure vero consuetudinis vel constitutionis hoc meum est, illud alterius.'

[65] *Dist.* 8 *dictum post* c.1, 'Quaecunque enim vel moribus recepta sunt, vel scriptis comprehensa, si naturali iuri fuerint adversa, vana et irrita habenda sunt.'

[66] Very few of the twelfth-century commentaries on the Decretum have been edited. However, many particular passages relating to natural law have been printed in modern works. Some important texts were included in S. Kuttner's seminal *Repertorium der Kanonistik, 1140–1234* (Vatican City, 1937). Others were collected by O. Lottin, *Le droit naturel chez Saint Thomas et ses prédécesseurs* (Bruges, 2nd edn.,

the apparent difficulties might be resolved. As Ricardus Anglicus pointed out, it was not inappropriate if *ius naturale* in one meaning of the term contradicted *ius naturale* in some other meaning.[67] (So private property might be contrary to natural law in one sense of the term, but in accordance with it in another sense.) It soon became a common exegetical technique among the early Decretists to provide long lists of all the possible meanings of the term *ius naturale* — including, perhaps, some that no one had thought of before. Huguccio explained the problem to his students near the beginning of his great *Summa* on the Decretum (*c*.1190):

> Note that not all the examples of *ius naturale* given here refer to the same meaning of *ius naturale*; therefore a prudent reader will carefully discern which example refers to which meaning. But lest the mind of some idiot be confused we shall carefully assign each one . . .

and he proceeded to do so. Already by 1160 Stephanus had found five meanings for *ius naturale* and, a little later, an English canonist gave nine, ranging from 'the order and instinct of nature' to an impenetrable metaphysical definition. 'Others have said that natural *ius* is an extra-predicamental something including both the mode of existing as essence and as being.'[68]

In reading these texts one encounters a persistently recurring problem. Gratian himself used the word *ius* consistently to designate systems of objective law in the opening chapters of the Decretum — e.g. he considered in turn natural law, customary law, civil law, military law, public law as different species of *ius*; but the canonists who commented on his texts lived in a world where, in everyday discourse, the word *ius* commonly meant a subjective right. Hence, in their commentaries, they would shift from one meaning to the other, unreflectively it seems, and without seeing any need for explanation, evidently confident that their meaning would be plain to contemporary readers. Thus, where Gratian discussed customary law as a form of *ius*, the Ordinary Gloss commented that a custom was not established by repeated usage unless there was actually an intention to establish it, and then added,

---

1931). The most ample collection of texts is provided by R. Weigand, *Die Naturrechtslehre der Legisten und Dekretisten* (Munich, 1967). But the authors interested in canonistic doctrines on natural law have not considered the importance of their texts for later theories of natural rights. Lottin observed (*Le droit naturel*, p. 97), 'Or, on ne voit nulle part ce dernier sense subjectif (du terme *ius*) dans la littérature du XIIe et du XIIIe siècle' (though his own texts hardly support this conclusion). In the following discussion I have taken some texts from Weigand. Where I have used my own manuscript transcriptions and Weigand provides a similar transcription from another source, or a partial transcription, I have given a cross-reference to *Naturrechtslehre*. (Weigand sometimes omits phrases which are significant for our argument.)

[67] *Summa ad Dist.* 1 c.6, MS Admont 7, fol. 3vb, 'Et nota quod non omnia exempla iuris naturalis hic posita referuntur ad eandem acceptionem iuris naturalis. Ergo prudentis lectoris erit caute discernere quod exemplum ad quam acceptionem iuris naturalis referatur. Sed ne ydiote animus in hoc confundatur, de quolibet diligenter assignabimus' (cf. Weigand, p. 214). Earlier, in his introductory remarks (MS Admont 7, fol. 2va), Huguccio wrote, 'His bene intellectis facile erit aptare sequentia contraria iuris naturalis, scilicet que ad quas acceptiones pertineant et referuntur'. For the comment of Ricardus see Weigand, *Naturrechtslehre*, p. 393.

[68] Weigand, *Naturrechtslehre*, pp. 148, 203, 'Alii dixerunt ius naturale esse quiddam extra predicamentale habentem simul modum existendi per se ut essentiabile res et ens.'

casually introducing the subjective meaning of *ius*, that this was true even when a person acted by virtue of his right (*iure suo*).[69] Another example occurs at the very first chapter of the Decretum (*Dist.* 1 c.1) where Isidore distinguished between divine natural law (*fas*) and human law. The natural law defined in Gratian's own opening dictum as the Golden Rule was clearly a precept, a divine command. But *fas* has rather the sense of what is permissible or allowable or rightful, and this meaning was suggested by Isidore's example, 'To pass through another's field'. The Ordinary Gloss, commenting on this, used the word *ius* to mean both a body of law and what was permitted by law — what we might call a right. 'It is permitted by divine law (*iure divino*), nevertheless it is not a right (*ius*) because it is not permitted by human law (*iure humano*).'[70] For us the concepts of objective law and subjective right are clearly distinguishable, but in medieval discourse the word *ius* could oscillate easily between the two meanings.

It is the same when we turn to the multiple meanings of the term *ius naturale* presented in the Decretist glosses. The everyday use of *ius* to mean a right, a rightful power, infected the language of the canonists when they came to write of *ius naturale*. They occasionally gave a Stoic interpretation of the term as meaning a force pervading the whole cosmos; usually they included Gratian's view that *ius naturale* was a code of moral law revealed through Scripture and also accessible to reason; but often they added a subjective definition of the term that was not evidently present in Gratian's texts at all.

A particularly influential discussion was presented by Rufinus, writing in about 1160:

> Natural *ius* is a certain force instilled in every human creature by nature to do good and avoid the opposite. *Ius* consists in three things, commands, prohibitions and demonstrations . . . It cannot be detracted from at all as regards the commands and prohibitions . . . but it can be as regards the demonstrations, which nature does not command or forbid but shows to be good, and this is especially so as regards the liberty of all and common property, for nowadays, by civil law, this slave is mine, that field is yours.[71]

---

[69] Gloss ad *Dist.* 1 c.5, '. . . etiam si suo iure id faceret . . .'.

[70] Gloss ad *Dist.* 1 c.1, '. . . fas est, id est iure divino permittitur, ius autem non est, id est non permittitur iure humano.' Later on, when Hostensis wanted to refer to a right derived from civil law, he wrote, '. . . ius de iure civile proveniens' (*Lectura ad* X.1.2.7). In the same passage he referred to a '. . . ius quod omnibus competit de iure naturali . . .'. The word glides from one meaning to another in a single terse phrase. I have often retained the Latin word *ius* in the English text above because frequently the sense cannot be rendered adequately either by 'right' or 'law'.

[71] *Die Summa Decretorum des Magister Rufinus*, ed. H. Singer (Paderborn, 1902), pp. 6–7. 'Est itaque naturale ius vis quedam humane creature a natura insita ad faciendum bonum cavendumque contrarium. Consistit autem ius naturale in tribus, scilicet: mandatis, prohibitionibus, demonstrationibus . . . Detractum autem ei non est utique in mandatis vel prohibitionibus . . . sed in demonstrationibus — que scilicet natura non vetat non prohibet, sed bona esse ostendit — et maxime in omnium una libertate et communi possessione; nunc enim iure civili hic est servus meus, ille est ager tuus.' On acquisition of property and natural law, see the texts collected by Weigand, *Naturrechtslehre*, pp. 307–61. Underlying much of the argumentation was the Roman law doctrine that, according to natural reason, *dominium* was acquired by

Rufinus used the word *demonstrationes* to mean 'descriptions', 'indications', of behaviour that was licit but not required. His explanation that community of property belonged only to the 'demonstrations' of natural law (which could be changed by civil law) was widely accepted. But both parts of his argument were very important, the initial subjective definition of *ius* and the following tripartite division. We need to consider each in turn.

'Natural *ius* is a certain force . . .'. We do not know the precise source of this formula if there is an earlier source (though, obviously, one is reminded of Cicero's *innata vis*). But, whatever the source, the definition had a great success, and it was taken up and reformulated, with frequent variations of language, by many later canonists. Odo of Dover (*c*.1170) wrote, closely following Rufinus:

More strictly, natural *ius* is a certain force divinely inspired in man by which he is led to what is right and equitable.[72]

For Simon of Bisignano:

Natural *ius* is said to be a force of the mind . . . the superior part of the soul, namely reason which is called *sinderesis*.[73]

For Sicardus:

Ius is called natural . . . from human nature, that is a certain force or power naturally instilled in man . . . [74]

Ricardus Anglicus explained:

Some say that natural *ius* is free will . . . others say that it is charity . . . others say that natural *ius* is the superior part of the soul, namely reason . . . We reject none of these.[75]

Richard Tuck suggested that Gerson was the first to define *ius* as an ability or faculty; but this language too occurs in the twelfth-century glosses. According to the English *Summa, In nomine*:

---

the first occupant of a *res nullius*. For further background see most recently Janet Coleman, 'Property and Poverty', in *The Cambridge History of Medieval Political Thought*, ed. J.H. Burns (Cambridge, 1988), pp. 607–48.

[72] Weigand, *Naturrechtslehre*, p. 161. 'In tertia significatione et strictiori dicitur ius naturale uis quedam diuinitus homini inspirata qua ad id quod iustum est et equum ducitur.'

[73] *Ibid.*, p. 173, 'Cum autem ius naturale dicatur esse uis mentis . . . Nobis itaque uidetur quod ius naturale est superior pars anime, ipsa uidelicet ratio, que sinderesis appellatur . . .'. For other texts identifying *ius naturale* as *sinderesis* see *ibid.*, pp. 177, 187.

[74] *Ibid.*, p. 184, 'Nam ius naturale dicitur . . . ab humana natura, hoc est quedam uis et potentia homini naturaliter insita ad faciendum bonum et uitandum contrarium.'

[75] *Ibid.*, p. 212, 'Dicunt enim quidam quod ius naturale sit liberum arbitrium . . . Alii dicunt quod sit caritas . . . Alii dicunt quod ius naturale est superior pars anime, ratio scilicet . . . Nullorum sententiam reprobamus.'

Natural *ius* is a certain ability by which man is able to discern between good and evil, and in this sense natural *ius* is a faculty . . . and this is free will.[76]

So far, of course, we are not dealing with an overt theory of natural rights; but it may already be evident that the subjective understanding of *ius* that Gerson took as the starting point of his rights theory, 'a faculty or power in accordance with right reason', associated with free will and synderesis, was no novelty of late medieval theology; it had already found ample expression in the glosses on the Decretum two centuries earlier.

Many Decretists included a definition of *ius naturale* as a kind of subjective force or power inherent in human personality, along with many other definitions. But the greatest of them all, Huguccio, was unusual in insisting that this was the one primary and proper meaning of the term. According to his definition, 'natural *ius* is called reason, namely a natural force of the soul . . .'. Huguccio added that, in a second sense, the term could be used to refer to the moral laws known through reason, which could be summed up in the Scriptural rule 'Do not do to others what you do not want done to yourself'.[77] All this seems conventional enough. Huguccio was apparently just following Gratian. But then the argument took a sudden turn. Huguccio declared sharply that this second meaning — Gratian's own meaning — was derived from an improper understanding of *ius naturale*. We ought to say that moral precepts are effects of natural *ius* or that they derive from natural *ius* rather than that they *are* natural *ius*.[78] Huguccio did not maintain a consistent distinction here between *ius* and *lex*; like his contemporaries he sometimes used the terms interchangeably.[79] But he was distinguishing clearly between a subjective and an objective sense of the term *ius naturale* and asserting that the subjective sense was the proper one. Moreover he was insistent about this. On Gratian's view of *ius naturale* as what was contained in the Old Law and the Gospel, he wrote: 'If audacity is granted, I will safely say that this is improperly called *ius naturale*.'[80] When he came to Isidore's specification of

---

[76] Kuttner, *Repertorium*, p. 202, 'Quarto modo dicitur ius naturale habilitas quedam qua homo statim est habilis ad discernendum inter bonum et malum: et secundum hoc dicitur ius naturale facultas — hoc est liberum arbitrium.' Kuttner printed parallel passages from two other related works which also described *ius naturale* as a faculty or ability (cf. Weigand, *Naturrechtslehre*, p. 197). See Tuck, *Natural Rights Theories*, p. 26, and Tierney, 'Tuck on Rights', p. 438.

[77] MS. Admont 7, fol. 2rb (Introduction), 'Ius ergo naturale dicitur ratio, scilicet naturalis uis animi ex qua homo discernit inter bonum et malum . . . Dicitur etiam secundo loco ius naturale iudicium rationis . . . et ut breuiter dicam, nolle aliis facere quod tiba non uis fieri . . .' (cf. Weigand, *Naturrechtslehre*, pp. 215–16).

[78] 'Sed in hac acceptione improprie dicitur ius naturale cum quodlibet talium qualia diximus contineri in hoc acceptione potius sit affectus iuris naturalis uel ab ea descendat uel ad ipsum ex iure naturali teneatur quis quam sit ius naturale' (fol. 2rb).

[79] As noted above (note 28), this was also typical of seventeenth-century usage. Moreover Hobbes's attempt at 'linguistic legislation' did not succeed. *Ius* continued to have both meanings as long as works on law or political theory were written in Latin. It is the same with Gerson. Although he distinguished between *ius* and *lex* when giving formal definitions he often used the words interchangeably in other contexts.

[80] 'Unde, si audatia detur, dico uerbum secure, quod hoc ius improprie dicitur naturale . . .' (fol. 2rb).

the varied contents of *ius naturale*, Huguccio declared, 'The things set out here are not natural *ius* or *iura* but each is an effect of natural *ius* or derives from it'.[81] For Huguccio, *ius naturale* in its proper sense was always an attribute of human persons 'a force of the soul'. His doctrine of natural *ius* was not based on cosmic harmony or, specifically, on Christian revelation but on a view of human nature as rational, self-aware, morally responsible.

In reading the language of the twelfth-century canonists or Gerson's later adaptations of it, one is often reminded of the Stoic doctrine of a natural law in man. But a decisive shift of meaning and emphasis occurred in the twelfth century. For some of the Stoics and for Cicero there was a force in man through which he could discern *ius naturale*, the objective natural law that pervaded the whole universe; but for the canonists *ius naturale* itself could be defined as a subjective force or faculty or power or ability inherent in human persons. Although such definitions do not in themselves express a doctrine of natural rights, once the term *ius naturale* was clearly defined in this subjective sense the argument could easily move in either direction, to specify natural laws that had to be obeyed or natural rights that could licitly be exercised; and canonistic argument soon did move in both directions. Stoic authors, when they wrote of *ius naturale*, were thinking mainly in terms of cosmic determinism; the canonists were thinking more in terms of human free choice. When the concept of *ius naturale* was associated in the canonists' glosses with words like 'power', 'faculty', 'free will', it was moving in a different semantic field of force so to speak, and took on new meanings. Stoic reflection on *ius naturale* never led to a doctrine of natural rights; canonistic reflection did so, and quickly.

To carry the argument further, we need to recall the common modern view that to have a right is to enjoy a sphere of personal liberty, a 'zone of autonomy', an area of licit choice where the right-holder is free to act as he pleases. Alongside the definitions we have considered so far of *ius* as a subjective moral force or power inhering in individuals, we also encounter this precise understanding of *ius naturale* in some of the twelfth-century glosses. The authors commonly took as a starting point the second part of Rufinus' definition, that we have not explored so far, the tripartite division of natural law into commands, prohibitions and *demonstrationes*. Often the 'demonstrations' were taken to be descriptions of a primeval state of affairs — the 'state of nature' familiar in many later natural law theories — which had been superseded by the later development of human law and government. Alanus even wrote, 'Positive law is always preferred to natural law', but he meant only natural law in this latter sense.[82] Sometimes, however, the third kind of natural *ius*, corresponding to Rufinus' 'demonstrations', was taken to be a permanently existing feature of the law (or right) of nature, a kind of natural *ius* that defined an area of permissiveness where rights could licitly be exercised, rather than a body of restrictive law.

[81] *Summa ad Dist.*1 c.6, MS Admont 7, fol. 3va, 'Nam ea que hic ponuntur non sunt ius naturale uel iura naturalia . . . Sed quodlibet tale est effectus iuris naturalis uel ab eo descendit . . .' (cf. Weigand, *Naturrechtslehre*, p. 219).

[82] Weigand, *Naturrechtslehre*, p. 318.

The Summa *Inperatorie maiestate* posed the standard problem that, according to Gratian's texts, private property instituted by human law seemed contrary to natural law. The author explained that natural law consisted of 'precepts, prohibitions, counsels and permissions'; since private property did not fall under the 'prohibitions' of natural law its introduction was licit. This led on to a consideration of property as a natural right. The author noted that *ius naturale* was sometimes identified with *ius gentium*, which also permitted acquisition of property. He concluded, 'The law of nature (*ius nature*) is called the law of nations (*ius gentium*) because, by dictate of nature rather than by command of a statute (*lex*), one has his right (*ius*).'[83] The oscillation between *ius* as meaning objective law and *ius* as meaning subjective right which we noted earlier in the Ordinary Gloss occurs here in the specific context of natural law and natural right.

Other early glossators of the Bolognese school defined natural *ius* as conduct that was 'licit and approved'. But the clearest use of such language to specify 'a zone of human autonomy', 'a neutral sphere of personal choice', is found in a group of English glossators of the 1180s who wove together in a new synthesis the idea of a permissive natural *ius*, Isidore's definition of *fas* at the beginning of the Decretum, and Paul's words to the Corinthians, 'All things are licit for me'. The author of the Summa, *In nomine*, who defined *ius naturale* in one sense as a faculty or ability, gave as another meaning of the term:

> *Ius naturale* . . . licit and approved, neither commanded nor forbidden by the Lord or by any statute, which is also called *fas*, as for instance to reclaim one's own or not to reclaim it, to eat something or not to eat it, to put away an unfaithful wife or not to put her away . . . whence, upon the words of the Apostle, 'All things are licit for me', Ambrose commented, 'By the law of nature' (*lege nature*).[84]

(Later on, Gerson would declare that the word *facultas* was particularly appropriate to define right in his subjective sense because (he thought) *facultas* was derived from *fas*.) The idea of natural right as a sphere of free choice was emphasized in another English gloss:

> *Ius naturale* . . . licit and approved though not commanded or prohibited by any statute, as to go through another's field or not to go, which is called *fas*;

---

[83] *Ibid.*, p. 165, 'Ius enim nature dicitur ius gentium quia de natura dictante, non de lege precipiente potius habet ius suum.'

[84] Kuttner, *Repertorium*, p. 202, 'Secundo modo dicitur ius naturale licitum et approbatum quod nec a Domino nec constitutione aliqua precipitur prohibiturve, quod et fas appellatur, ut repetere suum vel non repetere, comedere vel non comedere, dimittere uxorem infidelem cohabitare volentem vel non dimittere . . . Unde (super) illud Apostoli "omnia mihi licent" Ambrosius: lege nature.' The idea that *lex* could be permissive was ancient: see Digest 1.4.3 and *Dist.* 3 c.4 of the Decretum. The interesting twelfth-century development was the association of this principle with a doctrine of natural right.

to eat or not to eat, concerning which Paul said, when he spoke of the use of foodstuffs . . . 'All things are licit for me'; all things, he said, which concern food are licit by the power of free choice and by natural law (*lege naturali*).[85]

This understanding of natural right, which is also found in other contemporary English works,[86] became broadly diffused when it was incorporated into the widely read *Summa* of Huguccio.[87]

The association of *ius naturale* with Paul's text in 1 Corinthians broadened the apostolic teaching on Christian exemption from Jewish ceremonial precepts into a more generalized doctrine of natural liberties. (The same argument will recur in Ockham's natural rights theory.) It was not that Christianity first conferred rights on its followers; rather, by not imposing the restrictions of the Old Law it left them free to exercise their pre-existing natural rights. In the texts we have just quoted *ius naturale* plainly does not mean restrictive law; the term is used to mean what we should call a natural right — to eat what one chooses for instance. The right of nature in these texts is what is permitted by the law of nature.

In discussing modern rights language, Hart explained that a right defines an area where the agent is free to act as he chooses, to assert a claim or not to assert it. The canonists were making the same point — for them *ius naturale* could mean 'to reclaim one's own or not to reclaim it'. Christian Wolff wrote: 'The law (*lex*) of nature is called preceptive which obliges us to perform certain actions; it is called prohibitive when it obliges us to omit certain actions; it is called permissive when it gives a right (*ius*) to act.' We find this same doctrine expressed in very much the same language, scattered through the Decretist glosses of the twelfth century. Wolff added, 'What we have a right (*ius*) to do is called "licit".'[88] This again echoes a common canonistic definition of *ius naturale*. Michel Villey, describing the doctrine of individual rights which, he thought, could be formulated only after Ockham, wrote that such rights implied 'a quality of the subject, one of his faculties, a liberty, a

---

[85] *Distinctiones Bambergensis*, MS Bamberg Can 17, fol. 94ra, 'Ius naturale . . . quod licitum est et approbatum, quamuis nulla constitutione sit preceptum nec prohibitum veluti per agrum alienum ire vel non ire quod fas dicitur, commedere non commedere, de quo apostolus Paulus cum de usu ciborum loqueretur ut de idolatria dixit "omnia mihi licent", omnia dixit que ad cibum pertinent licent potestate liberi arbitrii et lege naturali.' (Cf. Weigand, *Naturrechtslehre*, p. 205.)

[86] See Kuttner, *Repertorium*, p. 202 and Weigand, *Naturrechtslehre*, p. 209. Also Ricardus Anglicus, *Summa quaestionum*, MS Zwettl 162, fol. 145r. 'Secundo modo licitum dicitur et approbatum nulla constitutione preceptum uel prohibitum. Unde Ambrosius "omnia mihi licent" lege nature, et Augustinus alibi, licent que non precipiuntur nec prohibentur' (cf. Weigand, *Naturrechtslehre*, p. 213).

[87] Huguccio gave the meaning *licitum et approbatum*, with the usual references to Paul and Ambrose, as a possible fifth definition of *ius naturale*. He preferred his own primary definition, discussed above (p. 634). See Weigand, *Naturrechtslehre*, p. 217.

[88] Wolff, *Institutiones*, pp. 22, 23, '*Lex naturae . . . permissiva*, quae jus dat ad agendum', '. . . ad quod agendum tantummodo jus habemus, *Licitum* dicitur'.

possibility of acting'.[89] This too was affirmed by the twelfth-century canonists as one of the many meanings of *ius naturale*.

In the period of transition from medieval to modern thought during the sixteenth century, both definitions of *ius*, as a zone of human autonomy or sphere of licit conduct, and as a faculty or power of the individual, were drawn together in the very influential work of Francisco Vitoria, a principal founder of the school of Salamanca. Vitoria, however, seems to have been unaware of the earlier origin of the doctrines that he had assimilated during his preceding years of study in Paris:

> *Ius* therefore . . . is nothing else than what is licit or what is licit by law . . . This is plain from Saint Thomas on 2.2 ae q.57 art 1 . . . And so we use the word when we speak. For we say, 'I do not have a right (*ius*) of doing this', that is, it is not licit for me; or again, 'I use my right . . .', that is, it is licit.
>
> Conrad (Summenhart) gives a broader definition of the word *ius* . . . He says that *ius* is a power or faculty pertaining to anyone according to the laws — Conrad takes this definition from Gerson.[90]

Vitoria correctly ascribed the definition of *ius* as a *facultas* to Gerson (though, as we have seen, it was not original with him). But the attribution of a definition of *ius* as a subjective right to Aquinas was quite mistaken; Aquinas taught no such doctrine. Vitoria, steeped in a scholastic tradition that had been shaped by juristic as well as by theological reflection, and concerned with the new rights problems of his own age, including those arising from the discovery of America, creatively reinterpreted St. Thomas, just as the canonists of the twelfth century, steeped in the problems and preconceptions of their own society, reinterpreted the ancient texts collected by Gratian. In their different ways, both Vitoria and the Decretists were engaged in 'noncanonical readings of canonical texts'.

Need and Natural Right: From Medieval to Modern

By 1200 the canonists had created a language in which natural rights theories could readily be expressed. Their 'speech acts' did not merely modify existing language; they would lead on to 'the creation and diffusion of new languages'. But one might still ask whether the canonists themselves defended any specific natural rights. Had they developed only a vocabulary of words or also a vocabulary of ideas that would persist in later discourse? So far we have considered only isolated definitions of *ius naturale*, only *paroles* one might say. To answer our question we need to consider the whole *langue*, the whole context of discourse, in which the words were

---

[89] M.Villey, 'La genèse du droit subjectif chez Guillaume d'Occam', *Archives de philosophie du droit*, IX (1964), pp. 97–127, p. 101.

[90] *Francisco de Vitoria, Commentaria a la Secunda secundae de Santo Tomas*, III, ed. R.P. Vicente Beltran de Heredia (Salamanca, 1934), p. 64, 'Jus ergo . . . nihil aliud est nisi illud quod licet vel quod lege licet . . . Patet hoc ex sancto Thoma supra q. 57 a.1 . . . Et ita nos utimur illud vocabulum cum loquimur. Dicimus enim: non habeo ius faciendi hoc, id est non mihi licet; item, jure meo utor, id est licet, Conradus . . . ponit late diffinitionem illius nominis "jus" . . . Dicit ergo quod jus est potestas vel facultas conveniens alicui secundum leges . . . Hanc diffinitionem accepit Conradus ex Gersone . . .'.

embedded, and the ways in which it was transmitted to later thinkers. If we tried to trace out all the threads that led from the web of medieval rights language to the fully formed natural rights theories of the seventeenth century we would have to explore many areas of discourse in which, by about 1250, particular rights were defended in terms of natural law. They would include rights to property, rights of consent to government, rights of self-defence, rights of infidels, marriage rights, procedural rights. (From the thirteenth century onwards, Roman and canon lawyers argued that the basic rules of legal procedure guaranteeing a fair trial were based on natural law, not merely on human enactments.) Another major theme would be the respective rights of individual and community within corporate groups, a topic long ago touched on by Maitland, and especially important because of the influence of corporation law on late medieval and early modern theories of the state. (For instance, when Ockham wanted to argue that a community could not surrender all the rights of its members to a sovereign, he based his position on a technicality of thirteenth-century canonistic corporation law.) Such an inquiry would remind us that the first rights theories were not derived from contemplation of the individual isolated from his fellows — *isolé sur son île comme Robinson*[91] — but from reflection on the right ordering of human relationships in emerging societies.

A full discussion of all these topics would go far beyond the possible scope of this paper. I would like therefore to consider just one example, concerned with the most fundamental right of all, the right of self-preservation, specifically the right of the poor to use the surplus property of the rich to sustain life in cases of extreme need. In this case one can trace a clear line of argument concerning a specific natural right from the twelfth century to the seventeenth century.

Among the church Fathers there was some discussion as to whether almsgiving was a work of justice or a work of charity;[92] but the twelfth-century canonists had no doubt that strict justice required a rich man to share at least his superfluities with those in need. The Decretum contained some striking texts on this obligation: 'Feed the poor. If you do not feed them you kill them.' 'A man who keeps more for himself than he needs is guilty of theft.' 'The use of all things that are in the world ought to be common to all.' 'No one may call his own what is common, of which if he takes more than he needs, it is obtained by violence . . . The bread that you hold back belongs to the needy, the clothes that you store away belong to the naked.'[93]

Such texts indicate plainly that the rich were considered to have a duty to the poor; but, as we have seen, for modern rights theorists, to be the beneficiary of a duty is

---

[91] The phrase is from J. Dabin, 'Droit subjectif et subjectivisme juridique', *Archives de philosophie du droit*, IX (1964), pp. 17–35, p. 20. The problem of individual and community in relation to rights theories is discussed in B. Tierney, 'Conciliarism, Corporatism, and Individualism: The Doctrine of Individual Rights in Gerson', *Christianesimo nella Storia*, IX (1988), pp. 81–111. On corporation theory and early modern ideas of the state see B. Tierney, *Religion, Law, and the Growth of Constitutional Thought* (Cambridge, 1982).

[92] For detailed discussion, with references to the earlier literature, see G. Couvreur, *Les pauvres. Ont-ils des droits?* (Paris, 1961).

[93] *Dist.* 86 c.21, *Dist.* 42 *ante* c.1, C.12 q.1 c.2, *Dist.* 47 c.8.

not necessarily the same thing as having a right. Medieval canonists understood this point too. A bishop might have a duty to grant a dispensation when circumstances warranted it, they pointed out, but the petitioner did not have a right to insist on the grant. One of the twelfth-century Decretists, distinguishing between duties and rights in a discussion on the claims of the poor, used precisely the example of a third-party beneficiary employed in Hart's modern argument. 'If I promise you to give something to someone else I am bound to give to the third party and I am naturally obliged to him; nevertheless he cannot bring suit . . .'.[94] The rich certainly had a natural duty to succour the poor; it was not so clear that the poor had a natural right that could be asserted against the rich.

The canonists first approached this question by asking whether a poor man in extreme need who took the goods of a rich one was guilty of the sin of theft. Characteristically, they addressed the problem first by probing the inner state of mind of the agent. Theft, by definition, required the taking of something from an unwilling owner. So the poor person would not be guilty of theft, Huguccio suggested, because 'he believes or should believe' that the owner would give him permission to take what was needed.[95] Couvreur maintained that, with this argument, Huguccio 'magisterially concluded from the duty of the rich to the right of the poor'.[96] But it was still a shadowy sort of right, based only on an unprovable hypothesis about the state of mind of the needy person. Huguccio made a greater contribution with a novel argument about the relationship between common ownership and private property — a persistent, nagging problem for commentators on the first distinctions of the Decretum.

So far we have considered the existence of private property in relation to natural law only as a sort of legal conundrum to be solved by juggling the various senses of *ius naturale*. The usual explanation was that common property was only a 'demonstration' of natural law, a primeval state of affairs that had passed way with the introduction of human law or divine positive law (as expressed in Commandments like 'Thou shalt not steal', 'Thou shalt not covet thy neighbour's house'). But there was another whole dimension to this problem for medieval moralists. 'The use of all things ought to be common to all.' 'No one may call his own what is common.' These texts, attributed by Gratian to St. Clement and St. Ambrose, spoke as if common property was a permanent feature of Christian society, informing it with charity and justice. There seemed an inherent conflict between the ideal held up by the Fathers and the realities of medieval life.

Huguccio was particularly unhappy with the idea of a natural law that could simply become obsolete, with no continuing relevance to the social and moral problems of

---

[94] *Summa Bambergensis ad Dist.* 47 c.8 (Couvreur, *Les pauvres*, p. 109), 'Nam et si stipulor tibi me daturum X alii, teneor quidem dare tertio et naturaliter obligor illi. Tamen illi non potest agere ad illa X . . .'.

[95] *Summa ad* C.12 q.2 c.11, MS Admont 7, fol. 243ra, 'Ego tamen credo quod non peccet quis in tali casu, scilicet cum utitur re alterius propter urgentem necessitatem . . . quia aut credit aut debet credere dominum esse permissurum . . . quo casu furtum non committitur.'

[96] Couvreur, *Les pauvres*, p. 91.

his own age. Such a doctrine did not fit well with his own preferred definition of *ius* as an intrinsic, permanent force of reason or moral discernment in the human soul. At one point he wrote, 'If you want to insist on the common explanation you may say that common possession of all things is from the natural law . . . that consists in demonstrations'.[97] But Huguccio did not think this was the real explanation. He preferred a new formulation of his own which he set out at the beginning of his *Summa* and reiterated several times in the course of the work:

When it is said that by natural *ius* all things are common . . . this is the meaning. By natural *ius*, that is in accordance with the judgement of reason, all things are common, that is they are to be shared with the poor in time of need. For reason naturally leads us to suppose that we should keep only what is necessary and distribute what is left to the needy.[98]

'*Communis . . . id est communicanda.*' 'Common . . . that is to be shared.' The words were endlessly repeated in later discussions. In this way of thinking, private property was a social institution involving natural obligations to others. Property could and should be private and common at the same time; private in the sense that ownership and administration belonged to the individuals, common in the sense that worldly goods had to be shared with others in time of need.[99]

Huguccio did not himself use this doctrine to assert a natural right of the poor to the superfluous property of the rich, but its relevance to the issue was perceived almost at once. Ricardus Anglicus, again discussing the case of a poor person in extreme need, wrote in the 1190s: 'Since by natural *ius* all things are common, that is to be shared in time of need, he is not properly said to steal.'[100] From this it was only a step to affirming explicitly the natural right of the poor. Around 1200 Alanus held that the poor man did not steal because what he took was really his own *iure*

---

[97] *Summa ad* D.1 c.7, MS Admont 7, fol. 3ra, 'Vel si vellis communi expositioni insistere, dicas, *communis omnium possessio*, id est quod omnia sint communia id est de iure naturali, eo scilicet quod licitum siue fas appellatur, scilicet quod consistit in demonstrationibus . . .'.

[98] *Summa* (Introduction), MS Admont 7, fol. 2va, 'Cum dicitur iure naturali omnia sunt communia . . . is est sensus . . . iure naturali, id est iudicio rationis approbante omnia sunt communia, id est tempore necessitatis indigentibus communicanda. Naturali enim ductu rationis approbamus nobis tantum necessaria retinere, reliqua proximis indigentibus debere distribuere . . .'. See also *Summa ad Dist.* 1 c.7, fol. 3ra, 'Communis possessio omnium, id est communicatio omnium que possidemus tempore necessitatis, hoc de iure naturali quod dicitur ratio . . .'. This doctrine of Huguccio, and its incorporation into the Ordinary Gloss of the Decretum was discussed in B. Tierney, *Medieval Poor Law* (Berkeley and Los Angeles, 1959). A little later Couvreur returned to the topic and printed a wealth of texts illustrating the wide diffusion of Huguccio's teaching. See Couvreur, *Les pauvres*, pp. 91–106, 141–54 and, for an extensive selection of Huguccio's texts, pp. 290–6.

[99] *Summa ad Dist.* 47 c.8, MS Admont 7, fol. 65ra, 'Quod est commune, id est tempore necessitatis aliis communicandum . . . Et secundum hoc idem est proprium et commune, proprium quoad dominium uel potestatem dispensandi, commune quia aliis communicandum tempore necessitatis.'

[100] Gloss *ad Comp. I*, 5.26.5 (Couvreur, *Les pauvres*, p. 92, n. 248), 'Nam cum iure naturali omnia sunt communia id est tempore necessitatis communicanda non dicitur proprie furari sed pretoris altissimi fungi . . .'. Ricardus was followed by many other canonists. See Couvreur, *Les pauvres*, pp. 92–4.

naturali — which could mean either 'by natural right' or 'by natural law'.[101] About the same time another glossator suggested that the person in need could 'declare his right for himself'.[102] Then Laurentius, followed by Vincentius Hispanus, wrote that, when the poor man took what he needed, it was 'as if he used his own right and his own thing'.[103] Finally, the doctrine entered the mainstream of medieval jurisprudence when Hostiensis reformulated it more sharply and included it in his very widely read *Lectura* on the Decretals. 'One who suffers the need of hunger seems to use his right rather than to plan a theft.'[104] Of course, it was a natural right that was being discussed.

In modern rights language, we have seen, a right can be defined in one sense as a 'rightful power'. This is essentially what the canonists were asserting for the person in want. If he used his own efforts to take what he needed from the superfluities of the rich he was acting rightfully in the sense that he was not guilty of sin in the eyes of God. But the situation was not wholly satisfactory from the point of view of the person in want; the secular judge would probably hang him. We need to consider therefore whether the poor man also had a 'rightful claim'. If he did not want to risk punishment for theft, could he only appeal to the 'love or piety or mercy' of the rich (to use Feinberg's modern language) or could he somehow demand, claim, insist upon his right? Huguccio doubted that he could. The problem was that none of the established forms of legal action covered this kind of case. Certainly the superfluities of the rich were owed to the poor, Huguccio wrote, but then he added: 'Many things are owed that cannot be sought by judicial procedure, such as dignities and dispensations and alms . . . but they can be sought as something due mercifully for the sake of God and piety.'[105] This opinion did not prevail however. Alongside the formal judicial procedures inherited from Roman law the canonists had developed an alternative, more simple, equitable process known as 'evangelical denunciation'. By virtue of the authority inhering in his office as judge, a bishop could hear any complaint involving an alleged sin and could provide a remedy without the plaintiff bringing a formal action. From about 1200 onwards several canonists argued that this procedure was available to the poor person in extreme need. He could assert a rightful claim by an 'appeal to the office of the judge'. The bishop could then compel

---

[101] Gloss *ad Comp. I*, 5.26.5 (Couvreur, *Les pauvres*, p. 161, n. 280), '. . . quod accipit suum iure naturali efficitur'.

[102] *App. Militant siquidem ad Comp. I*, 5.26.5 (Couvreur, *Les pauvres*, p. 118, n. 349), '. . . in tali articulo potest sibi ius dicere sicut et creditor si videat debitorem suum a civitate fugere . . .'.

[103] Vincentius, *ad Comp. I*, 5.26.5 (Couvreur, *Les pauvres*, p. 102), 'Hic res ista quam dicebat furari est communis, id est communicanda in tali articulo erat, et ideo iste eam accipiendo quasi iure suo et re sua utebatur.'

[104] Hostiensis, *Lectura in V libros Decretalium* (Venice, 1581), ad X.5.18.3, 'Unde potius videtur is qui necessitatem patitur uti iure suo quam furti consilium inire.' The text was later included in Johannes Andreae's *In quinque Decretalium libros novella commentaria* (Venice, 1601), *ad* X.5.18.3.

[105] *Summa ad Dist.* 47 c.8, MS Admont 7, fol. 65ra, 'Revera eis debentur, sed multa debentur que tamen peti non possunt ordine iudiciario ut dignitates et dispensationes et elemosine, sed possunt peti sicut debentur, scilicet misericorditer et intuitu dei et pietatis.'

an intransigent rich man to give alms from his superfluities, by excommunication if necessary. The argument gained general currency when it was assimilated into the Ordinary Gloss to the Decretum.[106] It was, as Couvreur wrote, an elegant solution. 'It provided a judicial sanction for the rights of the poor.'

These canonistic arguments about the status and claims of needy persons provide an explicit example of an early natural rights theory. Considered simply as theory, the doctrine was subtle and far-ranging. As with many supposed human rights nowadays, one can envisage serious difficulties in putting the theory into practice. But, however that may be, the canonists' teaching persisted and, from the thirteenth century onwards, it was drawn into philosophical as well as juristic discussions. Aquinas repeated that the poor person who stole in extreme need took what was really his, but without any overt reference to a subjective right of the poor person.[107] Godfrey of Fontaines, a little later, was quite explicit. The right to the necessities of life was not only a natural right but an inalienable right: 'By the law of nature (iure naturae) each one has a certain right (ius) in the common exterior goods of this world, which right cannot be licitly renounced.'[108] Ockham reformulated the doctrine of the rights of the poor in extreme need with explicit reference to the text of pseudo-Ambrose included in the Decretum, and closely paraphrased Huguccio in discussing it:

> In another sense temporal things belong to others because they are owed by necessity . . . that is they are owed by right reason. And in this way the superfluities of the rich belong to the poor . . . So are to be understood the words of Ambrose given at Dist. 47.[109]

Gerson wrote of a 'right of nourishing the body' and repeated that all things were common in case of necessity.[110] Vitoria restated the canonists' teaching but, again, mistakenly suggested that Aquinas taught a doctrine of subjective rights. 'Thomas

---

[106] Gl. ord. ad Dist. 47 c.8. On this whole question see Tierney, Medieval Poor Law, pp. 37–9 and Couvreur, Les pauvres, pp. 108–15.

[107] Aquinas, Summa theol. 2.2ae.66.7.

[108] Les Quodlibets onze-quatorze de Godefroid de Fontaines, ed. J. Hoffmans, Les Philosophes Belges, IV (Louvain, 1924), p. 105, 'Immo etiam propter hoc quod unusquisque tenetur iure naturae vitam suam sustentare . . . ideo etiam iure naturae quilibet habet dominium et quoddam ius in bonis communibus exterioribus huius mundi, cui etiam iuri renuntiare non potest licite.'

[109] Opus nonaginta dierum, ed. H.S. Offler, Guillelmi de Ockham opera politica, II (Manchester, 1963), p. 576, 'Aliter dicuntur temporalia esse aliquorum ex debiti necessitate . . . quia scilicet eis ex ratione recta debentur. Et isto modo superflua divitum sunt pauperum . . . Et sic intelligenda sunt verba Ambrosii, quae ponuntur di xlvii Sicut hii . . .'. In other contexts Ockham referred explicity to the right of the person in need, e.g. Opera I, p. 322, 'Nam quilibet in extrema necessitate constitutus habet ius utendi re consumptibile, sine qua de hac vita migraret . . .'.

[110] Gerson, Oeuvres, III, p. 156, '. . . dicimus titulum naturalem ad quem consequitur jus nutriendi corpus sic quod in ejus necessitate omnia sibi sint ad hoc communia'.

says that all things are common in extreme necessity. So if they are common I have a right to them.'[111]

Other Spanish scholastics of the school of Salamanca continued the medieval discussions about the rights of the needy and the duties of the wealthy with endless refinements of argument.[112] The right of a poor man to the surplus property of the rich still found a place in Locke's political theory:

> God, the Lord and Father of all, has given no one of his children such a Property in his peculiar portion of the things of this world, but that he has given his Brother a Right to the Surplusage of his Goods; so that it cannot justly be denied him when his pressing Want calls for it.[113]

Conclusion

The language of the canonists persisted in later political theory, though sometimes the original source of the language was forgotten. It was transmitted mainly in two ways. One way was through the encyclopaedic works of the late medieval lawyers. They were well known to those of the sixteenth-century Spanish scholastics who were jurists as well as theologians; and these writers in turn often influenced seventeenth-century rights theories. When Suarez, for instance, chose to formulate his doctrine of rights in terms of *ius in re* and *ius ad rem* he was well aware that he was using a long-established technical vocabulary. The other main channel of transmission was through the work of Ockham and other participants in the fourteenth-century dispute over Franciscan poverty.[114] Ockham relied more on earlier canonistic teachings than on his own innovative nominalist philosophy in formulating his theories on property and poverty and natural rights. He in turn influenced a whole school of late medieval theologians, including Gerson. When Ockham wrote on natural rights he was not trying to start a 'semantic revolution'. There was no need for a revolution. The canonists had already created a language in which sophisticated rights theories could be expressed. Ockham's role was to draw this language into the mainstream of Western political thought. None of the canonists themselves, we have noted, wrote an extended, coherent treatise on natural rights. Paradoxically, the closest thing we have to a 'great text' on canonistic political theory is Ockham's *Dialogus*.[115]

---

[111] Vitoria, *Commentaria*, III, p. 340, '. . . Sanctus Thomas . . . dicit quod omnia sunt communia in extrema necessitate. Si ergo sunt communia, habeo jus ad illa'.

[112] See K. Deuringer, *Probleme der Caritas in der Schule von Salamanca* (Freiburg, 1959).

[113] *John Locke. Two Treatises of Government*, ed. P. Laslett (Cambridge, 2nd edn., 1970), IV. 42, p. 188.

[114] Some of the others, besides Ockham, who contributed significantly to the growth of rights theories are discussed in the forthcoming papers, 'Marsilius on Rights' and 'Law and Rights in Decretales 5.40.12'.

[115] On Ockham's use of canonistic sources see B. Tierney, 'Ockham, the Conciliar Theory and the Canonists', *Journal of the History of Ideas*, XV (1954), pp. 40–70 and B. Tierney, 'Natural Law and Canon Law in Ockham's Dialogus', in *Aspects of Late Medieval Government and Society. Essays Presented to J.R. Lander*, ed. J.G. Rowe (Toronto, 1986), pp. 3–24. De Lagarde counted the citations in one book of

Still, the language of the twelfth-century Decretists was decisive for the future of rights discourse. To be sure no canonist presented as ample an array of natural rights as we find in some of the fully formed theories of the seventeenth century; but then no seventeenth-century theorist envisaged the whole catalogue of more or less worthy human aspirations that are included in our modern Universal Declaration of Human Rights. The story of natural rights language from the twelfth century to the present is one of constant growth and adaptation. One might say that, in the works of the Decretists, a distinctive mutation of thought and language occurred which gave rise to a whole new species of ideas, the species of natural rights theories. Individual examples of the species came to vary widely after a few generations, shaped by the experience of changing environments. Ideas that could adapt persisted. In some historical environments natural rights theories could not survive at all. Sometimes the seed fell on stony ground. Sometimes the theories that grew up were stunted and deformed.

Biological metaphor can carry us only so far. Historians do not have such elegant models to explain the development of ideas as scientists use in describing organic evolution. It is partly of course because cultural evolution is Lamarkian, not Darwinian. Acquired characteristics are passed on to succeeding generations. To put it differently, each particular rights theory was shaped partly as a response to a specific set of contingent circumstances. A real history of Western natural rights theories would have to be concerned as much with contexts as with texts. (In the Middle Ages alone we should need to consider the contexts of twelfth-century juridical humanism, of fourteenth-century Franciscan poverty disputes, of fifteenth-century conciliarism; then the discovery of the New World, the religious turmoil of the Reformation, and the English Civil War all provided new contexts in which rights theories could flourish.) But not everything was new in each succeeding context. That is why a historical tradition can be intelligible, something other than a mere sequence of unconnected Foucaultian archaeological layers. Language inherited from the past, shaped by old, perhaps forgotten contingencies, formed a part of the context within which each succeeding rights theorist lived and thought and wrote. Characteristics of language that were first acquired in the twelfth century persisted. The language of the Decretists was a part of the context for Ockham, Ockham's language for Gerson, Gerson's for Suarez. A text like that of Huguccio on private property and its responsibilities became 'an actor in an indefinite series of literary utterances'.

Carlos Fuentes wrote recently: 'There is no creation without tradition; the 'new' is an inflection of a preceding form; novelty is always a variation on the past.' It is true of course, and yet some variations are of decisive importance for the future. The semantic shifts of the twelfth century were of this kind. The medieval concern for subjective rights in practical everyday life reshaped the language in which discourse

---

the *Dialogus*; he found three references to Thomas Aquinas, twelve to church Fathers, sixty-five to Scripture, and three hundred and thirteen references to canon law. G. de Lagarde, *La naissance*, IV (Paris, 2nd ed., 1962), p. 52.

II

646

about natural right was conducted. By around 1200 many canonists were coming to realize that the old language of *ius naturale* could be used to define both a faculty or force of the human person and a 'neutral sphere of personal choice', 'a zone of human autonomy'. But they did not, like some modern critics of rights theories, expect such language to justify a moral universe in which each individual would ruthlessly pursue his own advantage. Like most of the classical rights theorists down to Locke and Wolff they envisaged a sphere of natural rights bounded by a natural moral law. The first natural rights theories were not based on an apotheosis of simple greed or self-serving egotism; rather they derived from a view of individual humans as free, self-aware persons, capable of moral discernment, and from a consideration of the ties of justice and charity that bound individuals to one another. Western rights theories have a respectable ancestry; they grew from good seed. Maybe they will continue to bring forth fruit. That will depend on the kind of environment we create for them in the years ahead. The texts of the twenty-first century on human rights will also be shaped by their contexts.

III

IUS AND METONYMY IN RUFINUS

A widespread point of view in modern scholarship holds that the idea of "right" (*dikaion, ius*) referred to an objective reality in Aristotelian philosophy and classical Roman law, that this meaning was faithfully preserved in the thought of Thomas Aquinas, and that the notion of *ius* as a subjective attribute of human persons, the source of modern rights theories, was a fourteenth-century deviation from this established tradition. Eventually, it is argued, the deviant doctrine found a home in the «Second Scholasticism» of sixteenth-century Spain.

This argument was worked out most fully in the many writings of Michel Villey.[1] He pointed out that, for Aristotle, *to dikaion* did not refer to a subjective faculty or to laws defining subjective rights; it meant rather "the just", the object of justice. This meaning was preserved by the classical Roman jurists in their definitions of *ius*. For Gaius, Villey pointed out, *ius* was not a subjective power but a thing, *res*. Similarly, when Aquinas gave a formal definition of *ius* (*Summa theol.* 2.2ae.57.1), he wrote that the word, in its primary sense, meant "the just" or "the just thing". As for *ius* understood in a subjective sense, Villey regarded this as a later, post-Thomist aberration. In an early article he associated it with the *cogito ergo sum* of Descartes and with Jesuit spirituality,[2] but in his subsequent work he emphasized especially the role of Ockham as the decisive innovator. Influenced by his nominalism and voluntarism, Ockham for the first time fused together the two disparate concepts of *ius* and *potestas*. Villey saw this as a «Copernican moment» in the history of legal phi-

---

[1] Villey's arguments, originally presented in many scattered articles, are conveniently summarized in two works of synthesis, *La formation de la pensée juridique moderne*, 4th ed., Paris, 1975 and *Philosophie du droit* 2 vols. 3rd ed., Paris, 1982. For a critical review of his theses see my *Villey, Ockham and the Origin of Individual Rights*, in: T. WITTE and F.S. ALEXANDER (eds.), *The Weightier Matters of the Law. A Tribute to Harold J. Berman*, Atlanta, 1988, 1-31.

[2] M. VILLEY, *Le «jus in re» du droit romain classique au droit moderne*, in: *Conférences faites à l'Institut de Droit Romain en 1947*, Paris 1950, 187-225 (190).

losophy. For Ockham, *ius* was not something inherent in the external order of things but specifically a subjective power of individuals.[3]

Louis Lachance presented a similar set of arguments.[4] He too emphasized the objective meaning of *ius* in Aquinas and treated the subjective understanding of the work as a later development associated with nominalism and voluntarism. For Lachance, the definitions of *ius* as meaning either a body of law or a moral power inherent in individuals, that we find in later legal philosophies, were only analogies. They departed from the real, primary meaning of the word. They were "improper" definitions.[5] Lachance particularly disliked a definition that he quoted from Suarez, «... *solet proprie ius vocari facultas quaedam moralis...*». Thomas never dreamed of including such a meaning even among the various derivative senses of *ius*, Lachance noted. He added that to define *ius* as a moral power was to make human will the rule of morality. Lachance argued that a moral power may indicate what is licit, permitted, not prohibited, but that this moral power is not itself *ius* in a strict sense; rather the faculty presupposes *ius* understood as what is just, which in turn is specified by laws aiming at the common good. It would turn things upside down to define *ius* as a moral power related to the good of the individual.[6]

Similar arguments recur in the most recent scholarly literature. In an article published in 1988, Dario Composta began by asserting, as an established finding of modern legal-historical research, that an objective concept of *ius* (*diritto*) prevailed from Aristotle to the fourteenth century. Subjective attitudes, Composta noted, could be expressed by words like *facultas, potestas, licitum est*, but they were not considered relevant in the definition of *ius* itself. A new attitude emerged in the fourteenth century in the work of Scotus and Ockham; *ius* was now understood primarily as a faculty or power identified with the individual will. Composta went on to discuss the interplay of the two concepts of *ius* that he had described in the Spanish scholastics of the sixteenth century, especially in Vitoria's view of *ius* as a faculty or power to do what is licit.[7]

Much of the argumentation presented by Villey, Lachance and Composta

---

[3] *La formation*, 252: «... il appartient à Occam... sans doute pour la première fois... de consacrer la jonction des idées de *droit* et de *pouvoir*...»; «Nous sommes ici-même au moment copernicien de l'histoire de la science de droit» (261).

[4] L. LACHANCE, *Le concept de droit selon Aristote et S. Thomas*, 2nd ed., Ottawa-Montreal, 1948; *Le droit et les droits de l'homme*, Paris, 1959.

[5] *Le concept*, 235; *Le droit*, 146-150.

[6] *Le concept*, 292-300; *Le droit*, 164-165.

[7] D. COMPOSTA, *Il concetto di diritto nell'umanesimo giuridico di Francisco de Vitoria O. P.*, in: C. SORIA (ed.), *I diritti dell'uomo e la pace nel pensiero di Francisco de Vitoria e Bartolomé de las Casas* (Milano 1988).

is sound and perceptive. But it neglects a whole relevant area of medieval jurisprudence. In this paper I want to call attention to a tradition of thought initiated by the canonist Rufinus that, before Aquinas and long before Ockham, had already emphasized a subjective understanding of *ius*, and specifically of *ius naturale*. The modern authors mentioned above all implicitly or explicitly denied the existence of such a juristic tradition. Composta observed that the Aristotelian understanding of *ius* persisted in Roman and medieval jurisprudence. Villey held that a subjective concept of *ius* did not find expression in the writing of academic jurists until Ockham provided a philosophy to justify it. Lachance wrote that the views of Aquinas «reflected a long and invariable juridical tradition» and that in his day, «juridical subjectivism was still unknown».[8] Such remarks ignore a significant body of twelfth-century Decretist texts in which *ius naturale* was defined in just the kind of language that Composta mentioned as irrelevant to the definition of *ius* before Scotus and Ockham - as *facultas, potentia, licitum* and, most commonly, *vis*. Many relevant texts have been printed and they are well known, at least to specialists in canon law;[9] but they do not seem to have been adequately assimilated into modern studies on the origins of natural law and natural rights theories. Among the twelfth-century Decretists Rufinus was unusual, not because he gave a subjective definition of *ius naturale*, which was common enough, but because he presented this definition, not merely as one possible meaning among several others, but as the primary and proper significance of the term. Moreover Rufinus seems to have been the first to formulate such a definition. For him, *ius* was, not primarily the objectively just, but «a certain force instilled into the human creature by nature to do what is good».[10] From this primary, subjective definition he derived, already in the twelfth century, the various meanings of *ius* discussed by Lachance and the other authors we have mentioned – *ius* as law, *ius* as a power inhering in a person, *ius* as the objectively just.

* * *

The English critic, William Empson, once wrote that a complex word can contain a whole «compacted doctrine».[11] It is true of course, but not the whole

---

[8] COMPOSTA, *Il concetto*, 275; VILLEY, *La formation*, 239; LACHANCE, *Le droit*, 150, 166.

[9] The most ample collection of relevant texts is in R. WEIGAND, *Die Naturrechtslehre der Legisten und Dekretisten von Irnerius bis Accursius und von Gratian bis Johannes Teutonicus*, München, 1967. Weigand's texts provide examples of all the subjective meanings of *ius* mentioned above.

[10] H. SINGER (ed.), *Rufinus von Bologna. Summa Decretorum*, Paderborn, 1902, 6 (see below n. 14).

[11] W. EMPSON, *The Structure of Complex Words*, Totowa, New Jersey, 1979, 39. I do not

truth. A word like *ius* can convey several different doctrines — at one extreme, let us say, the doctrine of Thomas Aquinas (*ius* as the objective «just thing»), at the other that of Thomas Hobbes (*ius* as the liberty to exercise a subjective power). Rufinus's concept of *ius* as an innate *vis* is different from either of these. It is neither the objective just thing of Aquinas nor the absolute liberty of Hobbes. Nor is it quite identical with the *facultas moralis* of Suarez. Rufinus's *ius* was primarily a force impelling us to do the good, not a power to assert a right (though it could also have this latter meaning). At any rate, Rufinus was certainly starting out from a subjective understanding of *ius* as an attribute of the human person[12] which was different from anything we find in Aristotle or, later, in Aquinas: *Est itaque naturale ius vis quedam humane creature a natura insita ad faciendum bonum cavendumque contrarium.*

Problems of interpretation arise when a word is defined in a new way so as to imply a set of interconnected ideas which are deployed in the ensuing text, but without an explicit account of how the ideas are related to one another or to the original definition. This is what we find in Rufinus. After the first firm definition of *ius* as an innate *vis*, he most commonly used the word *ius*, not in this precise sense, but rather to mean either *lex*, a law or body of laws, or alternatively to mean a subjective right. Rufinus did not invent the meanings of *ius* that he deployed after his own definition; the word came to him laden with past associations which were also familiar to his readers. A twelfth-century audience interested in canon law did not need to be told explicitly that the word *ius* could sometimes mean a body of laws as in *ius canonicum* and sometimes an individual or corporate right as in *ius eligendi*. So Rufinus could move unreflectively from one meaning to the other, confident that the connotation he intended in each case would be apparent to the audience he addressed.

But Rufinus was not simply following accepted usage. The unusual feature of his work is that he chose to introduce the discussion of *ius naturale* with his own new definition of the term, which clearly was not presented inadvertently or unreflectively. So when he went on at once to deploy the word *ius* with different meanings there was an implied assertion that they were all somehow related to the first meaning and so to one another. Rufinus himself

---

want to overload this brief paper with methodological considerations; for some further relevant discussion, see P. COSTA, *Iurisdictio. Semantica del potere politico nella pubblicistica medievale (1100-1433)*, Milano 1960; A. VAN HOVE discussed some metonyms of *ius* in *Prolegomena ad codicem iuris canonici*, Mechliniae-Romae, 1945, 6-7.

[12] Weigand noted this, *op. cit.*, 145: «Er fasst es also mehr in einem subjektiven Sinn».

suggested this in discussing human law when he wrote: «All the rivers of human righteousness flow back to the sea of natural *ius*».[13]

Rufinus, then, first gave a clear definition of the core meaning of *ius naturale* as he understood it; then he surrounded the core meaning with a cluster of derived and related meanings. His argument can best be understood as a series of metonyms, the figure of speech in which a word is used to convey a meaning that is not its primary one but somehow adjacent to the first meaning or connected with it by some association of ideas, as for instance a part for a whole, a cause for an effect, a place for an institution («the White House», «the Kremlin»). We need not suppose that Rufinus set out consciously to construct a series of such metonyms, it is rather that a modern reader can be helped to follow his thought if we bear in mind that this common figure of speech is often used unreflectively in everyday discourse, both medieval and modern.

Let us turn back to the text. I have said that Rufinus did not formulate his definition of *ius naturale* unreflectively. We can know this from the fact that he deliberately set aside two established definitions in order to shape his own preferred one. He mentioned Ulpian's Roman law definition, «natural *ius* is what nature has taught all animals», but dismissed it as irrelevant for his purpose. The text of Gratian that he was commenting on provided another definition of *ius naturale* as a moral precept, the Golden Rule of Scripture, «Do unto others as you would have them do unto you...». But Rufinus tacitly rejected this too. Instead, he gave his own new definition of *ius* as a «*vis... a natura insita*».[14]

Composta recently expressed amazement that a sixteenth century definition of *ius* by Ferdinando Perez (1587) did not include the objective sense of «the just». But this meaning is already lacking in our twelfth-century definition. After his first words, Rufinus continued with a further explanation: *Consistit autem ius naturale in tribus, scilicet: mandatis, prohibitionibus, demonstrationibus.*

---

[13] *Summa ad dictum Gratiani ante* c. 1, 7: «... *flumina honestatis humane redeunt ad mare iuris naturalis...*».

[14] *Summa ad dictum Gratiani ante* c. 1, 6. O. LOTTIN thought this definition could have been derived from Cicero, the *glossa ordinaria* to Romans 2.14, or a text attributed to Basil, *Le droit naturel chez Saint Thomas et ses prédécesseurs*, 2nd ed., Bruges, 1931, 14. Weigand suggested an analogy with the definition of Ulpian that Rufinus quoted but declined to adopt. The closest anticipation of Rufinus's language is certainly Cicero's *vis innata*; but Rufinus's doctrine is not the same as Cicero's. For Cicero there was an innate force in man through which he could discern *ius*. For Rufinus the innate force was itself *ius*. His definition may be compared with the «objective» one of Aquinas: «*Ius sive iustum naturale est quod ex sui natura est adaequatum vel commensuratum alteri*» (*Summa theol.* 2 2ae. 57.3). Aquinas knew of course a natural inclination in man to seek the good, but he did not identify the inclination with *ius*.

554

At once we encounter a problem. In what sense does *ius naturale*, understood as an innate force, «consist» of commands and prohibitions or of «demonstrations»? Commands, prohibitions, demonstrations are not component parts of a subjective *vis*; they are rather rules of conduct that can be discerned by the force in us making for good (*ius naturale* in its primary sense). The metonymic relationship is like that of cause and effect or more precisely of a faculty and the object of the faculty. (Thus, in English, the word sight refers primarily to the subjective faculty of seeing but it can also mean the thing that is seen, as in the phrase «a pretty sight»).

The division into commands and prohibitions on the one hand and demonstrations on the other was original with Rufinus. The commands and prohibitions are clearly laws, and, in discussing them, Rufinus identified natural *ius* with natural *lex*, using the terms interchangeably. He argued, quite conventionally, that the natural law that could be known to man intuitively was also revealed by God in the Ten Commandments and more perfectly in the Gospel: *Et propterea evangelium substitutum est ubi* ius *naturale... perficitur. Quoniam autem ista* lex *naturalis nudam rerum naturam prosequitur, ostendendo solummodo hoc in natura sui* equum *esse... ideo necessarium fuit − bonos mores succedere.*[15]

Rufinus was like Aquinas (and medieval authors generally) in noting that natural law, which specifies what is intrinsically just, needs to be supplemented by human laws. But the sequence of argument is different. For Aquinas the primary meaning of *ius* was «what is just». For Rufinus *ius* meant first an innate force in human persons; from this was derived a concept of *lex*; and from this a perception of what is just (*equum*). Aquinas's starting point comes at the end of Rufinus's argument.[16]

In the work of Rufinus the idea of *ius naturale* as natural law was clearly stated and often repeated. Eventually his further understanding of *ius naturale* as *demonstratio*, an area of allowed conduct where the laws neither commanded nor prohibited, would lead on to a concept of natural rights.[17] But this argument was not much developed by Rufinus himself, though he did refer to conduct that was licit and permitted by natural law,[18] the language that Lachance and Composta associated with later natural rights theories.

---

[15] *Ibid.*

[16] G. KALINOWSKI suggested a metonymic relationship in Aquinas's treatment of *ius* and *lex*. See, *Le fondement objectif du droit d'après la Somme théologique de Saint Thomas d'Aquin*, in: *Archives de philosophie de droit* 18 (1973), 59-75.

[17] This is discussed further in my article, *Origins of Natural Rights Language: Texts and Contexts, 1150-1250*, in: *History of Political Thought* 10 (1989), 615-646.

[18] *Summa ad Dist.* 1 c. 1, 8: «... *iure naturali, quo sunt omnia communia, licitum est transire*

Both objective laws and subjective rights were considered when Rufinus turned to the human forms of *ius* that supplemented natural *ius*. At the beginning of his work he explained carefully how the first body of human law, the *ius gentium*, was derived from the original *vis* inherent in human beings. The qualities that gave to human personality its pristine dignity, a sense of justice and a clarity of understanding, were obscured by sin; but the original *vis* — which Rufinus would shortly define as *ius naturale* — was not altogether extinct. It led men to deliberate together to form the *ius gentium*.[19] So here, through the medium of human agreement, natural *ius* in the primary sense of an innate *vis* was the cause of *ius* understood as a system of law.

When Rufinus discussed *ius* as subjective right he derived it from common consent or established law. The Roman people, threatened by anarchy, gave to the decemviri the supreme right (*summum ius*) of reshaping the laws. The law of guardianship gave to a tutor *ius et potestas* in relation to his ward. (*Pace* Villey, the concepts "right" and "power" were commonly associated in canonistic discourse.) Such usages seem related to the initial definition of *ius* in that, even when the word means a right or power as here, it is related to a good end, the good of the Roman people, the good of the minor under tutelage.

In these passages Rufinus was adapting the language of Roman law. But he was not just using it unthinkingly. He also made a distinctive contribution of his own to the understanding of *ius* as a subjective right. Discussing the status of ecclesiastical prelates, he carefully explored the meaning of *ius* in the sense of an authority or power inhering in a person. A bishop-elect, before his consecration had full power or full right in the sphere of administration, Rufinus wrote, even though he lacked the full dignity of his office: *... plenam potestatem habeat quoad administrationem non autem quoad dignitatis auctoritatem, et ideo iure plene administrationis potest aliquos... suspendere.*[20]

Here again *ius* and *potestas* were treated as interchangeable terms. Rufinus also deployed the careful distinction between authority and right of administration in another context when he considered papal-imperial relations.[21] A crucial text of Peter Damian, incorporated into the *Decretum* at *Dist.*

---

per agrum alienum». At *Dist.* 1 c. 7, 10, referring to the right of self-defense, Rufinus wrote: «... *vi vim repellere omnes leges omniaque iura permittunt»* (cf. *Dig.* 9.2.45.4).

[19] *Praefatio,* 4: «*Cum itaque naturalis vis in homine penitus extincta non esset... deliberavit homo cum proximis convenire... et certas pactiones inire: que quidem ius gentium appellantur».*

[20] *Summa ad Dist.* 23 c. 1, 52.

[21] *Summa ad Dist.* 22 c. 1, 47: «... *ius aliud est auctoritatis, aliud amministrationis...».*

22 c. 1 declared that Peter had received «rights of earthly and heavenly empire» — *terreni simul et celestis imperii iura.* (In the sphere of divine government too, the word *ius* could mean a divinely conferred right as well as a divinely promulgated law.) Rufinus explained that, in earthly matters, the pope had a right of authority in that he consecrated the emperor and judged him if he sinned. The emperor had authority «after» the pope and the office of administering «apart» from him. Thus Rufinus elegantly affirmed the pope's superiority while leaving to the emperor the actual management of temporal affairs. To explore this text in detail would take us into a new range of problems concerning spiritual and temporal power. It is an area where Alfons Stickler has written in magisterial fashion. In his early work Alfons Stickler pointed to the importance of Rufinus's text for medieval theories of empire and papacy. It is only a footnote to his work to add that Rufinus was also important in the development of juristic thought on the concept of *ius naturale.*

* * *

After Rufinus, the definition of *ius naturale* as an innate *vis* was often repeated by the twelfth-century canonists, usually as one of several possible meanings. Huguccio, however, again insisted on the subjective interpretation as the primary, essential sense of the term. Moreover Huguccio emphasized a point that was already implicit in Rufinus: the force in humans that corresponded to *ius naturale* was a force of reason — *ius naturale dicitur ratio, scilicet naturalis vis animi.* Similarly, for Rufinus, the *vis* instilled in the first man was «clarity of understanding».[22] As we have noted, the canonists also used other words besides *vis* to express the subjective sense of *ius* — e.g. *potentia, facultas, habilitas.* After Huguccio, the word that had most success was *instinctus,* understood specifically as an instinct of reason. The usage was suggested by a text of Isidore associating natural *ius* with an instinct of nature and by the distinction that Rufinus drew between a natural *ius* common to all animals and a natural *ius* peculiar to humans. Laurentius defined the latter as *instinctus rationis* and Johannes Teutonicus, in the *glossa ordinaria* to the *Decretum,* wrote of an instinct of nature proceeding from reason.[23] These words of Johannes were repeated and adapted in later writings. Raymond of Pennaforte wrote: *Ius na-*

---

[22] WEIGAND, *op. cit.,* 216. On Rufinus, Weigand commented: «Dabei scheint er sowohl an die Erkenntnis (Verstand) als auch an den Willen zu denken» (p. 145).

[23] WEIGAND, *op. cit.,* 253, 255. Johannes actually used the phrase «*instinctus nature ex ratione proveniens*» as an interpretation of the word «natural». But his successors commonly understood it as a definition of *ius naturale.*

*turale habet quinque acceptiones... Tertio modo dicitur instinctus nature prove-
niens ex ratione, et hoc dicitur equitas naturalis.*[24] Here *ius naturale* meant first a subjective instinct then the objective equity that the exercise of the instinct revealed. In modern writing we tend to dis-
tinguish carefully between subjective and objective senses of *ius* or "right"; a
medieval author could move easily from one meaning to the other without any
evident sense of disjunction. It seems to be another case of unreflective
metonymy.

Around 1300, Guido de Baysio for the first time included Aquinas's objective definition of *ius,* together with the various derivative senses that
Aquinas presented, in a formal commentary on the *Decretum.* But he also included the subjective definition of *ius naturale* as an «instinct of reason».[25]
Guido did not, however, overtly compare or contrast or attempt to reconcile
the different doctrines he presented. Early in the fourteenth century, Johannes
Monachus returned to the word *vis* and by a play on words – associating *vis*
with *virtus* - reached the conclusion that *ius* could mean a «virtuous» power.[26]
Thus the initial definition by Rufinus of *ius* as a subjective *vis* inherent in rational human persons gave rise to a whole tradition of canonistic commentary.

Let us turn back to the points raised at the beginning of this paper for a
few final observations. I have suggested elsewhere that Ockham's teaching on
natural law and natural rights was influenced more by the preceding body of
canonistic argumentation than by the tenets of his nominalist and voluntarist
philosophy.[27] Certainly the work in which he first developed his doctrine of *ius
naturale,* the *Opus nonaginta dierum,* is saturated with canonistic citations.[28]
This is a topic that requires further research; but the texts just cited suggest
one preliminary observation. The subjective definitions of *ius* that we find in
Suarez and other writers of the "second scholasticism" are usually taken to
imply a voluntarist understanding of the term, opposed to Thomistic rationalism, and Ockham is often seen as the source of this voluntarism. But as Folgado has pointed out, there is no concept of *ius* as unrestrained will in Suarez.[29]
And one may doubt whether Ockham taught such a doctrine. Perhaps we as-

---

[24] *Summa Iuris,* ed. J. RIUS SERRA, Barcelona, 1945, 23.

[25] GUIDO DE BAYSIO, *Rosarium,* Strasbourg, 1473, *ad Dist.* 1 c. 1, fol. 2va; *ad Dist.* 1 c. 7,
fol. 4vb.

[26] JOHANNES MONACHUS, *Glossa Aurea,* Paris, 1535, *ad Sext.* 1.6.16, fol. xci. On this text
see my *Villey* (above n. 1), 29.

[27] *Natural Law and Canon Law in Ockham's Dialogus,* in: J.G. ROWE (ed.), *Aspects of Late
Medieval Government and Society. Essays Presented to J.R. Lander,* Toronto, 1986, 3-24.

[28] *Opus nonaginta dierum,* in: H.S. OFFLER (ed.), *Guillelmi de Ockham opera politica,*
Vol. 2, Manchester 1963.

[29] A. FOLGADO, *Evolución histórica del concepto de derecho subjetivo,* Madrid, 1960, 51.

sume too readily that the very subtle speculations of some philosophers and theologians about the manner of coexistence of the divine will and the divine reason in God also determined the authors' teaching in the more mundane sphere of law and politics. Certainly, when Ockham formally defined *ius naturale* in either an objective or a subjective sense, it was reason that he emphasized, rather than will. For instance: *Ius autem poli vocatur aequitas naturalis, quae... est consona rationi rectae... hoc ius aliquando vocatur ius naturale.*[30] And again: *Ius autem poli non est aliud quam potestas conformis rationi rectae...*[31]

Rufinus or Huguccio or Guido de Baysio would not have been shocked by such expressions. To them, Ockham's definitions would have seemed to be merely variations on a familiar theme.

To sum up then: the subjective understanding of *ius*, which took on new meanings and new importance in early modern thought, was not just a late aberration from an Aristotelian doctrine that dominated medieval thought until the fourteenth century. Nor was it necessarily associated with a voluntarist philosophy. Alongside the Aristotelian tradition there existed, at least from the twelfth century onward, an alternative juristic tradition, which nurtured a different understanding of *ius*. The two currents of thought flowed together in the work of the sixteenth-century Spanish scholastics who transmitted the medieval heritage to the modern world.

---

[30] *Opus nonaginta dierum*, 574. Ockham used *ius poli* as well as the more usual *ius naturale* because the first phrase occurred in Nicholas III 's decretal *Exiit* on Franciscan poverty, a major text in dispute between Ockham and John XXII. The term *ius poli* comes from a text of Augustine included in the *Decretum* at C. 17 q. 4 c. 43 (cited by Ockham at 573).

[31] *Op. cit.*, 579. Gerson, perhaps influenced by Ockham, gave a similar definition. See his *De vita spirituali animae*, in: P. GLORIEUX (ed.), *Oeuvres complètes*, vol. 3, Paris, 1962, 141: «*Jus est facultas seu potestas propinqua conveniens alicui secundum dictamen rectae rationis. Itaque totalis et finalis resolutio materiae nostrae ad dictamen rectae rationis terminatur*». Suarez specifically listed this treatise of Gerson as a source of his own work. For a recent discussion of Gerson's rights theory see my *Conciliarism, Corporatism, and Individualism: The Doctrine of Individual Rights in Gerson*, in: *Cristianesimo nella storia* 9 (1988), 81-111.

IV

Religious Rights:
An Historical Perspective

I n the years since World War II religious liberty has been proclaimed
as a human right in several United Nations documents, and all the
major Christian churches have affirmed their commitment to the
same ideal. It was not always so. A leading scholar in this field observed
recently that "[f]or several thousand years the history of religion was
marked by religious intolerance and persecution." After mentioning specifically the persecutions of one another by Christians of various persuasions, he added: "Clearly religion and freedom have not been natural
allies."[2] This is the situation we have to bear in mind when we reflect on
the historical background to the modern idea of religious rights.

The Western experience that I want particularly to consider is in
some ways paradigmatic, since a doctrine of natural rights—or human
rights as we say nowadays—first grew up in the Christian West. Of
course, all the great religious cultures of the world have given expression
to ideals of justice and right order in human affairs, but they have not
normally expressed those ideals in terms of subjective natural rights. (It
would be hard, for instance, to imagine a Confucian Hobbes or Locke.)
Even in the West, a doctrine of religious rights emerged only painfully
and belatedly, out of a tradition that had earlier found it much easier to
acknowledge other kinds of rights. Nowadays it has become commonplace to maintain, as Pope John Paul II recently asserted, that religious
rights are the "cornerstone" of all other rights. But, viewed in historical

---

This chapter includes some paragraphs that I originally published in R. Davis, ed., *The
Making of Modern Freedom* (Stanford, 1994). I am grateful for permission from Stanford University Press to use the material here.

[2] James E. Wood, Jr., "Editorial: Religion and Religious Liberty," *Journal of Church and
State* 33 (1991): 226.

J. Witte, Jr. and J.D. van der Vyver (eds.), Religious Human Rights in Global Perspective, 17-45.
© *1996 Kluwer Law International. Printed in the Netherlands.*

perspective, religious rights came last; these rights were the most difficult to conceive of, let alone put into practice.

The Roman Catholic Church was the last of the great Christian denominations to embrace wholeheartedly the principle of religious freedom. This at least had the advantage that its leaders could form a mature and well-considered version of the doctrine. Hence the *Declaration on Religious Liberty* of Vatican Council II, promulgated in 1965, provides an appropriate starting point for our discussion:

> This Vatican Council declares that the human person has a right to religious freedom. This freedom means that all men are to be immune from coercion on the part of individuals or of social groups and of any human power . . . the right to religious freedom has its foundation in the very dignity of the human person as this dignity is known through the revealed word of God and by reason itself.[3]

This passage of the *Declaration* referred, in all-embracing fashion, not only to coercion by the state but by "any human power." It defined religious freedom specifically as a "right" and a right inherent in the human person, a natural or human right therefore. This natural right, discernible by human reason, was also said to be rooted in divine revelation and so intrinsic to the Christian faith. The *Declaration* contained only a bland and innocuous hint that these affirmations represented a radical reversal of a policy of religious repression that the Catholic church (and the mainstream Protestant churches too) had maintained for centuries. The hint came in an observation that the demands of human dignity "have come to be more fully known to human reason through centuries of experience." How true these words are can be gathered from a decree of another general council, promulgated in 1215, just 750 years before the *Declaration* of Vatican Council II. This is from the Fourth Lateran Council:

> We excommunicate and anathematize every heresy that raises itself against the holy, orthodox, and Catholic faith. . . . Secular authorities, as they wish to be esteemed and numbered among the faithful, ought to take an oath that they will strive in good faith and to the best of their ability to exterminate all heretics pointed out by the church.[4]

My task as a historian is to try to explain how we got from there to here, from the repression of heretics to a declaration on religious liberty. A skeptic, faced by the two conciliar texts, might observe that the Chris-

---

[3] W.H. Abbot, trans., *The Documents of Vatican II* (New York, 1966), 678-680.
[4] H.J. Schroeder, trans., *The Disciplinary Decrees of the General Councils* (St. Louis, 1937), 242.

tian religion evidently meant one thing in 1215 and something quite different in 1965. A more sympathetic observer might acknowledge that the church has indeed modified its teachings in the course of time but that this is only because the "centuries of experience" that Vatican II mentioned have led on to deeper insights into the truths that were originally proclaimed by the church's founder. As Jacques Maritain observed in discussing human rights, our understanding has increased "as man's moral conscience has developed."[5]

This idea of a growth of understanding in time is not a novel concept, based on modern historicism. In the thirteenth century the Franciscan theologian Peter Olivi wrote of the need for "new explication in the holy church of God—more and more through the course of time—of the sublime truths of faith." Olivi's master, St. Bonaventure, wrote of "seeds" of truth in scripture that slowly ripened in the minds of men, and he added that "Scripture and its mysteries cannot be understood unless the course of history is known."[6] Such writers were not arguing that divine revelation changes, but that human understanding of scripture deepens in the course of the centuries. We might add that some kinds of understanding, it seems, can be achieved only by undergoing specific historical experiences, sometimes harsh and bitter ones. This is especially true when we consider the theme of religious rights.

In the following discussion I want first to consider some aspects of early Christian teaching and then explain how, even in the medieval church, there were some developments of Christian thought that might seem favorable to a growth of religious liberty. (We shall find in the medieval period, for instance, vigorous assertions of the church's freedom from control by secular governments, strong affirmations of the value of individual conscience, and a newly emerging doctrine of natural rights.) Next I will try to explain why, for many centuries, such ideas were outweighed by an apparently insuperable body of counterargument favoring coercion of religious dissidents. Finally, we shall need to consider how a new—or renewed—ideal of religious freedom took root in the early modern era, with a glance at the relevance of all this historical experience for the global problems of our modern age.

The Early Church

From the beginning of the Christian era there were elements in Christian tradition that could lead on either to a doctrine of religious lib-

---

[5] Jacques Maritain, *The Rights of Man and Natural Law* (New York, 1943), 65.

[6] On the views of Olivi and Bonaventure see Brian Tierney, *Origins of Papal Infallibility*, 2d ed. (Leiden, 1988), 72-76, 109-114.

erty or to a practice of persecution. Jesus himself taught a doctrine of universal love. "I say to you, love your enemies, do good to those who hate you" (Matthew 5:44). Jesus disclaimed the role of a political Messiah, relying on coercive force, when he said: "My kingdom is not of this world" (John 18:36). And he offered a new kind of freedom to his followers: "You shall know the truth and the truth shall make you free" (John 5:32). Paul, too, wrote eloquently of "the freedom wherewith Christ has made us free" (Galatians 4:31). And perhaps an ideal of spiritual liberty was always implicit in the Judeo-Christian understanding of the human person as a morally autonomous individual, endowed with conscience and reason and free will. But if an ideal of religious freedom was always implicit in Christian thought, it was certainly not always explicitly asserted. There was always a potentiality for intolerance in the early Christians' disregard for all other religions, their conviction that they alone knew the one true God, that they alone were on the one true path to salvation, that all those outside the church were lost in a world of darkness and sin and error.

Still, a belief in the righteousness of one's own cause does not necessarily imply that one should coerce others into joining it. During the early days of the church Christians generally favored religious toleration, if only because they were so often the victims of persecution; but of course the situation changed dramatically after the emperors themselves became Christians. When Constantine issued the "Edict of Milan" in 313 he granted toleration to the Christian church and to all other religions "so that every man may worship according to his own wish." Later, the emperors adopted a more repressive attitude toward non-Christian religions; but, in the fourth century, Christian apologists like Hilary of Poitiers and Lactantius still defended the principle of religious freedom. And toward the end of the century, St. Martin of Tours bitterly condemned a group of bishops who persuaded the emperor to execute a supposed heretic, Priscillian. Perhaps the case for religious liberty was expressed most eloquently in the words of Lactantius.

> Liberty has chosen to dwell in religion. For nothing is so much a matter of free will as religion, and no one can be required to worship what he does not will to worship.[7]

A decisive turning point in patristic thought came in the teaching of Augustine (354-430). In 395, when Augustine became bishop of Hippo in north Africa, he found the church in that region divided by a bitter schism between orthodox Catholics and a dissident group known as Do-

---

[7] Lactantius, *De divinis institutionibus*, in *Patrologia Latina* (Paris, 1844), 6: col. 1061.

natists. Religious animosities gave rise to frequent civil disturbances, with riots and street fighting in the cities between the two factions. For years Augustine argued that only peaceful persuasion should be used to end the schism. Finally, however, he accepted the view of his fellow-bishops that the civil power should be called in to repress the dissidents. The works he wrote in defense of this policy seem to contradict his earlier writings where he had emphasized freedom in religious matters. But Augustine always maintained that he was seeking only the salvation of the heretics. "It is better to love with severity than to deceive with indulgence," he wrote. Augustine justified the use of coercion against heretics by citing the parable of Jesus about a rich man who prepared a great feast. When none of the intended guests would accept the invitations he sent out, the master dispatched his servants to bring in alternative guests. But the servants told him that there was still room at the table:

> Then the Lord said to the servant "Go out into the highways and hedges and compel them to come in" (Luke 14:23).

The key words for Augustine were the last ones (*compelle intrare*). In his interpretation, the guests who refused their invitations were the Jewish people; those who accepted voluntarily were the Gentiles who became Christians; and those who were "compelled to enter" were heretics who had left the church and could licitly be coerced into returning.[8] Modern historians who have studied Augustine sympathetically point out that he always preferred discussion and persuasion in religious controversies; that he did not favor the harshest penalties against heretics—he did not advocate the death penalty, for instance; that for him the purpose of coercion was not to punish but to win back the heretic to the true faith and so to ensure his ultimate salvation. Less sympathetic historians have designated Augustine as "the prince and patriarch of persecutors" and as "the first theorist of the Inquisition." Certainly his views remained enormously influential throughout the Middle Ages. For a thousand years the church pursued a policy of suppressing religious dissent. Before turning to that theme, however, we need to consider some aspects of medieval religion that could—and eventually did, though only after centuries of struggles and vicissitudes—contribute to a growth of religious freedom.

---

[8] *Writings on the Donatist Controversy. Library of the Nicene and Post-Nicene Fathers*, J. R. King, trans. (New York, 1887), 4:642.

Church and State

The most obvious way in which the leaders of the medieval church contributed (unintentionally of course) to the emergence of modern religious liberty was by their insistence on the freedom of the church from control by temporal rulers. In the Middle Ages there was never just one hierarchy of government exercising absolute authority, but always two—church and state as we say nowadays—often contending with one another, each limiting the other's power. This duality of government was a rather unusual development in human history. In societies larger than a tribal unit or a city-state the most common form of rulership has been some form of theocratic absolutism. The Pharaohs of Egypt, the Incas of Peru, the emperors of Japan were all revered as divine figures. The order of society was seen as a part of the divine order of the cosmos; the ruler provided a necessary link between heaven and earth. Typically, in such societies, religious liberty was neither conceived of nor desired.

Christianity was different from the beginning. It grew up in an alien culture, the sophisticated classical civilization of Greece and Rome. To become a Christian or to persist in the religion was a matter of free personal choice, often involving considerable self-sacrifice. For early Christians, the emperor was not a divine ruler but a persecutor of the true faith. The tension between Roman state and Christian church was expressed classically in the words of Jesus himself: "Render to Caesar the things that are Caesar's and to God the things that are God's" (Mark 12:17). In all ages Christians have remembered, too, the words of Peter: "We ought to obey God rather than man" (Acts 5:29). After the conversion of Constantine and the establishment of a Christian empire there was indeed a possibility for a time that the church might become merely a sort of department of religious affairs in an imperial theocratic church-state. But, as the imperial power crumbled in the West, the independent role of the church was vigorously reasserted by Pope Gelasius (492-496):

> Two there are, august emperor, by which this world is chiefly ruled, the sacred authority of the priesthood and the royal power . . . in the order of religion, in matters concerning the reception and right administration of the heavenly sacraments, you ought to submit yourself rather than rule.[9]

There were *two* authorities in the world; whole areas of religious thought and practice were excluded from the control of the temporal ruler. The text of Gelasius was assimilated into the medieval corpus of canon law and endlessly quoted and discussed in later disputes.

---

[9] Brian Tierney, *The Crisis of Church and State, 1050-1300* (New York, 1964), 13.

The whole issue of empire and papacy arose again when Charlemagne sought to establish a new theocratic empire (c. 800), and his claims were reiterated by his successors of the Ottoman and Salian dynasties of Germany. Claiming to be vicars of God on earth, the kings assumed the right to control their churches; they regularly appointed bishops in the lands they ruled and invested them with the ring and staff that were the symbols of spiritual office. When, from time to time, a German emperor invaded Italy and occupied Rome, he chose and appointed popes, just as he appointed other bishops.

The church seemed to be drifting into another form of theocratic monism. But a dramatic change came in the pontificate of Gregory VII (1073-1085). Gregory condemned the whole existing order of society as radically contrary to divine justice. He declared himself willing to fight to the death for the "freedom of the church," a phrase he used like a kind of battle-cry. To implement his policy, he forbade the prevailing practice of lay investiture (the appointment of bishops by kings) and so inaugurated a struggle that historians used to call the Investiture Contest but that is now often referred to simply as the Papal Revolution. Henry IV, king of Germany and later emperor, denounced Gregory as a pseudo-pope and a heretic; Gregory responded by deposing Henry from his kingship. The fight that ensued between pope and emperor was both a war of propaganda and a real civil war in Germany and Italy. At one point Henry had to humiliate himself before the pope at Canossa and humbly beg his forgiveness; but later his armies occupied Rome and drove Gregory into exile. In the end neither side could prevail and, after both of the original protagonists had died, a compromise peace was patched up in the Concordat of Worms (1122).[10]

The struggle between popes and kings was reenacted over and over again in the following centuries. After denouncing the theocratic pretensions of kings, the popes were often tempted to assert a theocratic role for themselves. Sometimes they put forward extreme claims to a kind of overlordship of Christian society in both spiritual and temporal affairs. The point is, however, that such claims were always resisted and never generally accepted by medieval kings or their peoples. The theocratic claims of the papacy reached a high-water mark in Boniface VIII's Bull, *Unam sanctam* (1302), with its uncompromising declaration: "It is altogether necessary for every human creature to be subject to the Roman pontiff."[11] But Boniface was defeated and humiliated in the struggle with the king of France that had been the occasion of his pronouncement.

---

[10] Ibid., 53-73.
[11] Ibid., 188.

24

Because neither side could make good its more extreme claims, a dualism of church and state persisted in medieval society and eventually it was rationalized and justified in many works of political theory. The French theologian, John of Paris, for instance, writing in 1302 (the year of *Unam Sanctam*) wrote a treatise *On Royal and Papal Power* which presented a carefully balanced dualism, assigning to each power its proper function. "The priest is greater than the prince in spiritual affairs," John wrote, "and, on the other hand, the prince is greater in temporal affairs."[12]

The persistent dualism in medieval society that we have described was far removed from a modern "wall of separation." In the Middle Ages, the powers of church and state constantly overlapped and interacted and impinged on one another; but the church remained committed to a radical limitation of state power in the sphere of religion. By the end of the Middle Ages, the Catholic kings had again acquired a large measure of control over church appointments; but, in the Reformation era, the revived theory of royal divine right was challenged by new forms of protest that led to new ways of asserting religious rights.

Freedom of the church from control by the state is one important part of modern religious liberty. But it is only a part. The *libertas ecclesiae* that medieval popes demanded was not freedom of religion for each individual person but the freedom of the church as an institution to direct its own affairs. It left open the possibility, all too fully realized from the twelfth century onward, that the church might organize the persecution of its own dissident members. And, when the interests of church and state happened to coincide, as they often did in dealing with heresy, there was room for a savage suppression of religious dissent. But, even during the centuries of persecution, there were some aspects of medieval thought and practice that could have been conducive to an alternative tradition of religious toleration.

For one thing, medieval canonists and moral theologians often upheld the overriding value of the individual conscience as a guide to right conduct. When Paul wrote: "Everything that is not from faith is sin" (Romans 14:23), the Ordinary Gloss to the Bible (the standard medieval commentary on the text) explained that the words "not from faith" meant "all that is contrary to conscience." In the twelfth century, Peter Abelard expanded the argument. He taught that to act against one's conscience was always sinful, even if the conscience erred in discerning what was right.[13] A century after Abelard, Thomas Aquinas addressed this same

---

[12] Ibid., 209.
[13] *Peter Abelard's Ethics*, D. E. Luscombe, ed. and trans. (Oxford, 1971), 55-57, 67, 97.

question. It might seem that we are not obliged to follow an erring conscience, he wrote, because we are not obliged to obey the command of a lower authority when it conflicts with that of a higher one; but conscience might favor our acting contrary to the law of God, who was the supreme authority. In reply, Thomas quoted the Ordinary Gloss to Romans 14:23 and explained that we are only obliged to follow the command of the higher authority when we *know* that it conflicts with our present judgment. An erring conscience could be formed in good faith if one were ignorant of the higher law. A person was always obliged to do what his conscience discerned as good, even though the conscience might be mistaken.[14]

The same doctrine was taught by the canonists. It was expressed in two judgments of Pope Innocent III (1198-1216) that were incorporated into the corpus of medieval canon law. The Ordinary Gloss to the Decretals, a work studied in law schools throughout Europe, explained their implication. "One ought to endure excommunication rather than sin . . . no one ought to act against his own conscience and he should follow his conscience rather than the judgment of the church when he is certain . . . one ought to suffer any evil rather than sin against conscience."[15]

We are not dealing here with a right to religious liberty but with a duty to obey one's conscience. Still, an emphasis on the primacy of the individual conscience was an important element in later theories of religious rights. The medieval position was that a person was right to follow his conscience but that he might suffer at the hands of the authorities if his conscience led him to illicit behavior. Similarly, in the modern world, individuals may be led by a sincere conscience to violate the law—as in some forms of civil rights or anti-war protest—but the law will hold them responsible for their actions. There is one further point: medieval moralists did not hold that people should act on mere subjective whims. Everyone was required to use the utmost diligence and every resource of knowledge and understanding to form a correct conscience. Failure to do this was sinful. In practice, it was assumed that most cases where an erring conscience led to illicit behavior involved culpable ignorance or culpable negligence.

In one sphere, the emphasis on individual conscience did lead to a degree of religious toleration. Medieval doctrine always taught that non-Christians could not be forcibly converted to Christianity. God's grace was a free gift, and it had to be freely accepted. In practice the only substantial populations of non-Christian people scattered throughout the

---

[14] Thomas Aquinas, *Summa theologiae*, 1.2ae.19.5.

[15] *Decretales Gregorii Papae IX cum glossis* (Lyons, 1624), gloss ad 5.39.44.

Western church were Jewish communities, and the principle of toleration was explicitly applied to them. The attitude of the medieval church toward the Jews, as toward heretics, was shaped by the teaching of Augustine, though in this case it had a more benign effect. Augustine held that, although the Jewish people had erred at the time of Christ, still it was God's will that they should always survive. They existed to give permanent independent witness to the divine law revealed in the Old Testament. They could also attest to the words of the prophets which Christians understood as foretelling the coming of Christ. (Infidels could not maintain that the Christians had just made up the prophecies about a coming Messiah when the Jews also affirmed their reality.) And accordingly, to fulfill this role, some of the Jewish people would exist until the end of time. The acceptance of this theology shaped the official attitude of the medieval church toward the Jews. They were indeed discriminated against—made to wear a distinctive dress, excluded from positions of authority in government—but they were allowed to have their own synagogues and to practice their own religion. The attitude of the papacy was one of toleration, grudging toleration no doubt, but still a recognition that Jews had a right to exist in a Christian society. The policy was defined by Gregory I (590-604) in a letter that became a part of the permanent canon law of the church.[16] "Just as the Jews ought not to be allowed more than the law concedes," he wrote, "so too they ought not to suffer harm in those things that the law does concede to them." From the beginning of the twelfth century onward it became customary for the Jewish community of Rome to obtain a restatement of Jewish rights from each new pope at the beginning of his reign. In the real-life world of the Middle Ages, needless to say, savage outrages against Jewish communities occurred all too often; but they were due to outbursts of mob violence or actions of secular rulers. They were contrary to the law and teaching of the church.

The Idea of Natural Rights

There was one further area in which medieval thinkers began to develop a doctrine that would be important for later theories of religious liberty—the idea that all persons possess natural rights.

No consensus exists among modern scholars about the origin of this doctrine or how it is related to the tradition of Christian thought. Jacques Maritain simply assumed that the idea of human rights was always implicit in the Judeo-Christian teaching on the dignity and value of each

---

[16] *Decretales*, 5.6.9.

human person.[17] At the opposite extreme, Leo Strauss focused on the supposedly atheistic philosophy of Thomas Hobbes, whom he regarded as the founder of modern rights theories, and concluded that the idea of natural rights was alien to the whole preceding classical and Christian tradition.[18] Disciples of Strauss will still maintain that "[t]he very idea of natural rights is incompatible with Christian doctrine."[19] But this view seems untenable if only because there certainly were Christian natural rights theorists before Hobbes—Suarez and Grotius for instance. An intermediate point of view, that has come to be widely accepted, was put forward by Michel Villey. He held that the idea of natural rights was indeed derived from Christianity but from a distorted and aberrant form of Christian thought, specifically from the fourteenth-century, nominalist and voluntarist philosophy of William of Ockham. Villey argued that Ockham inaugurated a "semantic revolution" when he interpreted the Latin word *ius* (right) as meaning a subjective power (*potestas*).[20] But subsequent research has shown that the association of "right" and "power" was quite common in earlier medieval jurisprudence. Before 1200, for instance, the canonist Huguccio wrote, concerning a bishop-elect: "He has the power (*potestas*) of administering, that is the right (*ius*) of administering."[21]

According to the most recent work, the origin of the later natural rights theories is to be found in the Christian jurisprudence of the late twelfth century, especially in the works of the canonists of that era.[22] The twelfth century was an age of renewal in many spheres of life and thought. New networks of commerce grew up. There was new art, new architecture, a new literature of courtly romance. Religious thought placed a new emphasis on the individual human person—on individual intention in assessing guilt, on individual consent in marriage, on individual scrutiny of conscience.[23] And in the secular sphere, at every level of society we find an intense concern for individual rights and liberties.

---

[17] Maritain, *The Rights of Man*, 64-66.

[18] Leo Strauss, *Natural Right and History* (Chicago, 1950), 166-202.

[19] "Walter Berns Comments," *This World* 6 (Fall, 1983): 98.

[20] Michael Villey, *La formation de la pensée juridique moderne*, 4th ed. (Paris, 1975), 252, 261.

[21] R.L. Benson, *The Bishop-Elect: A Study in Medieval Ecclesiastical Office* (Princeton, 1968), 118, n.5.

[22] Brian Tierney, "Origins of Natural Rights Language: Texts and Contexts, 1150-1250," *History of Political Thought* 10 (1989): 615-646; Charles J. Reid, "The Canonistic Contribution to the Western Rights Tradition: An Historical Inquiry," *Boston College Law Review* 33 (1991): 37-92.

[23] On the juristic implications of these attitudes see especially Harold J. Berman, *Law and Revolution: The Formation of the Western Legal Tradition* (Cambridge, MA, 1983).

28

Above all, the twelfth century was an age of legal renaissance marked by the recovery of the whole corpus of classical Roman law, and by the first adequate codification of the accumulated canon law of the church in Gratian's *Concord of Discordant Canons*, completed circa 1140. In the following decades a succession of great jurists, inspired by the old texts, found ways to express all the new impulses of their own age in juridical language. For us the crucial development was that the new personalism in religious life, and the everyday concern with rights in secular society, infected the language of the canonists when they came to discuss the concept of *ius naturale*, natural right. Earlier the phrase *ius naturale* had been understood in an objective sense to mean natural law or "what is naturally right." But the canonists who wrote around 1200, reading the old texts in the context of their more humanist, more individualist culture, added another definition. In their writings, *ius naturale* was now sometimes defined in a subjective sense as a faculty, power, force, ability inhering in individual persons. From this initial subjective definition, the canonists went on to develop a considerable array of natural rights. Around 1250 Pope Innocent IV wrote that ownership of property was a right derived from natural law and that even infidels enjoyed this right, along with a right to form their own governments.[24] Other natural rights that were asserted in the thirteenth century included a right to liberty, a right of self-defense, a right of the poor to support from the surplus wealth of the rich.[25] What was still notably lacking was a developed concept of religious rights.

By around 1300 a sophisticated legal language had grown up in which a doctrine of natural rights could be expressed. The next step was the assimilation of the juristic idea of rights into works of political philosophy. William of Ockham was indeed important here. He drew on the earlier canonistic tradition but went beyond it. One of his major contributions was to reshape the scriptural idea of evangelical liberty into a doctrine of natural rights. When Paul wrote about Christian freedom he meant freedom from the law of the Old Testament or freedom from sin, but Ockham used Paul's texts to argue for freedom from any tyrannical government, especially within the church. Not even the pope, he wrote, could injure "the rights and liberties conceded to the faithful by God and nature."[26] Ockham also developed a concept of "suppositional" or contingent natural rights, related to basic human needs, but applied in dif-

---

[24] *Commentaria Innocentii ... super quinque libros decretalium* (Frankfurt, 1570), ad 1.2.7, fol. 3v, and 3.34.8, fol. 429v.

[25] Tierney, "Origins," 638-44.

[26] "An princeps," in *Guillelmi de Ockham opera politica*, H. S. Offler, ed., 3 vols. (Manchester, 1956-74), 1:251.

ferent ways in different circumstances.[27] The idea could perhaps have some relevance for modern problems concerning the applicability of general norms in a world of cultural diversity.

Ockham's ideas were developed further by Jean Gerson, an eminent theologian who wrote around 1400. Gerson gave a very influential definition of *ius* as "a power or faculty belonging to each one in accordance with the dictate of right reason" and argued that, even in man's fallen state, humans retained many such rights.[28] Also, Gerson took up and developed further the idea that Christ's law was a law of liberty. In the existing church this was no longer the case, Gerson complained. On the contrary, Christians were oppressed by an intolerable burden of laws and regulations and obligations imposed by human authority, that is by the church hierarchy. Such enactments were like snares and nets to trap the soul, he wrote.[29] By fusing Paul's doctrine of Christian liberty with his own idea of natural rights, Gerson went on to argue that the essential obligation of a Christian was to accept freely the divinely revealed law of scripture and the natural law that his reason and conscience could discern. In the last resort one could exercise an inherent natural right of self-defense that no human law could take away against any oppressive authority, even an oppressive pope. Gerson's words sometimes have an almost modern sound, and his ideas were indeed very important in the growth of later natural rights theories. They were transmitted to the early modern world mainly by the Spanish scholastics of the sixteenth century, especially in the course of their debates about the rights of American Indians. Bartolomée de las Casas in particular tried to defend the Indians against subjugation and forced conversion by appealing to a doctrine of natural rights based on medieval legal and theological sources.[30]

Given all these aspects of medieval thought—an insistence on the primacy of the individual conscience, a rejection of forced conversion, a nascent theory of natural rights—one might reasonably hope that at least some medieval thinkers would have moved on from these premises to assert a full-fledged doctrine of religious liberty. Nothing of the sort happened. Every medieval writer who discussed this question saw heresy as a sin and a crime that was properly judged by the church and properly

---

[27] H.S. Offler, "The Three Modes of Natural Law in Ockham: A Revision of the Text," *Franciscan Studies* 37 (1977): 207-18.

[28] "De vita spirituali animae," in *Jean Gerson Oeuvres complètes*, P. Glorieux, ed., 10 vols. (Paris, 1960-73), 3: 141-42.

[29] Ibid., 129. On these views of Gerson see Brian Tierney, "Conciliarism, Corporatism, and Individualism: The Doctrine of Individual Rights in Gerson," *Cristianesimo nella storia* 9 (1988): 81-111.

[30] Brian Tierney, "Aristotle and the American Indians—Again," *Cristianesimo nella storia* 12 (1991): 295-322.

punished by the secular power. Even Gerson had no conception of religious freedom as we understand it; indeed, he participated in the trial and burning of John Hus. Gerson could defend the rights of Christians within the church, but it never occurred to him to assert that heretics had rights against the church. Before we can understand how real religious rights emerged in the early modern world, we need to consider why they were so persistently denied in the preceding centuries.

Heresy and Persecution

In his classic little book, *The Whig Interpretation of History*, Herbert Butterfield warned historians against "present-mindedness." We should not impose our own ideas on the past, he urged, but rather seek to understand each historical era "in its own terms." The sort of question we ought to ask, Butterfield suggested, is not: How did we get our religious liberty? But rather: Why were people in former ages so given to persecution?[31] It seems to me that both questions are legitimate ones for a historian, but obviously we cannot begin to address the first question until we have considered the second one. And it is not an easy question to answer.

In the late Roman empire, laws against heresy, sometimes imposing the death penalty on offenders, were enacted by imperial authority. But in the centuries after the fall of the empire there was little organized persecution, though heretics or people suspected of heresy were sometimes lynched by fanatic mobs. When cases came before church courts, the usual penalty was excommunication. A more systematic repression began from the twelfth century onward, even as new doctrines of natural rights were growing into existence. This was partly because of the spread of new heresies and partly because of the growing institutionalization of the church. As the church became more aware of itself as an ordered society with its own system of law and organs of government, it became less tolerant of those who rejected its authority. In 1199, Pope Innocent III declared, in the decretal *Vergentis*, that heresy was equivalent to treason.[32] Heretics were traitors to God, he wrote, just as others guilty of treason were traitors to the emperor. The most threatening heresy of the time was that of the Cathars or Albigensians who had come to dominate substantial areas of southern France. In 1208 Innocent counterattacked by unleashing the Albigensian Crusade, an invasion of southern France by Catholic forces from the north which perpetrated savage massacres in cities that were strongholds of the heretics and effectively destroyed the

---

[31] Herbert Butterfield, *The Whig Interpretation of History* (London, 1931), 18.
[32] *Decretales Gregorii* IX, 5.7.10.

Cathar civilization in Provence. Then, in 1215, Innocent's Fourth Lateran Council issued the general condemnation of heretics that I have already quoted. Secular governments also enacted harsh penalties against heresy. In 1231, Emperor Frederick II decreed that the appropriate punishment was death by burning; the words of his statute indicate the common attitude to heretics:

> Heretics try to tear the seamless robe of our God. They are violent wolves. . . . They are sons of depravity. . . . Therefore we draw the sword of vengeance against them. . . . Committed to the judgment of the flames, they should be burned alive in the sight of the people.[33]

Other rulers enacted similar legislation, and burning at the stake became the common punishment for heresy. About this same time, Pope Gregory IX (1227-1241) first began to commission groups of inquisitors, usually Dominican and Franciscan friars, to seek out and punish heretics. By the mid-thirteenth century, such inquisitors were at work in all parts of the church.

In some areas of political thought, medieval ideas were not so different from our own. Medieval people had quite well-developed concepts of representation and consent and government under law. But, when we turn to the idea of individual religious rights, their whole mindset was so alien to ours that it takes a considerable effort of historical imagination to enter into their world of thought. Perhaps we can find a starting point in a remark of the great legal historian, Frederic Maitland: "In the Middle Ages the church was a state." The church, he pointed out, had its own institutions of government, its own bureaucracy, its own laws and law courts. In the Middle Ages, secular political power was fragmented. The old Roman empire had passed away, and the attempt to found a medieval Christian empire had failed—partly indeed because of the struggle between popes and emperors that we have considered. National monarchies in France and England were only just beginning to grow into existence. The only bond of unity that held Western Christian society together was the bond of a common religion. Nowadays the focus of our loyalty is the state; we look to the state to protect our security and our liberty; to be a "stateless person" in the twentieth century is a most unhappy fate. The other side of the coin is that we do not tolerate people who are perceived of as traitors to the state. We charge them with treason; we inflict punishment on them, sometimes capital punishment in extreme cases. A plea of personal sincerity, that the traitor has acted from good motives, in accordance with his own conscience, is not a sufficient

---

[33] *The Constitutions of Melfi,* J. Powell, trans. (Syracuse, 1971), 7.

defense. Medieval people regarded heretics in much the same way; they held them guilty of treason to the church, and they treated them as traitors. When a common religion defined the whole way of life of a society, to reject it was to cut oneself off from the community, to become a sort of outlaw—and a dangerous outlaw from a medieval point of view.

When Thomas Aquinas first discussed the issue of heresy he began by presenting a series of apparently cogent arguments in favor of toleration.[34] In the first place, there was the parable of the wheat and the tares from Matthew 13. In this story the good grain and the weeds were allowed to grow together until the time of harvest lest, in destroying the weeds, some of the wheat was destroyed too. In commenting on this, Aquinas quoted John Chrysostom, an early church father, who had explicitly interpreted the text as meaning that heretics were not to be killed because, if this were permitted, some of the innocent would probably suffer along with the guilty. Again, Aquinas noted, canon law taught that Jews were not to be forcibly converted. Moreover, faith required the free assent of the will; and God himself had said, through the prophet Ezekiel: "I do not will the death of a sinner." Against all this, Aquinas quoted one text of Scripture, the one Augustine had already used: "Compel them to enter." And Aquinas understood it in the same sense as Augustine. The texts in favor of toleration applied to Jews and infidels; it was true that they could not be converted by force. But those who had already accepted the faith could be compelled to return to it if they fell into heresy. To explain this, Aquinas used the analogy of a vow or promise. A man could not be compelled to take a vow, but if he chose to do so he was obliged to fulfill it. In a later discussion, Aquinas compared heretics to counterfeiters of false money.[35] It was a more serious offense to corrupt the faith than to corrupt the currency, he argued. Hence, just as counterfeiters were executed, so too heretics could be put to death. Sometimes the health of the whole body required that a diseased limb be cut away.

John Noonan, discussing these texts from the standpoint of a lawyer rather than a theologian, has pointed out that they are based on a series of legal fictions and unpersuasive analogies. It was a fiction that persons baptized in infancy had freely vowed to accept the faith; the comparison between counterfeiters and heretics confused the material realm of property with the spiritual realm of truth; and the use of the phrase *compelle intrare* transferred the words from the context of a parable about the kingdom of God to a context of law and earthly jurisdiction.[36] However

---

[34] Aquinas, *Summa theologiae*, 2.2ae.10.8.

[35] Ibid., 2.2ae.11.3.

[36] John T. Noonan, Jr., "Principled or Pragmatic Foundations for the Freedom of Conscience," *Journal of Law and Religion* 5 (1987): 205.

cogent such objections may appear to us, one has to add that the arguments of Aquinas seemed entirely convincing to the medieval audience
he was addressing.

Medieval people were so convinced of the truth of their religion that
they could never see dissent from the accepted faith as arising simply
from intellectual error, from a mistake in judgment. They thought that
heresy must somehow stem from malice, from a perverted will that deliberately chose evil rather than good, Satan rather than God. Aquinas
wrote: "Unfaithfulness is an act of the intellect, but moved by the will."[37]
This was the root cause of the medieval hatred of heresy. The heretics
were seen, not only as traitors to the church but as traitors to God. To
medieval people it seemed that they had rejected God's truth and God's
love out of pride and self-love, the love of their own self-contrived errors.
They had set themselves on a path that could lead only to eternal dam-
nation and, unless they were restrained, they would lure countless others
to the same terrible fate. Elementary justice and charity, it seemed, required that they be rooted out. The Inquisition that pursued this task
with increasingly harsh and cruel measures, including the use of torture
to extort confessions, was accepted as a necessary safeguard of Christian
society.

Thinking about the Inquisition may remind us of two aphorisms that
Lord Acton quoted.[38] The first is the well-known saying of Mme de Staël:
"To understand all is to forgive all." The other, less indulgent, is from the
Duke de Broglie: "We should beware of too much explaining lest we end
up with too much forgiving." Neither aphorism is altogether satisfying
for a historian. Our task is surely to understand and explain as fully as
possible; but we do not have to condone everything that we have tried to
understand; and, when everything possible has been said in mitigation,
the medieval theory and practice of religious persecution will seem ab-
horrent to most modern people. Over a period of centuries, thousands of
persons were hunted down, tortured, and killed for a crime that, to us,
might seem a mere eccentricity of personal belief.

A critical observer, looking back over the history of the West for the
past thousand years and at the policies pursued in many parts of the
world during the present century, might suppose that persecution is a
normal pattern of human conduct. He might think that Butterfield had
got his question upside down after all. Perhaps the real question a historian has to answer is not: Why were they so given to persecution? But

---

[37] Aquinas, *Summa theologiae*, 2.2ae.10.2.

[38] Lord Acton, "Inaugural Lecture," in id., *Lectures on Modern History*, J.N. Figgis and R.
V. Laurence, eds. (London, 1906), 27.

rather: Why are we so committed to an ideal of religious liberty? This is the final topic that we have to consider.

The Emergence of Religious Rights

In the context of medieval life, religious persecution seemed both right and necessary. No one could see that "freedom of the church" could mean freedom of conscience for each individual Christian or that the duty to obey one's conscience might imply a right to act in accordance with it, or that a natural right to liberty was radically incomplete if it did not include a right to freedom of religion. The Reformation of the sixteenth century created a new historical context in which all these matters were reevaluated in the light of new understandings of Christian teaching shaped by new historical experiences in the centuries after Martin Luther's first protests.

The changes that came about were not due to any intangible "spirit of Protestantism" or to the specific teachings of the first great reformers. It would indeed be hard to discern any seeds of religious liberty in Luther's rantings against Catholics and Jews, or in Calvin's grim-lipped defense of persecution after the execution of Servetus. Luther, Calvin, Beza, Bullinger, Melanchthon all accepted the entirely conventional view of their time that heretics should be suppressed, just as their Catholic contemporaries did. Moreover, Lutheranism gave Europe the doctrine of the "godly Prince" whose duties included the suppression of idolatry and error; and Calvin introduced a new kind of clerical theocracy that could be as intolerant as the medieval church hierarchy. Religious liberty arose out of a play of contingent events that no one had planned and no one had foreseen.

Thomas Carlyle observed that new historical events do not spring from one single cause but from a whole web of causation, from "all other events, prior or contemporaneous."[39] Then, he noted, the new event combines with all the other ones to give birth to further change. This is the sort of situation we have to deal with in considering religious liberty. Between 1500 and 1700, a new web of causation was created. Europe experienced a series of savagely destructive wars of religion that ended in stalemates and a splintering of religious unity into innumerable competing sects. Eventually, this led on to a growth of national states that could command the loyalty of subjects who professed a variety of religious beliefs. But before that final outcome was achieved, religious groups who rejected an established faith found themselves persecuted in many coun-

---

[39] Thomas Carlyle, "On History," in *Critical and Miscellaneous Essays: Collected and Republished*, 7 vols. (London, 1872), 2:257.

tries—Huguenots in France, Roman Catholics and Puritan separatists in England, Lutherans in the Catholic principalities of Germany, and every kind of dissenter from Catholic orthodoxy in Spain.

In each country, the groups that were being persecuted sought toleration for their own beliefs; but these demands were not at first based on any devotion to religious liberty as such. The right and duty of the ruler to punish religious error was taken for granted; it was just that each group was convinced that it alone held fast to the truth. In England, an anonymous pamphlet of 1615 urged King James I to relax the laws against Puritans but to inflict the death penalty on Catholics.[40] At the other end of the religious spectrum, the Jesuit Robert Parsons protested against an oath of allegiance demanded of Catholics with an eloquent plea against coercion: "For he that should force a Jew or a Turke to sweare, that there were a blessed Trinity . . . against their conscience should synne grievously."[41] But Parsons was defending a church that persecuted religious dissidents wherever it had the power to do so. Each religious group believed that it should be tolerated because it was right and, usually, that its adversaries should be persecuted because they were wrong. Oliver Cromwell said, in a moment of exasperation: "Everyone desires to have liberty, but none will give it."[42] Looking back rather disdainfully on the whole situation, J.N. Figgis wrote of the competing sects: "It was . . . the inability of any single one to destroy the others, which finally secured liberty."[43]

There is truth in this, but it is not quite the whole truth. From the middle of the sixteenth century onward a few voices were raised in defense of a genuine religious freedom. Among Protestant groups, the Anabaptists and Baptists always condemned coercion in matters of religion. And the execution of Servetus for heresy in Calvin's Geneva (1553) evoked a response from Sebastian Castellio, *On Heretics, Whether they Should be Persecuted* that provided the first full-scale argument for freedom of conscience.

A century later, a volatile and complex situation that arose during the English Civil War made England for a time the principal forcing ground for the ideal of religious freedom. The Parliament that defeated Charles I was controlled by Presbyterians who wanted to impose, by force if necessary, a rigorous Presbyterian discipline on the English church. Their po-

---

[40] W.K. Jordan, *The Development of Religious Toleration in England*, 4 vols. (Cambridge, MA, 1932-40), 2:209.

[41] Ibid., 500.

[42] W. Abbott, ed., *The Writings and Speeches of Oliver Cromwell*, 4 vols. (Cambridge, MA, 1937-47), 3: 547.

[43] J.N. Figgis, *Churches in the Modern State* (London, 1913), 101.

sition was summed up in a statement of Thomas Edwards: "A toleration is against the nature of reformation, a reformation and a toleration are diametrically opposite; the commands of God given in his word for reformation do not admit of toleration."[44] But the armies that had won Parliament's victories were filled with members of dissenting sects—Congregationalists, Baptists, Unitarians, Fifth Monarchy Men, Muggletonians, and many others. They all demanded and, under Cromwell, enjoyed for a time a measure of toleration. Moreover, in the vast pamphlet literature that grew up, some spokesmen went further and began to argue for a real religious liberty for all, not just toleration for one group. The Presbyterian Richard Baxter, when serving as a chaplain to one of Cromwell's regiments, noted disapprovingly that, among the soldiers, "their most frequent and vehement disputes were for liberty of conscience as they called it; that . . . every man might not only hold, but preach and do in matters of religion what he pleased."[45] Perhaps the most impassioned plea came from Roger Williams, who had known persecution both in old England and New England. In *The Bloudy Tenent of Persecution*, Williams wrote:

> It is the will and command of God that (since the coming of his Sonne the Lord Jesus) a permission of the most Paganish, Jewish, Turkish, or Antichristian consciences and worships be granted to all men in all Nations and Countries.[46]

It was not unusual for seventeenth-century Protestants to urge toleration for "Jews and Turks." This was just a way of reaffirming the old medieval doctrine against forced conversion. But Williams was exceptional in his willingness to tolerate even Roman Catholics. He wrote that even Catholics had consciences "more or less," and that their consciences were to be respected. A man who converted to Catholicism in good faith might still be a "loving and peaceable" person, according to Williams.[47]

In the early modern world, the practice of persecution was attacked by three main lines of argument which we might characterize as based on skepticism, or on expediency, or on an appeal to the underlying principles of the Christian faith itself. The arguments were not all of equal value. The first two could lead on only to a plea for some limited degree of toleration; only the third could provide a basis for a principled commitment to an ideal of religious freedom.

---

[44] Thomas Edwards, *Antapologia* (London, 1641), 285.

[45] A.S.P. Woodhouse, ed., *Puritanism and Liberty: Being the Army Debates (1647-9) from the Clarke Manuscripts* (Chicago, 1951), 388.

[46] *The Complete Writings of Roger Williams*, 7 vols. (New York, 1963), 3:3.

[47] Ibid., 4:317, 508.

The skeptical approach was rooted in Renaissance humanism. The humanists began by dismissing all the finespun arguments of scholastic philosophy as dreary nonsense; then some of them carried over the same attitude in considering the arcane theological disputes that divided the Christian churches of their own day. This was the underlying attitude of Castellio. (Before writing his treatise on toleration he had composed another work on *The Art of Doubting*.) The skepticism of the humanists was not (at least not at first) a skepticism about the fundamental truths of Christian faith. Castellio wrote: "No one doubts that there is a God, whether He is good and just, whether He should be loved and worshipped. . . ."[48] On the other hand, the things that Christians did not agree about—doctrines concerning predestination, free will, baptism, the eucharist, the Trinity—were matters of controversy precisely because they were not clearly revealed in scripture. The truth about such things could not be known with certainty, Castellio thought. So it was futile and cruel for Christians to persecute one another over these matters. This line of argument was continued by the Italian, Acontius, and then, in mid-seventeenth-century England, by writers like William Walwyn and Francis Osborne.

The Huguenot exile, Pierre Bayle, presented a more radically skeptical attack on religious persecution. His work provides a link between the questioning of the Christian humanists and the more thoroughgoing skepticism of the Enlightenment, when a defense of toleration was often associated with indifference or hostility to all religious teaching. We should not underestimate our debt to the Enlightenment. No doubt, the skeptical mockery of a Voltaire was needed to expose the lingering cruelties and superstitions of established religion. But perhaps in the end skepticism is not enough. Humans are religious animals, and if their old faiths are worn away by too much doubt they are likely to invent new and more savage substitutes. The Enlightenment did not lead on to a new era of peace and harmony; it led to a reign of terror in revolutionary France and a new round of religious persecution.

The second line of argument in favor of toleration was simple expediency. This attitude was typified in Henry IV of France who changed his religion from Protestant to Catholic in order to gain the French crown but then, as a Catholic king, issued the Edict of Nantes (1598) that granted substantial liberties to Protestants. Henry's contemporary, Queen Elizabeth of England, also pursued a religious policy guided mainly by reason of state. Reasons of economic policy were cited too. The Spanish regent in the Netherlands, Don Juan of Austria, wrote in 1577: "The Prince of Or-

---

[48] Sebastian Castellio, *On Heretics*, Roland H. Bainton, trans. (New York, 1935), 294.

38

ange has always insisted . . . that freedom of conscience is essential to commercial prosperity."[49] The greatest theoretical exponent of the argument from expediency was the political philosopher Jean Bodin. He acknowledged that religious uniformity was desirable, and he did not doubt that the state could lawfully suppress religious dissent; but he argued that, when a new religion had become so entrenched that it could not be suppressed without a danger of civil strife, the most reasonable policy was to tolerate it.[50] A king's duty to maintain the public welfare took precedence over his obligation to uphold religious truth. A problem with the argument from expediency is that, in many circumstances, toleration is not the most obviously expedient course of action. Often it seems that the most effective way to maintain order and unity is to crush dissent. It was a rather unusual set of circumstances in the seventeenth century that made persecution so often ineffective. The argument from expediency left open the likelihood of renewed persecution when circumstances changed again.

The third argument for toleration was ultimately the most important one. Over and over again the idea was asserted—though not indeed generally accepted, for these are still dissident voices—that the practice of persecution was radically contrary to the teaching of Jesus himself. This argument was included in the works of many different thinkers. Castellio wrote of persecution that "Satan could not devise anything more repugnant to the nature and will of Christ." Pierre Bayle argued in a similar fashion. He framed his case for toleration as a commentary on the text, "Compell them to enter," the text that Augustine and Aquinas had used to justify persecution; but Bayle argued in a different spirit that to understand the words of Christ in this way was "contrary to the essential spirit of the Gospel itself."[51] Bayle was a man of skeptical temperament, but the same kind of argument was put forward by writers of fervent religious faith. Roger Williams presented various considerations in favor of religious freedom, but the fundamental one was that persecution was "directly contradicting the spirit and mind and practice of the Prince of Peace."[52]

The awareness that religious liberty needed to be grounded on Christian principles as well as on pragmatic considerations of expediency was well expressed in an English pamphlet of 1614. The author wrote: "A

---

[49] Quoted in H. Kamen, *The Rise of Toleration* (London, 1967), 149.

[50] Jean Bodin, *Six Books of the Commonwealth*, M. J. Tooley, trans. (Oxford, 1955), 4.7, 140-142.

[51] Castellio, *On Heretics*, 123; *Pierre Bayle's Philosophical Commentary*, A.G. Tannenbaum, trans. (New York, 1987), 1.3, 42.

[52] Williams, "Bloudy Tenent," in id., *Complete Writings*, 3:219.

man would think we had been schooled and whipt long enough to it by our calamities." That is to say, recent practical experience had shown the ill-effects of persecution. But the author added at once that "liberty of conscience is no new doctrine." Rather, he declared, it was "as old certainly as the blessed word of God."[53] The new exigencies of the time led discerning Christians to understand more deeply the implications of their old faith. The more learned authors quoted the early patristic texts in favor of religious freedom. Often the parable of the wheat and tares was cited as an argument for toleration. A Baptist pamphlet of 1661 declared that liberty of conscience was "a part of the Christian religion."[54] In the Netherlands, Dirck Coornhert, arguing against the skeptical views of Justus Lipsius, defended religious freedom as a part of the authentic teachings of Christ, and insisted that the truth of those teachings could be known with certainty.[55] Among the English writers, John Milton took up St. Paul's texts about Christian liberty, the texts that Ockham and Gerson had appealed to earlier, and derived from them an argument that the use of force in matters of faith was contrary to "the very weightiest and inmost reasons of Christian religion."[56]

In this new climate of opinion, when persecution was increasingly condemned as contrary to the teachings of Jesus, all the old medieval strands of argument about the freedom of the church from secular control, the overriding authority of conscience, and the existence of natural rights were taken up again and woven into new patterns. These arguments, I suggested earlier, could all have been conducive to a doctrine of religious liberty, but in the context of medieval life they never led on to that result. In the post-medieval world, in a new historical context, the arguments were carried further to conclusions that perhaps had always been implicit in them but that had never been explicitly affirmed.

The old claim that the church ought not to be controlled by secular rulers was now taken to mean that the civil magistrate had no right to interfere with any person's choice of religion. Protestant dissenters often

---

[53] "Religion's Peace," in E.B. Underhill, ed., *Tracts on Liberty of Conscience and Persecution (1614-1661)* (London, 1846), 10-11. The anonymous author continued, "War and its miseries have overspread all lands. Love, meekness, gentleness, mercy, the truest badges of Christianity, have been damned and banished; and, in their room, cruelty, hard-heartedness, respect of persons, prisons, tortures, etc., things that our blessed Lord and Master, and his apostles never (ap)proved . . . have had great sway for these many hundred years."

[54] "Sion's Groan," in Underhill, ed., *Tracts*, 379.

[55] Justus Lipsius argued that, since the truth concerning the matters that divided the Christian sects could not be known anyway, the civil magistrate was justified in punishing dissenters from an established church. Skepticism did not always lead to toleration! On the views of Lipsius and Coornhert see R. Tuck, *Philosophy and Government, 1572-1651* (Cambridge, 1993), 58.

[56] Woodhouse, *Puritanism and Liberty*, 227.

IV

pointed out that the magistrate was no more infallible than the pope or
the bishops. It followed that, as William Walwyn observed, "he who is in
an error may be the constrainer of him who is in the truth."[57] Another argument against government coercion of religion pointed out that progress in the understanding of divine revelation could be achieved only
through free and reasoned discourse. When Milton wrote of "the re-
forming of the Reformation itself" in a coming new age, he was arguing
specifically for freedom of the press.[58] Medieval theologians had sometimes envisaged a gradual progress in the understanding of scripture
through the course of the centuries. The new insight was that such progress required freedom of thought and expression.[59]

The view that any meaningful freedom of the church required that
the civil magistrates refrain from interfering in matters of religion was
widespread among members of the separatist groups in England. During
the army debates held at Whitehall in 1648, one of them declared: "No
man or magistrate on the earth hath power to meddle in these cases."[60] A
Leveller pamphlet written in the following year set out the same doctrine
that the First Amendment would eventually proclaim for Americans:

> [W]e do not impower or entrust our said representatives to . . .
> compell by penalties or otherwise any person to any thing in or
> about matters of faith, Religion or Gods worship or to restrain
> any person from the profession of his faith, or exercise of his Re-
> ligion according to his conscience. . . .[61]

Roger Williams, arguing against any sort of unified church-state, introduced the phrase "wall of separation" when he wrote of a "wall of separation between the Garden of the church and the Wilderness of the
world."[62]

Another strand of medieval argumentation that underwent radical
development in the early modern era concerned the authority of the individual conscience. In the middle of the seventeenth century, the prevailing view was still that religious disagreements sprang "from malice,

---

[57] W.B. Haller, *Tracts on Liberty in the Puritan Revolution, 1638-1647*, 3 vols. (New York, 1934), 3:70.

[58] John Milton, *Milton: Areopagitica*, J.W. Hales, ed. (Oxford, 1904), 45.

[59] Milton's contemporary, John Goodwin, also developed the idea of a progressive understanding of scripture. For him, "Revelation was an unfinished but progressive process of
indefinite duration." See W.B. Haller, *Liberty and Reformation in the Puritan Revolution* (New
York, 1955), 252.

[60] Woodhouse, *Puritanism and Liberty*, 141.

[61] "An Agreement of Free People," in W.B. Haller and G. Davies, eds., *The Leveller
Tracts, 1647-1653* (New York, 1944), 323.

[62] Williams, *Writings*, 1:392.

rooted in sin."[63] But by then alternative opinions were also being expressed. The Latitudinarian Anglican, Chillingworth, declared in 1638: "An honest man . . . a true lover of God, and of his truth . . . may embrace errour for truth."[64] In the subsequent years of civil war it became increasingly difficult for men of good will and good sense to believe that their neighbors, sometimes men they had fought with side by side in a common cause, were really inspired by active malice to do the work of the devil because of a disagreement about some obscure point of theology. Yet this belief in the malice of the dissenter had been the essential basis of the medieval abhorrence of heresy. When differences of religious opinion could be seen as effects of intellectual error rather than of perverted will, the way was open to reconsider the proper attitude to a mistaken conscience. William Walwyn took up the text "Whatever is not of faith is sin," the same text that medieval authors had used to defend the primacy of conscience, but arrived at a conclusion that no medieval theologian had reached: "[E]very man ought to have Liberty of Conscience of what Opinion soever."[65] Walwyn argued that a person's conscience could be directed only by his own individual reason. A person could not be compelled to believe as true something that reason and conscience told him was false. If, under compulsion, he acted against his conscience, he sinned; but, and this was the new twist to the argument, the one who compelled him was a party to the sin and was acting like a tyrant.[66] This became a common argument among those who defended freedom of conscience. Even an extreme royalist like Michael Hudson argued that a magistrate who compelled a man to act against his conscience forced him to commit the sin of hypocrisy, and that the magistrate himself was guilty of "sacrilegious intrusion upon those sacred prerogatives which God hath preserved unto himself."[67] The Anglican divine Jeremy Taylor argued at length that a person who followed an erring conscience did not sin in doing so and, again, concluded with a plea for religious freedom: "If God will not be angry at men for being invincibly deceived, why should men be angry one at another?"[68] Sometimes the forcing of a person's conscience was compared to physical rape; in the pungent language of Roger Williams it was "spirituall and soule rape."[69]

---

[63] Haller, *Liberty and Reformation*, 251. This was the opinion that John Cotton still maintained in his dispute with Roger Williams. See Williams, *Writings*, 3:42.

[64] W. Chillingworth, *The Religion of Protestants* (Oxford, 1638), 21.

[65] Haller, *Tracts on Liberty*, 3:67.

[66] Ibid., 3:71, 86.

[67] Hudson's views are discussed in Tuck, *Philosophy and Government*, 270.

[68] Jordan, *Toleration*, 4:405.

[69] Williams, "Bloudy Tenent," 3:219.

IV

The final outcome of all the new argument about conscience was a fusion of the new ideal of religious liberty with the older doctrine of natural rights. Freedom of conscience came to be seen as one of the natural rights of man, guaranteed by natural law and discernable by the "light of reason" or "light of nature." The parliamentary leader, Henry Vane, for instance, asserted that freedom of religion could be claimed "upon the grounds of natural right."[70] Roger Williams has also been called an extreme exponent of natural rights because of his all-embracing argument for freedom of conscience,[71] but this seems to be a misunderstanding of his position. I do not think Williams ever used the language of natural rights.[72] William Penn, however, did so, and with "classic clarity," according to Searle Bates. Penn wrote: "I ever understood an impartial liberty of conscience to be the natural right of all men. . . ."[73] He argued that the people did not and could not give up this natural right to any government formed by the original contract that first established a political society. Hence, subsequently, government could have no lawful power to invade this right of the individual. As one might expect, the constitution of Pennsylvania in due course echoed the words of the founder and proclaimed "a natural and unalienable right" to freedom of worship. As a Quaker, Penn stood outside the mainstream of the religious thought of his age, but his eminently respectable contemporary, Bishop Burnet, expressed a similar view: "I have long looked on liberty of conscience as one of the rights of human nature, antecedent to society, which no man could give up. . . ."[74] Going back to the roots of Christian tradition Burnet also undertook a translation of Lactantius and, in his preface to it, again argued for toleration. John Locke, too, in his influential *Letter Concerning Toleration*, wrote that "liberty of conscience is every man's natural right."[75] Outside England, Pierre Bayle defended the rights of conscience,[76] and Spinoza drew on his own idiosyncratic doctrine of natural rights in asserting an inalienable right to freedom of religion.[77]

---

[70] Henry Vane, *A Healing Question Propounded* (London, 1656), 5.

[71] Haller, *Tracts on Liberty*, 1:60.

[72] Williams relied on his own idiosyncratic understanding of scripture rather than on any appeal to natural rights in defending religious freedom. He inveighed against the "light of nature" in "The Examiner Defended," in Williams, *Writings*, 7: 242, "Come to the light of nature—and then I ask, if it be not a downright Doctrine of Free-will, in depraved nature?"

[73] M. Searle Bates, *Religious Liberty: An Inquiry* (New York, 1945), 297, quoting William Penn, *England's Present Interest Discovered* (London, 1679).

[74] Gilbert Burnet, *History of My Own Times*, 6 vols. (Oxford, 1823), 5:107.

[75] John Locke, *A Letter Concerning Toleration*, M. Montuori, ed. (The Hague, 1963), 95.

[76] Bayle, *Philosophical Commentary*, 161, 173, 193.

[77] "A Theologico-Political Treatise," in R.H.M. Elwes, ed., *The Chief Works of Benedict de Spinoza*, 2 vols. (London, 1883), 1:257.

By the end of the seventeenth century, reasonably adequate theories of religious rights had been formulated. Implementing them took much longer. Persecution became more sporadic in the eighteenth century, but it was not until the liberal revolutions of the nineteenth century that freedom of religion became widely established in the constitutions of Western states and not until the twentieth century that the major Christian churches proclaimed religious rights as an essential feature of the Christian faith itself.

Conclusion

The peoples of Western Europe slowly learned, through centuries of cruel experience, to acknowledge at least the practical necessity of tolerating religious differences among Christians; and, at best, they came to see religious freedom as an ideal inherent in their traditional faith. We need to ask in conclusion what relevance this distinctively Western Christian experience can have for a world of many religions and diverse cultures.

Some critics have suggested that all the brave new pronouncements about human rights, including religious rights, simply inflate Western concepts into universal values and then assume without question that such values are valid for all other societies, regardless of their histories and cultures. Perhaps, it is suggested, this is just another kind of Western chauvinism. On the other hand, it is evident that the whole world has willingly accepted some aspects of Western culture, notably Western technology. And Wolfgang Huber has argued that it would be merely arrogant for the West to export its material culture on a worldwide scale while assuming that other societies are incapable of appreciating Western ideals or learning from Western experience.[78] Technology itself, we may note, is a product of several centuries of distinctively Western cultural evolution; but the fruits of technology—a computer or an internal combustion engine—can easily be replicated in societies with quite different cultural traditions. The situation is evidently more complex when we consider the fruits of Western religious experience; it is easier to export an artefact than to implant an ideal. And certainly, in this sphere, communication could not be along a one-way highway. The West had to learn—or relearn—the practice of nonviolence from India, through Mahatma Ghandi. Modern Western ideas, including religious ideas, on respect for the environment and for all species of life, have been shaped in part by currents of Buddhist thought. Moreover, we should not expect to

---

[78] Wolfgang Huber, "Christianity and Democracy in Europe," *Emory International Law Review* 6 (1992): 35-53.

find Western ways of institutionalizing religious rights duplicated exactly in any African or Asian society (and, indeed, the institutional arrangements vary a great deal in the West from country to country).

Yet, for all this, the actual state of the world suggests that the lessons the West learned so painfully may indeed have a universal relevance. Evidently, the global utopia envisaged in the various United Nations pronouncements has not yet arrived. In some countries religious minorities are openly persecuted or at best denied full civic rights. New forms of religious fundamentalism inspire hatred and fear of all those outside the chosen group. In many regions, from Northern Ireland to Sri Lanka—in the republics of the former Soviet Union, in what was once Yugoslavia, in parts of the Islamic world—ancient religious animosities have fused with ethnic rivalries to produce new and explosive socio-religious compounds. The resulting violence ranges from individual assassinations to large-scale massacres to outright civil war. Religious conflict is a major cause of global disorder in the modern world. The recognition of religious rights is a necessity if a more peaceful world-order is ever to be achieved.

Obviously, all societies cannot reenact the specific experiences of early modern Europe that shaped the modern idea of religious rights; and indeed that would be a dismal prospect. But during the present century, people in all parts of the world have experienced for themselves the grievous effects of religious conflict and religious persecution. It would certainly be expedient to end such savageries. One might think that we too should have been "schooled and whipt by our calamities" into recognizing this. And perhaps a certain skepticism might be an appropriate response to the claims of the more fanatical fundamentalists. But modern pragmatism and modern skepticism seem insufficient to assuage the existing conflicts within religions and between religions. Perhaps the only answer for all peoples is the one that Christians discovered so painfully when they compared the words of Jesus with all the hatreds and cruelties of their contemporary world; that is, the need for a return to the original sources of religious tradition and a reconsideration of their implications in the light of our accumulated centuries of experience. Modern Christian pronouncements on religious rights base those rights on the dignity of human beings as children of God. But Mohammed, too, said: "Verily we have honored every human being." Jesus told us to love those who hate us, but Gautama Buddha also declared: "Hatred does not cease with hatred; hatred ceases only with love." Among all the founders of the great world religions we can find an attitude of respect and compassion for the human person that is the best argument—the only ultimately compelling one—for religious liberty. Often contingent historical

circumstances have distorted human understanding of the original revelations and intuitions that lie at the root of our religious traditions. Perhaps the best antidote for all the false fundamentalisms of our age might
be a true fundamentalism, a return to the words and spirit and example
of the great founders.

V

Aristotle and the American Indians-Again
Two Critical Discussions*

I. Introduction

In the years since Lewis Hanke published his excellent little book on *Aristotle and the American Indians* studies on the Indies Debates of the sixteenth century have multiplied (Vidal Abril Castello recently mentioned the «thousand and one» current articles on Vitoria and Las Casas).[1] Some old controversies have died away — one hears less now about Las Casas and the Black Legend — but some persist. Above all there is no consensus on one of the most important issues, the role of the Spanish scholastics in the transition from the Christian-Aristotelian thought world of the Middle Ages to the secularized culture of the Enlightenment. It is a great theme for any scholar concerned with the problems of «cristianesimo nella storia».

In a brilliant and paradoxical essay on the sources of Enlightenment thought, the American historian Carl Becker once argued that the Philosophes, who denounced Christian «superstition» so vehemently, in fact «at every turn... betray their debt to medieval thought without being aware of it».[2] More recently this theme has

---

* This paper is dedicated to Domenico Maffei in honor of his sixty-fifth birthday.
[1] L. Hanke, Aristotle and the American Indians, Chicago 1959. V. Abril Castello, Vitoria-Las Casas, confrontacion y proyeccion, in I diritti dell'uomo e la pace nel pensiero di Francisco de Vitoria e Bartolomé de las Casas, Milano 1988, 155-172. The articles in this volume provide a good overview of recent work on Vitoria and Las Casas. See especially the bibliographical article of Francesco D'Elia, Studi Lascasiani, dell'ultimo ventennio. Bibliografia essenziale ragionata, 309-321.
[2] C.L. Becker, The Heavenly City of the Eighteenth-Century Philosophers, New Haven 1932, 30. For criticism see R.O. Rockwood, Carl Becker's Heavenly City Revisited, Ithaca 1958.

been taken up by European scholars in debates about the «secularization» of Christian culture in the age of the Enlightenment and the «legitimacy» of such a process. Current discussions have centered around two themes, the origin of Enlightenment theories of natural rights and the origin of the Enlightenment idea of human progress. Some modern scholars have maintained that the Enlightenment concept of subjective natural rights — our modern «human rights» — was illicitly derived from a deviant form of Christianity, the late medieval voluntarism and nominalism of William of Ockham.[3] In this view modern rights theories are seen as a secularized form of Ockham's Franciscan thought. Other scholars have argued that the Enlightenment idea of progress was an illicit transposition of Christian eschatology to the secular sphere. Certainly Christianity substituted a linear conception of time for the classical myths of eternal recurrence; and, in the works of Joachim of Flora, Christian history was presented as a story of progress, moving from an age of the Father through an age of the Son to a coming age of the Holy Spirit. Writing in 1949, Karl Löwith maintained that the modern idea of progress was a secularized version of Joachim's salvation history.[4] This view was widely accepted until, in a spirited response defending the «legitimacy» of the modern age, Hans Blumenberg attacked the whole idea of secularization as a meaningful explanation of Enlightenment culture.[5]

In both these areas — theories of rights and theories of progress — the Spanish writings evoked by the first encounters with America may be seen as representing a transitional phase between medieval and modern thought. In the following critical discussions I want to

---

[3] This was the position of Michel Villey. On his work see my paper, Villey, Ockham, and the Origin of Individual Rights, in The Weightier Matters of the Law. A Tribute to Harold J. Berman, T. Witte and F. S. Alexander eds., Atlanta 1988. For a discussion of modern human rights theories as a form of secularized thought see Eutimio Sastre Santos, Derechos humanos y secularización en Francisco de Vitoria in I diritti dell'uomo e la pace..., 585-612, with extensive further literature. For Sastre, secularization means a shift from a «theocentric» to a «rationalistic» way of thinking. He argues that Vitoria's thought was not secularized in this sense.

[4] K. Löwith, Meaning in History, Chicago 1949.

[5] Die Legitimität der Neuzeit, Frankfurt 1966. I have used the translation of R.M. Wallace, The Legitimacy of the Modern Age, Cambridge, Mass. 1983, which includes a helpful introduction. For further discussion of Blumenberg's thesis and Löwith's response see R.M. Wallace, Progress, Secularization and Modernity: The Löwith/Blumenberg Debate, New German Critique 22 (1981) 63-79. See also J. Bennett, Unthinking Faith and Enlightenment, New York 1987, 18-21.

consider these two topics and the treatment of them by two modern authors, Philippe André-Vincent and Anthony Pagden. Each of them, I think, presents new interpretations of Aristotelian elements in the thought of Vitoria and Las Casas that are stimulating and interesting in themselves but that lead on to radical misunderstandings of the Spanish authors and their role in the emergence of the modern world.

II. Philippe André-Vincent, Las Casas and the Rights of Man

The role of Las Casas in the development of Western rights theories has often been debated. Luno Pena described the Spanish friar as a «precursor» of modern ideas on the rights of man and argued specifically that Las Casas' insistence on a natural right to liberty reflects his adherence to the Thomist tradition of rational natural law.[6] Edmundo O'Gorman argued in a contrary fashion that, in asserting a right to equality, Las Casas spoke «with the voice of Voltaire, Hume, and Rousseau», but that he achieved this only by breaking with the medieval Christian-Aristotelian synthesis of Aquinas.[7] André-Vincent's view is different from either of these. He maintains that Las Casas was indeed a faithful Thomist but that, precisely because he was a Thomist, he did not expound a doctrine of subjective rights.[8] The work of the French Dominican gains authority from his

---

[6] Luno Pena, Presupuestas historico-doctrinales de la teoria Las Casas de la libertad, in Las Casas et la politique des droits de l'homme, Aix-en-Provence 1974, 153-165.

[7] E. O'Gorman, Lewis Hanke on the Spanish Struggle for Justice in the Conquest of America, Hispanic American Historical Review 29 (1949) 563-571. For O'Gorman «Las Casas occupies a mid-way position between the scholasticism in which he was trained and the rationalism which he foreshadowed» (569). M. Mahn-Lot, Bartolomé de las Casas et le droit des Indiens, Paris 1982, 258, wrote (with a reference to André-Vincent) «Il faut se garder... de confondre le droit naturel de la théologie scolastique et le droit naturel moderne, celui de Grotius et des Encyclopédistes», but also «il y a une filiation indéniable des hommes des Lumières à l'école de Salamanque...».

[8] André-Vincent has presented his views in many books and articles. The ones cited below are Derecho de los Indios y Desarrollo en Hispano-America, Madrid 1974; Les révolutions et le droit, Paris 1974; Bartolomé de las Casas prophète du Nouveau Monde, Paris 1980; Les droits de l'homme dans l'enseignement de Jean Paul II, Paris 1983; La concrétisation de la notion classique de droit naturel à travers l'oeuvre de las Casas, in Las Casas et la politique des droits..., 203-213; La dialectique lascasienne du droit naturel concret, in I diritti..., 639-649. The last two papers provide especially clear, brief accounts of André-Vincent's position.

long engagement with Latin-American studies. It is only a historical aspect of his argument that I want to criticize.

According to André-Vincent the modern concept of «human rights» or «rights of man» is nowhere to be found in the work of Las Casas. He reaches this conclusion by applying to Las Casas a special variety of neoAristotelianism and neoThomism which was developed most fully in France by Michel Villey. The argument turns on a sharp distinction between «classical natural right» and «modern natural right». Classical natural right was the doctrine of Aristotle and Aquinas and of the whole Thomist school, the mainstream of medieval Christian thought, it is suggested. In this tradition the idea of right (*dikaion, ius*) has primarily an objective sense; it means «what is just», the just thing itself, what is justly due to someone. Modern natural right, on the other hand, takes *ius* as meaning primarily a subjective power inhering in human persons, giving rise to the subjective natural rights or rights of man that we encounter in eighteenth-century thought.[9] In discussing William of Ockham as a principal source of the modern doctrine, Villey emphasized especially Ockham's identification of right (*ius*) with power (*potestas*). He saw this as a revolutionary semantic innovation, a decisive break with the older tradition. Thus, for Villey, the idea of subjective rights was an aberration from the mainstream of medieval Christian thought. André-Vincent sees Las Casas as a faithful Thomist who remained safely within the mainstream.[10]

---

[9] La dialectique..., 639, «A qui cherche dans l'oeuvre de Las Casas le vocable "droit de l'homme", la première épreuve sera de ne l'y pas trouver: ni le mot, ni ses équivalents». La concrétisation..., 203, «A la suite de Saint Thomas d'Aquin, frère Barthélemy donne la première place dans sa pensée au concept objectif du droit». André-Vincent did acknowledge «affinities» between Las Casas and the thought of the French Revolution in Bartolomé de Las Casas prophète..., 247. But, when he discussed the historical development from the earlier movement to the later one, his main concern was always to emphasize the difference between scholastic objective right and eighteenth-century subjective rights. See his Jean Paul II..., 16, «En passant par le volontarisme de Suarez et par le rationalisme de Grotius ce droit objectif est devenu cette collection de droits subjectifs...».

[10] M. Villey, La formation de la pensée juridique moderne, Paris 1975⁴, 252, 261. See André-Vincent, Concrétisation..., 212 n.3 and Derecho de los Indios..., 88-89. André-Vincent wrote here that, although a doctrine of subjective rights existed from the time of Ockham, Vitoria was too good a Thomist to define right as a power of the subject. But in fact Vitoria accepted from Conrad Summenhart a definition of ius as «potestas vel facultas conveniens alicui secundum leges». Vitoria added that the word was often used in this sense in Scripture. See his De justitia, ed. V. Beltran de Heredia, I, Madrid 1934, 64.

The difficulty with this neat and simple dichotomy between Thomist and Ockhamist thought is that it ignores the whole world of medieval jurisprudence to which Las Casas turned so often in his arguments on behalf of the Indians. As I have argued in detail elsewhere, the idea of *ius* as meaning a subjective right, including specifically the identification of *ius* and *potestas,* was commonplace in canonistic writings in the centuries before Ockham.[11] Such language is scattered throughout the Gregorian Decretals and the medieval commentaries on them. There really is a doctrine of individual subjective rights in the writings of Las Casas but it is derived, not from Aquinas or Ockham, but from this other great storehouse of medieval thought.

By mid-thirteenth century the canonists had identified a considerable variety of rights inhering in individuals or corporate groups — property rights, marriage rights, rights of election, rights of waging war. Such rights could be either natural rights or civil rights, depending on whether they were derived from natural law or positive human law. It will suffice here to quote from a work of Innocent IV that Las Casas knew well and cited often. Arguing that a city could not ·arbitrarily deprive a cleric or even a layman of his property rights *(dominia),* Innocent wrote:

...such a statute would injure the right *(ius)* of another and a right that pertains to someone or is acquired by natural law *(ius)* as are *dominia* and obligations and such things. And it is not given by civil law as are legal actions...[12]

Here the word *ius* is used to mean both natural law and the rights defined by that law. Arguing similarly from natural law, and

---

[11] Origins of Natural Rights Language: Texts and Contexts, 1150-1250, History of Political Thought 10 (1989) 615-646. Luno Pena wrote that Las Casas' assertion of a right to liberty derived from natural law in the De regia potestate was based on the authority of Thomas Aquinas (Presupuestas, 156). It is true that Las Casas referred here to three texts of Aquinas. But in the same short chapter he cited twenty-one texts of Roman and canon law. All the texts which specifically related liberty and ius naturale are legal ones. See De regia potestate, ed. L. Perena etc., Madrid 1969, 16-20.

[12] Commentaria Innocentii... super libros quinque decretalium, Frankfurt 1570 ad 1.2.7, «...tale statutum esset in laesionem iuris alterius et eius iuris, quod ad aliquem spectat, vel acquiritur de iure naturali, ut sunt dominia, obligationes et huiusmodi. Et non datur a iure civili, vel ab imperatore ut actiones...».

from divine positive law, Innocent also maintained that even infidels could hold true *dominium*.[13] This was of course a central contention of Las Casas in his arguments on behalf of the Indians. Perhaps he could have argued his case entirely in terms of Thomist objective justice; in fact he chose to turn often to the canonistic tradition of subjective rights.

Kenneth Pennington has pointed out that the whole argument of Las Casas' treatise, *De thesauris,* one of his last major works, sometimes called his Testament, was built around a series of doctrines drawn from medieval canon law.[14] We can conveniently illustrate from this same treatise Las Casas' persistent appeal to the concept of subjective rights that André-Vincent found lacking in his work. It is as though the modern author had read Las Casas through Thomist spectacles that filtered out anything not in accord with Thomist principles.

In modern discourse, André-Vincent points out, we often use the term *droit objectif* to mean the rules of law, and *droits subjectifs* to mean the subjective rights defined by law. The first usage is common in Las Casas, he writes, but the second is never found in his works. Las Casas never used the word *droit* to mean a power or juridical capacity. Even when he referred to *iura* in the plural, we are told, he meant the laws of the Indians not their rights.[15] In fact, though, Las Casas referred specifically to the powers and jurisdictions of the Indians as rights (*iura*) which pertained to them by natural law.[16] Again, closely following the thought of Innocent IV, he wrote:

[13] Commentaria ad 3.34.8. Innocent went on, however, to argue that the pope could exercise jurisdiction over infidels if they violated natural law, a position that Las Casas rejected. On Innocent's text and its use by later authors see J. Muldoon, Popes, Lawyers, and Infidels, Philadelphia 1979.

[14] K. Pennington, Bartolome de las Casas and the Tradition of Medieval Law, Church History 39 (1970) 149-161.

[15] La concrétisation..., 204. «Par contre on ne rencontre jamais dans les écrits lascasiens le mot droit employé dans le sens derivé subjectif, celui d'un pouvoir, d'une capacité juridique attribuée ou reconnue par la loi au sujet... Ainsi quand on lit chez Las Casas "Les droits des Indiens"... il s'agit des lois des Indiens...», Writing in French, André-Vincent always uses the word droit when he refers to Las Casas' use of ius.

[16] Los tesoros de Peru, ed. A. Losada, Madrid 1958, 68. «Sed principatus et potestates, dominia et jurisdictiones quae sunt apud infideles... pertinent adeos lege naturali et gentium, quae *jura* lex evangelica... instaurauit, augificauit, firmauit...», (emphasis added).

...the rights (*iura*) of others which belong to each one by natural and divine law (*iure*) should be fixed and immutable... civil reason can extinguish civil rights but not natural ones.[17]

At another point he denounced any

...violation of the rights (*iura*) of those people since they pertain to them by natural law (*iure*) and the law of nations.[18]

These are typical passages. Throughout the *De thesauris*, Las Casas used the term *iura* to mean both the objective laws that define subjective rights or juridical capacities and the rights or capacities that are defined (jurisdiction, dominion, etc.). In reiterating the point that Las Casas did not use *ius* to mean a juridical attribute, André-Vincent observed that the friar did not claim for the Indians a «droit de...» a right of doing something. But Las Casas did use such language. He wrote that the Indians had a right of making war (*ius movendi bellum*) and a right or power of electing their own rulers (*Potestas et auctoritas vel ius eligendi*).[19]

According to André-Vincent, when Las Casas wanted to refer to the subjective attributes of the Indians he spoke of «powers» but not «rights». Thus he preserved the distinction between subjective and objective and the essentially objective meaning of *ius* in the tradition of Aquinas.[20] As we have just seen this was not always the case. Las Casas did sometimes identify *ius* with a subjective power. This usage was especially evident again when he deployed the canonistic terminology of *ius ad rem* and *ius in re*. He used this language to argue that the pope's grant of 1493 gave to the Spanish king a title or claim to the Indies (*ius ad rem*), but not a right of actually ruling them (*ius in re*). In referring to this latter *ius*, Las Casas described it as a «right... of royal power» or «the full power of exercising supreme jurisdiction» or «the exercise of royal power».[21] In each case the *ius* was understood as a *potestas*.

---

[17] Tesoros..., 80, «...aliena jura et quae unicuique de jure naturali et diuino competunt, fixa et immutabilia esse opportet... Quia ciuilis quidem ratio ciuilia jura perimere potest, naturalia vero non utique».
[18] Tesoros..., 92, «..ne fiant injuriae vel jurium illarum gentium violatio cum ad illas pertineant jure gentium et naturali...».
[19] Tesoros..., 206, 342, 344.
[20] Concrétisation..., 204 «Las Casas... parlera de capacités, de pouvoirs, non de droits. Ainsi sont maintenus la distinction du subjectif et de l'objectif et la primauté du sens objectif, selon la tradition thomiste et le droit naturel classique».
[21] Tesoros..., 196, 280, 284.

V

In the work of Las Casas, again according to André-Vincent, persons never appear as isolated subjects of individual rights. The right of the Indian people existed only «globally», in the whole. So, in this view, Las Casas was a prophet of the right of peoples rather than of the rights of man. He argued passionately for the liberty of the Indian people — he saw this as a necessary preliminary to their evangelization — but he never claimed liberty as an individual right.[22]

All this is only partly true. In the treatise *De regia potestate*, Las Casas wrote simply, «Liberty is a right implanted in men...».[23] When he discussed the whole ensemble of Indian rights in the *De thesauris* he repeatedly used the phrase, «rights of their natural kings and of single persons». The emphasis on a right to liberty in the *De thesauris* was especially strong when Las Casas discussed the need for the Indians to consent to the Spanish rule over them if that rule was to be legitimized. Here he deployed the legal phrase, *quod omnes tangit* («What touches all is to be approved by all»), a doctrine of Roman private law that had been developed into a broad constitutional principle by the medieval canonists. Las Casas now applied it to his American Indians. Whenever a free people was to accept some new obligation or burden, he explained, it was fitting that all whom the matter «touched» should be summoned and should freely consent. Then Las Casas added, echoing earlier canonistic doctrine, that a group of people could have a right either as a corporate whole or as separate individuals. In the first case the consent of a majority was sufficient; in the second case the consent of each individual was required.[24] Las Casas maintained that this latter kind of consent — *omnes et singuli* — was needed to legitimize Spanish rule over the Indians. The consent of a whole people could not prejudice a single person withholding consent. Especially where liberty was concerned, the case was «common to all and many as single individuals». It would detract from the right of each one (*juri uniuscuiusque vel singulorum*) if they all lost «sweet liberty». Rather than a majority prejudicing a minority in such a case the opinion of the minority

---

[22] Dialectique..., 640. Concrétisation..., 205, «Cette liberté... n'est jamais revendiquée comme un droit individuel».
[23] De regia potestate..., 17. See Q. Moreno, Pensiamento filosofico-politico de Bartolome de Las Casas, Sevilla 1976, 285-291.
[24] Tesoros..., 174, citing Innocent IV and Baldus.

dissenters should prevail.[25] This was an extreme doctrine of individual rights and especially of the right to liberty. It is an example of the intransigence that seemed to grow in Las Casas as he grew older. But it also shows how he could take old legal doctrines that were hardening into platitudes and use them in new ways to sustain a political theory based on liberty and equality.

André-Vincent argues that Las Casas was not concerned with any abstract rights of man in general but with particular concrete rights of the Indians that had been violated, rights that were rooted in Indian society and specific to Indian culture. He praises this realism of Las Casas and contrasts it with the abstract rights of Enlightenment theorists. The eighteenth-century revolutions in America and France, he suggests, appealed to a natural right devoid of realism. «Le réalisme de Las Casas lui tourne le dos».[26]

Again this seems only partly true. Las Casas was indeed concerned with violations of real rights of the Indians and he knew and valued the cultures of Indian peoples. But the contrast with eighteenth-century attitudes seems overdrawn. The American founding fathers were not concerned only with rights in the abstract but with some very concrete grievances of American colonists. They eventually defended their claims in terms of natural rights because an appeal to the common-law rights of Englishmen proved ineffective as a response to laws enacted by an English parliament.[27] In just the same fashion, Las Casas wanted to defend specific concrete rights of the Indians, but he found that he could do so most effectively by appealing to the underlying natural rights of all men.

The essence of André-Vincent's argument is conveyed in the words, «Le langage moderne des "droits de l'homme" est issu à travers des idéologies contraire de la grande tradition du droit naturel» — that is from ideologies opposed to the Thomist conception of ob-

---

[25] Tesoros..., 176, «...et omnes et singuli habent consentire... Nec si etiam omnes dum libet populo vel civitate consentiente non praejudicabunt uni solo non vocato aut non consentiente quod haec causa est communis omnibus et pluribus ut singulis maxime favore libertatis....». 180, «Immo etsi maior pars consentiat... quia faciunt contra libertatem; non praejudicaret non consentientibus, et esset standum minori parte nolenti consentire».

[26] Les révolutions..., 125. Dialectique..., 639.

[27] French writers also had concrete grievances but they turned more readily to the idea of natural rights because they had much less of a tradition of legal rights to invoke.

jective right.[28] Modern neoThomists find a doctrine of subjective natural rights asserted by Enlightenment thinkers who were hostile to traditional Christianity and to medieval scholastic thought. They do not find this doctrine of subjective rights in Aquinas. They therefore assume that the doctrine was alien to the medieval Christian tradition except in the «decadent» thought of Ockham and his school. But this approach distorts the whole history of Western rights theories. The language of natural rights was actually shaped in the legal renaissance of the twelfth century, when all the great legal traditions of the Western world were taking shape. It was transmitted to the modern world largely through the work of the great Spanish jurist-theologians of the sixteenth century. Over the course of time the idea of natural rights came to be associated with a variety of philosophies and applied in different historical contexts to serve different causes, sometimes conservative, sometimes revolutionary. For some modern Catholic writers, including André-Vincent perhaps, the present-day position is confused by the fact that recent pontiffs have enthusiastically embraced the Enlightenment language of natural rights that the Roman church frowned on for centuries.[29] A proper understanding of the origin of Western rights theories in the Catholic jurisprudence of the Middle Ages would perhaps make the present situation more intelligible.

One can share André-Vincent's impatience with the abuses of modern rights language. Too often liberal Western values are inflated into general principles of human conduct and then proclaimed as universal rights applicable to any society regardless of its culture, economy, or religion. But it is a good Thomist principle that *abusus non tollit usum*. There may still be a core of real human rights and good reason to insist on them in our modern world.

---

[28] Dialectique..., 649.
[29] André-Vincent, Les droits de l'homme dans l'enseigement de Jean Paul II, 22, argues that John Paul's concept of rights is «objective» rather than «subjective» and so quite different from that of the UNO Declaration of 1948. But there is no evidence of this in the papal texts that he presents. See e.g. John Paul's address to the UN in 1979 (p. 105) «La déclaration universelle des Droits de l'homme et les instruments juridiques tant au niveau international que national, dans un mouvement qu'on ne peut que souhaiter progressif et continu, cherchent... à définir au moins certains droits inaliénables de l'homme». The pope went on to list among these inalienable rights, a right to life, to liberty and security, a right to freedom of thought, of conscience, of religion, a right to property... It is hard to see how all this differs from some Enlightenment catalog of subjective rights.

V

III. Anthony Pagden. Ethnography and Cultural Evolution

In his book, *The Fall of Natural Man*, Anthony Pagden has turned aside from the old problems of law and political theory involved in the Indies debates to consider the rise of a new ethnography and a new concept of cultural evolution in the work of Vitoria, Las Casas, Acosta, and Lafiteau.[30] Clearly such a theme could be relevant to the second major topic mentioned at the outset of this paper, the relationship between medieval Christian thought and the modern idea of progress. In the following comments I want first to criticize Pagden's account of Vitoria's ideas on cultural development, which seem to me radically flawed, and then to explore some ideas suggested by his treatment of the later authors, especially Las Casas.

1) Vitoria and «Nature's Children»

Pagden dismisses rather summarily the considerable body of earlier writing in this field by Spanish authors. He finds their work marred by nationalist bias (in the case of Venancio Carro «to the point of worthlessness») and by «general theoretical errors». These earlier scholars, he complains, naively assumed that «the text ... is merely what is there on the page». Pagden proposes instead to recover a whole «forgotten and frequently misrepresented mindset».[31]

He begins with a theme discussed by many previous writers, the difficulties that sixteenth-century Europeans encountered in fitting

[30] A. Pagden, The Fall of Natural Man. The American Indian and the Origins of Comparative Ethnology, Cambridge 1986[2].

[31] Fall of Natural Man, 6,7. But, apart from the specific errors of interpretation noted below, Pagden himself misunderstands the whole thrust of Vitoria's treatise. He writes (Fall of Natural Man, 65), «There is no conclusion to Vitoria's relectio De indis, beyond the pragmatic observation that in the absence of any just title for the conquest, the whole intellectual inquiry would have to be dropped, because the Spaniards could never in fact abandon the Indies as this would bring "great detriment to the Spanish princes and is thus unacceptable to us"». But this was not Vitoria's conclusion. He wrote nothing about dropping the intellectual inquiry in the absence of a just title for conquest. Instead, he went on to argue that, even if there were no such title, profitable trade could continue between Spain and the Indies without any necessary diminution of royal revenues. See De Indis recenter inventis relectio prior in Obras de Francisco de Vitoria, ed. T. Urdanoz, Madrid 1960, 725.

V

the new experience of America into a preexisting, mainly Aristotelian framework of thought.[32] Pagden points out that the ensuing tensions eventually led writers on the Indies from a generally static view of human nature as essentially uniform to a more relativist approach. The new approach was moreover a kind of historical relativism in which «differences in place may be identical to differences in time».[33] The role of Vitoria in this development is discussed in the central chapter of the book called «From Nature's Slaves to Nature's Children».

The argument goes like this. Early defenders of the Spanish conquests in America appealed to Aristotle's doctrine of natural slavery; if the Indians were natural slaves, then the Spaniards could easily be presented as their natural masters. But Vitoria saw that the theory of natural slavery did not fit the facts of Indian life and, more fundamentally, he discerned an inherent contradiction in the theory itself.[34] (Creatures as inferior as Aristotle's natural slaves could hardly be human at all.) Yet the way of life of the Indians, especially their offenses against natural law and their primitive eating habits, suggested that they were something less than fully developed human beings. With the category of natural slavery no longer available to him, Vitoria made a decisive move by shifting the argument «from one branch of Aristotelian psychology (concerned with the mental status of slaves) to another (concerned with the mental disposition of children)».[35] This move liberated the Indian «from a timeless void of semi-rationality». Still using Aristotelian categories of thought, one could now see him, not as some subrational creature, but as a human being whose intellect was still in a state of becoming, still «potential» rather than «actual». So Vitoria's new insight «opened the way to an historical and evolutionary account of the Amerindian world».[36]

This account has been widely accepted. One reviewer praised «the seriousness with which Pagden reconstructs the classificatory theories of sixteenth-century Iberians». But the argument is all

---

[32] As Lewis Hanke wrote, Aristotle and the American Indians, 3, «They tended to look at the New World through medieval spectacles».
[33] Fall of Natural Man, 2.
[34] Ibid., 5, 94, 97, 106.
[35] Ibid., 3, 104.
[36] Ibid., 99, 104, 106.

wrong. Vitoria did not recognize an inherent contradiction in Aristotle's theory of natural slavery; he did not affirm that the Indians were nature's children; he did not regard their intellect as potential rather than actual; he did not shift from one path of Aristotelian psychology to another. In the following comments I have not tried to list every trivial mistake in Pagden's work but only to mention some errors that seem to indicate a real misunderstanding of Vitoria's mindset. The constructive purpose of such criticism is to rescue Vitoria's real thought from a cloud of misunderstandings.

Near the beginning of his book the author introduces the categories of *ius naturae*, law of nature, and *ius gentium*, law of nations. Sixteenth-century writers, he notes, were inclined to believe in universal social norms. Then, he explains further, «There might, of course, exist a wide variety of local customs (the *ius gentium* or law of nations was a record of such customs); but they had all to conform to a body of meta-laws, the law of nature, the *ius naturae*, itself».[37] This description of the *ius gentium*, a central category of thought in Vitoria's argument, is precisely upside down. The *ius gentium* was not a record of varied customs but the common core of universally accepted law that all peoples had in common, sometimes regarded as identical with natural law, more often as closely related to it.[38] It is disconcerting to encounter at the outset of the argument such a basic misunderstanding.

Perhaps it was just a slip. But further difficulties arise when the author returns to the concept of natural law that Vitoria derived from Aquinas. Pagden oversimplifies here in discussing the primary and secondary precepts of natural law. The secondary precepts, he notes, include all the rules by which a people regulates its day-to-day social behavior, «the way a man eats, the modes of address he uses... the clothes he wears and so on». For Pagden all these secondary rules are arrived at by «deduction» from the first principles of natural law. And so, «Every aspect of human behavior can thus be judged natural or unnatural».[39] But Aquinas held that there were *two* ways in which human laws could be related to natural law — ei-

---

[37] Ibid., 6.
[38] In the definition that Vitoria gave from Roman law, *ius gentium* was «what natural reason has established among all peoples» (Obras, 706).
[39] Fall of Natural Man, 62.

V

ther as conclusions deduced from premisses or as specifications of matters left undetermined by natural law. The wide variety of different human customs and practices typically fell into the second category. They were morally indifferent. As Aquinas wrote, «they have no other force than that of human law».[40] The point is worth pursuing a little further since Pagden applies his understanding of the secondary principles of natural law in lengthy discussions on the everyday practices of the Indians — especially their dietary practices — and on the implications of these practices for their supposed irrationality.

There is plenty of evidence that Europeans were often disgusted by the Indians «unsavory eating habits» and no reason to doubt that Vitoria shared this cultural prejudice. But Pagden attributes more to Vitoria than mere cultural prejudice. He suggests that, in formal theological discourse, Vitoria treated the Indians' habit of eating «inappropriate» or «unclean» or «unnatural» food as indicative of their subrational or semirational status, as implying an inability «to understand the world as it really is»[41] — all this of course leading up to the argument that, for Vitoria, the Indians were not mature human beings, but «children» of nature.

But the argument is flawed. Vitoria plainly taught that «no kind of food is or was prohibited to man by natural law». (The only exception he admitted was cannibalism, the eating of human flesh). Pagden however, confuses the issue by suggesting that, for Vitoria, some of the food taboos of the Old Testament, the «abominations of Leviticus», were moral precepts.[42] But Vitoria did not assert this. No Catholic theologian or canonist of his age could have asserted it. For all of them the moral precepts (*moralia*) of the Old Testament, like the commands of the Decalogue, were enduring norms. The food taboos of Leviticus were *cerimonialia*, which had passed away as regards their literal observance with the coming of the New Law (though they retained a symbolic significance). The passage that Pagden cites from Vitoria is there on the page, but it was presented only as a hypothetical objection to the position that Vitoria intended to sustain. His own position was set out a little further on, «... It is

---

[40] Summa theologiae, 1.2ae. 95.2.
[41] Fall of Natural Man, 74;
[42] Obras, 1010; Fall of Natural Man, 87 n. 179, referring to Obras, 1009.

answered... all these precepts are counted among the ceremonial ones as is clear from St.. Thomas».[43]

Another misinterpretation concerning the use of food occurs in a discussion on the effects of ingrained custom on a people's behavior. Pagden mentioned here the Greek church's prohibition against eating bloody meat and commented, «The fact that such a precept, for which (Vitoria) could find no explanation in natural law, *is* a custom gives it its authority», and, further, «Vitoria calculated that it would require six hundred years» for an ingrained custom to be eradicated. But this argument exists only in Pagden's imagination. The prohibition of the Greek church was based not on custom, but on apostolic legislation (Acts 15.29). Vitoria knew this of course. His point was, not that the prohibition had been established by custom, but that, in the West, it had been annulled by the institution of a contrary custom.[44] He mentioned that the apostolic law had still been asserted in the Western church six hundred years earlier and explained that a subsequent custom contrary to the law would take forty years to become established. Vitoria was making a legal argument about *consuetudo contra legem*, with the appropriate citations from Roman and canon law to illustrate his point. Pagden rightly tells us that in this kind of discourse a reference to some well-known text «could contain an entire subtext». But here the subtext is conveyed by legal allusions that the modern author has not troubled to explore; and they need to be explored by anyone who hopes to understand Vitoria's thought.

The underlying assumption that, for Vitoria, there was something immoral or irrational about eating the wrong kind of food is based in part on a misreading of the treatise, *De temperantia*. The Indians, Pagden explains, «ate creatures that were too low on the scale of being», such things as «rats, snakes, locusts», but Vitoria, it is argued, implicitly condemned such behavior. «The general drift of Vitoria's argument [in the *De temperantia*] is that the quality of the thing being eaten reflects the quality of the eater. Thus, it is "better"

---

[43] Obras, 1012. Vitoria, following Aquinas, also distinguished a third class of «judicial precepts» which had also ceased to be binding with the coming of the New Law.

[44] Fall of Natural Man, 100 and 230 n. 246. See Obras, 1013-1014. Vitoria thought that in the Greek church, even in the absence of a contrary custom, the prohibition could have lost its force through the operation of another legal doctrine, *cessante causa cessat effectus*.

to eat a cow than a cabbage...». Also, «The better a man is, the better... will be... the food he eats...».[45] But this is not really what Vitoria was arguing. Much of the *De temperantia* dealt with problems concerning the Carthusian Order. The Carthusians ate cabbages but not cows; their rule required a rigorous abstention from meat. But this did not mean, for Vitoria or any other Catholic writer, that they had adopted an inferior way of life. The «general drift» of Vitoria's argument was that all kinds of food are licit for humans in the age of the New Law. He quoted Matthew 15.11 «What goes into the mouth does not defile a man». Also the profession of faith drawn up for the Armenians at the Council of Florence, «We firmly believe that every creature of God is good and none to be rejected...». Also Peter's vision at Acts 10.12 of a vessel descending from Heaven, «And in it were all the four-footed beasts and creeping things of the earth and birds of the air, and there came a voice to him, "Arise, Peter, kill and eat"». Pagden sums up his argument by writing «Dietary norms... were a precise measure of a man's power of reason». But Vitoria wrote, «By no natural reason can it be known what if any food is prohibited».[46] It is no doubt true that the full meaning of a sixteenth-century text is not always conveyed simply by «what is there on the page». Still an ability to read what is there on the page is a useful preliminary qualification for a modern critic. To me it seems that the pages of vague anthropological musing about culture and diet and religion have no firm anchorage in Vitoria's texts. Pagden seems to be expressing a modern mindset of his own rather than eliciting a distinctive mindset of the sixteenth century.

Such errors are not negligible; but they do not necessarily invalidate Pagden's main thesis. Some practices of the Indians — their cannibalism and idolatry for instance — certainly were contrary to natural law as Vitoria understood it and could cast doubt on their rationality. It might still be true that Vitoria perceived an inherent contradiction in Aristotle's theory of natural slavery and so, to account for the Indians' behavior, turned from one path of Aristotelian faculty psychology to another and argued that the Indians were «nature's children» rather than «nature's slaves».

---

[45] *Fall of Natural Man,* 87, 88.
[46] *Fall of Natural Man,* 87; *Obras,* 1010. The texts from Matthew, Acts, and the Council of Florence referred to above follow at 1011, 1018.

But in fact there is no such argument in Vitoria's work. Far from questioning Aristotle's teaching on natural slavery he wrote, when first introducing the topic, «As Aristotle eloquently *and accurately* states, "Some are by nature slaves, namely those who are better fitted to serve than to rule"» (emphasis added).[47] Vitoria wanted to maintain that the Indians possessed their lands rightfully before the arrival of the Spaniards and he had to counter the Roman law argument that «a slave can have nothing of his own». He therefore distinguished sharply between the status of a natural slave and that of a person who was legally enslaved according to civil law. It was the latter kind of slave who could own nothing. Natural slaves were simple people, «not over strong in intellect», «better fitted to serve than to rule», but, according to Vitoria, Aristotle did not assert that they were «by nature in the power of another» and had «no dominion over themselves and other things».[48] It was a benign interpretation of Aristotle's doctrine but not a rejection of it. There was no suggestion, here or elsewhere, that Aristotle's teaching was incoherent. Vitoria did not argue that the Indians could not be natural slaves; rather he asserted that, even if they were, they still had property rights. He argued similarly at this point that children too could legally own property even though they were not fully competent mentally. The important distinction Vitoria made was between natural slavery and civil slavery. He did not distinguish between «nature's slaves» and «nature's children» in order to assign the Indians to one class rather than the other.

Vitoria also considered the status of another class of people whom he called *amentes*, those who were altogether witless, without the use of reason or hope of acquiring it. The passage is important for Pagden's argument because it was here that Vitoria introduced the Aristotelian language of potency and act in discussing the status of the Indians. But, again, the modern author misunderstands the

---

[47] *Obras*, 650 «Nam ut Aristoteles eleganter et accurate tradit aliqui sunt natura servi quibus scilicet melius est servire quam imperare».

[48] *Obras*, 665, «Aristoteles non intellexit quod tales, qui parum valent ingenio sint natura alieni iuris et non habeant dominium et sui et aliarum rerum. Haec enim est servitus civilis et legitima qua nullus est servus a natura». The point was that nobody could be naturally in a state of civil servitude, The same error concerning Vitoria's teaching was made by J.B. Killoran, Aquinas and Vitoria: Two Perspectives on Slavery in H.J. Johnson, ed., The Medieval Tradition of Natural Law, Kalamazoo 1987, 87-101 (96).

text. He introduces it by posing a central problem about Indian behavior. «If they were *irrationales* or *amentes*, what could account for their cities...? If they were rational men how could one explain their cannibalism...?» The answer for Vitoria, we are told, lay in the formal structure of the universe. «Like all matter man contains within himself both potentiality and actuality».[49] Such a description of «matter» does not inspire confidence in the author's grasp of the Aristotelian terminology used by Vitoria. Nor does his further exegesis of the text.

Vitoria's response to the problem he had raised about the rights of those without reason (*amentes*) was twofold. The achievements of the Indians proved that they were not in fact irrational; and, in any case, it would be impossible for a whole race of such humans to exist. To establish the latter point he appealed to the old adage that nature does nothing in vain. The argument went like this.

According to the truth of the matter they are not irrational (*amentes*) but they have the use of reason in their own way. This is clear because they have a certain order in their affairs, ordered cities, separate marriages, magistrates, rulers, laws... Also they do not err in things that are evident to others, which is evidence of the use of reason. Again, God and nature do not fail for a great part of a species in what is necessary. But the special quality in man is reason, and potency which is not actualized is in vain.[50]

The evident point is that the Indians cannot be a race whose rationality is potential rather than actual, because the existence of such a race would imply a failure of God and nature. But, slightly mistranslating the text, Pagden extracts from it the meaning that «their rationality is still in *potentia*».[51] He notes that «the utterance is gnomic», but it seems gnomic to him only because he is trying to make Vitoria say the opposite of what he actually meant. This initial error infects all the subsequent discourse about the Indians as nature's children. The argument that Vitoria regarded the Indians as a species of humankind whose faculties were potential rather than actual leads on to the central assertion that he moved «from one path

---

[49] Fall of Natural Man, 93.
[50] Obras 664, «Item, Deus et natura non deficiunt in necessariis pro magna parte speciei. Praecipuum autem in homine est ratio et frustra est potentia quae non reducitur ad actum».
[51] Fall of Natural Man, 94.

of Aristotelian faculty psychology to another, from a focus on slavery to a focus on childhood». But, in the passage discussed, Vitoria attributed to the Indians not a mere «potential» for rationality but an actual «use of reason».

Pagden also sees this passage as the place where Vitoria exposed an inherent contradiction in Aristotle's theory of natural slavery. But this is again a misunderstanding. Vitoria was not writing here about natural slaves, whose possible existence he had readily conceded, but about the different class of people whom he called *amentes*.

There remains to be considered the one text where Vitoria did compare the Indians to children. This, if any, is the passage that should establish Pagden's thesis. But one must note at the outset that Vitoria did not endorse the argument that he presented here. After listing seven «titles» that might justify Spanish rule in the Indies he hesitantly proposed one last one. «There is another title that cannot indeed be asserted, but that may be brought into the discussion, and some people think it valid. I affirm nothing about it, but I dare not condemn it altogether». The argument continued thus. Although the Indians were not an irrational people (*amentes*) — Vitoria had proved that earlier — still they might be so little removed from such a condition that they were incapable of conducting their own affairs. Then came the analogy with the children. If all the adult Indians had died and only children remained, then certainly some outside ruler could take charge of them for their own good. But if the grown up Indians who actually existed were more foolish than the children of other races, as some who knew them reported, then the same argument could apply to them. Then Vitoria added, «What has been said above, that some are by nature slaves, might also be useful for this argument».[52]

There are two points to make. Vitoria did not endorse the argument he presented; and, more fundamentally, the argument as presented does not sustain Pagden's thesis. Vitoria did not assert that

---

[52] Obras, 725 «...et ad hoc posset etiam prodesse illud quod supra dictum est, quod aliqui sunt natura servi, nam tales videntur omnes isti barbari, et sic possent ex parte gubernari ut servi». Vitoria was referring here to his previous discussion at Obras, 665. The point was that, even if the Indians were as foolish as natural slaves or children, this could not justify a plundering Spanish conquest — but it might justify a Spanish guardianship for the Indians' own good.

the Indians were nature's children rather than natural slaves. He did suggest that, if indeed they were, like children, incapable of managing their own affairs, then Spanish rule over them might be justified. But then he added the concluding remark about natural slaves as an additional argument that would support the same conclusion. Here again there was no assertion that the Indians belonged to the former category (children) rather than to the latter category (slaves). There was no «shift from one path of Aristotelian faculty psychology to another».

Pagden notes correctly at one point that Vitoria regarded the Indians' defects as a result of their bad upbringing, their «poor and barbarous education»; but he does not seem to realize that this contradicts his main thesis. If the minds of the Indians had been formed, or deformed, by a barbarous education, then adult Indians could not have had the unformed minds of children. It is unlikely that Vitoria really thought of the Indians as either nature's slaves or nature's children. His description of their achievements suggests that he did not see them as dull-witted natural slaves. His attribution to them of moral responsibility for their acts indicates that he did not regard them as children. Of course, colonists often do refer deprecatingly to indigenous peoples as «childish». But such unreflective usage is different from the formal Aristotelian argument that Pagden attributes to Vitoria.

Vitoria did not really need a new argument based on Aristotelian faculty psychology to explain the «perverse» practices of the Indians. Their behavior could readily be accounted for within the framework of traditional scholastic discourse. Thomas Aquinas had acknowledged that a whole people might fail to discern the principles of natural law that were in principle knowable by reason. (He gave as an example the ancient Germans who were said to have condoned theft). And it was a commonplace of Christian philosophy that human intellect had been clouded by original sin. This was how Vitoria saw the Indians. They were a pagan people, unenlightened by Christianity, sinning against natural law as Aquinas had taught might happen in such a case, but not thereby deprived of the right to their lands and goods.[53]

---

[53] In introducing this passage (Fall of Natural Man, 80), Pagden notes that Vitoria did not affirm the position presented there. But in other references he takes it for granted that the argument represented Vitoria's own opinion.

Pagden's attempt to find the origin of a doctrine of cultural development in the scholastic thought of Vitoria — in the supposed shift from one path of Aristotelian psychology to another — is misleading in several ways. It distracts the reader's attention from the real change that Vitoria made in the Christian-Aristotelian paradigm he inherited, the grafting of a theory of subjective rights onto the Thomist doctrine of natural law. Again, Pagden's thesis obscures the fact that the idea of cultural evolution grew up first, not in the schools of Europe, but among Christian writers like Las Casas who had actually lived and worked among the Indians. And, finally, Pagden's concern to derive cultural relativism from Aristotelian thought conceals the fact that Las Casas and his successors were indeed working within a Christian paradigm, a paradigm that included a concept of linear time and of human progress in time.

At his worst, Pagden can mistranslate a text, notice that there is something odd (or «gnomic») about his rendering of it, but still go on, quite undeterred, to build an edifice of speculation on his original error.[54] At his best though, once Vitoria is left behind, he offers perceptive and interesting reflections on the rise of new forms of historical anthropology in Las Casas and, later, in Acosta and Lafiteau. This is the final theme that I want to explore.

2) Las Casas and the Idea of Progress

Although the chapter on «Nature's Children» is placed at the center of Pagden's book it is not really essential to the discussion

---

[54] This happens again when Pagden discusses the varieties of barbarism classified by Las Casas. The friar's argument here followed an earlier one of Aquinas who quoted 1 Corinthians, 15, «If then I do not know the meaning of the language I shall be to him that speaks it a barbarian and he that speaks will be a barbarian to me». A little further on, making the same point, Aquinas wrote «...illi qui suum invicem sermonem non intelligunt barbari ad se ipsos dici possunt», «those who do not understand each others language can be called barbarians to one another». (Opera omnia, vol. 48, Rome 1971, A75). Pagden translates this, meaninglessly, as «all those who do not know their own speech... may be called barbarians in relation to themselves» (Fall of Natural Man, 128-9). He notes that this «may seem a rather puzzling observation», but goes on to make the same mistake in translating a passage of Las Casas' Spanish from the Apologética historia. This leads on to apparently sophisticated but really vacuous observations about «linguistic anarchy» and «social anarchy».

that follows. As Pagden himself noted, Las Casas argued «in a way that made no appeal to Aristotelian bipartite psychology».[55] Las Casas' argument took a different path. He believed passionately that the Indians could not become truly Christian unless they had the opportunity to choose Christ freely. But, in upholding their right to freedom and self-government, he had to overcome two major difficulties. Among the Indians there were peoples at very different levels of cultural development from the most primitive to the most advanced; and, even among the more advanced Indian societies, practices like idolatry and human sacrifice persisted, that might seem indicative of mere barbaric savagery.

Las Casas' response, well delineated by Pagden, was to argue that all peoples, and not only the Indians, had begun their existence in a primitive state, «wild, unsocial and ignorant». Then, through the exercise of reason and the occasional intervention of great leaders who arose in all nations, they slowly advanced in civility and all the arts of life. But, even among the most advanced civilizations before the coming of Christ, the practices of idolatry and human sacrifice persisted just as they did among the Indians. Las Casas concluded that those Indians who were still wild and ignorant were simply at an early stage of cultural evolution. The advanced Indian societies had reached the same stage of development as the great civilizations of the ancient world. Only the message of Christianity was needed to perfect their cultures. Las Casas' missionary zeal had led him to devise a new theory of cultural progress.

Given the great voyages of discovery around 1550 and the subsequent encounters of Europeans with so many new peoples, the growth of a comparative anthropology was perhaps inevitable. But it did not have to be a historical anthropology. This was a contingent development that calls for an explanation, and the preexisting Christian concept of linear time may be a necessary part of any adequate explanation. Pagden properly emphasized the historical dimension in the thought of Las Casas, Acosta and Lafiteau, but he was more interested in arguing that a comparative ethnology could be derived from Aristotelian premises than in reflecting on Christian doctrines of progress. I want therefore to suggest some further implications of his argument that he did not have occasion to discuss.

---

[55] *Fall of Natural Man*, 121.

Other modern authors have emphasized more than Pagden the role of Las Casas in the emergence of the modern concept of progress. George Sanderlin, for instance, wrote, «Las Casas... occupies an intermediate position between St. Thomas Aquinas and Jean Jacques Rousseau. For Aquinas, natural man was an unalterable substance... For Las Casas, however, natural man... was more of an entity in transition — a voyager on the sea of history... Las Casas looked beyond scholasticism toward the idea of progress — an ascent of humanity through the ages».[56] In similar fashion José Maravall declared, «Las Casas es como un Rousseau que permanece en la tradicion cristiana viva, de la cual el proprio Rousseau tal vez no es más que un fenomino de relativa secularización».[57]

The reference to secularization and the suggestion that, in the emergence of the idea of progress as well as in political theory, Las Casas was a transitional figure between medieval and Enlightenment thought, takes us back to the problem we mentioned at the outset. Can modern «progress» be explained adequately as a secularized version of Christian eschatology? And where do the Spanish scholastics fit into the recent argument about this question?

Ideas derived from Joachim of Flora's prophetic vision still had a wide currency at the time of the discovery of America. The conversion of newly discovered Indians was sometimes seen as a sign that the coming of the third age of the Holy Spirit was at hand. And, even as such dreams faded, the idea of progress in time persisted. In our own day it has become almost a platitude to say that «Joachimism is the ancestor of the modern idea of progress».[58]

In the work of Karl Löwith, as we saw, this idea was associated with the sociological category of «secularization»; the modern idea of progress was seen as a secularized version of Christian eschatology in its Joachimite form. But Löwith thought that the idea of progress was a mere illusion. He argued therefore that the transfer of

---

[56] G. Sanderlin, Bartolomé de las Casas: A Selection of His Writings, New York 1971, 112.
[57] J. Maravall, Antiguos y Modernas, Madrid 1966, 447. Maravall provides the best account of Las Casas and Acosta in relation to the emerging idea of progress. John H. Elliott has some excellent pages inspired in part by Maravall in The Old World and the New, 1492-1650, Cambridge 1970. R. Nisbet in turn quoted Elliott, History of the Idea of Progress, New York 1980, 146-147.
[58] John L. Phelan, The Millenial Kingdom of the Franciscans in the New World, Berkeley 1970, 59.

V

Christian eschatology to the sphere of profane history was radically illicit — «a mistaken Christianity»,[59] giving rise to a false view of human history and destiny.

Hans Blumenberg, presenting a counterargument in defense of the «legitimacy» of modern culture offered an alternative account of the origin of the concept of progress. He emphasized new ways of thinking stimulated by advances in astronomical science and by the *Querelle des anciens et des modernes*. More radically Blumenberg attacked the whole concept of secularization as Löwith understood it. The resemblances between Christian eschatology and Enlightenment progress were superficial, he suggested, the differences profound. Eschatology envisaged transformation of the human condition brought about through incursions of divine power from outside history; progress implied a continuous development through human strivings within the historical process. «It is impossible to see how one "expectation" could ever result in the other», Blumenberg wrote.[60] To establish a meaningful argument that Enlightenment progress was a form of secularized Christianity it was not enough to point to analogies. One had also to provide «evidence of transformation, of metamorphosis».[61] That is to say one had to show *how* the later idea was derived from the earlier through intermediate stages.

The sixteenth-century Spanish writers seem to provide just such a «metamorphosis» as Blumenberg demanded. In the work of Las Casas (and later in Acosta) we find examples of historical thinking that are rooted in Christian concerns, that take for granted the Christian concept of linear time, and that look with hope to a better age to come.[62] Yet they are not mere applications of Joachimite prophecy. Las Casas offered a kind of half-secularized theory of progress. He certainly believed in a history guided by divine providence. He thought that the coming conversion of the Indians was foretold in Revelations. Yet he was not a Joachimite. He was not

---

[59] Meaning in History, 203.
[60] Legitimacy..., 31.
[61] Ibid., 16.
[62] Las Casas' modern editor, Juan Perez de Tudela, found in his work «an anthropology of hope». Pagan and Christian concepts of time are too complex to be described adequately by the single words «circular» and «linear»; but this basic distinction is sufficient for the present argument.

writing just another version of sacred history based on Scriptural narrative and prophecy. His account of primitive humanity began with Cicero and Virgil rather than with Genesis.[63] His idea of progress included, not only a growth in religious understanding, but advances in all the arts of civilization and civic order, achieved by human striving in historical time. All nations, he held, made such progress «little by little, gaining experience of things» until they became wise and prudent and politically sophisticated.[64] That was why young peoples, recently settled in a new homeland, were bound to be wild and uncultured. Blumenberg wrote that, in a real doctrine of progress, we should expect to find at least «a coordinate relation between the quantum of time and the quality of the achievement».[65] That is just what we do find in Las Casas.

IV. Conclusions

Human history is a story of struggle between persistence and change, a struggle well exemplified in the transition from medieval culture to the world of the Enlightenment. The concept of a secularized Christianity can help us to understand the transition, but only if it is used with caution. One can sympathize with Blumenberg's protest against «secularization run wild».[66] We cannot simply take medieval Christianity as a prime datum, something given, whose secularization provides an adequate explanation for the thought-forms of modern civilization. Medieval culture itself was a compound of secular and religious elements, derived from Stoic and neoPlatonic and Aristotelian ideas as well as from Scripture and church fathers and theology. Earlier still, primitive Christianity too was shaped in part by secular Hellenistic influences. Secularization in the early modern world is only one phase of an incessant interplay between sacred and profane that has characterized Western culture throughout the centuries.

Still, there do seem to be certain ideas that took shape in the religious thought of the Middle Ages and that persisted into the secu-

---

[63] Apologética historia, ed. E. O'Gorman, Mexico 1967, 250-251.
[64] Ibid., 248.
[65] On a Lineage of the Idea of Progress in Social Research 41 (1974) 6.
[66] Legitimacy..., 15.

V

lar world of the Enlightenment; and they include the ideas we have been discussing concerning natural rights and human progress. We are left with the original question. Does the Christian origin of such doctrines compromise their legitimacy? Löwith assumed that secularization implied illegitimacy, that an idea transferred from the sacred sphere to the profane became inevitably degraded, disempowered. But this is not necessarily the case. It can often happen that a doctrine is first formulated in a religious framework of thought — perhaps could be first formulated only in a religious framework — and later is seen to have an independent value of its own and to be defensible on rational non-religious grounds. The legitimacy of the process depends on whether the rational arguments adduced for the doctrine are in fact valid.

The persistence of the doctrine of natural rights seems to me a rather straightforward example of licit secularization. The doctrine grew up in the Christian juristic culture of the Middle Ages. It was associated with Christian teachings on the value and dignity of each human person. Then the doctrine took on a new life in the course of the Indies debates and was assimilated (rather uneasily perhaps) into the Aristotelian-Thomist thought-world of the Spanish scholastics. From then onward, one can trace clearly enough the stages of secularization, beginning with Grotius who saw that the ideas of natural law and natural rights could be detached from the whole context of scholastic thought in which they had earlier been embedded. (Grotius not only wrote «Even if there were no God...»; more radically, he sometimes argued as if there were no Aristotle).[67] Even at the height of the Enlightenment the article on *Droit Naturel* in the *Encyclopédie* still echoed the language of Gratian and Aquinas as well as of Hobbes and Locke.

To present the modern idea of progress as a licit secularization of Christian thought is a more problematical undertaking. The idea of ineluctable progress leading inevitably to a golden age in the future is not defensible on rational grounds. So a simple transfer of Joachimite eschatology to the sphere of secular thought would in-

---

[67] Later seventeenth-century thinkers (e.g. Pufendorf) admired Grotius precisely because his argument did not depend on «the dogmas of Aristotle». See R. Tuck, The «Modern» Theory of Natural Law in A. Pagden (ed.), The Languages of Political Theory in Early-Modern Europe, Cambridge 1987, 99-119.

deed seem illegitimate; and the argument that the modern theory of progress is a form of secularized Christianity has normally been presented as such a transfer.[68] The secular factors that Blumenberg emphasized in the emergence of the idea of progress from the seventeenth century onward are evidently important. And Blumenberg's argument that such elements in early modern culture could justify a more defensible, more modest doctrine of progress is attractive. Such a doctrine would envisage only a likelihood of continuing progress in the future brought about through human effort and «self-assertion». Still it is hard to see how the seventeenth-century developments could have led on to an idea of open-ended progress at all without an underlying, taken-for-granted acceptance of the Christian conception of linear time.[69] So the question we must ask is not just whether the idea of progress is «a mistaken Christianity» (in Löwith's phrase) but rather what role a residual secularized Christian way of thinking may have played — along with various other factors — in the emergence of the modern idea, especially in its more modest, defensible form.

The Spanish writers of the sixteenth century would have to find a place in any adequate answer to the question. In reading Löwith and his critics one might suppose that Joachim's eschatology was the only Christian theory of progress. No attention is paid to less colorful medieval theories of «development of doctrine», which envisaged a slow growth from generation to generation in the understanding of Christian truth, achieved through human intellectual effort and continuing «until the end of the world» as Henry of Ghent wrote in the thirteenth century.[70] Also the Spanish historiography we have discussed was not taken into account in the debate between Blumenberg and Löwith. But, in considering the nature of Christian influence on the emergence of the idea of progress, we do not have to make an unlikely leap from Joachimite eschatology to Enlightenment rationalism. The substantial body of historical writing evoked by the

---

[68] As Blumenberg observed, Legitimacy..., 14 «It has become almost a fashionable pastime to interpret expectations of political redemption, like those typified by the Communist Manifesto, as secularizations either of the biblical paradise or of apocalyptic messianism».
[69] The early modern achievements that, in Blumenberg's view, stimulated the idea of continuing progress could have been seen only as a later phase of a recurring cycle.
[70] Summae quaestionum ordinarium... tomos prior, Paris 1520, fol. LXVIIIr. On Henry's views, see my Origins of Papal Infallibility, Leiden 1988², 133-140.

V

European encounter with America — some of it well-known in the
eighteenth century — provides an intermediate level «of Christian
reflection on human progress in historical time».

In both spheres that we have considered, the idea of natural
rights and the idea of progress, Las Casas was a transitional figure.
Moreover the two concepts were fused together in his thought. He
insisted on the Indians' natural rights to liberty and equality in order
to facilitate their conversion to Christianity; the rights were not intended to serve the ends of a static society but to make possible the
further progress of the Indian peoples. Blumenberg was right to protest against «secularization run wild». But Edmundo O'Gorman was
right too when he maintained that, in the areas we have considered,
«sixteenth-century Spain is the bridge over which European culture
passed from the medieval to the modern shore...».[71]

---

[71] «Lewis Hanke» (above n. 7), 566.

VI

PUBLIC EXPEDIENCY AND NATURAL LAW: A FOURTEENTH-CENTURY DISCUSSION ON THE ORIGINS OF GOVERNMENT AND PROPERTY

The Sum of the Matter betwixt Mr. *Hoadly* and Me is this, I think it most Natural that *Authority* shou'd *Descend*, that is, be *Derived* from a *Superiour* to an *Inferiour*, from *God* to *Fathers* and *Kings*, and from *Kings* and *Fathers* to *Sons* and *Servants*: But Mr. *Hoadly* wou'd have it *Ascend*, from *Sons* to *Fathers* and from *Subjects* to *Sovereigns*; nay to *God* Himself, whose *Kingship* the Men of the *Rights* say, is *Derived* to *Him* from the *People*! And the *Argument* does Naturally Carry it all that Way. For if *Authority* does *Ascend* it must *Ascend* to the *Height*.[1]

THIS PARADOX was presented by Charles Leslie, a brilliant contemporary critic of John Locke's theory of natural law and natural rights. Walter Ullmann, with his characteristic learning and insight, has shown us in many distinguished studies how the problem of ascending and descending powers discussed here by Leslie had already been posed centuries earlier in the religious and political thought of the Middle Ages.[2] Indeed the English seventeenth-century debate echoed strangely – as it were in a different key – a theme that had already been clearly enunciated in Western political theory in the years around 1300. Moreover the earlier debate, like the later one, concerned not only political authority but also property rights, 'dominion' understood to mean both jurisdiction and ownership. The really complicated problems arose, as Michael Wilks has pointed out, when constitutional theorists began to argue that such rights came from both God and the people, that they somehow ascended and descended at the same time.[3]

In this paper we shall be concerned with an aspect of the medieval debate. But we must note at the outset that the resemblances between the discussions of the early fourteenth century and those of the late

---

[1] Charles Leslie, *The Finishing Stroke, Being a Vindication of the Patriarchal Scheme of Government* (London, 1711), p. 87, quoted by John Dunn, *The Political Thought of John Locke* (Cambridge, 1969), p. 63, n. 1.

[2] My own first attempt at historical writing, written under Dr Ullmann's supervision nearly thirty years ago, dealt with the best-known medieval exponent of the 'ascending' thesis, Marsilius of Padua.

[3] M. Wilks, *The Problem of Sovereignty in the Later Middle Ages* (Cambridge, 1963), p. 202.

seventeenth century are not merely coincidental. Throughout the whole medieval period the 'descending' thesis was implicit in the accepted Christian conception of the universe to this extent at least: no one denied that licit dominion came ultimately from God. But from about 1250 onward the problem arose of combining this apparently self-evident doctrine with new versions of the 'ascending' thesis based on the Aristotelian teaching that society and the state were natural to man. In the ensuing discussions, a cluster of ideas emerged that would have a continuous history of development in Western constitutional thought down to the time of Leslie and Locke.

Early modern debates on the origins of government and property centred around three themes: divine right, natural law, and public utility. Proponents of divine right, like Leslie, maintained that all licit rights of jurisdiction and ownership were derived from God directly or through his agents on earth.[4] Natural law theorists, like Locke, argued that legitimate government was based on consent and that legitimate property rights arose whenever a man mixed his own labour with material things. Such arguments did not convince the theorists of divine right. How could any man be licitly subjected to another, they asked, unless God, the lord of all, had established rulers among men? And how could any man licitly claim property for himself unless God, the owner of all, had granted the property to him?[5] (Arguing against Locke's labour theory of acquisition, his critics pointed out that even a man's own person belonged to God.) At a later stage of the discussion, utilitarian thinkers attacked the whole doctrine of natural rights and natural law from a more radical perspective. Beccaria argued that human law, especially penal law, could not and should not seek to exemplify abstract principles of natural justice but should aim solely at promoting public utility. And Bentham, rejecting all theories of natural rights, constructed an alternative doctrine of government by consent based on the utilitarian principle that only the whole community would most clearly perceive and most effectively pursue its own self-interest.

Historians have often noted that both the natural law theories and the divine right theories of the early modern world had medieval antecedents. Medieval anticipations of later utilitarian doctrines have

---

[4] For these views and Locke's counter-arguments see John Locke, *Two Treatises of Government*, ed. P. Laslett (Cambridge, 1967), pp. 174–89, 213–17.

[5] *Ibid.*, p. 111.

Public expediency and natural law

been less often noticed (though legal historians at least will be aware
that the concepts of *utilitas publica*, *necessitas*, and *status regni* (or *status
ecclesiae*) were very familiar to medieval Roman and canon lawyers).
The work to be considered below, a fourteenth-century *Tractatus de
Legibus* attributed to Durandus of St Pourçain, is interesting for its
persistent emphasis on utilitarian arguments.[6] The author quoted often
from Aristotle and Thomas Aquinas (as well as from Roman and
canon law) but he did not present just one more medieval natural-law
theory of the state. On the contrary his work is most interesting at the
points where he anticipated later criticisms of such theories. The
Tractatus shows how far a medieval author could go in constructing a
purely utilitarian theory of law, government and property, and also
the difficulties of conducting such an enterprise within a framework of
medieval presuppositions. The discussion moved from a conventional
account of *ius naturale* and *ius gentium* to a highly pragmatic theory of
human legislation. When applied to problems of political theory, the
author's arguments led to a nuanced doctrine of government by
consent and, most interestingly, to an unusually detailed consideration
of property rights in natural law and in civil law. We shall consider
these topics in turn.

6 The arguments against Durandus's authorship were given by J. Koch, *Durandus de S. Porciano*,
O.P. (Münster, 1927), pp. 177–8. His discussion is persuasive but not conclusive. Koch presents
the following six arguments. (I have added responses to them.) (1) The treatise is more loosely
organised than Durandus's other works. But it seems doubtful that the surviving text presents
the full work as the author wrote it. See (5) below. (2) The author seems more a jurist than a
philosopher. But there is no display of juristic learning in the work. It includes only well-known
texts of Roman and canon law which are found in other fourteenth-century works on political
theory written by philosophers. (3) The author expresses views that are not found in Durandus's
other works. But this point lacks substance. Even medieval authors did not invariably repeat
themselves. (4) The author refers to the *populus romanus* and *res publica* which suggests that he
was Italian. But he also presents an argument for hereditary monarchy which might suggest
that he was French. (5) The author often states that he has discussed controversial points
elsewhere and sometimes no such discussions can be found in Durandus's certainly authoritative
works. This is important but not decisive. The author sometimes uses indeterminate phrases
like *probavi alias*, but sometimes writes more explicitly, e.g. *ut supra innui* (fo. 15vb), *dixi in hac
materia* (fo. 16ra), *ut superius dicebatur* (fo. 17ra). It is not always possible to find corresponding
passages in the surviving text of the *Tractatus*. Of course they could also refer to some lost work
of Durandus. (6) The author quotes Thomas Aquinas extensively. But he often disagrees with
Thomas's views. Johannes de Turrecremata, who probably acquired the Vatican MS about
1420 (Koch, *Durandus*, p. 177, n. 1), attributed the work to Durandus. See his *Repertorium super
Decretum* (Venice, 1578), *ad Dist.* 1 c. 9. It seems that the question of authorship should be
regarded as still open. Certainly the tone and substance of the treatise seem in keeping with
Durandus's cognomen (*Doctor Resolutissimus*) and with his epitaph (*durus Durandus*). The
Tractatus was printed by J. Barbier (Paris, 1506), fo. 10r–23r. In the following notes I have
collated the printed text with MS Vatican Barb. lat.869, pp. 77–93 (omitting very minor
variations of spelling and word order).

Thomas Aquinas defined natural law as a 'participation of reason in the eternal law'. He regarded *ius gentium* as a form of human law, closely related to natural law and derived immediately from its principles. All positive human law, he maintained, was derived from natural law either as a conclusion from a premise or as a determination of something left indifferent in natural law.[7] The author of the *Tractatus de Legibus* agreed with Thomas about the definition of natural law. But since *ius gentium* was defined in the Digest precisely as 'what natural reason has established among all men' he could see no grounds for distinguishing between *ius gentium* and *ius naturale*. Both were common to all men and were immutable. Both were based on 'natural reason', on 'nature itself considered absolutely', on the intrinsic 'nature of a thing', or on the nature of the case, we might say (*natura rei*). Accordingly, for him, *iura gentium et iura naturalia non distinguuntur*.[8] This departure from Thomas's classification was perhaps more a matter of words than a serious disagreement in substance. (The author agreed with Thomas that *ius gentium* was different from the 'primeval' natural law which applied to animals as well as to men.[9]) The real difference came with the treatment of human law. The author of the *Tractatus* accepted the common opinion that human law, unlike natural law, varied with time and place, but he did not agree with Thomas that human law was derived from natural law. On the contrary it was based on a different foundation. 'Civil law does not take nature (*natura rei*) as its foundation, but rather public expediency, so that there public expediency occurs as the whole cause of establishing its conclusions.' Accordingly *ius naturale* and *ius gentium* were 'formally distinguished from civil law'.[10]

These propositions were set out at the beginning of the treatise. From there onward the whole argument was conducted in terms of

---

[7] *Divi Thomas Aquinatis Opera Omnia*, ed. L. Vives (Paris, 1874–1889), *Summa Theologiae*, 1a2ae.91.2, 1a2ae.95.4, 1a2ae.95.2. All subsequent quotations from Aquinas are taken from this edition.

[8] 'Ius gentium secundum legum descriptionem est illud quod ratio naturalis constituit inter omnes homines.' (fo. 10ra) (cf. *Dig*. 1.1.9); '. . . talia recipiunt natura rei pro fundamento . . .' (fo. 10va); 'Prima conclusio est quod iura gentium et iura naturalia non distinguuntur . . . iuris naturalis et iuris gentium fundamentum est natura ipsa absolute considerata' (fo. 10vb).

[9] *Tractatus*, fo. 10vb. Cf. *Summa Theologiae*, 2a2ae.57.3. The problems of definition arose from the differing usages of the terms *ius naturale* and *ius gentium* that occur in the Institutes and Digest.

[10] 'Ius ciuile uero non accipit sic naturam rei pro fundamento illo (primo, MS 77b) sed magis expedientiam publicam ita quod expedentia publica concurrit ibi pro totali cause in constituendo istas conclusiones' (fo. 10va) (cf. *Dig*. 1.1.11).

Public expediency and natural law

public expediency. The words *expediens, expedientia, utilitas* are scattered over every page of the treatise. (The specific phrase *expedientia publica* occurs more than thirty times.) As a first example of his doctrine the author considered a point of penal practice. Natural law indicated that a criminal should be punished, but it did not specify the precise punishment, e.g. that a thief should be hanged. The specification of the punishment belonged to human law.[11] This is of course a familiar medieval example. Thomas Aquinas also used it. But the author of the *Tractatus* pressed his argument in an unusual way by insisting that human law had to mete out a punishment determined solely by public expediency. Let us suppose, he suggested, a polity in which there were few men and an abundance of goods. In those circumstances it would not be necessary to hang thieves. Some other penalty could be assigned. But if there was a large population and a shortage of material goods, then it would be expedient to hang thieves for even small offences. Later the author noted that in some places men were more prone to theft than in others and that it would be expedient to punish them more severely in such places.[12]

The example of theft was only an illustration in a general theory of penal law based on expediency. The author did not deny that a given offence merited a particular degree of punishment from the nature of the offence itself. But he held that it was no business of the human judge to enter into such calculations. One could argue that divine judgment and divine punishment were necessary precisely because human judgments could not concern themselves with abstract justice. Emperors could not be 'true punishers' (as God was). There was 'no way in the world' that they could know the proper penalty that should be assigned in a particular case.[13] Human law measured punishment according to public expediency, divine law according to justice.[14]

The author also applied his theory of expediency rather oddly to

---

11 'Nam aliqua expediunt uno tempore que non expediunt alio, ut quando est raritas hominum in policia et sunt bona ad uitam super excrescentia non impedit (expedit, MS 77b) tunc quod pro furto aliquis suspendatur sed debet aliter castigari. Et aliter quando est multitudo hominum quasi super excrescens et bona terre pauca, expedit quod suspendatur etiam pro modico furto' (fo. 10va). The author often used the word *policia* in preference to *civitas* or *respublica*.

12 'homines in aliquo loco sunt magis inclinati ad furtum quam in alio (loco *add.* MS 85b), ergo expedit quod puniantur magis scilicet per suspendium' (fo. 17ra).

13 'imperatores puniunt homines pro suis delictis qui non sunt punitores ueri, nam per nullam rationem mundi possunt cognoscere certum gradum pene imponende . . .' (fo. 16va).

14 'Nam lex humana . . . in punitionibus faciendis mensurat secundum expedientiam publicam . . . et quantum exigit expedentia publica . . . Sed lex diuina imponit penam delinquenti ut aliquid iustum . . .' (fo. 19vb).

marriage law. Marriage could be viewed on several levels. The actual act of generation pertained to the primeval natural law common to men and animals. Consent in marriage pertained to the *ius gentium* (the natural law proper to man). But the indissolubility of marriage was a provision of civil law introduced for the sake of public expediency. It did not have its origin in the 'nature of the thing'. Rather nature suggested that an infertile marriage should be dissolved. But a man would more readily undertake noble deeds for his own good and the good of the state if he had someone to share his misfortunes (should any befall him) and to succour him in time of need.[15] In a later discussion the author suggested that, if a population grew too large in relation to the available resources, marriage might be prohibited for a time.[16]

Some precepts of natural law were indeed included in human legislation, the author acknowledged, but this was because they promoted the health of the state. In such cases it might be said that the legislator acted only as a teacher declaring the law, but this was not the whole truth, for the emperor's declaration had binding force, unlike that of any private doctor.[17] Still such enactments did not derive their justice solely from the emperor's promulgation; they could be seen to be just beforehand by natural reason. Other laws, however, acquired a quality of justice only from the fact that they had been promulgated.[18] In general, civil procedure was not regulated by natural reason but, to borrow the phrase of a later jurist, by 'the artificial reason of the law'. For instance, natural reason could not prove that the evidence of two witnesses established a fact as true; such evidence had to be accepted

[15] 'Item est actus iuris ciuilis quantum ad aliqua ibi introducta propter expedientiam publicam ut quod non sit separatio uiri a muliere. Hoc non est secundum natura rei ... Attamen propter expedientiam publicam est introducta impossibilitas separationis. Nam uir citius facta laudabilia ad bonum suum et policie aggredietur si sciat aliquem participare in suis infortuniis supposito quod aliqua sibi contingat (continguant, MS 79a) et qui succurret sue necessitati' (fo. 11vb).

[16] 'Nona conclusio est quod in conclusionibus iuris naturalis sunt gradus ita quod alique conclusiones sunt magis naturalis aliis ... Uellent aliqui dicere quod posset recipere mutationem, ut si multitudo hominum esset super excrescens secundum quantitatem bonorum deberet usque ad tempus prohiberi ad matrimonium. Quid hic dicendum non assero. Et secundum hoc sequitur quod alique conclusiones iuris gentium debent magis dici (dici magis esse, MS 80a) naturales quam alique que sunt de iure naturali primeuo ... ut ista conclusio quod deus sit diligendus' (fo. 13va).

[17] 'inter ea que facienda sunt in policia ad saluandum policiam quedam sunt que essent facienda secundum se ... non per consuetudinem set magis naturaliter indita rei' (fo. 10ra); 'Quia diximus quod in conclusionibus iuris naturalis non interuenit imperator nisi per modum doctoris declarantis. Hoc posset male intelligi ... nam sue declarationi oportet stare quod non esset de alio ...' (fo. 12vb).

[18] The author specifically discussed the law of *usucapio* as legislation based on public expediency rather than on natural reason (fo. 12va).

Public expediency and natural law

as if it were true for the sake of public expediency.[19] Legal science was not a subordinate branch of moral philosophy. It was an autonomous discipline deriving its conclusions, not from one first principle (*bonum humanum*) as many doctors taught, but from two basic principles – the good and the expedient.[20]

We need not pursue all the applications of the doctrine of expediency that occur throughout the *Tractatus*.[21] The underlying argument was always the same, that expediency required the elaboration of a structure of purely human legislation which was not deduced or deducible from natural law. Yet the author insisted that men living within such a framework of human laws continued to be bound by natural law before God.[22] For him, we might say, *expedientia non tollit naturam*. The author of the *Tractatus* did not acknowledge any opposition between the two basic principles upon which all law was founded in his theory – nature and expediency. Rather he argued that the two principles could be reconciled in a broader generalisation – that men should always do what was pleasing to God. The conclusions of law established what was pleasing to God in two ways, immediately from natural law, and mediately from considerations of public expediency. Laws based on expediency were pleasing to God because it pleased God that those things be done which promoted the well-being of the whole.[23]

This may seem an optimistic conclusion. Common sense suggests that sometimes the demands of expediency might conflict with the precepts of natural law. It remains to consider how far this difficulty did arise in connection with the two problems raised at the outset of

19 'sed solum talia recipiuntur ac si essent uera propter expedientiam publicam' (fo. 12rb).
20 'ista principia scilicet bonum ex natura rei et expedientia publica fundant omnes conclusiones morales siue legales sint siue non . . . Et ex hoc improbaui quod communiter dicitur a doctoribus quod ipsa legalis scientia est subalternata morali philosophie . . .' (fos. 15vb–16ra). 'bonum humanum . . . non est subiectum in legali scientia licet communiter asseratur . . . bonum et expedientia publica assumuntur ut subiectum ad demonstrandas omnes conclusiones legales' (fo. 16rb).
21 E.g. servitude based on public expediency (fo. 11vb); exceptions to natural law for reasons of expediency (fo. 15vb); validity of customs based on expediency (fo. 19vb). The author acknowledged that in practice some human laws were neither natural nor expedient. The definition of *ius*, he wrote, described what laws ought to be, not what they always were (fo. 11ra). Further discussion of the legislator's will as source of human law at fos. 13rb, 16vb.
22 Even the emperor was so bound, 'a legibus iuris naturalis imperator non est absolutus . . .' (fo. 12vb).
23 'illa (principia) reducuntur in unum primum, scilicet in amabilitatem diuinam . . . Et ideo de his dicitur quod sunt quedam diuina prouidentia constitute . . . alia uero per medium scilicet per expedientiam publicam. Unde amabile est deo quod fiat illud quod est ad salutem totius . . .' (fo. 16vb).

this paper, the origin of human government and the origin of private property. Were such institutions rooted in natural law or in expediency, in nature or in convention? Evidently the thought of our author could have been developed in either direction. We may add that his teaching on the will of God as the ultimate source of all law could have been developed into a 'descending' theory, his teaching on human nature and human needs into an 'ascending' theory.

Let us begin with the origin of licit government. Thomas Aquinas had provided no definitive solution to the problem of political obligation. Rather he hinted at two quite different solutions, both of which were developed independently by the philosophers of the next generation. In some contexts Thomas wrote that men were inherently unequal, ranked in a hierarchy that was part of the hierarchical order of the whole universe. The right of some men to rule others could then be based on their status in the hierarchy.[24] And since the whole hierarchy depended on God it was not difficult to develop from this side of Thomas's thought a thoroughly theocratic 'descending' theory of government like that of Aegidius Romanus. But in other contexts Thomas wrote that all men were by nature equal.[25] One could deduce from these texts that licit authority could only be based on consent and so arrive at the radical 'ascending' theory of popular sovereignty later developed by Marsilius of Padua.

The author of the *Tractatus de Legibus* took an intermediate position. His discussion favoured an 'ascending' thesis but it was complicated by his usual concern for the dual claims of nature and expediency. On one point he was quite clear. The constituting of a ruler was not a matter of natural law but of civil law.[26] In defending this view the author

---

[24] *Summa Contra Gentiles* 3.81, 'Quia vero homo habet intellectum et sensum et corporalem virtutem, haec in ipso ad invicem ordinantur, secundum divinae Providentiae dispositionem ad similitudinem ordinis qui in universo invenitur . . . Ex eadem ratione et inter ipsos homines ordo invenitur; nam illi qui intellectu praeeminent naturalitur dominantur.' See also *Summa Theol.* 1.96.4, 2a2ae.104.1, *II Sent.* 44.1.3; *De Regno* 1.9.

[25] *Summa Theol.* 1.109.2, 'Ad tertium dicendum quod daemones non sunt aequales secundum naturam; unde in eis non est naturalis praelatio; quod in hominibus non contingit, qui natura sunt pares'; 2a2ae.10.11 'dominium et praelatio introducta sunt ex iure humano . . .'; 2a2ae.12.2 'dominium introductum est de iure gentium . . .'. On natural equality see also 2a2ae.104.5; *II Sent.* 6.1.4; and, on servitude as a product of human law, *Summa Theol.* 1a2ae.94.5; *IV Sent.* 36.1.2. Modern authors, by emphasising one set of texts or the other have been able to present Aquinas as an extreme theocrat or an extreme democrat.

[26] The author did not emphasise even the natural origin of society as such. Indeed his remarks sometimes have an almost Hobbesian flavor. 'Item nisi essent iudices statim homines procederent ad bella (arma, MS 79b)' (fo. 12rb). Again, unless a threat of divine punishment existed 'homines . . . intantum sunt nati ad sequendum suos motus quod nunquam submitterent se ad uoluntatem alicuius principis immo sine freno sequerentur concupiscentias suas' (fo. 19rb).

Public expediency and natural law

addressed himself to the question that Thomas had left open. What if there were one man in a society clearly superior to all others? It would be natural, he replied, that such a man should be honoured and followed in some things, but not that he should be sole ruler in the sense that all men had to obey his laws in all matters.[27] The argument on this point was not based on natural liberty and equality as in the more radical theories of the time but on an old-fashioned Aristotelian position. It was conceivable that some one man might know more than any other individual about the direction of public affairs, but not that one man should know more than the whole collectivity of men, including himself and others. Therefore it was inherent in the nature of things that rights of government should reside in the whole community.[28] But at once the claims of expediency arose. All the members could not assemble together and if they did assemble they would hardly agree. It was expedient therefore to transfer power to a ruler.[29]

The next question followed inevitably. Was this 'translation of power' revocable? The answer seems inevitable too given the whole structure of the argument. The ruler's power was immediately revocable if it ceased to serve the end of public expediency.[30] It was not to be lightly revoked on account of personal defect in the ruler – change of rulers might do more harm than good – but a ruler was to be deposed if his offence was such as to 'infect the whole polity', if for instance he became a heretic.

The author also considered the relative merits of elective and hereditary rulership. Again his argument balanced the natural against the expedient. It was 'more natural', he wrote, that succession should

---

27 'Decima conclusio est quod constitutio principis non est naturalis sed ciuilis. Uerum est quod si esset unus homo in mundo omnibus hominibus melior (melior omnibus, MS 80a) bonum est secundum constitutionem naturale quod ipse honoretur et quod ipse principaretur quantum ad quedam. Sed quod ipse simpliciter principetur et quod alii omnes eius obediant legibus in omnibus non est secundum naturam rei' (fo. 13vb).

28 'Nam licet sit unus homo in mundo melius cognoscens illa que possunt esse ad directionem populi, tamen non (nullus, MS 80b) est in mundo qui simpliciter omnia ita (omnia illa possit esse ita, MS 80b) possit cognoscere sicut faceret tota collectio hominum ipsius et aliorum. Et ideo magis esset secundum naturam rei quod totus populus haberet rationem principis. Et esset simile ac si esset unum animal habens ualde multos oculos . . .' (fo. 13vb). Cf. Aristotle, *Politics*, 3.11.2 (1281b).

29 'Tamen propter expediens quia non possunt congregari omnes et congregati uix consentirent fuit expedientius contrarium' (fo. 13vb).

30 'Translatio potestatis translate in imperatorem est reuocabilis ex una causa . . . statim quod cessaret expedientia posset reuocari, ut puta si essent pauci homines equalis sciencie qui faciliter congregarentur et faciliter conuenirent' (fo. 13vb). The author noted that future generations were bound by the initial consent of the populus. 'Et ita populus sequens reputatur idem cum populo preterito' (fo. 17va).

be by election, for natural reason indicated that the best man should rule and election was better adapted to secure this result than hereditary right. He brushed aside the argument that, because a good man would generate a good heir, hereditary kingship was really more natural. (Astrological influences might interfere with the act of generation.) 'And so', the author concluded, 'election is always more natural.' But then came the usual qualification. Perhaps in his own time hereditary rule was more expedient because, if men could not come together to elect, they might remain without a head.[31]

There is evidently a tension here between the 'ascending' and 'descending' theses and between the claims of the natural and the expedient. An argument for natural popular sovereignty ends in a defence of expedient hereditary monarchy. But the tension is not too disruptive. The 'natural' right of a people to govern itself is not extinguished by the 'expedient' transfer of power to a ruler since the people never lose the natural right to revoke that power. Here again we might adapt St Thomas and say, *expedientia non tollit naturam*.

The situation is more complicated when we turn to the problem of property. The author devoted substantial sections of his work to this question and they contain some of his most idiosyncratic arguments. Virtually all medieval thinkers adhered to the common Stoic–Patristic tradition which described 'the common possession of all things' as a tenet of natural law. Obviously then a problem arose of explaining how private property could licitly be established by human law. Thomas Aquinas offered one widely accepted solution. He argued thus. The statement that by natural law all things are possessed in common meant only that natural law did not assign specific possessions to particular men. There was no positive precept of natural law which forbade such division. Hence the right of individual ownership was not contrary to natural law, but was rather an addition to it devised by human reason.[32] The author of the *Tractatus de Legibus* presented a quite different argument. The idea that individual property rights exist in

---

[31] 'Duodecima conclusio est quod constitutio principis per electionem est magis naturalis quam per progeniei successionem ... semper est electio magis naturalis licet forsan alia magis sit expediens pro hoc tempore quia homines non possunt conuenire ad electionem et ita remanerent membra sine capite' (fo. 14ra).

[32] *Summa Theol.* 2a2ae.66.2. Thomas held that the use of property (as distinct from possession) remained common according to natural law in the sense that a man was required to share goods with those in need. On canonistic doctrines see my *Medieval Poor Law* (Berkeley and Los Angeles, 1959). A good general survey of medieval doctrines in this area is provided by G. Couvreur, *Les Pauvres ont-ils des droits?* (Rome, 1961).

Public expediency and natural law

natural law is sometimes supposed to be a contribution of the natural rights school of the seventeenth century. In fact our author presented such a doctrine three centuries earlier. His theory was a very odd one however. The author did not argue, like so many later thinkers, that human law was created to preserve natural rights. On the contrary, he asserted that the requirements of public expediency required human law to set up a system of civil rights in property quite different from the rights that existed under natural law.

The author's fundamental premise was that rightful ownership was based on virtue, so his theory could find a place in the broad spectrum of medieval doctrines of dominion founded on grace.[33] In his first approach to the problem he wrote that, although division of property as it actually existed in the world was not based on natural law, still natural law did indeed define individual rights of ownership. For, according to natural law, property ought to be subjected to the will of good men rather than bad (and, the author added, a man was called the owner of a thing precisely when it was subjected to his will so that he could claim it against others). But it was not in accord with nature, rather against nature, that a bad man should claim goods as his own against a better one. That claim could only be based on public expediency. The text of the Digest stating that division of property was introduced by the *ius gentium* had to be understood therefore in the sense that *ius gentium* (which the author equated with natural law, as we have noted) upheld the right of the good against the bad, but not vice versa. Also natural reason urged that, other things being equal, a man could claim as his own what he acquired by his own labour.[34]

In a later discussion the author summed up his teaching thus: *In rebus naturalibus melior . . . potest dici dominus rerum diuisim et distinctim et alii non sic.* For instance, if there were two men and only sufficient resources to support one, the better man would have a 'distinct and separate right' against the other by natural law. The reason for this was

---

[33] The most obvious source for such a doctrine would be Augustine's phrase, 'iure divino . . . cuncta justorum sunt' (Ep. 93c.12, PL XXXIII. 345), but the author does not cite this.

[34] 'Bene (Unde, MS 79a) apparet secundum naturam rei quod debet esse aliqua distinctio quantum ad hoc quod res magis submittantur uoluntati meliorum quam peiorum. Sed quod pessimus possit distinguere res suas contra meliorem non apparet quod illud possit dici secundum naturam rei . . . Et sic (Ideo, MS 79a) intelligendum est (est *om*. MS 79a) quod est fundata propter expedientiam publicam . . . Et cum dicitur *ff de iusticia et iure* 1. *ex hoc iure* quod distinctio dominiorum est ex iure gentium intelligo . . . quantum ad hoc quod melior potest condistinguere aliquam rem contra minus bonum et uti ea . . . Item cum aliquid est acquisitum ex industria mea naturalis ratio dictat quod ego possum illud condistinguere contra alium ubi cetera paria essent' (fo. 12ra).

simple. God was the lord of all things; God loved the better man more; therefore God would want him to use the goods in question.[35] The argument that the other man might have acquired a natural right by his labour had no force here, for God always had a superior right. Subsequently the author wrote that God had dominion even over our own persons,[36] thus anticipating one of the arguments that, centuries later, would be directed against Locke's labour theory of property. The author also maintained that a bad man claiming a property right against a good one in time of necessity was a thief and a murderer.[37]

How then could one defend the traditional teaching, 'By natural law all things are common'? They were common, the author replied, in the sense that they were distributed from a common source, God, who was no respecter of persons. That is to say, no one was excluded from acquiring a just title to property by natural law. If a better man had a greater right, the worse man had only to improve himself. As soon as he became as good as the other he acquired an equal right and, if he became better, he acquired a superior right. Property was also common by natural law in the sense that natural law rejected the division of property that actually existed among men.[38]

Let us turn next to property in civil law. The author's teaching was summed up towards the end of the treatise. 'Although things are common by natural law as set out above, nevertheless because of men's wickedness it was expedient for the state (*reipublice*) that rights of ownership (*dominia*) be distinguished.'[39] In several preceding discussions

[35] 'Dico quod magis bonus . . . habet unum ius distinctum et diuisum contra alium' (fo. 14rb).
[36] 'Nec obstat quod res sit acquisita industria alterius quia deus semper magis habet ius in re . . .' (fo. 14rb). 'Unde sicut de rebus ita nec de se ipso plenum et totale habet dominium (plenum . . . dominium *om.* MS 83a) quia omnia sunt dei' (fo. 14ra).
[37] 'Tertia conclusio est quod minus bonus diuidens rem quam habet contra magis bonum in casu necessitas est uere fur . . . et uere homicida' (fo. 14vb). Cicero had posed the question whether a wise man in great need could take the goods of some idle, worthless person (*De Officiis*, 3.6) and decided that he could do so, not for his own sake but for the sake of the common weal. For medieval discussion of this text see Couvreur, *Les Pauvres*, pp. 22–9. The doctrines evolved from it are quite different from those of the *Tractatus de Legibus*.
[38] 'Qualiter ergo intelligendum est quod res sunt communes . . . sunt communes quia exhibende sunt per receptum (respectum, MS 82a) ad medium commune scilicet deum qui est totum ens et (qui MS 82a) non est acceptor personarum. Et ideo si ille melior habeat plus iuris quam alius, faciat se alius meliorem, et si ad equalitatem bonitatis se reducat habeat ius equale. Si autem (autem *om.* MS 82a) ad maiorem, habebit ius (ius *om.* MS 82a) maius, et sic (etc, MS 82a) in aliis. Item sunt communes per negationem distinctionis que nunc est secundum qua minus bonus diuidit rem suam contra magis bonum' (fo. 14rb).
[39] 'licet enim res sint communes inspecto iure naturale eo modo quo in superioribus est declaratum, tamen expediens fuit reipublice occasione malicie hominum quod dominia rerum distinguerentur' (fo. 22vb).

Public expediency and natural law

the author had made it clear that the rights guaranteed by civil law could not be the same as those that arose from natural law. The emperor could not discriminate among so many men to determine the relative goodness of each. But the well-being of the polity required that the emperor or people make some division. Otherwise each man would claim to be better than others and often the strong would kill the weak. It was opportune therefore to so divide things that a man who was able to acquire more should have more.[40] Such a division was accordingly made 'by the consent of men or of one acting on behalf of the community'.[41] The division might assign property rights to good men or bad. But normally the less good men would have greater riches because they were more solicitous about acquiring material things.[42] The constant assumption of the argument was that rights in civil law could not and would not coincide with rights in natural law. There were two different structures of rights, one 'descending' from God, the other 'ascending' from popular consent.

The author applied his ideas in a variety of ways. He accepted the common view that in time of necessity superfluities were common according to natural law. (That is to say, even a good man could not claim his superfluous possessions against those in extreme want.) This led him to develop an interesting theory of poor relief.[43] The author also showed how, on his theory, it would be possible – though not expedient – for the pope to claim a universal right of dominion.[44]

---

[40] 'Non enim sufficeret imperator ad considerandum circa quemlibet hominem ille habebit tantum, alius tantum propter multitudinem super excrescentem hominum et quia difficile esset cognoscere circa quodlibet indiuiduum gradum quem habet in genere boni' (fo. 12ra). 'Unde in tanto populo ut nunc est non posset fieri ut semper melior haberet plus iuris in rebus. Quilibet enim assereret (se esse *add*. MS 82b) meliorem et alii minus boni qui sepius corpore sunt robustiores, alios interficerent. Ergo oportuit ut distinguerentur res ita quod qui posset plus acquirere plus habet . . .' (fo. 14va).

[41] 'ex consensu hominum uel alicuius habentis vicem populi fuerunt distincta dominia' (fo. 22ra).

[42] 'minus boni regulariter habundant pecuniis quia magis solliciti sunt circa acquisitionem rerum (rerum *om*. MS 82b)' (fo. 14vb). This served as a proof that usury was against natural law. The man in need who had to borrow money would normally be better than the rich man who lent. But by natural law the money belonged to the better man. Therefore it was wrong to charge him usury.

[43] Officials should be appointed in each city to help those in extreme need. Fear of want made men cowardly and it ought to be alleviated. In the last resort it was licit for one in extreme need to steal (fo. 22ra). If a man fell into want through his own fault, to help him might encourage idleness. But if there were signs of penitence the man should be helped. He might reform and become useful to the state. Public authorities could punish the idle (fo. 22vb).

[44] Jesus Christ was lord of all things by natural law but not by civil law (fo. 14ra). Similarly the pope was lord of all by natural law but this did not prejudice the temporal lordship of kings (fo. 14rb). It was possible that the most perfect man might choose for a time to be lord of all by civil law as well as by natural law (fo. 15rb). But regularly the pope ought not have

It would be interesting to explore all these ramifications of thought. But our main concern is with the tension between natural law and public expediency in the system of the *Tractatus*. On one point the author was entirely in agreement with later exponents of natural rights theories. 'The Obligations of the Law of Nature cease not in Society', observed Locke.[45] So too, in the thought of our medieval author, the natural right of ownership pertaining to a good man was 'a divine right, wholly immutable' which could not be changed 'by the act of the ruler or of anyone else'.[46] Moreover, laws of the emperor contrary to natural law were not to be observed. This may seem to contradict the whole doctrine of property rights in civil law that we have so far described. But, the author explained, imperial laws decreed only that goods should be treated for purposes of civil administration as if they were held separately, since public expediency required this. The emperor's laws did not deny that it was intrinsically good for a man to know his own natural status and refuse to claim his property against a better man. Human law did not destroy the rights and duties that existed before God.[47]

The system seems neatly balanced so far between nature and expediency, between moral rights and legal rights. But when the author tried to work out the detailed implications of his arguments he encountered severe difficulties. These were especially apparent when he discussed the problem whether a man could licitly assert rights derived from natural law against the rights of another derived from civil law. If a better man seized the property of a less good man, property which both needed equally, did he commit an offence?[48] Obviously he did according to civil law. The judge would hang him, our author observed quite contentedly. Without temporal punishments for offences

civil dominion. He would inspire more confidence as an exemplar if he lived modestly. Men needed both kings and pontiffs and it was better if their functions were not confused (fo. 17rb).

[45] John Locke, *Two Treatises*, ii.xi. 135 (ed. Laslett, p. 375).

[46] '. . . illud ius est ius diuinum totaliter immutabile ita quod facto principis uel alicuius alterius non potest mutari . . .' (fo. 14va).

[47] 'imperator condendo leges suas, si esset contrarius legi naturali, leges suas non essent tenende . . . non dicunt quominus semper bonum est quod quilibet congnoscat statum suum naturalem et non condiuidat res suas contra meliorem eo. Sed dicunt quod expedientia publica exigit quod proinde obseruentur ac si essent distincta quantum ad executiones faciendas' (fo. 15va); 'Et aduertendum quod imperator non remouet illud ius quod causabitur in ordine ad deum necque illud ligamen' (fo. 14vb).

[48] 'Sed pone quod (quod *om.* MS 92a) unus bonus habet unam rem (rem *om.* MS 92a) que precise est sibi necessaria, uenit magis bonus qui similiter est in articulo necessitatis, nunquid potest ab alio furari uel subrepere?' (fo. 22rb).

Public expediency and natural law

against civil law there would be constant dissensions and fighting among men. The people might even depose a prince who refused to punish such offences. But, the author observed, some would hold that the better man in our example did not offend before God. This implied, however, that civil laws were not binding *in foro conscientiae*.[49] Hence others would argue that, since God had given the better man strength to support himself, and the existing system of property rights was established by popular consent, he did indeed sin. But then again it might be argued that God sometimes gave much greater strength to the less good man and this could only be so that he should support both himself and the better man too.[50] The argument continued indecisively with further points of casuistry.[51] It is not a very satisfying discussion.

Indeed, at this point a real conflict arose in the author's thought that he was not able to resolve satisfactorily. Evidently, on his theory, any attempt to maintain natural rights in a civil society would lead to anarchy. Civil law could not abolish such rights but equally it could not permit them to be asserted. Still more confusingly, it was not even clear whether the assertion of natural rights against civil rights was morally justified. We are not dealing here with the situation envisaged by Thomas Aquinas – a definition in human law of a matter left undetermined by natural law. In this area natural law had made its determinations and human law imposed a conflicting set of obligations. At the end of his treatise the author explicitly rejected the argument of Aquinas that no positive precept of natural law required goods to be held in common. Natural law did require common ownership in the peculiar sense that the author had given to the phrase.[52] His very last

49 'Hic uellent forsan aliqui dicere quod posset. Et dicerent quod duplex est furtum, quoddam punibile eternaliter . . . Aliud est furtum punibile solum temporaliter ut in hoc casu. Unde iudex suspenderet eum et puniret temporaliter quia secundum hoc contingeret multociens nisi essent punitiones quod alicui (quia aliqui MS 92a) subirent necessitates et essent dissensiones et bella inter homines uel forsan quod populus procederet ad depositionem principis nisi ipsum puniret. Sed secundum hoc leges ciuiles etiam quantum ad prohibita non ligarent in foro conscientiae' (fo. 22rb).

50 'Uel dicatur quod non poterit iuste auferre ita quod utroque modo erit furtum uerum. Nam licet sit melior tamen ex quo deus dedit uirtutem prouisiuam ad conseruationem sui esse (utrique add MS 92a) et diuisi (diuisim, MS 92a) sunt dominia de consensu populi . . . magis uidetur amabile deo quod ipse moriatur . . . Sed illud non uidetur ualere quia interdum minus bono communicata est maior prouisiua potentia et magis bono nulla uel quasi, et non uidetur hoc aliud esse nisi ut ille prouideat sibi et alii magis bono' (fo. 22va).

51 E.g. if two men were starving could the better one 'use' the other (as food?).

52 'Dicunt aliqui quod res non sunt communes iure naturali positiue sed solum negatiue pro quanto oppositum scilicet distinctio diuiciarum non est de iure naturali. Non credo hoc uerum nam per rationem naturalem supra est probata communitas rerum secundum intellectum ibi expositum' (fo. 23ra) (see above, n. 38).

argument restated the underlying tension of the whole treatise. 'It is true that by natural law things are common. Nevertheless it is expedient that some division be made.'[53]

We shall not be surprised that the author of the *Tractatus de Legibus* failed to achieve an altogether harmonious synthesis if we remember how many different elements of thought he tried to include in one systematic treatise. The author tried to combine a doctrine of divinely sanctioned natural law with a theory of public utility that, in later times, would provide a potent weapon for critics of all natural law doctrines. He was equally concerned with the theoretical doctrine of government by consent and with the practical demands of expediency in shaping the form of a particular polity. Moreover the author was as interested in natural rights as in natural law. He saw the force of the Lockean argument about labour as a source of natural right in property but casually dismissed it with the same arguments that Locke's critics would use centuries later. He wanted to give due weight to both the 'ascending' and 'descending' theories of government and property.

We cannot regard the author of the *Tractatus* as a 'forerunner' of any one particular system of modern thought. But he did present various strands of argument that would be woven into different patterns in the theories of many later and more famous political thinkers. Walter Ullmann has given us the salutary reminder that, before the rediscovery of Aristotle's *Politics*, medieval men had no more idea of the state than they had of the steam engine. It is only a small footnote to his thought to add that, once they did recover the concept of the state, the men of the later Middle Ages began at once to identify and to attack the central problems that would preoccupy Western political theorists for the next several hundred years.

---

[53] 'Ergo hoc est uerum quod iure naturali res sunt communes. Tamen expediens est quod ibi sit aliqualis distinctio scilicet illa que dicta est supra' (fo. 23rb).

VII

Canon law and Church Institutions
in the late Middle Ages

When I was first asked to give this paper I accepted cheerfully. I envisaged a simple bibliographical survey covering all the recent work on late medieval canon law. It seemed easy. Then, as the time of the Congress approached, I began to realize that my task was not only difficult; it was almost impossible. And worse, it seemed impossible for two contradictory reasons. From one point of view there was too little material, from another far too much.

Too little, because by the early fourteenth century the internal development of the *Corpus iuris canonici* had reached its conclusion. A historian of that period no longer has the exciting task of tracing the evolution of an organically growing system of law. Canon law professors in the universities continued to write massive commentaries of course. Like modern academics they would rather publish than perish. As with some modern cases, it is not the volume but the value of their contributions that may be called into question. The situation is conveyed in the title of the modern book that covers our period most adequately—that of Paul Ourliac and Henri Gilles. It is called *La période post-classique.*[1] The classical era is over. It is at best a silver age we have to deal with, perhaps a leaden age. I myself, when young and impatient, once described late medieval canonistic commentary as a form of decadent scholasticism. But let me quote a greater authority. Gabriel Le Bras once complained about the 'dessicating methodology' of the post-glossators and observed crisply that 'the epoch of the Great Schism ... provides no material for a historian of canon law'.[2] You can see that my task is impossible. There is nothing to talk about.

---

[1] Paul Ourliac and Henri Gilles, *La période post-classique (1378-1500)* (Histoire du droit XIII; Paris 1971).
[2] Cited in Ourliac and Gilles, 5.

And yet, from another point of view, there is so much. Those vast elephantine commentaries of the later canonists touched on every aspect of medieval religious and social life. Very many modern historians have used them as source material in reconstructing the whole medieval world-picture—sometimes in unexpected ways. I recently opened a book called *Love and marriage in the age of Chaucer.*[3] It turned out to be largely a disquisition on the licitness of sexual love according to the canonists and the influence of their ideas on *The Canterbury tales.* If I were to try to discuss all the recent modern works that have used late medieval canonistic source material in one way or another I should be reduced to reading out titles from the standard bibliographies. So I have made a selection of two broad areas of recent research to discuss—conciliar ecclesiology, including ideas on representation, corporatism, infallibility; and social theory, including topics like poor relief, usury, sexual morality, marriage. And I gave up any thought of attempting a detailed bibliographical survey in each area. I will mention some recent studies but they are intended only as examples to illustrate the points I want to make.[4] It seemed more useful to try and construct a conceptual framework—to find a way of looking at the late medieval world—within which the canonists' achievement can be understood and appreciated.

There are several choices. Perhaps the most common approach among medievalists is to see the fourteenth century as an age of gloom and doom, tormented by famine, plague, war, and, finally, schism in the Church. One is reminded of Yeats's lines:

> Things fall apart. The centre cannot hold.
> Mere anarchy is loosed upon the world.

And worst of all was the anarchy in peoples' minds. Ockham's nominalism, in this view, destroyed Aquinas's beautiful synthesis of faith and reason. Man could know nothing except his own sense impressions of individual objects. The institutions of the Church seemed to be falling apart. And so, amid widespread despair, there grew up a generation filled with 'a hunger for certainty, a hunger for truth' in the words of Heiko Oberman. In this view we should see late medieval canon law, in

---

[3] H.A. Kelly, *Love and marriage in the age of Chaucer* (Ithaca-London 1975).
[4] Although I have not presented a detailed bibliographical survey the notes and bibliographies in the works cited should provide an adequate introduction to recent literature on the various topics discussed.

the manner of Le Bras, as the sterile product of a decadent culture. That would be one conceptual framework.

But just mentioning Oberman's name will remind us that there is another quite different way of looking at our period. Oberman and many other recent authors have offered a much more positive evaluation of late medieval thought. Oberman sees our age as one of creative new life, preparing the way for the great achievements of the Reformation era. (One of his articles is called 'The birthpangs of the modern era').[5] In such a framework we might see our late medieval canonists also as creative figures, courageously reshaping their old tradition to face new problems, as Zabarella for instance faced the problem of the Great Schism.

But neither account is wholly satisfactory. Each is too one-sided. To understand our late medieval canonists we need to put them in a framework that includes the elements of truth in both approaches. And I thought we might do this best by borrowing and adapting the notion of a paradigm and of paradigm shift that Thomas Kuhn first applied to the history of science.[6] (It is an overworked concept nowadays, but it may still be useful as a heuristic device.) You will remember the argument. Intellectual activity is normally carried on within an accepted paradigm—a world picture, a *Weltanschauung*. There are always anomalies—apparent contradictions within the paradigm, or areas where the paradigm does not fit the real world—but for a long time it is taken for granted that they can be overcome by further research. Indeed it is the perception of anomalies within a paradigm that constantly stimulates new reflections and investigations. (In our canonistic world one can recall how generations of decretists contentedly ruminated over the apparent anomalies in Gratian's Decretum.) But as the paradigm grows more and more all-embracing the anomalies, instead of disappearing, grow more and more intransigent. In the end the whole paradigm has to be abandoned. Copernicus replaces Ptolemy. Einstein replaces Newton. And so too the paradigmatic world-picture of our medieval canonists will break down amid the changes of the sixteenth century.

By the late Middle Ages the canonists' paradigm had grown very ambitious. During the twelfth century, canon law emerged as a discipline separate from theology, but throughout the later Middle Ages there were persistent attempts to draw together canonistic and theological materials

---

[5] Heiko A. Oberman, 'The shape of late medieval thought: the birthpangs of the modern era', *Archiv für Reformationsgeschichte* 64 (1973) 13-33.

[6] Thomas S. Kuhn, *The structure of scientific revolutions* (Chicago 1962).

in broader syntheses which sought to provide a systematic, all-embracing account of the nature and structure of Christian society—a coherent body of ecclesiology and social thought which could satisfy the pervasive hunger for truth, for certainty that was so characteristic of the age.

The process of integration began, I think, in the disputes between mendicant friars and secular masters at the University of Paris in the 1250s. A secular theologian like Guillaume de St. Amour drew extensively on canonistic materials in seeking to combat the new claims of the friars. Just a little later on we can observe the beginning of a complementary process, the use of theological material by the canonists. Around 1300, Guido de Baysio used Thomas Aquinas and Alexander of Hales to explicate Gratian's doctrine of natural law.[7] So there, in a formal canonistic commentary, we find leading theologians of the Dominican and Franciscan orders intertwined with Huguccio and Hostiensis and Innocentius.

After this the pattern becomes common. Alvarus Pelagius was a canonist by training who used theological sources; Augustinus Triumphus was a theologian who used canonistic materials. All the major authors of *summae confessorum* were ambidextrous so to speak—they had to be knowledgeable about both theology and canon law. John Baconthorpe, the leading theologian of the Carmelites wrote *Quaestiones canonicae.* But Baconthorpe's master, Guido Terreni provides a still more striking example. Guido was an ardent defender of Pope John XXII in the disputes of the 1320s. Pope John's adversaries often appealed to canonistic texts. So, to refute them, Terreni wrote a commentary on the whole of the Decretum, bringing an unusual patristic erudition to bear on Gratian's texts.[8] His commentary remains unpublished. I can think of nothing that would contribute more to our understanding of late medieval ecclesiology than an edition of Terreni's work.

In mid-fifteenth century the pattern was repeated. The great theologian Johannes de Turrecremata, a leading defender of the papacy in the later stages of the conciliar movement, also wrote a massive commentary on the Decretum which incidentally made use of the earlier work of Guido Terreni. Nicholas of Cues provides a different kind of example. He was a professional canonist by training and his great conci-

---

[7] Guido de Baysio, *Rosarium* (Strasbourg 1478) ad Dist. 1, c.6, c.7.
[8] The work is discussed in my *Origins of papal infallibility, 1150-1350* (Leiden 1972). Thomas Turley is preparing a monograph on Terreni based on his Cornell Ph. D. dissertation, *The ecclesiology of Guido Terreni* (1978).

liar treatise, *De Concordantia catholica* can only be fully appreciated as a very original exercise in canonistic scholarship. But Nicholas went on to achieve greater fame as a philosopher and theologian. Antony Black writes that Panormitanus, the greatest canonist of the Council of Basle, 'wished ... to introduce into canonistics a more serious study of theology'.[9] Black and other recent authors have insisted that late medieval conciliarism was essentially a theological movement of thought rather than just a juridical theory; and they are right in a way of course. We must not be chauvinistic in pressing the claims of the canonists. But I have come to think that perhaps the distinction is not really meaningful. The greatest works of Basle conciliarism are hybrids. Whether written by a professional canonist or a professional theologian they draw on both traditions of thought.

I know of course—someone will be yearning to tell me—that the disciplines of theology and canon law did remain distinct in the schools. There were vast regions of theology that had nothing to do with canon law and aspects of canon law, like court procedure, that had nothing to do with theology. But in the area that I am discussing—and it is a central area involving the whole ordering of Christian society—late medieval thinkers were striving after a synthesis of the two disciplines, an all-embracing paradigm. And, to go back to the beginning of my argument, it was just at this point that the anomalies within the paradigm became insuperable. Ideas which had happily coexisted with one another, which had been regarded as complementary, in earlier canon law came to seem starkly opposed in the later period. The earlier paradigm had been one of consensus and of concord (to borrow Gratian's word), a harmonious, justly ordered Christendom—one united Christian people growing in faith and knowledge under the universally accepted leadership of pope and bishops. The paradigm never corresponded precisely to reality of course. That is the nature of paradigms; that is why paradigm-shifts eventually become inevitable. But for a time it provided a persuasive framework within which canonistic thought and church policy could be conducted.

By the time of Basle the paradigm was falling apart. But before I go on with this let me say just a word or two about some recent work on the canonists of this period. Thomas Morrissey has been producing a valuable

---

[9] A. Black, *Council and commune. The conciliar movement and the fifteenth-century heritage* (London 1979) 93.

series of articles on Cardinal Zabarella.[10] Thomas Izbicki has given us a new monograph on Turrecremata's ecclesiology.[11] Among more general works Giuseppe Alberigo provides an overall view of the whole period in *Chiesa conciliare*.[12] He is faithful on the whole to Jedin's earlier portrayal of a good council of Constance and a bad council of Basle but there is a long and sympathetic treatment of Nicholas Cusanus. Werner Kramer also deals extensively with Cusanus in his book *Konzens und Rezeption* which presents a much more sympathetic view of Basle.[13] This book is dense with references to fifteenth-century authors and to modern work on them. Antony Black also presents a favorable view of Basle in *Council and commune* which includes a substantial chapter on Panormitanus. Both Panormitanus and Cusanus are considered at length in Arnulf Vagedes' book, *Das Konzil über dem Papst* with, again, very extensive references to other less famous fifteenth-century canonists. Joachim Stieber's *Pope Eugenius IV and the Council of Basel* deals mainly with papal diplomacy but there are long bibliographical appendixes touching on all the major conciliar thinkers. They are treated again in the broad-ranging work of H.J. Sieben, *Traktate und Theorien zum Konzil*.[14]

Such works can provide guidance to the maze of modern literature. Let me return to my broader theme, the conciliar epoch as a time when the stresses within a paradigm became intolerable. The most obvious symptom of this was the overt conflict of pope and council. In 1216 Johannes Teutonicus wrote a pregnant phrase in his ordinary gloss to the Decretum: 'Where matters of faith are concerned ... a council is greater

---

[10] Thomas E. Morrissey, 'Cardinal Zabarella on papal and episcopal authority', *Proceedings of the First Patristic, Medieval, and Renaissance Conference* (Villanova 1976) 39-52; 'The decree «Haec Sancta» and Cardinal Zabarella', AHC 10 (1978) 145-76; 'After six hundred years: The Great Western Schism, conciliarism and Constance', *Theological Studies* 40 (1979) 495-509; 'Franciscus Zabarella (1360-1417): Papacy, community and limitations upon authority': *Reform and authority in the medieval Church*, ed. Guy F. Lytle (Washington, D.C. 1981) 37-54.

[11] Thomas M. Izbicki, *Protector of the Faith. Cardinal Johannes de Turrecremata and the defense of the institutional Church* (Washington, D.C. 1981).

[12] Giuseppe Alberigo, *Chiesa conciliare. Identità e significato del conciliarismo* (Brescia 1981).

[13] Werner Krämer, *Konzens und Rezeption. Verfassungsprinzipien der Kirche im Basler Konziliarismus* (Münster 1980).

[14] Arnulf Vagades, *Das Konzil über dem Papst? Die Stellungnahme des Nikolaus von Kues und des Panormitanus zum Streit zwischen dem Konzil von Basel und Eugen IV* (Paderborn 1981); Joachim W. Stieber, *Pope Eugenius IV, the Council of Basel and the secular and ecclesiastical authorities in the Empire* (Leiden 1978); H.J. Sieben, *Traktate und Theorien zum Konzil. Vom Beginn des Grossen Schismas bis zum Vorabend der Reformation* (Frankfurt 1983).

than a pope'.[15] But I think he meant only that a pope surrounded by the bishops of a council was greater than a pope alone. He was suggesting the supremacy of pope-in-council. Of course there was a possibility—and Johannes perceived it—that the pope and bishops might disagree. The canonists went on discussing this point for centuries, usually in discussions on Dist. 4 c.3 of the Decretum. They discussed it contentedly, complacently, ingeniously, without undue anxiety. It was a nice little problem for the schools, a little anomaly within their system of thought. It didn't seem to threaten the whole system or to have much bearing on real life. But by the time of Basle rival theorists had exaggerated each side of the argument; and they stood opposed to each other not only in theory but in a practical struggle for supreme power in the Church. One could no longer choose pope-and-council. It had to be pope *or* council.

One can explore this theme further in relation to the various technical problems within the general framework of conciliar theory that I mentioned earlier. I want to consider three in turn—representation, corporatism, and infallibility. As for representation—the word is so multifaceted that it is hard to attach a specific meaning to it. But in a recent little article in *Concilium* I tried to invent a sort of typology based on three different kinds of representation that we encounter in medieval thought and practice—personification, delegation and mimesis.[16] We have representation by personification when a community is conceived of as symbolized by its head; delegation is when a community confers its authority on a representative by an act of election or consent; by mimesis I meant that an assembly can represent a community as a kind of microcosm of it, by including in its composition members of all the classes and groups that make up the large-scale community. These kinds of representation can occur in any human community. In addition, for the medieval Church in particular, an adequate attendance of bishops seemed especially important, since they were held to bear the authority that Christ had originally conferred on the apostles. All these concepts existed in the works of the decretists writing around 1200. The notion of personification was evident in their use of Augustine's teaching that when Peter received the keys he stood *in figura ecclesiae*, as a symbol of the Church. The decretists also taught that a corporate body could delegate its authority to a proctor with a mandate of *plena potestas*. The idea of mimesis

---

[15] Gloss ad Dist. 19 c.9.
[16] Brian Tierney, 'The idea of representation in the medieval councils of the West', *Concilium* 19 (1983) no. 8/9, pp. 25-30.

was implicit in their adaptations of the old Roman law principle, *Quod omnes tangit*—'what touches all is to be approved by all'—which some decretists interpreted as meaning that even lay people were to be invited to general councils when matters of faith were to be considered. All these ideas coexisted harmoniously in decretist glosses and they could moreover coexist harmoniously in real-life representative assemblies. At the Fourth Lateran Council in 1215 the pope personified the unity of the Church; some 400 bishops met with representatives bearing the delegated authority of chapters, collegiate churches, cities and kingdoms; and the whole assembly provided a credible microcosm or mimesis of Christian society.

But it was all different by the time of Basle. One still finds the three different types of representation discussed in the theoretical writings of the time, but none of them could justify the claims of the council actually assembled at Basle in its later stages. The council did not then represent the Church in any previously understood sense of the term. The paradigm exemplified in the Fourth Lateran Council had disintegrated. The last defenders of Basle fell back on affirming a mystical unity between council and universal Church based on a vague philosophical realism. They seem to have assumed that there was a kind of spiritual essence of the Church separate from the persons of individual members and that this essence was mysteriously concentrated in the assembly at Basle.[17]

It was not theoretically impossible to weave together the three earlier types of representation in a coherent conceptual structure, and Nicholas of Cues did so in his remarkable *Concordantia catholica*. There was an element of mimesis in his argument that any Catholic could attend the council. The two other forms of representation, delegation and personification, were fused in his teaching that each bishop was established as a symbol or 'figure' of his church precisely by election and consent. Even at the beginning of the Church, Nicholas wrote, the apostles first chose Peter before Christ appointed him as their head. The precise source of this odd doctrine has only recently been identified. It comes from a commentary on the Decretum by a fairly obscure Irish canonist of the mid-thirteenth century, Johannes de Fintona and it might be interesting to find out if Fintona had any other such odd ideas.[18] But to return to

---

[17] On the philosophic realism of Basle conciliarists see the works of Black and Krämer cited nn. 9, 13 supra.

[18] G. Kallen (ed.), *De Concordantia catholica* in *Nicolai de Cusa Opera omnia* XIV (Hamburg 1963) 284. Kallen did not identify the precise source of Nicholas's doctrine. It is

Nicholas. His work was, as I said, conceptually coherent. It preserved all the elements of the earlier paradigm. The trouble was that it was hopelessly out of touch with reality; and Nicholas's later turn to papalism suggests that he became well aware of the fact.

One modern author has suggested that Nicholas's disillusion with Basle and turn to Eugenius can be explained by his growing interest in Renaissance philosophy. But one might just as sensibly argue the opposite way and say that the fundamental intuitions of his philosophy were derived—perhaps unconsciously—from his experience at Basle. After all, the basic theme of his first major philosophical treatise, *De docta ignorantia*, is that human thought does not correspond adequately to true reality. If one studies the thought of the *Concordantia catholica* and then looks at the true reality of Basle, one can well understand how the author might have acquired that conviction.

But to return to representation and its problems. A medieval paradigm was changing. All the earlier elements of thought that went into it would survive and would indeed reemerge in various forms of secular constitutionalism; but they could no longer be held together in a coherent, workable ecclesiology. Either one abandoned the old theories in order to defend the existing fact, like the late defenders of Basle, or one went on elaborating the old paradigm, like Nicholas of Cues, but at the price of losing touch with reality.

Let me turn now to the second major area of conciliar thought —what I have called corporatism. By this I mean the application of the rules of corporation law concerning small-scale associations—chapters, guilds, communes—to describe the structure of large-scale societies, the universal Church and the political association of the state. Or, similarly, the application of corporation ideas to the ruling body of such a society, a general council, or the pope and college of cardinals, or a secular assembly of estates. Joseph Canning has recently discussed the application of corporation theory to Italian city states by Baldus, and almost every modern work on conciliar thought discusses corporatism to some degree. But Antony Black has developed this theme with particular care in his *Council and commune* and in his new book *Guilds and civil society in European political thought*.[19] Black has observed that if the con-

---

found in Johannes de Fintona's *Lectura ad Dist.* 50 c.53, MS Reims, Bibliothèque de la Ville 686, fol. 40rb. Nicholas knew the text through a quotation in Guido de Baysio's *Rosarium.*
[19] A. Black, *Guilds and civil society in European political thought from the twelfth century to the present* (Ithaca-London 1984). For *Council and commune* see n. 9 supra.

58

ciliarists did not have a paradigm of the republic to inspire them they did have a paradigm of the commune. But at this point a problem arises which can lead us to another set of anomalies in late medieval thought. The model of a commune could serve very well to establish the subordination of the pope to a general council or to the whole Church. But this model did not explain adequately the role of the pope as divinely ordained head of the Church, a doctrine that all the mainstream conciliarists wanted to preserve. A commune or guild created its own ruling offices, but the Church did not create the papacy. As Gerson wrote, 'The whole community of men, excluding Christ, could not institute this power as it can institute imperial power or royal ... or other purely secular powers'.[20]

Before I pursue this further, let me turn to another kind of work on corporation theory. Lawrence Duggan has investigated the history of the cathedral chapter of Speyer from the thirteenth century onward. Starting out from the classical canon law which assigned substantial rights of counsel and consent to a cathedral chapter he shows how at Speyer the chapter came to exercise substantial rights of government within the principality, 'acting in cooperation, or at loggerheads with the bishops'. The chapter's power in the later Middle Ages was rooted in the canon law of the twelfth and thirteenth centuries, Duggan points out. He further notes that 'the chapter served throughout the period as the chief restraint on princely excesses and as the principal guardian of the common interests of the principality'.[21] The point I want to make is that we have here a perfect example of canonistic corporation theory applied to the government of a large scale community. But this does not mean that Speyer was developing on the model of a commune; it was rather, we might say, a sort of limited monarchy. The important point about this is that when conciliarists or political theorists appealed to corporation law, there were always two basically different kinds of corporation model that they could use. In the simple guild all power inhered in the members and was bestowed temporarily on elected officials; in the quintessentially canonistic corporation structure of bishop-and-chapter the chapter elected the future bishop but it did not create the power of his office. In the subsequent conduct of affairs the two parties, bishop and chapter, head and members, came together as independent or at times interdependent enti-

---

[20] P. Glorieux (ed.), *De potestate ecclesiastica* in *Oeuvres complètes* VI (Tournai 1965) 225.

[21] Lawrence G. Duggan, *Bishop and chapter. The governance of the bishopric of Speyer to 1552* (New Brunswick 1975) 181.

ties, each with its own inherent rights, each at times requiring the cooperation of the other. Applied to large scale government the first corporation model led to republicanism, the other to limited or constitutional
monarchy. Neither model was wholly adequate for the conciliarists. If
they used the corporation model of a commune or guild they could not
explain adequately the role of the pope as divinely ordained head of the
Church. If they used the corporation model of bishop-and-chapter they
could not justify the subordination of pope to council that they wanted to
assert. Hence the major conciliar writers often moved between the two
models, sometimes overtly, sometimes implicitly appealing to one or the
other, and this helps to produce the impression of strain, of uncertainty
in addressing the fundamental problems of papal power that one often
encounters in their work. The same tension or anomaly persisted in
much early modern secular constitutional theory. Maitland once observed that 'political theory in its infancy is apt to look like sublimated
jurisprudence'. The sublimation of corporation law into constitutional
thought is a particularly good example. But it is a complicated one. And
we shall never fully understand the process unless we realize that not just
one but two kinds of corporation law were being sublimated.[22] It would
be much more useful to pay attention to this problem in future work
than to go on regurgitating stale arguments about the 'fiction theory' and
'realist theory' of corporations.

The final problem of ecclesiology that became intransigent and irre-
solvable in the conciliar crisis was the location of unerring authority in
the Church—the problem of infallibility as I called it though really, so
far as the canonists were concerned, the problem was rather a lack of
infallibility. The root of this problem was the common decretist teaching
that, although the pope was supreme judge in matters of faith, an individual pontiff might fall into heresy. This impeded the development of
theories of papal infallibility, though there were attempts to formulate
such theories in the later Middle Ages. (This was an age with a 'hunger
for certainty', a 'hunger for truth'). At the end of the thirteenth century
the great Franciscan theologian, Peter Olivi deployed all Gratian's texts
on the pope as supreme judge in matters of faith, but used them to support a new proposition—that the Roman pontiff was to be obeyed as an
unerring norm—'tamquam regula inerrabilis'. In the next generation this

---

[22] The two types of corporation structure and their implications for ecclesiology and
political theory are discussed in my book, *Religion, law, and the growth of constitutional
thought, 1150-1650* (Cambridge 1982).

doctrine was used both by the dissident Franciscans who rebelled against Pope John XXII—they sought to prove that the decisions of John's predecessors were irrevocable—and by one of the pope's chief defenders, Guido Terreni, the Carmelite theologian I mentioned who made himself such a good canonist that he could write a major commentary on the Decretum. So here again we find two great theologians reflecting on canonistic sources and deriving new conclusions from them. But this new, expanded paradigm of papal authority had surprisingly little success among the canonists themselves. Even ardent papalists in the fifteenth century continued to argue, not that the pope could never err, but that the faith of the Church would persist in spite of papal errors. I might mention an example that was quoted by that redoubtable old scholar George Coulton, who deserves to be remembered on this occasion, not only for his own considerable if controversial merits, but as a fellow of our host institution, St John's College. Coulton quoted a passage of the Franciscan inquisitor James of the March, inveighing against the rebel Fraticelli. Their error was to hold that all the popes since John XXII had been heretics. Against this, James confidently proclaimed his version of the true Catholic faith: that there could never be two heretical popes in succession. Of course, James conceded, any individual pontiff might be a heretic and might continue to bear the papal office as a heretic and might seduce all the simple people into error. But one could be sure that his successor would put things right.[23] The implication was that one could never be sure of the teaching of any particular pope at any particular time. It seems cold comfort for a generation that was hungering for certainty.

A revived doctrine of papal infallibility began to find acceptance only from the time of Cajetanus onward, and this development has been admirably traced by Ulrich Horst through the sixteenth and seventeenth centuries. His main work lies outside our chronological boundaries, but Horst has also written good studies on the late medieval period. (I think, incidentally, that he has radically misunderstood the teaching of Peter Olivi, but that is a matter to be taken up on another occasion).[24] The point for the moment is that Horst's work once more illustrates the uncertainty and lack of consensus on papal authority among fifteenth-

---

[23] G.G. Coulton, *Life in the Middle Ages* (2nd ed. Cambridge 1928) I 235.
[24] Ulrich Horst, *Unfehlbarkeit und Geschichte* (Mainz 1982). Horst's earlier studies are listed at p. xxvii. On Olivi see pp. 219-34. See my criticism of Horst in *Theological Studies* 46 (1985) 315-28.

century canonists and theologians. And a recent study by Jeffrey Mirus on discussions concerning papal heresy around 1500 shows how this persisted to the very eve of the Reformation.[25]

Where could a Catholic find certain truth? Conciliarists insisted that popes could err and papalists insisted that councils could err. (The work of H.J. Sieben, cited above, is especially valuable for its extensive treatment of the problem of conciliar infallibility). One outcome was a widely diffused doctrine—propounded first by the great canonist Panormitanus —that no church institution could be relied on to define the faith with certain truth. The opinion to be followed was the one most consistent with Scripture, even if that opinion was proclaimed by only a single private individual.

Panormitanus reached this conclusion by combining in a new fashion two old, twelfth-century decretist doctrines. One held that the faith could never become extinct, though it might survive in only one single person. The other was concerned with reception of doctrine. Generally the decree of a pope or council was to be accepted in preference to the teaching of an individual church father, but in an exceptional case, where the teaching of the father was better supported by Scripture, his view should prevail. The issue arose, not over some great matter of faith, but in connection with a teaching of Jerome on a point of marriage law.[26] Among the decretists, it seems to me, these teachings were not inspired by any distrust of the institutional structure of the Church. Rather they formed a coherent paradigm. The doctrine of indefectibility, affirming that the Church would survive all vicissitudes, was, after all, ancient and orthodox. And the doctrine of reception really expressed a confidence that the Church would in fact receive and build into its structure of law all the sound teachings of the past that were consistent with Scripture. Indeed, it seemed that Gratian had succeeded in doing this.

But the old doctrines took on a new significance when Panormitanus deployed them amid the fifteenth-century conflicts of councils and popes. Then they seemed to cast doubt on every established authority. As for the council, it could err because the true faith might survive only in one single person. As for the pope, 'in matters concerning the faith,' Panormitanus wrote, 'the opinion of one private person should be preferred to the opinion of a pope if he is supported by better reasons and authori-

---

[25] Jeffrey A. Mirus, 'On the deposition of the pope for heresy', AHP 13 (1975) 231-248.
[26] C.36 q.2 c.8.

ties from the Old and New Testaments.' But there was another twist to the argument. The pope himself might be the one individual supported by better reasons and authorities, and in that case his view should be preferred to that of a council. So the argument was multifaceted. It could be used to attack either side in the continuing controversies. And this helps to explain its popularity. The doctrine of Panormitanus was discussed some time ago by Knut Nörr and most recently by Hermann Schuessler who showed how widely diffused his teaching became in the century before the Reformation.[27] It even penetrated into the popular handbooks for confessors like the *Summa* of Angelo de Chiavassio.[28]

Eventually late medieval ecclesiology simply bifurcated. Some elements were developed by Cajetanus into a theory of papal infallibility, others were developed in a very different fashion by Luther, who appealed to the authority of Panormitanus in asserting the overriding authority of Scripture. Here again an earlier paradigmatic structure of ideas revealed an inherent instability in the course of its late medieval development. Joseph Lortz, the historian of the Reformation, once observed with commendable reticence, that there was a certain 'lack of clarity' in late medieval thought. We shall understand the Reformation even better as we come to appreciate more fully the extraordinary fragility of Catholic ecclesiology at the beginning of the sixteenth century.

There is another whole area I promised to discuss where the use of late medieval canonistic sources is proving very fruitful—I mean the area of social history, including the 'new social history' as we Anglophones persist in calling it. (We usually mean just the good old, time-tested approach of the *Annales* school.) Here the most useful sources are not the treatises and glosses of academic lawyers but the records of local church courts and the popular handbooks for confessors. Such writings provide a kind of bridge between ideas and reality. A recent article in this genre by Giovanni Ricci in the 1982 volume of *Annales* has indeed the subtitle 'Entre l'histoire des idées et l'histoire sociale'.[29] I suppose the classic example of this kind of work—constructing social history from church records—is Le Roy Ladurie's famous *Montaillou* based on the inquisito-

---

[27] Knut Nörr, *Kirche und Konzil bei Nicolaus de Tudeschis (Panormitanus)* (Köln-Graz, 1964); Hermann Schuessler, 'Sacred doctrine and the authority of Scripture in canonistic thought on the eve of the Reformation': *Reform and authority* (n. 10 supra) 55-68.

[28] Schuessler, 'Sacred doctrine' 65.

[29] Giovanni Ricci, 'Naissance du pauvre honteux: entre l'histoire des idées et l'histoire sociale', AESC 38 (1982) 158-77.

rial records of Jacques Fournier. It seems to me a major work of historical imagination—I will not say of historical fiction, though it does need
to be read with the cautions suggested by Leonard Boyle and others.

In beginning to discuss social history, I am moving into an area
where I have little specialist expertise so I hope those of you who have
worked in this field will supplement what I have to say later on. Even to
an amateur it is obvious that the topics which have most interested medieval canonists and their modern historians are the inevitable ones—money and sex. Or, to put it more formally, economic affairs and marital
relations (and extra-marital relations of course).

In the economic sphere much work continues to appear on the
theory and practice of poor relief. When I worked on this subject many
years ago it seemed to me that here again we encounter a paradigmatic
structure of thought worked out in the twelfth and thirteenth centuries
which was no longer really applicable to the actual circumstances of the
later Middle Ages.[30] And much of the most recent work has been devoted
to exploring the necessary changes that were made in various cities and
regions during the early modern period. For the Middle Ages as a whole,
Michel Mollat, who has contributed so much in this field, has provided a
brief overview in *Les pauvres au Moyen Age* with a good bibliography,
especially of works in French.[31] An interesting recent article from the
point of view of methodology is the one I have just mentioned, by Giovanni Ricci, 'Naissance du pauvre honteux', which deals with the problem of a respectable person who falls into want and is ashamed of his
poverty. Ricci reviews the earlier canonistic literature on this topic and
then shows how changing social realities in the later Middle Ages led to
a new concern with the problem in the actual functioning of charitable
institutions.

In areas like usury and the just price, an earlier group of scholars
—e.g. De Roover, Schumpeter and Sapori—showed that many concepts
of classical economics had their origins in medieval scholasticism. No
one nowadays will doubt the creativity of medieval writers in this field,
but here too new doubts and difficulties were arising in the fifteenth century. There is a good account of the earlier scholarship in an article of
Julius Kirshner in *Annales* for 1975 [32] and I have found that Kirshner's

---

[30] Brian Tierney, *Medieval poor law. A sketch of canonical theory and its application in England* (Berkeley-Los Angeles 1959).

[31] Michel Mollat, *Les pauvres au Moyen Age. Etude sociale* (Paris 1978).

[32] Julius Kirshner, 'Les travaux de Raymond de Roover sur la pensée économique
des scholastiques', AESC 30 (1975) 318-38.

subsequent articles provide a most helpful introduction to current problems and recent literature in the field. Much of it deals with figures like San Bernardino and Sant'Antonino and Angelo de Chiavassio, influential moralists who were at home with both law and theology; and, again, the most interesting recent work deals not just with abstract doctrine but with the interplay between theory and practice. Let us take a recent monograph of Kirshner to illustrate the kind of themes that arise. It is called, 'Pursuing honor while avoiding sin,' and it deals with the Monte delle Doti of Florence.[33] The Monte delle Doti was a public investment fund intended to provide for future dowries. A father who invested 100 fl. at the birth of a daughter was promised 500 fl. in fifteen years time when the girl was approaching marriageable age. This works out to a very high rate of interest; so naturally there was a catch. If the girl died, the father's investment reverted to the commune. In 1433, however, this rule was changed—the investment reverted to the girl's father or brother —and the interest rate was raised still higher. This made the Monte a very attractive and popular investment vehicle; unfortunately it became increasingly difficult for the fund to meet its obligations and finally, in 1488, it was declared insolvent.

The interesting thing for us about this case is the controversial literature it evoked and the variety of issues involved—marriage, dowry, honor, usury, public finance. San Bernardino and Sant'Antonino both condemned the Monte, though on different moral grounds apparently. Sant' Antonino seems to have thought that it was too risky and San Bernardino that it was not risky enough. Angelo de Chiavassio, author of the very popular *Summa angelica*, first condemned the fund, then changed his mind and wrote a lengthy *consilium* in favor of it. In all these writings we find again a fusion of law and theology; and again it is symptomatic that the fusion did not lead to any generally agreed solution within an accepted paradigm. On the contrary, as Kirshner writes, 'By the end of the fifteenth century the *forum internum* was teeming with conflicting judicial counsel'.[34] The uncertainty, the uneasiness I spoke of was not limited to academia. If an ordinary person went to confession to find out whether he was committing sin and on the road to hell, the answer he

---

[33] *Pursuing honor while avoiding sin. The Monte delle Doti of Florence* (Quaderni di Studi senesi, 41; 1978). For a related article, with references to more recent work, see Kirshner's 'Storm over the Monte Commune: genesis of the moral controversy over the public debt of Florence', AFP 53 (1983) 219-76.
[34] *Pursuing honor* 58. Kirshner adds: '... few citizens, even those capable of cauterizing self-criticism, could be confident that they had avoided sin'.

got would depend on whom his confessor had been reading lately. It must have been tiresome in an age when everyone really believed in hell. Although canon law sources are relevant for every aspect of medieval social history the most obvious area where they are quite indispensable is the study of marriage, the family, relations between the sexes. There has been a flood of work in this field in recent years. Among the general surveys one might think first of Foucault and his *History of sexuality*.[35] We don't normally think of Foucault as a practitioner of canonistic studies. And yet he does take as a starting point for his work the theory and practice of the medieval sacrament of penance. Moreover he deploys here his familiar argument about the interplay of knowledge and power. Foucault argues that, over and over again in history, discourse that seems to be concerned with truth or knowledge is really being used as an instrument of power. And in medieval penance he finds a perfect example. He even invents a new hyphenated word 'knowledge-power' (*savoir-pouvoir*). Medieval penance, he writes, was 'a form of knowledge-power'.[36] But he never mentions, nor do the fashionable writers who comment on Foucault, that the concept and the very language itself are rooted in medieval canon law—in Gratian's Decretum in fact. Discussing the power of the keys, Gratian observes—you will remember the phrase—'Not only knowledge is required but also power': *non solum scientia sed etiam potestas*.[37]

There is much more overt reliance on canonistic sources in some of the far-ranging studies of J.L. Flandrin.[38] His writing is typical of much recent work in that it deals not only with marriage but with every aspect of human sexuality—prostitution, rape, impotence, homosexuality, contraception. A good guide to recent work on all these topics is provided by a collection of essays edited by James Brundage and Vern Bullough.[39] On particular topics, the work on homosexuality that has attracted most

---

[35] Michel Foucault, *Histoire de la sexualité. La volonté de savoir* (Paris 1976).
[36] A similar view is expressed in T.N. Tentler, 'The Summa for confessors as an instrument of social control': *The pursuit of holiness*, ed. C. Trinkaus & H. Oberman (Leiden 1975). For further work on the *summae confessorum* see Leonard Boyle, *Pastoral care, clerical education and canon law, 1200-1400* (London 1981).
[37] Dist. 20 dictum ante c.1.
[38] See, most recently, J.L. Flandrin, *Le sexe et l'Occident. Evolution des attitudes et des comportements* (Paris 1981); *Un temps pour embrasser. Aux origines de la morale sexuelle occidentale (6e-11e siècle)* (Paris 1983). Flandrin promises to continue this survey down to the later Middle Ages.
[39] Vern L. Bullough and James Brundage, *Sexual practices and the medieval Church* (Buffalo, N.Y. 1982).

interest, at least in America, is that of John Boswell.[40] Boswell argues that homosexuality was generally tolerated in the Christian world of late antiquity and the early Middle Ages, with a more hostile attitude emerging only from the thirteenth century onward. This is his version of an accepted paradigm breaking down in the late Middle Ages. The book is engaging and genuinely learned but I doubt whether the canonistic references really establish the author's argument. After all, Gratian insisted that homosexuality was even more 'unnatural' than incest.

On contraception, the earlier work of Philip Ariès and others was largely replaced by the standard book of John Noonan. A more recent approach is that of P.P.A. Biller in the journal *Past & Present* for 1982.[41] I mention these particular topics because, apart from the intrinsic importance of the subject matter, such writings on sexuality raise more general problems for a historian of canon law. For instance, argument about the 'unnatural' practices of homosexuality and contraception involves the whole problem of nature as a guide to conduct, with implications for our understanding of all the other varieties of canonistic natural law theory. John Boswell brings out this point very well. Another general problem involved in the handling of this material, is raised by Biller when he discusses Philip Ariès' argument that a *mentalité* favoring contraception could not emerge in a pre-technological society. Ariès thought that he could understand the medieval *mentalité* simply by studying great works of literature. Biller suggests that humbler sources might be more relevant—the *summae confessorum* that were actually read by parish priests who had the task of forming their people's minds on moral questions. And so again we are led back to canonistic materials as valuable sources for social history.

This is most especially true as regards the central institution of marriage itself. The development of canonistic doctrine on matrimony was well worked out by earlier scholars like Dauvillier, Esmein, and Le Bras. Recent work has been concerned mainly with actual practice in local church courts—e.g. Helmholz and Sheehan for England, Gottlieb and Lefebvre-Teillard for France, Rudolf Weigand for Germany.[42] Here again

---

[40] John Boswell, *Christianity, social tolerance and homosexuality* (Chicago 1980).

[41] P.P.A. Biller, 'Birth control in the West in the thirteenth and early fourteenth centuries', *Past & Present* 94 (1982) 3-26. This is mainly a review article discussing the work of Ariès, Noonan, Flandrin, Herlihy and others.

[42] Richard Helmholz, *Marriage litigation in medieval England* (Cambridge 1974); M.M. Sheehan, 'The formation and stability of marriage in fourteenth-century England:

we might interpret the records as evidence of growing tensions within an accepted paradigm. In principle, for instance, marriages were indissoluble but Lefebvre-Teillard points out that the rule was surprisingly easy to evade. In the nature of things, when we investigate court records we are dealing with exceptions rather than the norm, but the exceptions seem to have been very numerous. Many problems arose out of the canonistic doctrine of consent. You will remember how the doctrine developed in the twelfth century. A binding, sacramental marriage was constituted by simple exchange of consent between two parties without any other formalities. The only qualification was that the words exchanged had to be words of present consent (*de presenti*). Words referring to the future created only a betrothal. Now this might seem a fine illustration of a twelfth-century paradigm—a paradigm that has been called humanism. In many spheres of life there was a new emphasis on individual human personality, individual will, individual conscience—and marriage by the sole uncoerced consent of two individuals fits into the pattern beautifully. But it gave rise to grievous difficulties in practice. The problem was that, although canon law condemned secret marriages, it recognized them as valid if they occurred. Beatrice Gottlieb regarded this as a great paradox —that a marriage could be valid although illicit. Yet this situation arises often enough in sacramental doctrine. The real paradox was that the canonists had invented a form of marriage which of its nature could not be canonically proved. Two witnesses were required to establish a question of fact. But if a couple disagreed about whether a marriage had taken place secretly and one party sought to prove it in court, in the nature of things there could not be two witnesses. Gratian saw this difficulty and the Ordinary Gloss commented that the judge had to decide according to the rules of law, not according to his conscience.[43] Probably many valid marriages were set aside for want of proof. If the partners then married other spouses their marriages were canonically valid but invalid before God. Or again, a partner in a long-established marriage might seek an annulment on the ground that he had previously contracted an informal

---

Evidence of an Ely register', *Mediaeval studies* 33 (1971) 228-63; Beatrice Gottlieb, 'The meaning of clandestine marriage': *Family and sexuality in French history*, ed. R. Wheaton & T.K. Hareven (Philadelphia 1980) 49-83; Anne Lefebvre-Teillard, 'Règle et réalité dans le droit matrimonial à la fin du Moyen-Age', RDC 30 (1980) 41-54; Rudolf Weigand, 'Zur mittelalterlichen kirchlichen Ehegerichtsbarkeit. Rechtsvergleichende Untersuchung', ZRG Kan. Abt. 67 (1981) 213-47.

[43] Gloss to C.30 q.5 dictum post c.9.

clandestine marriage. This is not mere hypothesis. Many such cases came before the courts. Lefebvre-Teillard found that the most common ground alleged in nullity cases was a previous clandestine marriage, and Helmholz found the same situation in England. The difficulties of proof in such cases were horrendous. So it might turn out that the judge would order a couple who were not really married to live together—actually in adultery; or he might separate a couple who were in fact really married. There was no agreement as to what precise words created a marriage bond. If a man said 'I take you as my wife', that was clear enough. But what if he said, *Volo*: 'I want to take you as my wife.'? Was that *de presenti* or *de futuro*? The canonists disagreed. And of course often the language that lovers used was quite informal. Helmholz cites this exchange from a Canterbury court record. 'She said to him ... «There is no man in the world I love more.» And he said, «I am grateful to you. And I love you»'.[44] This is from a suit for enforcement of a marriage contract. Were they really married? Who can tell?

Moreover it was not enough simply to determine what words were used. Angelo de Chiavassio muddied the waters further. 'If both parties had the intention of contracting *de presenti* there will always be a marriage even if the words sounded like *de futuro*'.[45] This is getting us to the border of linguistic philosophy, and indeed Helmholz found it helpful to quote J.L. Austin on 'performative' speech acts at one point. How could one be sure of the precise intention behind hasty, perhaps half-forgotten words of love spoken years before without any knowledge of canonistic subtleties? Some of the cases that came before the courts involved perjury and collusion but many were based on genuine doubt about an existing marriage. To all the uncertainties spawned by late medieval canon law—in an age that hungered for certainty, hungered for truth—we may add this final one. Many couples all over the Christian world may have been uncertain whether they were actually married or not.

It could not last of course. Marriage law was reformed at the Council of Trent for Catholics and, in different ways, for all the new Protestant groups of the sixteenth century.[46] And this leads on to my final observation. At the outset I tried to avoid a simplistic picture of the late Middle

---

[44] Helmholz, *Marriage litigation* 7.

[45] Cited in Gottlieb, 'The meaning of clandestine marriage' 78 n. 38.

[46] Charles Donahue has pointed out to me that the canonical form of marriage by present consent persisted in England until the eighteenth century and eventually gave rise to the form of common law marriage still recognized in a few American states.

Ages as simply an era of gloom and doom or as one of unfettered progress. It was an era of great tensions. But the tensions, the uncertainties of the age did not lead on to continuing decay but to reform, to a new world of thought and action and farflung adventure. A paradigmatic change in human culture is not necessarily a change for the worse—though some obdurate medievalists still may think this one was. But there is a further point that may encourage even them. A new paradigm does not abandon all the content of the old one; rather the new assimilates the old and uses it in fresh ways. Our late medieval canon law did not cease to exist somewhere around 1500. It lived on in the early modern world, most obviously in the great Spanish school of jurist-theologians, but in many other milieux too, adapted to the different purposes of a new age. Some elements of canonistic ecclesiology survived in French Gallicanism, some in counter-Reformation papalism and some even in Protestantism. Luther burned the canon law but he quoted Panormitanus. Canonistic conciliar thought influenced Calvinist political theory. Canonistic economic doctrines influenced all the major thinkers, Catholic and Protestant, of the new age. However we choose to evaluate the changes in the transition from medieval to modern civilization, we shall never understand those changes unless we learn to study with some sympathy and insight those vast, elephantine works of our late medieval canon lawyers.

VIII

"TRIA QUIPPE DISTINGUIT IUDICIA . . ." A NOTE ON INNOCENT III'S DECRETAL *PER VENERABILEM*

IN 1202 Count William of Montpellier persuaded the archbishop of Arles to intercede with the pope concerning the legitimization of the count's bastard children. It was not that he wanted his boys to be eligible to become priests, the usual reason for a papal dispensation *ex defectu natalium*; the count was anxious that his children should enjoy all the rights of legitimate offspring in the temporal sphere as well. Pope Innocent III had recently granted this privilege to the children of King Philip II by Agnes de Meran, and Count William hoped to obtain a similar favor.

The pope refused this request. He had just reached an agreement with Philip about the king's matrimonial difficulties and no doubt did not wish to provoke him anew by an officious intervention in a case that evidently pertained to the royal jurisdiction. But Innocent III was not content to leave the matter at that. He wanted there to be no doubt that the pope did have extensive powers in secular affairs even though he was not choosing to exercise them in this particular case. Hence his reply to Count William was cast in the form of the famous decretal *Per Venerabilem*[1] in which Innocent took advantage of this relatively trivial occasion to inject into the mainstream of mediaeval canon law a series of far-reaching pronouncements concerning the juridical rights of the pope in secular disputes. The decretal was included first in the unofficial compilation of Alanus[2] and then in the officially promulgated collection of canons known as the *Compilatio Tertia*.[3] Innocent ensured that no jot or tittle of his carefully chosen terminology should pass into oblivion or lack adequate canonistic exegesis when he sent a copy of this compilation to the university of Bologna with instructions that henceforward it was to be used "tam in iudiciis quam in scholis."[4] The pope's phrases were indeed discussed eagerly in the schools by generations of mediaeval canonists; more recently their implications have been debated with almost equal vigor by modern historians.

[1] Potthast 1794; Migne, *Patrologia Latina*, ccxiv, 1130–1134. A somewhat abbreviated version of *Per Venerabilem* was included in Gregory IX's *Liber Extra* (*X*) at 4.17.13. (We have used the edition of Lyons, 1624, which included the *Glossa Ordinaria* of Bernardus Parmensis together with some interpolations from later canonists.) The text of the decretal was also printed in W. Molitor, *Die Dekretale Per Venerabilem Innocenz III. und ihre Stellung im öffentlichen Recht der Kirche* (Münster, 1876), pp. 243–247.

[2] *Collectio Alani* 4.12.2. Cf. R. von Heckel, "Die Dekretalensammlungen des Gilbertus und Alanus nach den Weingärtener Handschriften," *Zeitschrift der Savigny-Stiftung für Rechtsgeschichte, Kanonistische Abteilung*, xxix (1940), 116–357, and S. Kuttner, "The Collection of Alanus: A Concordance of Its Two Recensions," *Rivista di Storia del Diritto*, xxvi (1953), 37–53.

[3] *Compilatio Tertia* 4.12.2 in *Quinque Compilationes Antiquae* ed. E. Friedberg (Leipzig, 1882), p. 128. The manuscripts of the *Compilatio Tertia* and its glosses cited below are listed in S. Kuttner, *Repertorium der Kanonistik* (Vatican City, 1937), pp. 355–368.

[4] Friedberg, *Quinque Compilationes*, p. 105.

The decretal was full of meat. Innocent's apparently innocuous, incidental comment that the king of France recognised no temporal superior provided a canonical basis for a whole theory of the independence of national kingdoms from the empire, which in turn has given rise to an elaborate controversy among modern historians about the origins of national sovereignty in Europe.[5] As for the immediate occasion of the letter, the pope held that authority to legitimize for spiritual functions necessarily included a capacity to legitimize in the temporal sphere as well "because for spiritualities greater care and authority and worthiness are required." This also gave rise to an important canonical controversy.[6] But the greatest significance of the decretal for students of mediaeval political theory lies in the fact that, having made these points and having protested that he had no wish to usurp the jurisdiction of another, Innocent went on to give a more general explanation of the pope's right to intervene in secular affairs:

Rationibus igitur his inductis regi gratiam fecimus requisiti, causam tam ex veteri quam ex novo Testamento trahentes quod non solum in ecclesie patrimonio (super quo plenam temporalibus gerimus potestatem) verumetiam in aliis regionibus, certis causis inspectis, temporalem iurisdictionem casualiter exercemus.[7]

The Old Testament proof was a passage from Deuteronomy (xvii. 8–12) "If thou perceive that there be among you a hard and doubtful matter in judgment between blood and blood, cause and cause, leprosy and leprosy; and thou see that the words of the judges within thy gates do vary: arise and go up to the place which the Lord thy God shall choose. And thou shalt come to the priests of the Levitical race and to the judge that shall be at that time . . . And thou shalt do whatsoever they shall say." The New Testament was cited (Matthew xvi. 19, "Whatsoever thou shalt bind on earth it shall be bound in heaven") to demonstrate that in the new dispensation the apostolic see was evidently the "chosen place" of God, and the pope himself the judge who presided there. And so Innocent reached his conclusion:

Tria quippe distinguit iudicia: Primum inter sanguinem et sanguinem, per quod criminale intelligitur, et civile. Ultimum inter lepram et lepram per quod Ecclesiasticum, et criminale notatur. Medium inter causam et causam, quod ad utrumque refertur, tam Ecclesiasticum quam civile; in quibus cum aliquid fuerit difficile, vel ambiguum, ad iudicium est Sedis apostolicae referendum: cuius sententiam qui superbiens contempserit observare, mori praecipitur, id est per excommunicationis sententiam velut mortuus a communione fidelium separari.[8]

---

[5] On this controversy see "Some Recent Works on the Political Theories of the Medieval Canonists," *Traditio*, x (1954), 594–624, and most recently, F. Calasso, *I glossatori e la teoria della sovranità*, 3rd ed. (Milan, 1957).

[6] " . . . cum maior in spiritualibus tam providentia quam auctoritas et idoneitas requiratur. . . . " For the canonists' discussions on this point see Molitor, *op. cit.*, pp. 11–18, W. Ullmann, *Medieval Papalism* (London, 1949), pp. 105–106, S. Mochi Onory, *Fonti canonistiche dell'idea moderna dello stato* (Milan, 1951), pp. 209–214.

[7] X. 4. 17. 13; Migne, *PL*, ccxiv, 1132.

[8] X. 4.17.13; Migne, *PL*, ccxiv, 1133. A. Hof called attention to the similarity between Innocent's claim here and the appellate jurisdiction attributed to the emperor in Roman law, " 'Plenitudo potestatis' und 'Imitatio imperii' zur Zeit Innocenz III," *Zeitschrift für Kirchengeschichte*, lxvi (1954–55), 39–71 at 64.

The interpretation of this passage is of crucial importance for the whole much-controverted question whether Pope Innocent III was essentially "dualistic" or "hierocratic" in his theory of the relations of church and state. It was already well established that in the strictly ecclesiastical sphere all "hard and doubtful matters," the so-called *causae arduae*, were to be referred to the apostolic see for decision. The question is whether Innocent was simply extending that claim to the sphere of secular jurisdiction or whether his words were intended to convey some other meaning. It happens that the two outstandingly superior textbooks on mediaeval political theory in current use offer distorted interpretations of the pope's words and that the distortion has not been discussed, nor the passage adequately analysed in any of the recent specialist works on Innocent's political theory. A note of correction therefore seems in order.

A. J. Carlyle saw in *Per Venerabilem* only a claim that "in cases of conflict between the spiritual and temporal jurisdiction, the spiritual power is to decide."[9] C. H. McIlwain similarly supposed that the "third judgment" referred only to those matters that were "in the first instance concurrently within the jurisdiction of both temporal and spiritual courts." With his usual discernment, however, McIlwain added that this was not the only possible interpretation of the passage. "If the words 'in these' . . . refer back to all three kinds of jurisdiction, then the interpretation above is wrong, and Innocent IV later added practically nothing to the claim of his predecessor."[10]

Innocent III's grouping of clauses does suggest that he intended the "in quibus" to refer particularly to the third type of judgment. But it seems quite certain that he did not intend to exclude the first two types of cases from papal jurisdiction, and there can be no reasonable doubt that, in the third class of cases, he intended to include all lawsuits, whether ecclesiastical or secular, and not merely those cases that had an ecclesiastical as well as a secular aspect.

As to the first point, one has only to consider the nature of the first two types of judgment. One of them was "ecclesiasticum et criminale." That is to say it had reference to criminal cases that fell within the jurisdiction of the spiritual courts, such as heresy or sacrilege. Obviously the pope was not intending to exclude himself from the role of judging such cases; the very essence of the papal position was to be supreme judge, *iudex ordinarius omnium*, at least in spiritualities. The other class of criminal cases mentioned, "inter sanguinem et sanguinem," was defined as "criminale . . . et civile." That is to say it referred to crimes like murder or assault normally cognizable before a secular judge. But Innocent could not have intended to exclude matters of this kind from the sphere of papal judgment for, in the decretal *Novit* (1204), he explicitly claimed the right to intervene in such

---

[9] R. W. and A. J. Carlyle, *A History of Mediaeval Political Theory in the West*, II (London, 1909), 233. Cf *ibid.*, p. 232, "[Innocent] urges that the Pope occupies the position of the priest in the Deuteronomic legislation, and that this principle applies especially to those cases where there is any uncertainty whether the matter belongs to the ecclesiastical or the secular authority."

[10] C. H. McIlwain, *The Growth of Political Thought in the West* (New York, 1932), p. 232, n. 1. F. Kempf regarded the third judgment as referring to mixed cases but took it for granted that the *in quibus* referred back to all three kinds of judgment, *Papsttum und Kaisertum bei Innocenz III* (Rome, 1954), p. 258.

cases *ratione peccati*. A crime of violence was also a sin, and all cases involving sin pertained to the papal jurisdiction according to Innocent.[11] The ambiguous definition of the third class of cases ("inter causam et causam quod ad utrumque refertur tam ecclesiasticum quam civile") offers greater difficulties of interpretation. The first argument against the view of Carlyle and McIlwain that Innocent's words referred only to cases where the spiritual and temporal jurisdictions overlapped is an *argumentum ex silentio*. It did not occur to any contemporary canonist that the pope's phrases could possibly have the meaning attributed to them by the modern historians. The point is of some significance, for several of the early commentaries on the *Compilatio Tertia* were written by canonists who are known as convinced dualists, e.g., Laurentius Hispanus, Vincentius Hispanus, and Johanes Teutonicus. These men were all interested in defending the essential autonomy of the secular power against the hierocratic views of contemporaries like Alanus and Tancred who maintained that supreme spiritual and temporal power were united in the pope. If Innocent's words could have meant to a contemporary merely that the pope was claiming jurisdiction when some "ambiguity" arose concerning a case which was "concurrently within the jurisdiction of both spiritual and temporal courts," either Laurentius or Vincentius or Johannes would have been delighted to point out the fact. None of them did so. Laurentius, the only one who referred specifically to the words of Deuteronomy in his glosses on *Per Venerabilem*, did maintain that the text was not necessarily a vindication of Alanus's extreme hierocratic doctrine of papal power, but he adopted a different line of argument to establish his point.

Regionibus. Scilicet cum requirimur et hoc probat auctoritate deuteronomi cum scilicet variatum est inter iudices, arg. supra, *de foro comp. Licet.* la.

Usurpare. Immo licet ex certis causis. Non ideo ordinarius quo ad temporalia, arg. supra, *de officio ordinarii, Pastoralis* §*Ex parte*. la.[12]

[11] Potthast 2181; Migne *PL*, ccxv, 325-328; *Comp. III*, 2.1.3; *X*. 2.1.3. "We do not intend to judge concerning a fief . . . but concerning sin, the judgment of which undoubtedly belongs to us . . . Now we can proceed in this fashion against any criminal sin to recall the sinner from vice to virtue, from error to truth, but especially so when it is a sin against the peace which is the bond of charity." In canonical discussions of the pope's right to judge secular suits the *ratio criminis* was always mentioned as one ground justifying such action. Cf. *infra*, p. 52.

[12] Cited by Vincentius Hispanus, *Apparatus ad Comp. III*, MS. Melk 333, fol. 227rb (with the siglum la [urentius]). The glosses occur in garbled form in the mixed apparatus of Karlsruhe Aug. XL, fol. 208va and were also cited by Bernardus Parmensis in his *Glossa Ordinaria ad X*. 4.17.13 s.v. *Certis causis*. For the glosses on *Per Venerabilem* in the so-called Laurentius apparatus to the *Comp. III* see F. Gillmann, *Des Laurentius Hispanus Apparat zur Compilatio III* (Mainz 1935). The dispute concerning the authorship of this apparatus and of the other glosses attributed to Laurentius by later canonists is not of the first importance for our argument. (The relevant literature is cited by A. M. Stickler, "Laurent d'Espagne," *Dictionnaire de droit canonique*, vi (1955), col. 364.) The point is that, so far as we know, none of the early glossators of *Per Venerabilem* thought it possible to extract a dualistic significance from the sentence beginning "Tria quippe distinguit iudicia." Those of them who did adhere to the dualist position preferred to concentrate on the earlier part of the decretal, arguing that the claim to legitimize did not in itself constitute an assertion of direct temporal power. See, e.g., the glosses cited by Gaines Post, "Some Unpublished Glosses on the Translatio Imperii and the Two Swords," *Archiv für katholisches Kirchenrecht*, cxvii (1937), 403-429 at p. 428 and those referred to *supra*, n. 6.

52   *Innocent III's Decretal* Per Venerabilem

The distinction Laurentius made was not between secular cases and mixed cases but between appellate jurisdiction and ordinary jurisdiction. Alanus, on the other hand, maintained that the pope was "iudex ordinarius . . . et quoad spiritualia et quoad temporalia."[13]

The argument that ecclesiastical courts could exercise jurisdiction in mixed cases (the so-called *ratio connexitatis*) was, of course, not unfamiliar to canonists of the early thirteenth century. Indeed one may doubt whether Innocent would have thought it necessary to invoke Peter and Paul and an Old Testament prophet to establish such a relatively modest claim. We can demonstrate further that he conveyed a different meaning to contemporaries by considering some comments on the *ratio connexitatis* itself. From about 1215 onwards it became a common practice among the decretalists to present lengthy lists of all the cases in which papal jurisdiction could be exercised in the temporal sphere. Such lists invariably mentioned the *ratio connexitatis* and they invariably mentioned the decretal *Per Venerabilem*. But they did not cite *Per Venerabilem* in support of the claim to jurisdiction *ratione connexitatis;* it was always cited as the basis of a quite different claim. Thus Tancred wrote (citing Laurentius in the first part of his gloss):

This is one case in which the ecclesiastical judge can concern himself with matters of secular jurisdiction, namely when no superior is to be found. Another is when the secular judge neglects to render judgment or do justice. A third is when any matter is difficult and ambiguous and the judges differ, as below in the title *Qui filii sint legitimi, Per venerabilem.* La(urentius). Fourth, when it is a matter of land subject to the jurisdiction of the church. . . . Fifth, if it is according to custom . . . . Sixth, in all ecclesiastical crimes . . . . Seventh, when any case is referred to the church through denunciation by reason of crime, as above in the previous title, *Novit.* Eighth, when the secular judge is suspect and accused . . . . Ninth is the reason of connection, for an ecclesiastical judge can judge concerning dowry by reason of the fact that he has jurisdiction in matrimonial cases, as above in the title *De dote post divortium, De prudentia.*[14]

[13] Gloss *ad Comp.* I, 2.20.7, MS. Karlsruhe Aug. XL, fol. 13vb. This famous text was first printed by J. F. von Schulte in *Sitzungsberichte der kaiserlichen Akademie der Wissenschaften in Wien, philos. hist. Klasse*, LXVI (1870), 89. It has been frequently cited in more recent works. Alanus's comment on *Per Venerabilem* itself expressed the same outlook, " . . . secundum nos Papa super principem est etiam in temporalibus et ideo habet potestatem legitimandi quoad actus seculares," MS. Vercelli 89, fol. 108va cited by A. M. Stickler, "Sacerdozio e regno nelle nuove ricerche," *Miscellanea Historiae Pontificiae*, XVIII (1953), 1–26 at p. 23. The most recent discussion of Alanus's political theory is also by Stickler, "Alanus Anglicus als Verteidiger des monarchischen Papsttums," *Salesianum*, XXI (1959), 346–406. This article presents a valuable analysis of the two recensions of Alanus's apparatus, *Ius Naturale*.

[14] "Iste est ergo unus casus in quo iudex ecclesiasticus potest se immiscere seculari iurisdictioni, scl. cum superior non invenitur. Alius est, cum iudex secularis negligit iudicium vel iustitiam facere ut J. c. prox.; ar. XXIII q. iv, administratores. Tertius cum aliquid fuerit ambiguum et difficile et variatur inter iudices: J. qui filii sint legit., per venerabilem la. § quartus, cum est de terra supposita iurisdictioni ecclesie. . . . Quintus, si est de consuetudine. . . . Sextus in omni crimine ecclesiastico. . . . Septimus, cum per denuntiationem ratione criminis aliqua causa ad ecclesiam defertur, ut S. tit. prox., novit. Octavus, cum iudex secularis est suspectus et recusatur. . . . Nonus est ratio connexitatis, quia potest iudex ecclesie iudicare de dote, ex quo cognoscit de matrimonio ut S. de dote post divortium, de prudentia" (*Apparatus ad Comp. II*, 2.1.3, MS. Vat. lat. 2509, cited by Stickler, "Sacerdozio e regno," p. 24). The first part of the gloss, attributed by Tancred to Laurentius, occurs separately in MS. Karlsruhe Aug. XL, fol. 152va.

This gloss was copied with little variation by Goffredus Tranensis and Bernardus Parmensis, and its substance repeated by Innocent IV and Hostiensis.[15] Each of them cited the decretal *De Prudentia* on the law of dowry to illustrate the *ratio connexitatis*, while each cited *Per Venerabilem* in support of the much more vague and far-reaching claim to a jurisdiction in secular cases whenever the issues proved "ambiguous" or "difficult" or when the judges were at odds with one another.

Finally, when the canonists did come to gloss in detail the words "Tria quippe distinguit iudicia" their interpretations regularly explained the third judgment as referring to cases which were *either* secular *or* spiritual, not both secular and spiritual at the same time. Innocent IV described the three judgments in this fashion:

Sanguinem. A judgment is between blood and blood when the accuser says it is proved that the defendant has shed blood, that is, has committted any civil crime, let us say homicide, adultery, theft or anything of that sort. *Inter lepram et lepram.* When the accuser says, "You are infected with the leprosy of heresy," that is, with any ecclesiastical crime, let us say simony, sacrilege, or anything similar, and the accused denies it. *Inter causam et causam.* When the plaintiff says, "You owe me [a sum] from a loan or contract," or some similar civil action. Or, again, [when the plaintiff says] "You are bound to pay tithes to me" or "I have the right of patronage in this church," or some similar civil and ecclesiastical action, but the defendant denies it. For in all these matters, if anything shall be difficult or ambiguous recourse is to be had to the apostolic see.[16]

There were thus really four types of cases involved — criminal actions which could be either ecclesiastical or secular, and civil actions which could likewise be divided into ecclesiastical cases or secular cases. The lack of symmetry in Innocent III's exposition in which both types of civil suit were lumped together under one heading arose simply from the structure of the text of Deuteronomy that he was expounding.

Hostiensis and Abbas Antiquus reproduced almost verbatim the comment of Innocent IV and a very similar explanation was given by Boatinus Mantuanus.[17]

---

[15] Goffredus Tranensis, *Apparatus ad X.* 2.2.10, MS. Vienna, Staatsbibliothek 2197, fol. 35ra; Bernardus Parmensis, *Glossa Ordinaria ad X.* 2.2.10; Innocent IV, *Commentaria in V Libros Decretalium* (Venice, 1570), ad X. 2.2.10, p. 238; Hostiensis, *Summa Aurea* (Lyons, 1568), ad X. 2.2, fol. 107va.

[16] "*Sanguinem.* Inter sanguinem et sanguinem iudicium variatur cum accusator dicit probatum est quod reus sanguinem fudit, id est aliquod crimen civile commisit, puta homicidium, adulterium, furtum vel aliquod aliud simile. *Inter lepram et lepram,* cum accusator dicit, infectus es lepra haeresis, id est aliquo crimine ecclesiastico, puta simonia, sacrilegio vel consimili et accusatus negat. *Inter causam et causam,* cum actor dicit, teneris mihi in centum ex mutuo vel commodato vel consimili civili actione, vel etiam, teneris mihi ad decimas praestandas vel habeo iuspatronatus in hac ecclesia vel alia consimili actione civile et ecclesiastica, reus autem negat; nam in his omnibus, si quid difficile vel ambiguum fuerit ad sedem apostolicam recurrendum est . . . ." (*Commentaria ad X.* 4.17.13, p. 574).

[17] Hostiensis, *Commentaria ad X.* 4.17.13 (interpolated in *Glossa Ordinaria,* ed. *cit.* col. 1544); Abbas Antiquus, MS. Vatican Borgh. 231, fol. 115va; Boatinus Mantuanus, MS. Vienna, Staatsbibliothek 2113, fol. 126va. "*Per quod criminale intelligitur et ciuile* i.e. crimen ciuile ut si dicatur, tu sanguinem exegisti et probetur et reus negat. Si de hoc dubitetur recurrendum est etc. *Per quod ecclesiasticum et criminale notatur* i.e. crimen ecclesiasticum ut heresis, symonia etc., ut si quis dicat se probasse aliquem esse hereticum et reus negat et de hoc dubitetur recurrendum est etc. *Ad utrumque refertur tam ecclesiasticum quam ciuile,* ecclesiasticum ut si agatur de decimis et de hoc dubitetur,

I do not think that there can be any question here of a "hierocratic" distortion of Innocent III's original meaning. No other meaning had been suggested. The mid-thirteenth-century canonists were merely giving concrete examples to illustrate an interpretation that had been taken for granted by their predecessors.[18] The principal reason why a modern reader might suppose that the third type of jurisdiction was intended to apply only to mixed cases lies in the fact that the immediate occasion of the decretal was a matter of legitimization, which did fall into this category. But, in the paragraph that we have been considering, Innocent III had turned aside from the issue of Count William's offspring to offer some general observations about the nature and extent of papal jurisdiction. It was not the habit of the canonists to relate such observations solely to the subject matter of the decretal in which they occurred; rather they sought to educe from them general rules of law, as in the comments of Tancred just cited. Innocent III himself was of course well aware of this decretalist technique. In general, it seems to me, the argument that Innocent's true meanings were misunderstood or distorted by the canonists of the next generation should be viewed with extreme caution. The pope was himself a trained canonist and a legislator of genius. He knew exactly what legal implications the canonists would find in the terms he chose to use, and we must surely suppose that he had a shrewd understanding of the effects they were likely to have on the long-range growth of canonical thought.[19]

---

ciuile ut si probaui quod debes mihi X et tu negas et de hoc dubitetur, recurrendum est etc." Paulus Hungarus, in his *Notabilia ad Comp. III*, briefly observed that *Per Venerabilem* referred to a three-fold division of legal cases and added that there existed a fourth class of cases known as "mixed," "Nota quod triplex est species causarum, scilicet criminalis, ciuilis et spiritualis . . . . Quarta species est mixta ut matrimonia . . . ." (MS. Melk 333, fol. 226vb). The only canonist I have noticed who used the word "mixed" to describe Innocent's third class of cases is Johannes de Deo in his *Casus ad X. 4.17.13*, MS. Vatican lat. 2343, fol. 46va. "Tertio dicit quid sit inter lepram et lepram et dicit quod est iudicium ecclesiasticum et criminale (et ciuile!), et quid sit inter sanguinem et sanguinem et dicit quod est iudicium criminale et ciuile, et quid sit inter causam et causam et dicit quod mixtum iudicium, scilicet tam ecclesiasticum quam ciuile et qui pape obedire noluerit in predictis per ex-communicationis sententiam condempnatur." This preserves the ambiguity of the decretal itself, but, even in this case, I think the meaning Johannes intended to convey was the same as that of the other canonists cited, i.e., the third judgment was "mixed" in that it referred to both ecclesiastical and to secular cases.

[18] One possible source of misunderstanding lies in the use of the word *civilis* in *Per Venerabilem*. The third class of cases included all "civil suits" (as we should say) as distinct from criminal suits. Innocent III, however, was consistently using the word *civile*, not in opposition to *criminale* but in opposition to *ecclesiasticum*. That is to say he used *civile* as a synonim for *seculare*. Some of the canonists thought it necessary to point this out, e.g., Tancred, *Apparatus ad Comp. III*, 4.12.2, Florence, Laurenziana S. Croce IV sin 2, fol. 223va, s.v. *Civile*, and Bernardus Parmensis, *Glossa Ordinaria ad X. 4.17.13*, s.v. *Civile*. Others, like Paulus Hungarus, cited above, used *civilis* in a different sense to distinguish civil cases from criminal cases. Innocent IV's comment contained both usages, but in an additional gloss on the word *criminali* he made it clear that he had understood Innocent III correctly, "*Criminali*. Idem vult intelligere criminale et civile non diversa . . . " (*Commentaria*, p. 238). This minor confusion of terminology does not seem to indicate any underlying confusion of thought. The much more common canonistic usage was indeed to oppose *civilis* to *criminalis*. Many examples are given by Stickler, "Imperator Vicarius Papae," *Mitteilungen des Instituts für Österreichische Geschichtsforschung*, LXXII (1954), 164–212 at pp. 177–179.

A new period in the study of Innocent's political ideas began with the publication in 1940 of Maccarrone's *Chiesa e stato*, the first work that seriously attempted to analyse his thought within its canonistic framework. Subsequently major contributions by Mochi Onory, Kempf, Stickler, and Tillmann have clarified our understanding of many doubtful points.[20] It seems arguable, however, that all of these writers have been unduly influenced in their exegesis of *Per Venerabilem* by a natural inclination to defend Pope Innocent III against the charge of seeking worldly power as an end in itself. They are anxious, that is to say, to establish that the great pope was not actuated by motives of gross worldly ambition, but that all his interventions in the political sphere were inspired "by motives of a spiritual order" (a favorite phrase of Mochi Onory). Let us acknowledge at once that Innocent's intentions were probably of the best. It is, heaven knows, no mean task to try to build the City of God on earth. But it also remains true that, after his pontificate, many theologians and some popes did become committed to a doctrine of papal temporal power that was repugnant to the consciences (as well as the interests) of most mediaeval princes and prelates, that this papal claim produced a destructive tension in mediaeval Catholicism, and that Innocent III's decretals played a significant part in its development. The problem of whether he had good intentions is one issue, primarily psychological; the problem of what exactly he did claim in the secular sphere is another, primarily canonical. Both are important, but to endeavor to solve the second problem merely on the basis of a conviction about the first leads only to confusion.

This seems especially the fault of Mochi Onory. Above all he failed to see — and this is true of Maccarrone too — that there was a radical difference between a papal claim to exercise indirect power in temporal affairs and a claim to exercise direct power in certain exceptional circumstances which the pope himself undertook to define.[21] It was quite consistent with the dualist theory to emphasise that an exercise of spiritual jurisdiction by the pope might sometimes, indirectly, produce effects in the temporal sphere. A sentence of excommunication launched against a king for some specifically ecclesiastical offense like sacrilege might, for

---

[19] This aspect of Innocent III's legislative activity was well emphasized by L. Buisson, *Potestas und Caritas* (Cologne-Graz, 1958), p. 67.

[20] M. Maccarrone, *Chiesa e stato nella dottrina di papa Innocenzo III* (Rome, 1940); H. Tillmann, *Papst Innocenz III* (Bonn, 1954) and "Zur Frage der Verhältnisses von Kirche und Staat in Lehre und Praxis Papst Innocenz' III," *Deutsches Archiv*, IX (1951), 136–181. The relevant works of Mochi Onory, Kempf, and Stickler are cited *supra*, n. 6, n. 10, n. 13. Kempf also maintained the essential dualism of Innocent III's political theory in "Die päpstliche Gewalt in der mittelalterlichen Welt," *Miscellanea Historiae Pontificiae*, XXI (1959), 117–169 at pp. 139–140. For the views of some other modern historians see A. Walz, "Papstkaiser Innocenz III. Stimmen zur Deutung," *Miscellenea Historiae Pontificiae*, XVIII (1954), 127–138.

[21] Maccarrone, *op. cit.*, pp. 109–110, treated papal jurisdiction *ratione peccati* as essentially similar to the jurisdiction, *certis causis inspectis*, claimed in *Per Venerabilem*, and claimed that neither involved any direct exercise of papal temporal power. Similarly Mochi Onory, *op. cit.*, p. 276, referring to the views of Laurentius, "Sostentore del principio della *iurisdictio divisa*, e del carattere essenzialmente indiretto dell' *auctoritas in temporalibus* del pontifice (. . . *nisi in subsidium, cum secularis est negligens, vel imperio vacat* . . . .)"

example, have political repercussions. But it was surely not consistent with the dualist position for a pope to claim that he could exercise jurisdiction in secular cases whenever the case happened to be a "difficult and ambiguous" one (as was claimed in *Per Venerabilem*) or whenever the temporal judge was negligent or suspect or the office of emperor vacant (as Innocent suggested in the decretal *Licet*):

> Si vacat imperium, si negligit, ambigit, an sit
> Suspectus iudex . . .

as Hostiensis put it, summarising Innocent III's doctrine.[22]

It is hard to see how a pope could claim to judge secular cases even in such circumstances, or to enforce his sentences with coercive sanctions, unless he supposed that the nature of his office was such as to include jurisdiction over the purely temporal issues involved. Helene Tillmann is the only modern writer who has emphasised the important distinction between indirect power and direct power exercised *in certis causis,* but even she obscured its full implications by maintaining that the papal claim was rooted in the medieval doctrine of necessity.[23] Innocent III certainly did know the Roman law tag, "Necessitas legem non habet," and he could have used it as the basis of a claim to temporal jurisdiction in exceptional circumstances. But the fact is that he did not choose to do so. The legal doctrine of necessity, if applied to the transfer of cases between secular and ecclesiastical courts, might have had uncomfortable consequences. It could after all have worked both ways. No thirteenth-century pope would have conceded that the emperor could judge a spiritual case (on the ground that "necessitas legem non habet") whenever the ecclesiastical judges found the matter "difficult and ambiguous" or when the papacy happened to be vacant. Innocent III, therefore, preferred to base his claim on the quite different ground that he was the vicar of one who was a priest after the order of Melchisedech — and Melchisedech was of course both priest and king.[24] On this theory the pope could judge secular cases when he considered it appropriate to do so simply because regal jurisdiction inhered in his office (and, correspondingly, the emperor could not judge spiritual cases because he possessed no spiritual jurisdiction).

Friedrich Kempf avoided this conclusion in his discussion of *Per Venerabilem*

---

[22] Hostiensis *ad X.* 2.2.10 (the decretal *Licet*), interpolated in *Glossa Ordinaria, ed. cit.,* col. 547.

[23] "Zur Frage," p. 139. Kempf referred to Tillmann's distinction but attached little importance to it (*op. cit.,* p. 264, n. 4). In another context he ignored it altogether, "Er übt in diesem Fall wiederum nur *casualiter, certis causis inspectis* seine *potestas indirecta in temporalibus* aus" (p. 279).

[24] "Eius vicarius, qui est Sacerdos in aeternum secundum ordinem Melchisedech, constitutus a Deo Iudex vivorum et mortuorum. Tria quippe distinguit iudicia. . . ." The explanation put forward by Maccarrone of the basis of Innocent's claim seems to me quite unconvincing: " . . . la presente decretale ha come fondamento diritti storici e consuetudinarii. . . . Infatti, come abiamo accenato il principio del ricorso all' autorità ecclesiastica in determinati casi e chiaramente basato sulla legislazione giustinianea. . . ." (*op. cit.,* p. 123). Maccarrone's own preceding exegesis of *Per Venerabilem* emphasized its essentially theological basis. In the decretal *Novit (supra,* n. 11) Innocent did refer to Roman law as a possible basis for the exercise of temporal jurisdiction by the pope, but brushed it aside as irrelevant. "In humility we pass over what Theodosius decreed . . . since we do not depend on any human constitution but rather on divine law, for our power is not from man but from God."

by stressing the voluntary nature of the jurisdiction involved. He did not argue that Innocent was claiming merely *iurisdictio voluntaria* in the most technical sence of that term (as opposed to *iurisdictio contentiosa*)[25] but he did maintain that, in *Per Venerabilem*, Innocent asserted the right to judge a secular case only when all the parties in the case voluntarily selected him as an arbitrator. There seems nothing in the decretal itself to support such a view. Its tone is quite different — "cum aliquid fuerit difficile vel ambiguum ad iudicium est sedis apostolicae recurrendum cuius sententiam qui superbiens contempserit observare mori praecipitur. . . . " Kempf also argued that *Per Venerabilem* must be interpreted in the light of Alexander III's decretal *Cum Sacrosancta*, and so understood in a dualist sense.[26] In this earlier decretal Alexander replied to a series of questions from the archbishop of Rheims. The last one enquired whether an appeal from a secular judge to the pope was valid and the pope replied: " . . . etsi de consuetudine ecclesiae teneat (appellatio), secundum iuris rigorem credimus non tenere." Kempf sees in this a definitive acknowledgment by the papacy of the autonomy of secular jurisdiction. Alexander did not, however, make any pronouncement at all in his decretal on the essentially theological issue of the inherent temporal power which might, or might not, be attributed to the papacy on the basis of such scriptural texts as Matthew xvi. 19. He indicated only that, as a matter of law, there was no adequate basis in the existing canons for a general right of appeal (though the custom of a local church sufficed to make the appeal valid). It was quite open to a future pope, who held on theological grounds that Christ had conferred on the papacy a supreme temporal jurisdiction, to enact such canons as he thought necessary to define the circumstances in which that jurisdiction would in fact be exercised. That is exactly what Innocent III did.

A. M. Stickler has insisted that the very occurrence in canonistic works of lists of "exceptional" cases in which secular jurisdiction would be exercised directly by the pope proves that, even in mid-thirteenth century, the canonists acknowledged in principle the autonomy of the secular power; and he suggested that the presence of such lists in the writings of extreme hierocrats like Tancred and Hostiensis reflects an unresolved tension in their thought.[27] It is true that some dualist writers did hold that the fact of papal jurisdiction in secular cases being exercised

---

[25] This was a possible line of argument. On the specific issue of legitimization Vincentius Hispanus wrote, "Per hoc non probasse iurisdictionem habere temporalem cum legitimare aliquando sit iurisdictionis uoluntarie" (MS. Melk 333, fol. 226v). In Roman and canon law *iurisdictio voluntaria* referred to a fictitious suit where there was no real dispute between the parties (as in cases of manumission or adoption) as opposed to *iurisdictio contentiosa*, where there was a real dispute between the parties. Vincentius did not suggest that the subsequent exegesis of Deuteronomy referred only to cases that fell under the *iurisdictio voluntaria*. Both Molitor (*op cit.*, pp. 59–61) and Kempf (*op. cit.*, pp. 260–262) discussed this point and both came to the conclusion (Kempf reluctantly) that the passage beginning "Tria quippe distinguit iudicia" could not be regarded as referring to *iurisdictio voluntaria* in this technical sense.

[26] Kempf, *op. cit.*, p. 262. Cf. Stickler, "Nuove ricerche," pp. 7–8, "Sacerdozio e regno," p. 14, and "Concerning the Political Theories of the Medieval Canonists," *Traditio*, VII (1949–51) 450–463 at p. 455. The relevant portion of *Cum Sacrosancta* was included in the *Liber Extra* at 2.28.7.

[27] "Sacerdozio e regno," p. 27, "Concerning the Political Theories," pp. 458–460.

only occasionally and in exceptional circumstances constituted an argument in favor of their own point of view. But their position was a very uneasy and illogical one, and it was natural enough that, after a generation's discussion of Innocent III's legislation, a major shift had occurred in canonistic thinking from the prevailing dualism of the late twelfth century to the dominant hierocratism of the mid-thirteenth. As we have argued, some of the "exceptional" cases were consistent with a dualist position, but some were not. On the other hand, the detailed definition of specific cases in which papal jurisdiction would be exercised directly in temporal affairs was entirely consistent with the most extreme hierocratic theories. Any court that claims a supreme appellate jurisdiction needs to define the circumstances in which it will in fact entertain appeals. It is quite possible to possess jurisdiction legitimately without exercising it in all cases; it is not possible to exercise jurisdiction legitimately in any case without possessing it. We may add that the listing of these exceptional cases occurs not only in the works of the canonists (whose technique of presenting scattered comments on a given topic in widely separated contexts could easily lead to inconsistencies) but also in the orderly exposition of the hierocratic theme by a systematic philosopher like Giles of Rome, who evidently saw no inconsistency in this procedure. Giles maintained that all power, spiritual and temporal, was vested in the pope, that sometimes he wielded his temporal authority directly but more commonly permitted it to be exercised by secular rulers. He went on to mention seven specific cases (based on the canonical exceptions) where the pope actually exercised the universal temporal jurisdiction that pertained to his office, one of them being the "hard and doubtful" matter referred to in the decretal *Per Venerabilem*.[28] Once again there is no question here of a hierocratic distortion of the pope's original meaning. Innocent himself had indeed spelled out precisely the same doctrine towards the end of *Per Venerabilem* itself: "Paul also, that he might expound the plenitude of power, wrote to the Corinthians saying 'Do you not know that you shall judge angels? How much more the things of this world.' And so [the pope] is accustomed to exercise the office of secular power sometimes and in some things through himself, sometimes and in some things through others."

Innocent did not consider it appropriate or desirable to exercise his jurisdiction over spiritual affairs and over temporal affairs in precisely same fashion, and he pointed this out in *Per Venerabilem*. In the ecclesiastical sphere he was *iudex ordinarius omnium;* in the temporal sphere he had no intention of burdening the papal curia with a mass of petty feudal litigation that, by legitimate custom, belonged to the courts of secular rulers. He did want to ensure that the temporal jurisdiction of the papacy could be invoked whenever a secular case had political implications involving the peace and good order of Christendom, and his various decretals provided a canonical basis for appeals in all such cases. Again, Innocent did take it for granted that, under the pope, secular rulers had a permanent and necessary role to play in the governance of Christian society, and that this role was a part of the divinely ordered scheme of things. He assumed that two hier-

---

[28] R. Scholz, *Die Publizistick zur Zeit Philipps des Schönen* (Stuttgart, 1903), p. 81.

archies of administration were necessary for the government of the Christian world but, in his view, both hierarchies culminated in the pope. If this constitutes dualism, as some modern students of Innocent's thought seem to suppose, then all the mediaeval popes and all the most papalist of mediaeval theologians were dualists. It did not occur to Innocent III or his successors that it lay within their competence simply to abolish the offices of all secular rulers and themselves assume the exercise of all temporal power. But it also lay quite outside their competence, in the ecclesiastical sphere itself, to abolish the office of bishop and rule all the affairs of the church through papal delegates. Either innovation would have grievously perturbed "the general state of the church," which was not permitted to a pope or any human legislator.[29]

The recent work on Pope Innocent III has been much concerned with relating his ideas to their mediaeval background. This is all to the good. It needs to be emphasised that the theory of papal power he propounded bore little resemblance to modern positivist theories of sovereignty and still less to modern totalitarian theories of despotism. We shall, however, eventually come to a full understanding of Innocent's position, not by minimising his plainly stated claim to temporal power, but by relating that claim to the complex of doctrines concerning natural law, counsel and consent, *status ecclesiae,* and customary rights that mediaeval popes as well as their critics took for granted.

[29] On this see "Pope and Council: Some New Decretist Texts," *Mediaeval Studies,* xix (1957), 197–218, which has references to other recent literature.

IX

Two Anglo-Norman Summae

The *Summa Prima primi* and the *Summa Quamvis leges seculares* were described by Kuttner and Rathbone in 1951 as two intimately related works of the Anglo-Norman school which were deserving of closer examination in future studies. These *summae* were significant, it was pointed out, as introducing a new stage in the literary output of the English schools, a stage marked by the reception of Bernard of Pavia's Breviarium and by a close dependence on Huguccio as the principal guide for the interpretation of the Decretum.[1] The texts

---

[1] S. Kuttner and E. Rathbone, 'Anglo-Norman Canonists of the Twelfth Century,' *Traditio* 7 (1949-1951) 279-358 at 327. Cf. Kuttner, *Repertorium* 204-206.

of the two *summae* have now been transcribed and collated in preparation for an eventual edition. This work makes it possible to explain their relationship to one another and to Huguccio. It also opens up a fresh set of problems concerning the connection between the *Summa Prima primi* and a little-known *Summa Duacensis* in MS Douai 649, fol. 96ra-140vb (*D*).

Prima primi and *Quamvis leges seculares* each occurs in only one manuscript, in London BM Royal 11.D.II, fol. 321ra-332ra (*L*) and Paris, St. Geneviève 342, fol. 185ra-187va (*P*) respectively. In both cases the *summa* is found as a kind of appendix on the last folios of a volume whose contents otherwise consist of the Decretum with glosses.[2] Both *summae* are written in hands of the early thirteenth century. The text in *P* is copied in a non-scribal hand by a writer who had no understanding of the material before him, and it contains innumerable scribal corruptions. *L* presents a far more legible and accurate transcription for the *Prima primi*.[3] This latter work is much the more extensive of the two. It covers the whole of the Decretum except for Causa 1, *De poen.* and *De cons. Quamuis leges seculares* covers only D.1-D.85 and is not complete even for that section of the Decretum. (There is no commentary, e.g. on D.15-24, D.28-30, D.34-37, D.47-49, D.57-60, D.72-73, D.83-84). The use of Huguccio and the Comp. I in both works provides a *terminus a quo* for the two *summae* of *c*.1191. There is no evidence that *P* was composed later than the early 1190's. *L*, on the other hand, cites two decretals of Innocent III promulgated in 1203.[4] An analysis of the contents of the two works suggests a probability that *L* was indeed composed about a decade after *P*.

P opens with the prologue *Quamvis leges seculares* which is not found in *L*. This prologue proves to be closely dependent on that of the *Summa Omnis qui iuste*, a fact which provides further evidence for the English origin of *P*.[5]

Omnis qui iuste	P
...Et *quamuis* ad eam partem *sciencie que in iudiciis* consistit legum secularium pericia plurimum prestat *adminiculum*, ecclesie tamen dei ad statum eius sobrie regendum et incolumnem seruandum iura propria sufficiunt...	*Quamuis* leges seculares illi *scientie que in iuditio* uersatur non modicum afferant *adminiculum*, in forma tamen iudicii ab eo uidetur accepisse principium qui in principio creauit celum et terram...
Primam namque animaduersionis sententiam dominus protulit cum *in initio creature humane primorum parentum culpas districtius*	Per factum enim domini forma incepit iudicii qui <*in*> *initio humane creature primorum parentum culpa<s> districtius re-*

---

[2] *L* has the *Glossa ordinaria* in the recension of Bartholomaeus Brixiensis (*Repertorium* 106). The gloss composition in *P* combines glosses of the Huguccio period with younger materials. Cf. Kuttner, 'Bernardus Compostellanus Antiquus,' *Traditio* 1 (1943) 277-340 at 286.

[3] There is a change of hand in *L* at fol. 329ra line 61.

[4] Fol. 327vb: 'Tenet enim appellatio... nisi hoc hodie immutatum sit ab innocentio ut in extra. de sententia excummunicationis, Per tuas' (Po. 1830; 3 Comp. *h.t.* 5.21.14 [X 5.39.40]; Alanus 1.19.1 [W app. 18], whose title is 'de officio iudicis ordinarii'); fol. 331ra: 'Cognoscens uxoris consanguineam, si ignoranter, non separatur..., si scienter... separatur... Set hoc totum est immutatum ab innocentio ut in extra. <de> diuortiis, Per tuas' (Po. 1836; Alanus 4.10.1, whose title is 'De eo qui cognouit consanguineam uxoris sue').

[5] Another point is that, in referring to C.9 q.2 c.10, *P* has *Londiniensis* for *Lugdunensis*.

requisiuit et illorum uterque *delicti* sui cau- quisiuit et *uir in feminam* et *femina in*
sam in alium extra *refudit, uir in feminam,* serpentem delicti causam refudit.[7]
femina in serpentem.[6]

(Both works continue with the same series of scriptural citations to illustrate the divine origin of ecclesiastical jurisdiction.) After this opening *P* presents a second prologue, *Prima primi,* substantially the same as the prologue in *L* and (after the opening sentences) closely dependent on Huguccio. From this point on, *P* and *L* frequently 'overlap.' There are long passages which are almost identical in both works but also frequent divergencies. Of the total material on D.1-D.85 contained in the two works, about 60 per cent is common to both, about 30 per cent occurs only in *L,* and about 10 per cent only in *P.* The common material is virtually all derived from Huguccio. Moreover, the material which is added in *P* but not in *L* is likewise derived from Huguccio. That is to say, the whole of *P* after the prologue is simply an incomplete summary of Huguccio's *Summa.* On the other hand, the passages that occur only in *L* are for the most part made up of non-Huguccio material.

The author of *L* used excerpts from Huguccio's *Summa* to provide a framework for his own work, but interpolated into it views sharply opposed to those of Huguccio. Quite frequently he cited Huguccio and then curtly dismissed the Bolognese master's opinion with 'Hoc non approbo,' or, alternatively, he embarked on a detailed counter-argument introduced by a phrase like 'Magis credo' or 'Set ego credo.' He disagreed with Huguccio, for instance, on the definition of natural law, on the pope's authority to interpret Scripture, on the deposition of a criminal pope, on the requirement of good faith in prescriptions, on the indispensability of vows.[8] The views expressed in *L* are sometimes both trenchant and unusual. The very first words of the *summa,* after the prologue, present a doctrine on natural law which not only differs from Huguccio's but reads like a deliberate rebuke to contemporary English canonists like Honorius, who had devoted much ingenuity to multiplying the possible connotations of the term *ius naturale.*[9] The author of *L* swept aside all such subtleties:

> Hic notandum quod multi multas circa ius naturale inutiles proposuerunt distinctiones, plures uocabuli significationes assignando. Sufficit enim hec unica acceptio ut dicatur ius naturale quod procedit ex prima natura sine corruptione, secundum quod scilicet homo uiueret si Adam non peccasset... Si hanc acceptionem semper tenueris ab intelligentia non deuiabis.[10]

His views on certain other questions also seem quite out of the ordinary.[11]

---

[6] MS Rouen 743 (E 74) fol. 1[ra].

[7] Fol. 185[ra]. The text is emended from a corrupt reading in *P,* 'Per factum enim forma deum ...'

[8] *Summa Prima primi ad* D.1 (fol. 321[ra]), D.20 (fol. 321[rb]), D.40 (fol. 322[ra]), C.16 q.3 (fol. 329[rb]), D.85 (fol. 324[rb]).

[9] 'Anglo-Norman Canonists' 355.

[10] Fol. 321[ra].

[11] Notably the comments *ad* D.20 and *ad* D.40 cited below. The doctrinal significance of these passages is discussed in my article, 'Pope and Council: Some New Decretist Texts,' *Mediaeval Studies* 19 (1957) 197-218.

486

I have not been able to trace any close connection between the characteristic teachings of this author and those current in any of the known circles of English canonists of the late twelfth century. One naturally finds occasional points of agreement between *L* on the one hand and the Caius glosses, the *Summa Omnis qui iuste*, the works of Honorius or Ricardus Anglicus on the other. But there is no evidence of direct borrowing from any of these sources or of close connection between any of them and *L*. Apart from Huguccio the author of *L* apparently used only one source — the *Summa Duacensis*. His own *summa* is a pastiche of passages from these two works, with the Huguccio material forming about two-thirds of the whole.

The *Summa Duacensis* itself was discovered by Professor Kuttner in 1938 and its existence was briefly mentioned in this Bulletin for 1957.[12] It is a work in the form of a pure *summa*, probably of French provenance and written after the Comp. I and Huguccio. It does not, like *L*, cite Innocent's decretals of 1203 in discussing the law of marriage and the law of appeals. The whole Douai manuscript, which contains, *inter alia*, the *Distinctiones* of Ricardus Anglicus and a substantial *Summa quaestionum*, will require more detailed analysis before the provenance and dates of its contents can be established with certainty;[13] but it seems probable that the *summa* which concerns us was written towards 1200 and that it provided a direct source for *L*.

Before this relationship can be demonstrated satisfactorily, it is necessary to return to the problem of the connection between *L* and *P*. Although their contents diverge so considerably, and although all the material common to both (except the opening lines of the prologue *Prima primi*) is derived from Huguccio, they are not independent works that used Huguccio as a common source. In both *summae* the Huguccio material is normally presented in the form of terse paraphrases, not in the form of extracts literally copied. The texts of *L* and *P* are consistently much closer to one another than either of them is to Huguccio. A typical example is this from D.13.[14]

Huguccio	L	P
Quidam dicunt quod aliquis potest esse perplexus *inter* duo *mortalia* ut *Iudei* qui interficiendo Christum peccauerunt mortaliter. Si *non interfe*cissent, similiter peccassent mortaliter quia fecissent contra conscientiam que dictabat eis quod tenerentur illum ad interficiendum, *cum in lege diceretur, ' Quicumque fecerit se filium dei morte moriatur.'*	*Quod uera sit perplexitas inter mortalia primo* arg. *infra eadem c. 1* et 2. *Item Iudei credebant se obsequium prestare* deo *cum in lege* eorum *diceretur, ' Quicumque fecerit se filium dei moriatur,' et ita non interficiendo peccarent.*	Hec di. § 1. *Quod uera sit perplexitas* etiam *inter mortalia primo* ut *infra eadem c. 1. Item Iudei credebant se obsequium prestare cum in lege* ipsorum *diceretur, ' Quicumque se fecerit filium dei morte moriatur,' et ita non interficiendo peccarent.*

---

[12] *Traditio* 12 (1957) 466.

[13] On some other contents of Douai 649 see 'Anglo-Norman Canonists' 315.

[14] Admont MS 7, fol. 16ra; *L*, fol. 321rb; *P*, fol. 185rb. The word *hec* in *P* is a misreading for the arabic numerals 13 (read as h').

Here the close interconnection between L and P is much more apparent than the dependence of both of them on Huguccio. L, the later and more complex work is not the source of P. Nor does P represent the source directly used by L since it lacks any comment on a considerable number of distinctions for which L presents a summarizing comment derived in the usual fashion from Huguccio. Evidently there was an intermediary, X, a summary of Huguccio's *Summa* which both L and P used as their direct source.

There is a peculiarity in L which sheds further light on the transmission of the Huguccio material in *Prima primi*. This work very commonly embarks on a discussion of some passage in the Decretum with a phrase like 'Hic dicitur' but without any indication at all of what the 'Hic' refers to. It is always possible to identify the passage of the Decretum under discussion, but sometimes, when a *capitulum* or *dictum* in the middle of a long distinction is involved, the task is quite a tedious one. P (and Huguccio) almost invariably identify the passage under discussion by citing its initial word in the usual fashion. The explanation for the absence of such identifying words in L would seem to be that the version of X used by the author of *Prima primi* had been transcribed in the form of a marginal gloss to the *Decretum*. In place of an identifying initial word, a pair of symbols could then have been used linking each gloss to the appropriate text of the *Decretum*. At one point in L such a symbol has in fact been transcribed at the beginning of a comment, though it is meaningless in the context of a *summa*.[15]

It seems possible to construct with reasonable certainty the content of the common source of L and P. Since both these works contain the prologue *Prima primi* and the comment 'Lex anglicana punit eum qui interfecit non hostem' at D.50, this material was presumably in the common source X, and its presence there suggests that X was composed in England. The author of P added to X an additional prologue, based on that of the English *Summa Omnis qui iuste*, but added almost nothing of his own to the subsequent text. L, on the other hand, frequently interpolated material from D.

We can now return to the relationship of L and D. The interpolations from D that occur in L seem to have been made for two quite separate reasons. Sometimes the author of L found no comment in X on a section of the Decretum which he thought needed comment. On other occasions he found the views of Huguccio expressed clearly enough in X but wished to express a dissenting opinion.

The most clear-cut example of the first situation is at C.23-C.26, where L depends on D and not at all on Huguccio. Evidently L's source, X, was prepared from the early recension of Huguccio's *Summa*, which lacked comment on these *causae haereticorum* as well as on C.1, *De poen.* and *De cons.* (all of which are lacking in L also). Another series of examples is provided by the cases where P lacks all comment on a succession of distinctions. At the corresponding points in L one finds either simply a terse summarizing comment derived from Huguccio or else a comment of this kind followed by material interpolated from D. Thus, at D.21 (lacking in P), we find:[16]

---

[15] *Summa ad* D.1, fol. 321[ra].

[16] Admont MS 7, fol. 24[vb]; L, fol. 321[rb]; D, fol. 97[ra-rb]. The comment of Huguccio on c.4, *Inferior*, is quite different from that of L and D.

Huguccio	L	D
Hic intitulatur di. xxi in qua tractat de ministris canonum et generaliter de omnibus ecclesiasticis ordinibus, ostendendo *qui sint ministri canonum et quot* sint *ordines ecclesiastici et unde habuerunt originem. Offitia quoque* eorum <et> *interpretationes* nominum eorum auctoritate isidori interserit. *Ad ultimum* addit quod qui est in maiore ordine et dignitate *non potest iudicari* ab eo qui in minore ordine uel dignitate constitutus est, unde, quia *papa* omnibus preest *a nemine iudicari* potest.	Cum a principio 15 dis⁻ tinctionis egerit de origine et auctoritate ecclesiasticarum constitutionum, ab hoc loco, principale propositum aggrediens, agit de ministris ecclesie, docens in hac 21 di. *qui sint ministri canonum et quot ordines ecclesiastici et unde originem habuerunt. Officia quoque* et *interpretationes* appellationum assignat. *Ad ultimum* uero ab hoc loco 'inferior' ostendit quod maior a minore *iudicari non potest*, et sic *papa a nemine iudica*bitur.	Dictum est de iure ecclesiastico. Set quia parum est iura nosse si persone quarum gratia sint institute ignorantur ut Inst. De iure naturali, in fine (*Inst.* 1.2.12), subiungitur de personis ecclesiasticis, de earum nominibus et offitiis et que quibus preponantur.
	Inferior: ...*Ex* hoc *colligitur quod* qui *potest ligare et soluere et econtra.* Item habetur ff. *De re iudicata l. 3* (D.42.1.3), *ff. De regulis iuris* l. *Nemo qui* (D.50.17.3). *In casu tamen necessitatis* aliud *inuenitur...* Item secus *in episcopo accusato, qui a coepiscopis potest absolui, non condempnari...*	Inferior: ...*Item* quod *ex* capitulo isto *colligitur, quod* quicumque *ligare potest et soluere et econtra.* Generale est id quod dicitur, C.(!) *De re iudicata l. 3, D. De regulis iuris, Nemo qui. In casu tamen necessitatis* secus *inuenitur...* Idem *in episcopo accusato, qui a coepiscopis absolui potest, condempnari non* potest sine auctoritate pape...

It would seem that the common source of *L* and *P* summarized Huguccio's teaching much more amply at some points than others. Often, when *X* provided only a very terse comment for a series of distinctions, *P* omitted the material altogether as of little siginificance. *L* also found the comment inadequate but preferred to amplify it with interpolations from his second source, *D.*[17]

A clear illustration of the second kind of interpolation, when the author of *L* had Huguccio's opinion before him but wished to dissent from it, occurs at D.20.[18]

---

[17] This pattern of interpolations from *D* at points where *P* lacks any comment on a distinction occurs frequently in *L*, e.g. at D.15, D.21, D.30, D.36, D.47, D.48, D.52, D.58, D.60, D.62.

[18] Admont MS 7, fol. 24rb; *L*, fol. 321rb; *D*, fol. 97ra.

Huguccio	L	D
Nunc autem in hac distinctione *querit de expositione sacre scripture et de canonibus et decretalibus, que quibus preponi debeant. Postea* ponit solutionem et dicit *quod* quantum ad causas decidendas *preualent* canones et decretalia, quantum ad sacram scripturam *interpretandam preualent expositiones sanctorum patrum. In* expositionibus enim *sacre scripture* preualet auctoritas *sanctorum patrum, in causis decidendis preualet* auctoritas romanorum *pontificum.*	In 20 distinctione primo *querit de expositioni*bus *sacre scripture et de canonibus et de decretalibus, que quibus debeant preponi. Postea* respondet *quod in interpretationibus sacre scripture preualent expositiones sanctorum patrum, in causis* uero *decidendis* ubi desideratur auctoritas *preualent* statuta *pontificum.* Hu.	Dictum est de decretis et decretalibus epistolis. Agitur hic de expositoribus sacre scripture. Hos Gratianus summis pontificibus in causarum decisione postponit, in expositione sacre scripture preponit.
	Magis credo quod pape auctoritas *in utroque* preferatur. *Licet enim sint uera que dicunt* sancti patres, *non tamen sunt autentica nisi a summo pontifice confirmata... Cum enim possit papa quedam iura euangelica* et *apostolica et legalia mutare... fortius eius interpretationi standum est.*	Set falso, quia *in utroque* postponendi sunt. *Licet enim sint uera que dicunt non tamen sunt autentica nisi a summo pontifice confirmata... Cum enim* possit papa etiam *iura quedam euangelica et legalia* uel *apostolica mutare, fortius* potest interpretari, et *eius interpretationi standum est.*

The best example of all of this interweaving of *Duacensis* material for a didactic purpose is provided by the discussions on the treatment of a criminal or heretical pope which occur in Huguccio and in *L, P,* and *D* at D.40. *P* introduces the subject by explaining that Huguccio's treatment of the matter was controversial, but the subsequent text is simply a point by point summary of Huguccio's opinions, at no point dissenting from them. The author of *L,* with the same summary of Huguccio before him, began by transcribing it, then interpolated a dissenting opinion from *D,* and finally returned at the end of the passage to the Huguccio material. It may be noted that this is a case where *P* gives a precise reference to the words of the Decretum under discussion, which is lacking in *L.* Indeed, these passages in themselves illustrate very effectively the relationship of Huguccio to *P,* of *P* to *L,* and of *L* to *D.*[19]

---

[19] *P,* fol. 185vb; *L,* fol. 322ra; *D,* fol. 99ra. The texts of *L* and *D* are printed more fully in *Mediaeval Studies* 19.217-218. The lengthy comment of Huguccio is printed in *Foundations of the Conciliar Theory* (Cambridge 1955) 248-250 and in J. F. v. Schulte, *Die Stellung der Concilien, Päpste und Bischöfe* (Prague 1871) 262-264. It should be noted that there are close verbal parallels between the *Summa Duacensis* and the corresponding passage in the

P

§40 'Si papa'. Multa hic dicta ab Hu. non placuerunt. § 'a nemine est iudicandus.'

Nota si papa admonitus uelit resipiscere a nullo potest excusari(!) *uel* condempnari ...*et siue hoc sit heresis siue aliud crimen notorium. Secus si publice predicet et ammonitus nolit corrigi ut hic...*
Set ecce, papa confingit nouam heresim.
Aliquis uult probare ut *sit heresis. Papa dicit quod est fides catholica. Estne audiendus qui uult probare?* Credo *quod non, arg. 24 Q. 1 Quociens.*

Ego tamen credo *quod de quolibet notorio* possit *accusari et dampnari sicut de*

L

Nota quod si papa admonitus uelit resipiscere a nullo potest accusari *uel* dampnari... *et hoc siue sit heresis siue aliud crimen notorium. Secus si publice predicet et ammonitus nolit corrigi ut hic...*
Set ecce, papa confingit nouam heresim.
Aliquis uult probare quod *sit heresis. Papa dicit quod est fides catholica. Estne audiendus qui uult probare?* Hu. dicit *quod non, arg. 24 Q. 1 Quociens.* Set magis credo contrarium. Hoc enim casu *debet iudicem eligere et sub eo litigare. Licet enim legibus sit solutus debet tamen legibus uiuere.* Quod *si nolit* credo quod *sine eo ecclesia* possit *disceptare* et iudicare. *Et eo inuento quod* papa *sit hereticus, nisi* coreptus *resipiscat,* ecclesia potest ipsum condempnare et deponere. *Secus si alias male faciat et corrigi nolit. Tunc enim non restat nisi dolor et gemitus. Ratio diuersitatis est* quia *causa fidei omnibus communis* est *ut 96 di. Ubinam, et eo inuito potest ecclesia decidere questionem fidei ut hic.*

§ Hu. tamen dicit *quod* papa *de quolibet* crimine *notorio* potest *accusari et*

D

Quod autem dicitur papam posse accusari si fuerit in fide deuius, large accipit Y (Huguccio) nomen fidei ut etiam possit accusari de omni crimine notorio, et dicitur tunc deuiare a fide, i.e. facere contra doctrinam fidei... Sic etiam omnis mortaliter peccans dicitur Christum negare... Set secundum hoc nullum uel modicum esset pape privilegium. Propterea dicendum simpliciter quod in nullo casu accusari potest propter defectum iudicis superioris...

Et quid si contendat heresim non esse quod predicet? *Debet iudicem eligere et sub eo de hoc litigare. Licet enim legibus solutus sit debet tamen legibus uiuere...* Et quid *si nolit? Credo* quia *sine eo* debeat *ecclesia* deliberatiue, non iudicialiter, *disceptare et eo inuento quod heresis sit,* papa correctus, *nisi resipiscat* papa desinit esse ipso iure. *Secus si alias malefaciat et corrigi nolit. Tunc enim non restat nisi dolor et gemitus. Ratio diuersitatis est* quoniam *causa fidei omnibus* indicitur esse *communis ut* xxvi(!) *di. Ubinam, et eo inuito potest ecclesia questionem fidei decidere.*

'short version' of Alanus' apparatus *Ius naturale.* The text of Alanus is also printed in *Mediaeval Studies* 19 (1957) 218.

heresi, quando scilicet am-monitus non uult cessare...	*dampnari sicut de heresi quando scilicet non uult ammonitus cessare...* Hoc non credo.
Item aliqui nouerunt pape crimen occultum...	*Item aliqui nouerunt pape crimen occultum....*

From this point the arguments in *P* and *L* continue in almost identical terms.

To sum up: *P* and *L* are based on a common source, a summary of Huguccio made in the English schools. *P* is made up almost entirely of material transcribed from this summary, while *L* is a conflation of its Huguccio material with passages borrowed from the *Summa Duacensis*. *P* represents an earlier stage in the reception of Huguccio, when the need was simply to present the key points in the Bolognese master's work in a more assimilable form than the vast and unwieldy *Summa* itself. *L* represents a later stage when mere assimilation had given way to critical comparison and evaluation.

X

Hostiensis and Collegiality

A complete account of the doctrine of collegiality in the thirteenth century would make a complicated story. Older canonical doctrine held that Christ had originally conferred authority on all the apostles and had also designated Peter as their head. In the existing Church the bishops, as successors to the apostles, formed one body united with Peter's successor, the pope, in the governance of the Church. During the middle years of the thirteenth century this traditional teaching came under attack from two directions — from advocates of extreme papal centralization and from advocates of episcopal particularism. The controversy was centered in the University of Paris. It began with the bitter disputes of the 1250s between mendicant and secular masters and broadened into a general debate concerning the pope's power to authorize the preaching and pastoral work of the friars throughout the universal Church. In the course of this debate mendicant theologians argued that Christ had originally conferred jurisdiction on Peter alone and that, in the existing church, bishops were mere servants of the pope. The episcopalists cited in reply all the standard texts which, traditionally, had been taken to mean that Christ conferred authority on all the apostles simultaneously. But they did not deploy such texts in order to stress the corporate union of the bishops with the pope. They used them rather to defend the autonomy of each individual bishop in his own diocese. Ideas akin to the modern doctrine of episcopal collegiality found virtually no support at this time.

In these circumstances a different theory of collegiality grew up — based on an earlier tradition derived from Humbert and Peter Damian — a theory which substituted the college of cardinals for the college of bishops as the collegiate body divinely established to rule the Church in association with the pope. This theory offered the possibility of retaining the advantages of papal centralization without abandoning the ideal of collegiate government. Its greatest exponent was the canonist Hostiensis. Twenty years ago I discussed his views in connection with the subsequent growth of conciliar thought.[1] More recently several other scholars — among them Leclerc, Alberigo and Congar — have commented on the very high claims that Hostiensis made for

---

[1] 'A Conciliar Theory of the Thirteenth Century', *Catholic Historical Review* 36 (1951) 415-40 ; *Foundations of the Conciliar Theory* (Cambridge 1955) 149-53.

X

the Sacred College.[2] However this widely accepted interpretation of Hostiensis' thought has been sharply challenged by John Watt in a series of articles that have appeared over the past fifteen years.[3] Watt maintains that Hostiensis presented a strictly monarchical rather than a collegial theory of Church government. In this paper I shall try to re-state Hostiensis' doctrine of collegiality and to respond to Watt's arguments concerning it.

In the first place, it is interesting that Hostiensis developed his theory of the cardinals' authority without any attack on the traditional prerogatives of the episcopate. Other writers of this period were beginning to call the cardinals successors of the apostles. Hostiensis reserved that traditional title of honor for the bishops. He did not hesitate to call the bishops vicars of Christ. Moreover he wrote that each bishop entered into a marriage bond with the universal Church as well as with his local church. This idea could have served as the basis for a theory of the bishops as participants with the pope in the government of the universal Church. But Hostiensis never developed his thought in that direction. A bishop's administrative responsibilities were concerned solely with his local church. A bishop who did not preside over a local, particular church had a part in the universal episcopate 'in number, in honor, in dignity' — but not in administrative responsibility. So far as the administration of the universal church was concerned, Hostiensis treated the bishops only as subjects of the pope, not as co-rulers with him.[4]

Hostiensis' position was made clear at the beginning of his *Commentaria*. Discussing the *Proemium* of the Decretals he wrote that all bishops stood in place of the apostles and all could be called vicars of Christ but that all were

---

[2] J. Lecler, 'Pars corporis papae', *Mélanges H. de Lubac* II (Paris 1964) 183-98; G. Alberigo, *Cardinalato e collegialità* (Florence 1969) 97-109; Yves Congar, 'Notes sur le destin de l'idée de collegialité. . .', *La collegialité épiscopale* (Paris 1965) 118-27.

[3] J. Watt, 'The Early Medieval Canonists and the Formation of Conciliar Theory', *Irish Theological Quarterly* 24 (1957) 13-31; 'The Theory of Papal Monarchy in the Thirteenth Century', *Traditio* 20 (1964) 179-317; 'The Term Plenitudo Potestatis in Hostiensis', *Proceedings of the Second International Congress of Medieval Canon Law* (Vatican City 1965) 161-87; 'The Constitutional Law of the College of Cardinals: Hostiensis to Johannes Andreae', *Mediaeval Studies* 23 (1971) 127-57. This last article reached the conclusion that 'the canonist tradition from Hostiensis to Johannes Andreae was in general agreement that papal government was monarchic and not oligarchic'. Unfortunately Watt has not discussed in any of his studies the views of Laurentius expressed in the *Glossa Palatina*. Laurentius was the most vigorous defender of the rights of the Sacred College in the generation before Hostiensis.

[4] See G. Alberigo, *Lo sviluppo della dottrina sui poteri nella chiesa universale* (Rome 1964) and the comments of Pio Fedele, 'Primato pontificio ed episcopato con particolare riferimento all dottrina dell'Ostiense', SG 14 (1967) 349-67.

subject to the pope as the pre-eminent and principal vicar.[5] Then, when he first introduced a discussion on the cardinals at X 1.5.3, he explained — with a reference back to his first comment — that the cardinals, like the pope, shared in the 'solicitude for the state of the universal Church'. Later he wrote that 'through them the whole world is ruled', and that they participated in the papal plenitude of power.[6] How could such assertions be justified? Every theory of Church government presented in the thirteenth century claimed to be founded on a scriptural basis and that of Hostiensis was no exception. It is again interesting that he avoided all the 'collegial' texts which had commonly been used in the past to establish the direct divine origin of episcopal authority. Instead he developed his case for the cardinals by giving a new interpretation to a text of Saint Paul quoted by Innocent III in the decretal *Per venerabilem*: 'Do you not know that we shall judge angels? How much more the things of this world.' Innocent used the text to justify the excercise of papal authority in temporal affairs. Hostiensis focussed his attention on the plural form of the verb *iudicare*.[7]

> It is not said *iudicabis* in the singular but *iudicabitis* in the plural in order that not only the pope but also the cardinals should be included in the expression of the plenitude of power.

This was the crux of Hostiensis' position. He was not arguing — like some of his contemporaries — that, just as the pope succeeded to Peter's position, so the cardinals succeeded to the position of the other apostles. His assertion was rather that the cardinals shared in the succession to the Petrine office itself. Together with the pope they 'constitute the Roman Church' which is the head of all others.[8]

Having established to his own satisfaction that, according to divine law, the headship of the universal Church was indeed a collegial headship Hostiensis developed his theory of the cardinals' authority with little further reference to

---

[5] *Commentaria* (Venice 1581), fol 3va: '. . . Omnes sunt loco apostolorum . . . unde et episcopus vicarius Cristi dicitur . . . sed papa specialiter per excellentiam dicitur episcopus quia super omnes est . . . et praecipuus ac principalis est vicarius Iesu Cristi'.

[6] *Com. ad* X 1.5.3, fol 34vb: '. . . cardinales communem impendunt solicitudinem pro statu ecclesiae generalis sicut et papa. . .', 1.24.2, fol. 129rb: '. . . per eos regitur totus mundus . . .'; 4.17.13, fol. 40rb: 'Participant ergo cardinales plenitudini potestatis. . .'.

[7] *Com. ad* X 4.17.13, fol. 39va: 'Unde et dictum est non *iudicabis* in singulari sed *iudicabitis* in plurali ut non solum papa sed et cardinales includerentur etiam in expressione plenitudinis potestatis. . .'. Innocent's original text used the correct scriptural form *iudicabimus*. This was changed to *iudicabitis* in the text incorporated in the *Decretales* upon which Hostiensis was commenting.

[8] *Com. ad* X 2.24.4, fol 126ra: '. . . papa et ipsi constituunt Romanam ecclesiam. . .'.

Scripture.[9] Instead he relied on specifically juridical arguments derived from the Roman law concerning the status of the senate and from the canon law of corporations which he himself had done so much to develop. On the basis of such analogies Hostiensis was able to conclude that the cardinals were 'part of the body of the lord pope', 'tanquam sibi invisceratis', 'so united with the pope that they are one and the same with him'.[10]

In spite of all this John Watt has felt able to argue that 'there is no word here to say that it was obligatory on the pope to share his power' and that the Sacred College 'did not *de iure* share in the plenitude of power'.[11] He supports this position essentially by two arguments, one based on Hostiensis' references to corporation law, the other on his use of the term *plenitudo potestatis*. To me such an interpretation seems totally excluded by the texts which I have already cited. Of course Hostiensis did not treat the pope as a mere equal of the cardinals. The pope enjoyed a unique status as head of the Sacred College. And yet Hostiensis stated over and over again that supreme powers of government over the church were vested in the college as a whole and not in the pope alone. Evidently, however, there must be some ambiguity in these texts since Dr. Watt can interpret them in a quite different sense. Fortunately, Hostiensis — in typical decretalist fashion — provides us with ample material for arriving at a correct understanding of his texts. Over and over again in his work a terse, perhaps ambiguous comment is followed by references to other sections of the Decretals and we are told to study the things 'that are read and noted' there for a full explanation of his position. By following this procedure we can hope to arrive at a clear and definitive interpretation of Hostiensis' views on the Sacred College.

Let us consider first the argument from corporation law. Dr. Watt commented at one point in his discussions on Hostiensis: 'His view of papal authority cannot be explained satisfactorily in terms of any alleged "normal rules of corporation law".'[11a] This I must confess I cannot understand, for it was Hostiensis himself who alleged the 'normal rules of corporation law' in order to explicate his views on the status of pope and cardinals. These analogies were not invented by Hostiensis' modern interpreters. Hostiensis' most important text declared:[12]

---

[9] He quoted Scripture extensively only at X 4.38.14 in order to prove that the cardinals did not lack a head during a papal vacancy since Christ himself was their head.

[10] *Com. ad* X 2.24.4, fol 126ra; 5.23.33, fol 86vb; 5.6.17, fol 33va.

[11] 'Plenitudo' 169 ; 'Constitutional Law' 134.   [11a] 'Constitutional Law' 136.

[12] *Com. ad* X 4.17.13, fol 39va: '. . . multo magis et multo excellentius maior est unio inter papam et collegium Romanae ecclesiae quam etiam inter aliquem alium patriarcham et capitulum suum, quod dic ut notatur infra *De privilegiis, Antiqua, respon. 1* (5.33.23) et tamen patriarcha sine consilio fratrum non debet ardua expedire ut patet in his quae leguntur et

... The union between the pope and the college of the Roman Church is much greater and more excellent even than that between any other patriarch and his chapter as is noted below, *De privilegiis* c. *Antiqua*. And yet a patriarch ought not to settle difficult matters without the counsel of his brothers as is made clear in the things that are read and noted above, *De his que fiunt a prelato*, c. *Novit* and c. *Quanto*. Much more then is it fitting for the pope to seek the counsel of his brothers . . .

On this Watt has two comments. Firstly Hostiensis used the word *decet* — it is fitting — to describe the pope's duty to consult with his cardinals and this excluded the idea that consultation was actually obligatory. Secondly Hostiensis used the word *consilio* rather than the stronger *consensu*. It might seem that there is indeed some ambiguity here. But Hostiensis has told us precisely where to turn for a full exposition of his views on these questions. When we turn to X 3.10.4 (*Novit*) we find an interpretation of the words *non decet*. When used in the context of corporation law, Hostiensis tells us they mean ' It is not fitting, not licit and not expedient'.[13] Hostiensis' understanding of the word seems quite different from Watt's. As to the word *consilio*, in his commentary on X 3.10.5 (*Quanto*), Hostiensis certainly distinguished between counsel and consent in commenting on the words 'cum eorum consilio . . . [negotia] eadem pertractes', but he also provided a careful specification of the matters in which a patriarch required the actual consent of his chapter. The general rule Hostiensis arrived at in discussing the meaning of the words *de consilio* in this context was that a prelate needed to take counsel in almost everything and he required actual consent in 'alienations and other major affairs'.[14] This is the explanation to which Hostiensis refers us when we seek a more precise understanding of his view that the union between pope and cardinals was even closer than that between any other patriarch and his chapter.[15]

Hostiensis' view that plenitude of power — understood as the supreme authority to govern the Church — resided in pope and cardinals as a collegiate body was made especially plain in his treatment of the cardinals' role during a

---

notantur supra, *De his quae fiunt a praelato*, *Novit* (3.10.4) et c. *Quanto* (3.10.5). Multo fortius ergo decet papam consilia fratrum suorum requirere . . .'.

[13] *Com. ad* X 3.10.4, fol 45rb. Commenting on the words 'Unde non decet te omissis membris aliorum consilio in ecclesiae tuae negotiis uti', Hostiensis wrote: '. . . Per hoc probatur quod nec decet, nec licet . . . nec expedit . . .'.

[14] *Com. ad* X 3.10.5, fol 45va: 'Dic ergo quod aliud est consilium sine quo nihil aut modicum gerere debet episcopus, aliud consensus qui non requiritur nisi in alienationibus . . . et aliis maioribus . . .'.

[15] In using the words *decet* and *consilio*, Hostiensis was adhering strictly to the language of the decretals he cited. Presumably he chose these two particular decretals because they were addressed specifically to a patriarch — the Patriarch of Jerusalem.

vacancy. Referring once again to the rules of corporation law he held that plenitude of power then resided with the Sacred College. The only problem was to define in what ways the cardinals were to exercise this power before a new pope was elected. At one point Hostiensis wrote that they did not have to concern themselves with cases especially reserved to the pope. When we consult the list of such cases to which he refers us we find that, likewise, the pope did not deal with such matters without consulting the cardinals.[16] The doctrine is quite clear. In normal situations these affairs were to be handled by pope and cardinals acting together. But Hostiensis was also quite clear that 'at least in cases of great necessity' the cardinals could actually exercise the plenary jurisdiction of the Roman See during a papal vacancy.[17]

It remains true that Hostiensis nowhere specified in precise detail all the powers that the cardinals could exercise during a vacancy just as he never specified in precise detail the cases in which their counsel sufficed and those in which consent was required. The reason is plain enough. The general principles regulating such matters could be deduced from the doctrines of corporation law to which Hostiensis referred us so often. But, in the case of any specific church, local custom was also an important factor. And the custom of the Roman church concerning the mode of participation of the cardinals in the collegial authority of the apostolic see was by no means stable and fixed in the time of Hostiensis. The custom was evolving, and it was evolving in the direction of a greater authority for the cardinals. Hostiensis had no intention of checking this beneficient evolution by premature and over-vigorous definitions. He explained this at the end of his discussions on the cardinals' powers during a vacancy:[18]

> I write these things to confute those who seem to annihilate the power of the cardinals altogether; it is not that I intend to limit their excellent authority precisely or to bind it by any certain rules.

We can now turn to Dr. Watt's second major point, Hostiensis' use of the term *plenitudo potestatis*. The crucial text is Hostiensis' comment on X 3.4.2. Here Hostiensis wrote that customarily the pope did not and, according to some, he could not excommunicate a cardinal without the counsel and consent of the other cardinals. In a later discussion Hostiensis suggested that this was

---

[16] *Com. ad* X 5.39.26, fol. 111ra: 'Cardinales non habeant se intromittere de casibus qui Romano pontifici specialiter reservantur, de quibus no. supra, *De excessibus praelatorum, Sicut unire'* (5.31.8). For Hostiensis' comment on X.5.31.8 see below n. 23.

[17] *Com. ad* X 5.38.14, fol. 104vb: 'Sed numquid collegium cardinalium habet iurisdictionem papae et etiam exercitium ipsius . . . tu teneas quod sic, saltem in his quibus de grandi necessitate evidenti et imminenti provideri oportet . . .'.

[18] *Com. ad* X 5.38.14, fol 105ra: '. . . non ut eorum authoritatem excellentem intendam praecise limitare vel aliquibus certis regulis alligare . . .'.

indeed his own opinion by writing that a cardinal could not be judged by anyone 'except the pope and his colleagues'.[19] However at the end of the first passage he wrote:[20]

> However this may be, I plainly confess that plenitude of power resides in the pope alone as above, *De usu pallii*, c. *Ad honorem.*

Dr. Watt takes this to mean that the pope could not possibly have needed the consent of the cardinals since he alone possessed plenitude of power. But this interpretation is defeated by the context itself. What Hostiensis wrote rather was this: Whatever we hold about the need for the consent of the Sacred College in the excommunication of a cardinal, it remains true that plenitude of power resides in the pope alone. But this seems self-contradictory. If we hold that the pope needs consent for certain actions how can we say that he alone has plenitude of power? And above all, how could Hostiensis write here that plenitude of power resided in the pope alone when he had plainly stated elsewhere that the cardinals participated in the plenitude of power?

The explanation is simple enough and once more it was provided by Hostiensis himself. The phrase *plenitudo potestatis* had several meanings. It could mean the supreme authority to rule the Church — and in this sense *plenitudo potestatis* inhered in pope and cardinals as a collegiate body. But the phrase could also indicate a state of personal immunity from all human judgment — and this was a personal prerogative of the pope. When Hostiensis wrote 'Plenitude of power resides in the pope alone' it was this second meaning that he had in mind. He made this clear by referring us to c. *Honorem* (X 1.8.4). There he defined the pope's *plenitudo potestatis* as a power so great that, however much the pope sinned, he could be judged only by God, provided that he did not actually fall into heresy.[21] In the passage that we have been considering Hostiensis was discussing the deposition of members of the Roman church. He wrote first that a cardinal could be judged only by the pope, and that perhaps the consent of the Sacred College was also necessary. Then he added that the pope enjoyed a unique personal prerogative of immunity

---

[19] *Com. ad* X 3.5.19, fol 18 *bis* vb: '. . . ipsi cardinales una cum papa omnes iudicent nec iudicari possint ab alio quam a papa et suis collegiis '.

[20] *Com. ad* X 3.4.2, fol 10va: '. . . papa non consuevit nec etiam potest secundum quosdam aliquem de cardinalibus excommunicare . . . sine aliorum suorum fratrum consilio et consensu . . . Quidquid tamen dicatur, hoc de plano fateor quod in solum papam [*sic*] plenitudo residet potestatis, supra, *De usu pallii, Ad honorem* (1.8.4)'. Hostiensis also gave a reference to X.3.8.4 where this doctrine was repeated. See below n. 27. On Watt's analysis of the term *plenitudo potestatis* see J. W. Perrin, 'Legatus, the Lawyers and the Terminology of Power in Roman Law', SG 11 (1967) 461-89 at 487-9.

[21] *Com. ad* X 1.8.4, fol 86ra: '*Plenitudinem*: Tantam quod quantumcumque peccet (dummodo a fide non exorbitet) citra Deum a nemine iudicatur . . .'.

from all human judgment provided that he did not deviate from the faith. The exposition was quite straightforward and consistent with what Hostiensis had written elsewhere about the powers of the Sacred College.[22]

But if God exempted the pope from all human judgment did he not *ipso facto* loose him from all human restraints by the cardinals or any one else? For Hostiensis this was true only in the sense that, if the pope chose to sin by departing from the divinely willed plan for the collegial governance of the Church, his punishment was reserved to God alone. Let us consider one final text. At X 5.31.8 Hostiensis wrote that the pope could not act without consulting the cardinals by his 'ordinary power' but that he could do so by his 'absolute power', and he added a reference to X 3.8.4.[23] Here again we are dealing with a phrase that had at least two meanings. *Potestas absoluta* could refer to an exercise of sovereign power outside the ordinary course of law which was essential to preserve the welfare of the whole community in a case of extreme necessity. Hostiensis was familiar with this usage and discussed it at length[24] — but he did not refer to this discussion when he wrote that, by his absolute power, the pope could act without the cardinals. Instead he referred to a passage in which he had described the exercise of absolute power by the ruler in a quite different way as an arbitrary, tyrannical, sinful procedure. This discussion took as its point of departure the Roman law principle, *Princeps legibus solutus est*. As I have argued elsewhere, to thirteenth-century jurists and theologians, this phrase did not mean that the ruler was freed from the

---

[22] If we accepted the view that *plenitudo potestatis* in the above passage necessarily referred to a general authority to rule the Church we should have to fall back on Alberigo's suggestion that the words *solum papam* did not certainly exclude the cardinals. This position is more reasonable than it appears at first glance. In medieval discourse the phrases like *solus papa* did not necessarily refer to the pope all by himself, separated from other people. They could indicate rather that certain collegiate acts could not be carried through without the participation of the pope. Thus Aquinas asked whether the promulgation of a new creed pertained 'to the sole authority of the supreme pontiff' and replied in the affirmative. But his explanation was that creeds were promulgated in general councils and that only the pope could convoke such councils (*Summa*, 2.2 q.1 art. 10). There was a similar usage in canon law. C.24 q.1 c.12 declared that a question of faith was to be referred to Peter alone (*non nisi ad Petrum*). But the canonists often explained that the highest authority in matters of faith was not the pope by himself but rather a general council or the universal Church. Among the Roman lawyers, Accursius observed on the phrase *solis imperatoribus* that '. . . haec dictio *solis* non excludat populum Romanum' (Cod. 1.14.1). However, the explanation of Hostiensis' words given in the text above seems to me the correct one.

[23] *Com. ad* X 5.31.8, fol 72vb: 'Sed nec papa haec . . . consuevit expedire sine consilio fratrum suorum, i.e. cardinalium, nec istud potest facere de potestate ordinaria, arg. supra *De his quae fiunt a praelatis, Novit* (3.10.4), licet secus de absoluta, supra *De concessione praebendae, Proposuit* (3.8.4)'.

[24] *Com. ad* X 3.35.6, fol 134ra.

common obligation to obey the laws.[25] It meant rather that, if he ignored this obligation, no human tribunal could impose coercive sanctions on him.[26] As Thomas Aquinas wrote, clearly and simply, the prince was freed from the 'coercive force' of the law but not from its 'directive force'. This was the teaching of Hostiensis too. At X 3.8.4 — the passage to which he referred us after stating that by his absolute power the pope could act without the cardinals — Hostiensis wrote:

> The pope has so great power that if he says and does whatever he pleases he cannot be accused or condemned by man provided that he is not a heretic.

But this was only to say that God had reserved judgment for himself. A pope who persisted in such arbitrary rule could expect a 'terrible judgment' and 'more intolerable torment' than any lesser man.[27] This was the fate that Hostiensis envisaged for a pope who tried to rule as an absolute monarch, without the co-operation of the cardinals.

After the decree *Lumen gentium* of Vatican Council II it is hardly necessary to point out that an ecclesiology of collegiality does not necessarily exclude an emphasis on papal headship in the Church. It is not clear to me that the fathers of the recent council succeeded in achieving an altogether satisfactory and definitive reconciliation of the ideas of papacy and collegiality. Perhaps Hostiensis too did not succeed in reconciling perfectly his Roman law theory of sovereignty with his doctrine of collegial headship in the Church. But one thing at least is clear. In the view of Hostiensis God did not establish only a single papal monarch to rule his Church. Rather he established a collegiate body of pope and cardinals. And in this Sacred College 'all rights of government over the Church were vested by a direct act of the divine will'.[28]

---

[25] 'The Prince Is Not Bound by the Laws: Accursius and the Origins of the Modern State', *Comparative Studies in Society and History* 4 (1963) 378-400; 'Bracton on Government', *Speculum* 38 (1963) 295-317.

[26] The term *potestas absoluta* was also used in this sense by Henry of Ghent. John Marrone disucusses his view in a forthcoming article in *Mediaeval Studies*.

[27] *Com. ad* X 3.8.4, fol 35ra: 'Papa sui ipsius tantam potestatem habet quod si faciat et dicat quicquid placuerit, accusari non potest necque damnari ab homine dummodo non sit haereticus . . . si sic decesserit iudicium terribilius imminet et intolerabilior cruciatus . . .'.

[28] *Foundations of the Conciliar Theory* 151.

XI

The Idea of Representation in the Medieval Councils of the West

EVEN BEFORE the great body of new writing on Church councils stimulated by Vatican Council II, several scholars had called attention to the importance of medieval councils in the general history of Western representative government. Maude Clarke, for instance, wrote, 'The Fourth Lateran Council put the representative principle into action on a scale and with a prestige which made it known throughout the whole of Western Europe.' Similarly Georges de Lagarde noted that '. . . it is difficult to follow the evolution of representative doctrines in civil society while ignoring the evolution of the same doctrines in the Church'.[1]

Such observations point to a truth, but they also indicate a problem. The practice of representative government has become so taken-for-granted in our political culture that we sometimes forget what a complex bundle of concepts the word 'representation' implies. All language is representation—the verbal sign represents a perceived reality. Art is representation, either of external reality or internal vision—and symbolic art represents in a special sense. An attorney represents his client. An actor represents the character he impersonates.

For the theory of representative government, three meanings of the word 'representation' seem especially important. The first is *symbolic representation or personification*, as when a whole community is taken to be figuratively present in the person of its head. In this sense a constitutional monarch is held to represent his people when he makes a State visit abroad. The second meaning of our term can be defined as *mimesis*. Here an assembly is considered to represent a whole society because it faithfully mirrors in its composition all the varied elements that make up the society, rather as a map imitates, feature by feature, the physical terrain it depicts. (This idea was summed up by the American Federalist, James Wilson, when he wrote: 'The legislature ought to be the most exact transcript of the whole society.') The third meaning of 'representation' is *delegation or authorisation*, as when a community confers on an individual the right to act in its name by a specific act of election. This third meaning is especially significant for modern political representation, but in medieval thought the other two meanings were at least as important.

The definitions we have mentioned so far are relevant in discussing the representation of any large-scale community. But, in considering the Church in particular, other issues arise. Here we are dealing with a society conceived of as a mystical body whose head is Christ, a body informed by the Holy Spirit. Any person or assembly with a credible claim to represent the Church must act in a manner consonant with the guidance of the Spirit. Again, Christ established from the beginning a structure of authority among his followers. Any credible representation of the Church must be seen to embody this divinely conferred authority.

In medieval writing, from the twelfth-century canonists to the fifteenth-century conciliarists, we encounter a substantial body of commentary on the relationship between pope and council, with a constant assumption that a general council could indeed represent the universal Church; but there is relatively little exploration of the abstract theory of representation, of the precise manner in which the whole Church could be considered to be present or represented in a council. Instead we find different concepts used by different authors and sometimes by the same author in different contexts, but without much analysis. It was only at the end of the medieval epoch that Nicholas Cusanus drew together all the earlier strands of thought in a coherent theory.

The idea of representation as personification—the symbolisation of a community in its head—was prominent in the writings of twelfth-century Decretists. Their teaching was based on a text of Augustine, incorporated in the Decretum at C. 24 q. 1 c. 6: 'When Peter received his keys he signified holy Church.' Commenting on this, Simon de Bisignano emphasised the principle of personification: 'In the person of Peter the Lord spoke to the universal Church.'[2] In another formulation of the same idea, Augustine wrote that Peter 'bore the figure of the Church' (figuram gestabat ecclesiae), and this phrase, too, was often recalled by the canonists.[3] The idea that Peter symbolised the Church did not necessarily have any 'democratic' connotations. It could indeed be developed in an extreme monarchical sense, as in the later phrase of Augustinus Triumphus: 'The pope, who can be called the Church. . . .' But the canonists were deterred from pursuing this monarchical argument to all its logical conclusions by their reflections on the indefectible faith of the Church. An individual pope could err (they all believed) but the faith of the whole Church could never fail. The papacy therefore did not provide a completely adequate representation of the Church for all purposes, and the question arose whether some other institution could represent the Church more perfectly. The usual answer of the Decretists, writing around 1200, was that a general council could represent the Church more adequately than the pope, at least where matters of faith were concerned.

A common starting-point for their discussions was provided by Dist. 15 c. 2 of the Decretum, a text of Pope Gregory the Great which declared that the canons of the first four general councils were to be revered 'like the four gospels' because they were 'established by universal consent'. Referring to this text, Johannes Teutonicus wrote, in the Ordinary Gloss to the Decretum: 'It seems that the pope is bound to summon a council of bishops, which is true where the faith is concerned and then a council is greater than a pope.'[4]

But the Decretists did not explain at all clearly why the council represented the Church more reliably than the pope who 'bore the figure of the Church', or how the council embodied 'universal consent'. Did Gregory's phrase mean that the whole Church subsequently accepted the canons that the four councils promulgated? Or did the councils faithfully mirror in their composition the structure of the universal Church? Or was it rather that each bishop brought a delegated authority conveyed by the consent of his church? (The word consensus was commonly used in early discussions on the election of bishops.) Or did each bishop personify his local church as the pope personified the whole Church? (The canonists were familiar with this conception through Cyprian's phrase: 'The bishop is in the church and the church is in the bishop.') Are we dealing with a doctrine of reception or of representation? And, in the latter case, did Gregory have in mind mimesis or delegation or personification or some other concept? Instead of discussing such questions the canonists simply assumed an identity between the council and the Church. Thus the author of the *Summa Parisensis* described a general council as 'the whole Church under the presidency of the pope'.[5]

The Ordinary Gloss reveals some uncertainty about the proper composition of general councils. At one point Johannes Teutonicus wrote conventionally that 'A general council is constituted by the pope . . . together with all the bishops'; but in another context he cited the Roman law maxim, *Quod omnes tangit* ('What touches all is to be approved by all'), as an argument that, when matters of faith were to be discussed, lay rulers also were to be summoned to councils.[6] Apparently it was not clear that a council of bishops alone could faithfully represent all the members of the Church. At about this same time the canonists were adapting another Roman law term in developing their doctrine that a corporate group could be fully represented by a proctor with a mandate of *plena potestas*. The two phrases, *Quod omnes tangit* and *plena potestas*, passed from canonistic writing into general medieval usage and are often encountered in connection with secular representative assemblies during the thirteenth century; but the Decretists did not deploy them in any systematic analysis of the representative function of general councils.

While canonistic theory was in this rather inchoate state, Pope Innocent III actually summoned the Fourth Lateran Council, the greatest representative assembly of the medieval world. Some 400 bishops and over 800 abbots attended from all parts of Christendom. Moreover, along with these prelates, Innocent also expressly summoned representatives of cathedral chapters and other collegiate churches, because, he wrote, matters concerning them were to be discussed at the council. Christian lay rulers were also invited to attend and among those represented by envoys were the emperor-elect Frederick II and the kings of England, France and Hungary. Some of the Italian cities also sent envoys. Innocent's great council combined all the forms of representation that we have considered. The pope as head of the assembly symbolised the unity of the Church; elected representatives brought the delegated authority of their communities; and the members as a whole formed a kind of microcosm—or mimesis—of the Christian world. The council formulated a new statement of Christian doctrine and promulgated a substantial body of reform legislation; but it did not theorise about the basis of its own authority or about its capacity to represent the universal Church.

The most important development during the century after the Fourth Lateran Council was a gradual juridicising of the theological concept of the Church as a mystical body. The *corpus mysticum* came to be conceived of more and more as a legal corporation, in which the head exercised an authority that inhered in the whole body of members.[7] Many elements of thought contributed to the development of this idea. The texts of Augustine on Peter as a symbol of the Church could be understood in this sense. A scriptural basis was found in Matt. 18:15-18: 'If your brother sin against you, go . . . tell it to the church. . . .' Roman law taught that the emperor received his authority from the people and, around 1200, some canonists applied this principle analogously to the pope. (Laurentius explained that, although the jurisdiction inherent in the papal office came from God, the Church elected the particular individual who was to hold the office.) Besides all this, the newly discovered political theory of Aristotle emphasised the natural capacity of a community to provide for its own government.

Between about 1300 and 1350 three influential theories of representation were put forward which we can associate conveniently with John of Paris, Marsilius of Padua, and William of Ockham, and also with the three principles of representation that we have defined—personification, delegation, and mimesis. John of Paris, who is well known as an early exponent of conciliar theory, maintained that the college of cardinals—as well as a general council—could represent the church or 'act in place of the church'.[8] We seem to have here an extension of the idea that the church was symbolised in its head;

but now the head is considered to be not the individual pope but the corporate Roman church. Some later authors introduced the idea of delegation by suggesting that the cardinals should be elected from all the provinces of the Church.

Marsilius of Padua developed the most extreme medieval theory of representation as delegation. He held that, in both civil and ecclesiastical society, the authority to make law and institute rulers inhered by right in the whole community or its 'weightier part'. The 'efficient cause' of any legitimate ruler's authority was the consent of his community. Marsilius denied that Christ had established in the Church any ruling offices endowed with coercive authority. The papacy therefore was of merely human origin; the pope, as a delegate of the Church, could be corrected and if necessary deposed by a general council. The council itself was composed of elected members 'representing the corporate body (*universitas*) of the faithful by the authority conceded to them'.[9]

William of Ockham acknowledged the divine institution of the papacy but he too upheld the right of the Church to defend itself against an erring pontiff. His theory of representation included the idea of delegation but especially emphasised the principle we have called mimesis. For Ockham, a council consisted of '. . . divers persons bearing authority on behalf of all parts of the whole. . . .' The participation of the laity was especially important for Ockham. He even had the Master in his *Dialogus* argue to a dubious Disciple that women could properly attend general councils, 'because men and women are one in the faith, which touches all'.[10] However, Ockham's final contribution to the theory of representation was a negative one. He argued that, although a council represented the Church, its powers were not identical with those of the whole congregation of the faithful. Even a general council was only 'part of the church'. Hence, even a general council could err in faith.

The final systematisations of medieval representative theory are found in the conciliar writings of the fifteenth century. The theories and practices developed then were influenced both by earlier teachings and by the practical exigencies of the Great Schism.[11] All the leading conciliarists maintained—unlike Marsilius of Padua—that Christ had established in his Church a ruling hierarchy of pope, bishops and priests. Yet, to end the Schism, they needed to assert that a council could exercise authority over any member of the hierarchy, including the pope. The famous decree *Haec sancta* of the Council of Constance suggested a solution: 'This holy Synod . . . representing the Catholic Church, holds power immediately from Christ. . . .' It was precisely because the council represented the Church that it could exercise the authority Christ had implanted in the Church. At Constance, this thought was developed most fully by Gerson. He held that all the essential ruling offices of the church were established by Christ at least 'in germ'—papacy, cardinalate, patriarchate, archiepiscopate, episcopate, and priesthood. A council therefore consisted of all these 'hierarchical states' assembled together.[12] But the power of such a council was necessarily greater than that of a pope because papal power was included in the council and 'a whole is greater than a part'.[13] Gerson defined a general council as 'an assembly made by legitimate authority of every hierarchical state of the whole Catholic Church, no faithful person who seeks a hearing being excluded'. This is essentially a doctrine of representation by mimesis; it differs from Ockham's theory in the emphasis on hierarchical authority and the minimal role ascribed to the laity. (In real life, of course, lay power was very influential at Constance, notably in the person of King Sigismund.)

Nicholas Cusanos presented the most systematic and far-ranging of the conciliar theories a little later at the Council of Basle. Hubert Jedin described his work as 'a grandiose vision of the church as a divine cosmos, in which two fundamental forces are at work: the Holy Spirit and human freedom'. By insisting that the guidance of the Holy Spirit in the Church was manifested through the consent of the community, Cusanus was able to combine the ideas of representation by personification and representation by delegation in a unified theory. To be sure Christ himself had established the ruling offices of pope and bishops; and just as the pope 'figured' or symbolised the whole Church, so each bishop symbolised his local church. 'The bishop signifies and represents (the church) as a public person.' But it was precisely election and consent that established a prelate as symbol and representative of his church. 'All power is judged divine . . . when it arises from a common consent of the subjects.'[14]

The idea of mimesis was present in Cusanus' work in the now common idea that all classes of the Christian community had a right to attend councils. Nicholas emphasised the role of the bishops and, like Gerson, minimised that of the laity; but, in his ideal scheme of Church government, the laity formed the base of a vast pyramid from which authority extended upward through representation and consent to all levels of the hierarchy. Parish priests were to be chosen with the consent of the laity, bishops by the clergy with concurrent consent of the laity, metropolitans by bishops with consent of the clergy, and cardinals by the metropolitans with the consent of the bishops. Finally the cardinals should elect a pope with the consent of the metropolitans.[15]

The connection between consent and personification appears again in Cusanus' theory of the supremacy of a general council. The pope, he wrote, signified the Church but he did so only very confusedly. The members, bearing a more immediate consent of their communities, represented them and together represented the whole Church more truly and certainly. Finally, the guidance of the Holy Spirit rendered the council infallible in defining the faith, and the presence of the Spirit manifested itself in the harmonious conduct of the assembly. 'Where there is discord there is no council.'[16]

When we compare Cusanus' ideal with the reality of Basle it is easy to understand why he eventually became a supporter of Pope Eugene IV. The Council of Basle was full of discords and it did not represent the Church in the way Cusanus envisaged. The prelates, who represented local communities, were outnumbered many times over by private doctors of theology and law who often represented no one but themselves. The later leaders of the council turned away from Cusanus' complex arguments to assert again a simple identity between the power of the Church and that of council—regardless of its composition. Sometimes they asserted that the council actually *was* the mystical body of Christ. But this was not so much a coherent theory of representation as a denial that any such theory was needed to uphold their claims.

In the end the ideas of the great medieval churchmen on representative government had more influence in the secular sphere than in the Church itself. The failure of Basle proved that a council cut off from the pope could not carry through the much needed reform of the Church; but the subsequent history of the Renaissance papacy showed that the popes could not reform the Church without a council that credibly represented the Christian world.

Notes

1. M. V. Clarke *Medieval Representation and Consent* (London 1936) p. 296; G. de Lagarde 'Les Théories représentatives du XIVe-XVe siecle et L'Église', in *Études presentées à la Commission Internationale pour l'histoire des Assemblées d'États* (Rome 1955) 65-75. For modern literature on conciliarism see F. Oakley 'Natural Law, the *Corpus Mysticum* and Consent in Conciliar Thought' in *Speculum* 56 (1981) 786-810, and G. Alberigo *Chiesa Conciliare* (Bologna 1981). On medieval representation see especially *Der Begriff der Repraesentation im Mittelalter: Stellvertretung, Symbol, Zeichen, Bild*, ed. A. Zimmermann (Berlin 1971) and H. Hofmann *Reprasentation. Studien zur Wort- und Begriffsgeschichte von der Antik bis ins 19 Jahrhundert* (Berlin 1974).

XI

2. Latin originals of all the canonistic texts quoted in this article are printed in my *Foundations of the Conciliar Theory* (Cambridge 1955).

3. For further references see *Foundations*, p. 35, n. 1.

4. Goss *ad Dist.* 19 c. 9.

5. *Summa Parisiensis*, ed. T. P. McLaughlin (Toronto 1942) p. 4.

6. Goss *ad Dist.* 17 *ante* c. 1 and *ad Dist.* 96 c. 4.

7. The idea was eventually expressed in classical form by Cardinal Zabarella. 'The pope has plenitude of power . . . not alone but as the head of a corporate body, so that the power is in the corporation fundamentally and in the pope as the principal minister through whom this power is expressed . . .' (see *Foundations*, p. 225).

8. *De potestate regia et papali* ed. J. Leclercq (Paris 1942) pp. 215, 254, 257. The idea that the cardinals were 'parts of the pope's body', 'one and the same with him' had been formulated earlier by the canonist Hostiensis.

9. *Defensor pacis* ed. C. W. Previté-Orton (Cambridge 1928) p. 320.

10. *Dialogus* in M. Goldast *Monarchia S. Romani Imperii* (Frankfurt 1614) pp. 603, 605.

11. Thus the cardinals could rely on a substantial earlier tradition when they claimed to exercise the authority of the Roman church in summoning the council of Pisa. But the system of voting by 'nations'—on the model of universities—at the council of Constance was not based on any sophisticated theory of representation; it was simply a tactical device to prevent domination of the council by the numerous Italian prelates.

12. *De ecclesiastica potestate* ed. P. Glorieux in Jean Gerson *Oeuvres complètes* VI (Turnai 1965) pp. 222, 240, 241.

13. Gerson held that this principle held good 'whether there is a pope or whether he is lacking through natural or civil death'. He was relying on the doctrine that the power of the head of a corporate body devolved to the members in case of vacancy or delict (p. 222).

14. *De concordantia catholica* ed. G. Kallen in *Nicolai de Cusa opera omnia* XIV (Hamburg 1963) pp. 58, 348.

15. *Ibid.* pp. 200-203.

16. *Ibid.* pp. 194, 199, 200.

XII

HIERARCHY, CONSENT, AND THE
"WESTERN TRADITION"

SAMUEL BEER DESERVES OUR RESPECT and gratitude for his many distinguished studies on modern British and American history. But his venture into medieval thought, "The Rule of the Wise and Holy: Hierarchy in the Thomistic System,"[1] calls for a Critical Response. Medievalists find their work amply rewarding on the whole; but they share one common frustration. No one pays the slightest attention to anything they write—except other medievalists. Yet everyone feels competent to pass judgment on medieval achievements, or to decry the lack of them.[2] Professor Beer begins with a simple assertion that the Americans of 1776 turned their backs on the whole preceding tradition of Western thought when they opted for a system of government by consent, "For more than 2000 years nearly all leading minds had rejected popular government. Classical philosophy had taught the rule of the wise, Christian theology the rule of the holy. Medieval thinkers had combined the two ideas" (p. 391). The subsequent argument is based on an analysis of the thought of Thomas Aquinas, which is taken to be characteristic of medieval thought in general. Beer points out that Aquinas viewed the whole universe as a vast hierarchy of being. Such a hierarchical order was evidently based on inequality. Transferred to the political sphere, this way of thinking implied that political obligation was based on the inherent superiority of a ruler—his holiness or wisdom.

There are two lines of objection to this whole argument. In the first place it presents a very one-sided picture of Aquinas's thought. In the second place (and this is much more important) it assumes that the ideas of Aquinas were characteristic of all medieval political theory.

The first objection need not detain us overlong, though Aquinas

POLITICAL THEORY, Vol. 15 No. 4, November 1987 646-652
© 1987 Sage Publications, Inc.

certainly emphasized popular participation in government more than Beer suggests. Aquinas laid down as the first principle of rightly ordered rule in any state or people that all should have some share of it.[3] Some modern interpreters have succeeded in extracting a fully fledged theory of government based on consent from his writings.[4] Moreover, Aquinas certainly did not teach consistently that people should obey their rulers, "not because they understand the truth and goodness of the law, but because they recognize the authority of the lawgiver" (p. 417). The whole familiar Thomist argument about whether subjects are obliged to obey an unjust law implies that they are expected to make a judgment about the law's "truth and goodness."[5]

I do not want to labor these points too much. The work of Aquinas is like the Bible in this, that one can prove anything out of it by an adroit selection of texts. The interpretation of Aquinas's political theory remains controversial; and his thought certainly did contain the hierarchical doctrines that Beer emphasizes. (To me it seems that they coexist uneasily with the more "constitutionalist" elements in Aquinas's work and that, in this sphere, he did not achieve or even attempt an all-embracing synthesis.)

My second line of objection is the weightier one. Even if we were to concede that there is no real idea of government based primarily on consent in Aquinas's work, that would not prove that the doctrine was lacking in medieval thought generally. Aquinas was a great thinker, but the idea that he was *the* one great thinker of the Middle Ages is an invention of modern neo-Thomism. It would have startled anyone at the University of Paris in the thirteenth century. Yet this notion seems to have somehow infected much of the political science discipline in America. Courses on the history of political theory often dwell lovingly on Plato and Aristotle, glance at Augustine, then take flight over the uncharted ocean of the next 1000 years until the teacher can alight happily in the familiar terrain of Machiavelli and Hobbes and Locke. Thomas Aquinas provides the only resting place on the way.

This approach makes it impossible to understand the origins of modern political theory. A major defect is that it ignores the massive work of the medieval jurists that provided the real foundation for medieval and early modern theories of government. Beer mentions John Adams's *Dissertation on the Canon and Feudal Law*, but he leaves us to infer that Adams was quite correct in seeing these medieval legal systems as mere instruments of tyranny. This is absurd of course. For many decades it has been platitudinous to point out that feudal ideas contributed to later doctrines of government by consent and of individual rights. Magna Carta was a feudal document. As for the canonists, a considerable body of recent work—some of it by American scholars—has emphasized their major contribution to Western constitutional thought, especially through their teachings on representation and consent.[6] A text at *Dist.* 4 of Gratian's *Decretum* gave rise to endless debate about popular consent to legislation.[7] The maxim of Roman private law, *Quod omnes tangit* ("What touches all is to be approved by all") was applied to the authority of General Councils by canonists from the twelfth century onward and so was transformed into a basic principle of representative government. The phrase, with its new meaning, passed into English usage and was still cited in the struggle of the 1640s.

Canonists did not teach that ruling power in the church was derived from personal holiness—a saint did not have jurisdiction over his bishop. Nor was it derived from sacramental orders—a person without Holy Orders or in lower orders might exercise jurisdiction over a priest. Nor was it derived from individual wisdom—any church Father could be wiser than a pope. When the canonists asked where jurisdiction did come from, they normally emphasized election. In another variation of the *Quod omnes tangit* phrase they held that "he who is to rule over all should be chosen by all."[8]

Let us turn to the political philosophers and theologians. Professor Beer notes that Aquinas's doctrine of "essences" was a "necessary premise" of his hierarchical theories, and he also mentions in passing that nominalist philosophers rejected Aquinas's doctrine on this point. One might expect then, on Beer's own argument, that alternative political theories would exist.[9] This was indeed the case. I will limit my argument to the specific question raised by Beer. Did ruling authority inhere in certain persons by virtue of their own intrinsic qualities, requiring only to be acknowledged by their subjects? Or did licit rulership arise only from consent, active consent that is, not just deference to an already existing authority?

It happens that this precise question was often asked by medieval writers. Marsilius of Padua (ca. 1325) argued that, because all good government was rule over voluntary subjects, it followed that such government had to be established by consent. Marsilius considered the argument that superior wisdom gave a title to rule and overtly rejected it. A ruler acquired power solely by election, "not by his knowledge of the laws, his prudence, or moral virtue."[10] The individual qualities of the ruler were not the most important consideration. Civil obedience was directed primarily to the laws and government as such, only secondarily to the person of the ruler.[11]

Marsilius of Padua was in some way a radical thinker for his age, but on this question of government by consent he was no lonely maverick. A few years before Marsilius wrote, his eminently respectable contemporary, Herveus Natalis, Master-General of the Dominican Order, had presented an essentially similar argument (ca. 1315). Herveus explained that ruling power did not inhere in a wise person as such. A prudent man could help to direct affairs by counsel and teaching, but he could not oblige others to obey him. For Herveus an essential feature of political jurisdiction was that it created obligation. The ruler had the right to *oblige* his subjects.[12] When Herveus asked where this right could come from, he replied, "Only through consent of the people." His argument was simple. If ruling power was not held by consent it was held by violence. "But no right is acquired by violent possession."[13] Herveus envisaged a sort of two-stage process. A people could first consent to establish a governing authority, then consent to institute a particular person in the office they had created. (Incidentally Herveus was the first author, so far as I have noticed, to define government in terms of legislative, judicial, and executive powers.)

Duns Scotus argued on similar lines (ca. 1300). The decision of a prudent man did not in itself bind a community. Just lawmaking required both prudence and authority. And political authority was justly derived from "the common consent and election of the community." Scotus imagined a crowd of unrelated strangers coming together to build a city. There would be no natural paternal authority among them but they would need some sort of rule. Hence, he suggested, they might all submit themselves by consent to one ruler or each submit himself to the authority of the whole community.[14]

Durand of St. Pourçain offered another variation of the argument.[15] Even if there were one man in all the world better and wiser than any other person it would not follow that all should obey his laws. There would always be more wisdom inhering in the whole community than in any one outstanding individual. Therefore, it was natural that political authority should remain with the whole community; but because of the practical difficulties of exercising such authority in common, public expediency normally required that it be conferred on a ruler. By the same token, if the ruler's power ceased to serve the end of public expediency it could be revoked.[16] The author went on to develop an unusual theory of civil government derived from consent and based wholly on utilitarian considerations.

William of Ockham also had his own characteristic variation on the common theme of government by consent. While insisting on consent as the true source of authority, most medieval writers (like modern ones) assumed that one purpose of the electoral process was to identify the person best qualified for office. In his *Dialogus* (ca. 1340), Ockham chose to consider the difficult situation that would arise if there were no person who deserved election by his own merit. He went on to argue that simple election and consent could institute a ruler over his equals in such circumstances.[17]

One could go on and on. The real problem is not that Beer presents the neo-Platonic elements in Aquinas's work incorrectly; it is that he bases sweeping conclusions on an inadequate appraisal of medieval thought as a whole. All through the Middle Ages there were two attitudes—not just one—to the problem of equality and inequality. One could emphasize that hierarchical ranking was necessary in an ordered society; or one could emphasize that, because all men shared a common humanity, they were all by nature equal, and also by nature free (for no one had a natural right to dominate his equals). Both positions were ancient, one Platonic, the other Stoic. Both could be defended in terms of Christian doctrine. The two attitudes coexisted side by side in the twelfth and thirteenth centuries and they still coexisted in the seventeenth and eighteenth centuries. The distinctive feature of medieval thought was not that it preserved the old notion of hierarchy but that it introduced a radical innovation by using the egalitarian concept as a foundation for new legal and philosophical theories of government by consent.

Medieval consent theory is a major source of the tradition that the seventeenth-century opponents of Stuart absolutism developed and passed on to the American Founding Fathers. To contest Professor Beer's argument is not just to quibble about recondite details of medieval political theory. It is a question of seeking an understanding of the past that can render our modern world intelligible. The real problem is to explain why Western culture developed a political tradition radically different from that of all the other great world civilizations. The problem can hardly be addressed meaningfully unless we realize that the decisive shift in ways of thinking occurred in the Middle Ages, mainly between 1100 and 1350. The shift is intelligible only when we relate it to the circumstances of that age—the conflicts between popes and kings, the simultaneous growth of religious individualism and corporative institutions, the rise of cities, the emergence of more centralized monarchies in church and state, the recovery of ancient political thought and its radical transformation to suit the needs of a new age.[18]

The Americans of 1776 had often forgotten the remote origins of the tradition that shaped their consciousness, that had given birth to the ideas of consent and obligation they took for granted. The task of a historian is precisely to restore our collective memory.

NOTES

1. *Political Theory* 14, no. 3 (August 1986): 391-422.

2. Professor Beer could have found abundant medieval material that implicitly contradicts his thesis in a standard old work like R. W. and A. J. Carlyle, *A History of Medieval Political Theory in the West*, 6 vols. (Edinburgh and London: William Blackwood, 1903-1936). More recently I wrote a little work of synthesis that attempted to present some contemporary understandings of the precise issues that Professor Beer addresses—medieval thought on hierarchy and consent and "mixed government," and the relevance of that thought for the Western tradition as a whole. The book was reasonably well received by the usual circle of medievalists. It was widely reviewed. A Japanese translation has just appeared. An Italian translation is on the way. But such current work somehow just does not enter the consciousness of modern historians who feel moved to write about medieval ideas.

3. *Summa theologiae*, 1. 2ae. 105. 1.

4. For example, G. Bowe, *The Origin of Political Authority* (Dublin: Clonmore and Reynolds, 1955). On Aquinas's theory of mixed government, see, most recently, James M. Blythe, "The Mixed Constitution in Aquinas," *Journal of the History of Ideas* 47 (1986): 547-65.

5. *Summa theologiae*, 1. 2ae. 96.4.

6. It will suffice to mention the contributions of Gaines Post, collected in his *Studies in Medieval Legal Thought* (Princeton, NJ: Princeton University Press, 1964).

7. *Decretum Magistri Gratiani*, ed. E. Friedberg (Leipzig: B. Tauchnitz, 1879), *Dist.* 4 *dictum post* c. 3, "Laws are instituted when they are promulgated; they are confirmed when they are approved by the practice of those using them."

8. *Decretales Gregorii P. IX*, ed. E. Friedberg (Leipzig: B. Tauchnitz, 1879), I. 11.6.

9. It seems to me, though, that there is less direct correlation between metaphysical doctrines and political theory than Beer supposes. On the difficulties inherent in this approach, see Charles Zuckerman, "The Relationship of Theories of Universals to Theories of Church Government in the Middle Ages: A Critique of Previous Views," *Journal of the History of Ideas* 36 (1975): 579-94.

10. A. Gewirth, *Marsilius of Padua: The Defender of the Peace*, 2 vols. (New York: Columbia University Press, 1951-1956), 2: 61.

11. Gewirth, *Marsilius of Padua*, p. 74.

12. *De iurisdictione*, ed. L. Hödl (Munich: M. Hueber, 1959), p. 15.

13. *De iurisdictione*, p. 16.

14. *Opus Oxoniense* in *Opera Omnia* (Paris: L. Vives, 1891-1895), 18: 266.

15. Or pseudo-Durandus. The authorship is disputed.

16. *Tractatus de Legibus* (Paris: no imprint, 1506), fol. 13rb.

17. *Dialogus* in M. Goldast, *Monarchia S. Romani imperii*, vol. 2 (Frankfurt: Conrad Biermann, 1614), III. 1.2. 13-17, pp. 798-803.

18. For a recent survey, see Harold J. Berman, *Law and Revolution: The Formation of the Western Legal Tradition* (Cambridge, MA: Harvard University Press, 1983).

XIII

ARISTOTLE, AQUINAS, AND THE IDEAL CONSTITUTION

The comments of Thomas Aquinas on problems of human governance covered a broad range of topics. In this paper we shall consider only one of them, Aquinas' adaptation in medieval Christian terms of the classical idea of a mixed constitution. The subject has a special interest as an illustration of a broader theme, the interplay of secular and religious ideas in the growth of western constitutional thought.

The theory of a mixed constitution asserted most typically that the best form of government was a mixture of monarchy, aristocracy, and democracy (though sometimes only two of these forms were included). The theory is ancient of course and distinctly secular in origin. It is found, applied to the state, in Aristotle, Cicero, and Polybius among others. The ancient idea was revived in secular Renaissance thought in Florence and Venice. It passed to England where, in 1642 on the eve of the Civil War, Charles I formally declared that the government of England was a mixed constitution. The idea remained alive and important in American eighteenth-century thought. All this secular theory has been elaborately explored in modern scholarship. But there is a whole chapter of medieval ecclesiastical thought about the mixed constitution which has hardly been explored at all and which needs to be explored if we are to understand all the sources of later constitutional theory. The major development is that in classical thought the idea of a mixed constitution was applied only to city-states. In the Middle Ages it was applied to larger entities, to the universal church or to national kingdoms, and so took on a different form. The democratic element had to involve a representative body which in turn formed part of a complex central government. Thomas Aquinas contributed significantly to this development.

We sometimes think of Thomas as a great synthesizer, a man who took all the current ideas of his age and wove them into coherent, self-consistent structures of thought. When one studies his political theory and ecclesiology the first impression is just the opposite. Thomas seems fascinatingly original but quite incoherent. Indeed, the question of whether he is coherent or not is a central one for any scholar who investigates Thomas' thought on the ideal constitution. The problem is of course that Thomas never wrote a complete treatise on political theory (his work *De Regno* was left unfinished) and he never wrote a systematic treatise on ecclesiology at all. Yet Thomas did write a great deal in scattered contexts on problems of governance in both church and state. To anticipate for a moment, it seems arguable that, when the scattered fragments are brought together, a clear, self-consistent doctrine emerges in the field of secular constitutional thought. But it is much more difficult to discern such a consistent doctrine in the sphere of ecclesiology.

2

The principal text of St. Thomas on the idea of a mixed constitution, comes at a point in the *Summa Theologiae* where Thomas considers the form of government established for the children of Israel in the days of Moses. Royal government, Thomas argues, is the most perfect form since monarchy most closely imitates the divine rule of the universe. But God did not establish a king over Israel from the beginning. Therefore, it would seem, he gave an imperfect form of government to his "Chosen People." In response to this, Thomas writes that, in discussing the best form of government, two things must be considered. First that all should have some part in government, since this makes for peace and stability. Second, one must consider the type of political regime to be adopted.[1] We can explore these two points further by comparing what Thomas says here with various relevant comments scattered in other parts of his work.

In the passage that we have just mentioned Thomas defends widespread popular participation in government by referring to Aristotle. But in other contexts he cites scriptural and patristic authority to reach the same conclusion. He discussed, for instance, St. Paul's argument on the different states and offices in the church, "As in one body we have many members but all the members have not the same office, so we being many are one body in Christ." Then at the end of the discussion he applied the Pauline argument specifically to secular government. "... an earthly commonwealth is the better preserved by a distinction of duties and states, since thereby the greater number have a share in public action. Wherefore the Apostle says that 'God hath tempered us together that ... the members might be mutually careful for one another.'"[2]

In another passage, Thomas asked whether an independent people had the right to change existing laws by practicing new customs, another form of popular participation in government. There were various arguments against this right. Human law was based on natural and divine law, and so should not be changed. An individual act against the law was wrong; therefore a multiplicity of such acts, constituting a custom, could not be right. Only rulers could make law, while customs were established by private individuals. Against all this Thomas cited only one authority, but this one text proved quite decisive. "St. Augustine says 'The customs of the people of God ... are to be considered as laws. And those who throw contempt on the customs of the Church ought to be punished.'"[3] Again an argument from ecclesiology is used to settle a point of political theory. Thomas seems to move between the two spheres almost unconsciously.

Let us consider one more example. In considering legislative activity Thomas states that there are different kinds of law-making in different kinds of constitutions. In a monarchy statutes are issued, in an aristocracy senatorial decisions, in a democracy, plebiscitary decrees. Then he adds that there is another form of government made up of all the preceding ones, and that this is the best form. In this kind of government law is sanctioned by elders and commons.[4] The authority for this is St. Isidore of Seville. So once more a patristic authority settles a point of secular political theory. In fact Isidore did mention law sanctioned by elders and commons but he did not relate this definition to the idea of a mixed constitution. That is Thomas' own gloss on the text.

In considering the governance of the children of Israel, you will recall Thomas raised two topics for discussion. The first was that all the people should participate in government. That position seems clearly and consistently defended from sacred as well as secular sources in other parts of his work. The other question concerned the type of regime to be established — and Thomas would go on to argue in favor of a mixed regime. But here a problem arises. Thomas himself raised the objection that monarchy was the best form of government because it most closely resembled the divine government of God. Moreover, this was not just an isolated comment. In various other contexts Thomas, with evident sincerity, defended monarchy as the best form of government. In the *Summa Contra Gentiles* he wrote, "He who excells in intellect naturally rules" (with references to both Aristotle and Solomon). And again, "The best form of government for a multitude is that it be ruled by one." (Thomas argues here from the ends of government, which are peace and unity.)[5] And, again, in the *De Regno,* "The members of the body are moved by one heart ... among bees there is one king ... and in the whole universe God is maker and ruler of all, so if art imitates nature it follows that a multitude of men should be ruled by one (king)."

Such texts led McIlwain to conclude that Thomas' real preference was for pure or absolute monarchy.[7] At least it might seem that there is some indecision, some incoherence between these texts and those that favor mixed government. To this we can respond that no contradiction would have been apparent to a thirteenth-century person. Kings in the secular sphere and prelates in the church commonly ruled with the advice and consent of their councils or chapters. This was not merely a matter of common practice. As a matter of principle too various systems of thirteenth-century law asserted a unique status for the monarch while still defending a right of others to participate in government. Canon law taught that only the pope was supreme head of the church but Hostiensis maintained that the cardinals also were included "in the expression of the plenitude of power," and the *Ordinary Gloss* to the *Decretum* declared simply that where matters of faith were concerned a general council was greater than the pope alone.[8] Roman law declared that only the emperor could make law but Accursius held that the Senate also should participate in legislation.[9] Bracton held that in England the king had no equal or superior but he also held that laws were established "by the counsel and consent of the magnates and the common engagement of the state."[10] Thomas knew something of Roman and canon law. He could hardly have known Bracton's English law, but Bracton was describing a situation common in feudal law, a situation which obtained also in Cyprus, the kingdom to which Thomas addressed his treatise *De Regno*. There too the highest authority inhered in a court made up of the feudal barons, with the king presiding.

In a thirteenth-century context of thought then, there seemed no inconsistency in defending monarchy as the best form of regime while insisting that others beside the monarch should participate in government. To return to our initial discussion on the children of Israel: Thomas argues that God did indeed establish the most perfect form of government for them. Monarchy is the best simple form of government, he acknowledges, but a simple monarchy is improved when elements of aristocracy and democracy are added to it. After referring to Aristotle again Thomas wrote:

> Hence the best form of government in any city or kingdom is where one is set in authority on account of his virtue to rule over all; and under him are others ruling on account of their virtue; and nevertheless such a government belongs to all both because the rulers can be chosen from all and can be chosen by all.

4

Then, by some slightly strained exegesis of Deuteronomy and Exodus, he demonstrates that such an Aristotelian regime was indeed established for Israel. Moses ruled over all, so he was a kind of king. But he was assisted by 72 elders who formed an aristocracy. And the elders were "chosen from all the people" and "chosen by the people" so there was also present an element of democracy. Thomas sums up: "For this polity is well mixed: from kingship, since there is one at the head of all; from aristocracy in so far as a number of persons are set in authority on account of their virtue; from democracy, that is, the power of the people, in so far as the rulers can be chosen from the people and the people have the right to choose their rulers."[11]

Gilson wrote on this passage, "(Thomas) derives his politics from Scripture and Aristotle and presents them in a text which (is) ... A typical example of those doctrines which he would lead us to believe he has borrowed and which, nevertheless, are to be found nowhere save in his works."[12] Thomas really had made a distinctive contribution. He quotes Aristotle and the Bible but the precise doctrine he presents does not really exist in either of his sources. It is a new synthesis. Thomas has not just decked out an Aristotelian idea in Old Testament dress. He had adapted the idea in the process of adopting it. Aristotle did indeed mention a threefold form of mixed government in connection with the constitution of Sparta, but all his more detailed discussions dealt only with a mixture of aristocracy and democracy. Aristotle was basically interested in securing a stable balance of class-interests in the state. Thomas was more interested in uniting in one government the excellences proper to each simple regime. Monarchy ensured unity, aristocracy wisdom, and democracy liberty. Thomas also introduced a kind of 'checks and balances' approach in his commentary on Aristotle's *Politics*. The mixed regime was best, he wrote, because each element checked, "tempered," the other two.[13] Again, while many classical authors suggested that there should be a democratic element in the ideal constitution, they did not suggest that the democratic element consisted in a right of the people to choose the monarchic and aristocratic elements. But such an idea does begin to suggest modern constitutional theory where a complex central government derives its authority from the consent of the people. And it is in this form, after passing through a filter of Christian theology, that the idea of a mixed constitution was most influential for the future.

When Thomas introduces a representative element into his theory of the mixed constitution his thought reflects in part the practices of his own day. Though most medieval monarchies were hereditary, some rulers were elected, including the greatest ones of all, pope and emperor. Also some rulers were beginning to experiment with representative assemblies, and church councils played a regular role in ecclesiastical government. But Thomas' ideal constitution does not correspond precisely to that of any thirteenth-century polity. (The closest analogue indeed is the governance of his own Dominican Order.) Thomas seems to have taken the common practices of his day, reflected on them in the light of his own understanding of Aristotle and the Bible, and offered a new generalization, one that was stimulating enough to influence theories of constitutional government in both state and church for the next several centuries.

So far so good. Thomas has constructed a coherent theory of the ideal constitution and he has constructed it in a way that admirably illustrates the themes we are pursuing — the interplay between religious and secular thought, and the interplay between old ideas and existing institutional realities in the thirteenth century. But now a further problem arises. Did Thomas regard his theory of a mixed constitution as applicable also to the government of the church? It seems that logically he should have done so. He wrote clearly enough that the church was ruled by the best constitution,[14] and if the best constitution was a mixed government then, one might suppose, this should have been the constitution of the church. One could pose various a priori objections to this position but they seem to me without substance. One might argue that monarchy in the state had to be tempered with aristocracy and democracy only in order to avoid tyranny, and that this problem did not arise in the church. But for a century before Thomas the canonists had been writing at length on the danger of a pope falling into notorious crime or heresy and on the steps that could be taken against such a papal tyrant. Thomas never discussed the question at all, but we cannot take his silence as implying a commitment to a novel and highly untenable doctrine of papal impeccability.

Again, one might argue that authority in the church came from God, authority in the state from the people. But the church was in principle a structure of elective offices. And thirteenth-century thinkers had already formulated the doctrine — still widespread in seventeenth-century thought — that authority in both church and state could be derived from God through the people. One might argue that norms of government for the state and norms of government for the church were quite different subjects, the one to be investigated by natural reason, the other to be determined by divine revelation. But in Thomistic thought one does not expect reason and revelation to contradict one another. Moreover, Thomas was not averse to drawing parallels between secular and ecclesiastical polities. In his commentary on the Psalms he compared the church in some detail to an earthly *civitas*.[15] Also, Thomas plainly indicated that reason and revelation coincided in this sphere when he described the form of government he found in the Old Testament as both approved by Aristotle and established by divine law. And finally it seems relevant that this was the form of government given by God specifically to the children of Israel. For Thomas as for any thinker of his age Israel in the thirteenth century was not constituted by the scattered remnant of the Jews but by the church itself, the congregation of the faithful, the new people of God.

There seems no a priori reason then why Thomas should not have regarded his doctrine of a mixed constitution as applicable also to the government of the church. Whether he actually did so regard it is another question. And evidently the question can not be decided solely on the basis of the Old Testament texts we have mentioned so far. Some elements of the old law were swept away by the new. The crucial question that remained was: what kind of government did Christ actually institute among the apostles and the first disciples? And it happened that a bitter controversy on this point broke out at the University of Paris just at the time when Thomas was first teaching there in the 1250's. The controversy concerned the privileges that the popes had conferred on the new orders of mendicant friars, including Thomas' own Dominican Order. Equipped with their papal privileges the friars were able to preach and administer sacraments in parishes throughout the church without permission of the local clergy. In 1252 the secular masters at the University of Paris, who had their own grievances against the friars, began to argue that the papal privileges were contrary to the divine constitution of the church since they undermined the authority of bishops and priests, an authority which, they claimed, had been established by Christ himself.[16]

The defenders of episcopal rights in the 1250s did not yet use the Aristotelian language of a mixed regime, but they did argue that Christ had established a pluralistic form of government for his church. They accepted the headship of Peter and the popes after him, acknowledging that Christ had first singled out Peter individually in the famous text at Matt. 16:18-19 when he said "Thou art Peter ..." and "Whatsoever thou shalt bind on earth it shall be bound in the heavens." But the episcopalists pointed out that Christ had conferred on all the apostles the same kind of power that he had first promised to Peter when he said to all of them at Matt. 18:18 "Amen I say to you, whatsoever you bind on earth it shall be bound in heaven" and again when he said to all of them at John 20:22-23 "Receive the Holy Spirit. Whose sins you shall forgive they shall be forgiven them ..." Hence, they argued, in the existing church the bishops, the successors of the apostles, also received their powers directly from Christ. Bishops were indeed subordinate to the pope. The pope as head of the church directed them in the use of their authority. But the authority itself was divinely conferred and could not be destroyed by the pope. Such ideas could be — and eventually were — restated as a doctrine that Christ had established a mixed constitution for the church.

In opposition to such arguments the more extreme defenders of the friars — most notably St. Bonaventure — maintained that the pope alone received authority directly from God and that all other jurisdiction in the church was derived from him. This 'derivational theory' could be defended in two ways. It could be argued that, in the words Christ spoke to all the apostles, he conferred on them only the sacramental power of orders. while he gave jurisdiction, the actual power of governing, to Peter alone. Alternatively, it could be argued that Christ did indeed confer jurisdiction on all the apostles but that, in the existing church, the pope ruled as vicar of Christ. Hence just as the first apostles received their authority from Christ, subsequent bishops received their authority from the pope. In both forms, the theory was one of pure monarchy, quite incompatible with any idea of a mixed constitution for the church.

It is very hard to determine the position of Thomas himself in these controversies.[17] His first treatment of the question, in his early commentary on the *Sentences,* expressed a very clear derivational theory. In a famous text usually cited to illustrate his views on the problems of church and state, Thomas considered different types of subordination, and wrote:

> A superior power and an inferior can be related in two ways. Either the inferior power stems totally from the superior ... and in this way the power of God is related to all created power ... so also the power of the pope is related to all spiritual power in the church since the various grades of dignity in the church are disposed and ordered by the pope himself, whence his power is a kind of foundation of the church as appears at Matthew 16....Again, a superior and inferior power may be so related that both stem from a certain supreme power which subjects one to the other as it pleases ... and the powers of bishops and archbishops are related in this way since both descend from the pope.[18]

Also in the commentary on the *Sentences* Thomas wrote:

> Some distinguish between a key of orders which all priests have and a key of

jurisdiction in the judicial forum. Christ, however, gave each to Peter at Matt. 16 and from him (the key) descends to others who have either.[19] But about the same time that he was writing these passages, Thomas wrote a tract in favor of the friars, *Contra impugnantes,* and in that work he carefully refrained from arguing that bishops derived their episcopal authority from the pope. Instead, he wrote in conciliatory fashion that the friars, even when equipped with papal privileges, should seek a bishop's permission before undertaking pastoral work in his diocese.

Moreover, the commentary on the *Sentences* itself is not without difficulties. Thomas' discussion in that work on John 20:23 is a masterpiece of tactful ambiguity:

> For absolution from sin a two-fold power is required, the power of orders and the power of jurisdiction. The first power indeed exists equally in all priests, but not the second. Hence when Christ gave to all the apostles together the power of remitting sins at John 20 this is understood to be the power which stems from orders....But to Peter he gave the power of remitting sins individually at Matt. 16.19 so that it might be understood that he has the power of jurisdiction before the others *(prae aliis).* The power of orders in itself however extends to all things to be absolved and therefore the Lord said indeterminately, "Whose sins you shall forgive", understanding however that the use of that power ought to be subject to the disposition of Peter, presupposing the power conferred on Peter.[20]

Thomas says here that Christ gave to all the apostles the power of orders but he does not precisely say who gave them the power of jurisdiction which was the really difficult question. No one at the time would have objected to the view that the use of sacramental orders was subject to papal control.

In yet another comment on the *Sentences* Thomas wrote, "The pope has plenitude of power like a king in his kingdom; but bishops assume a share of the solicitude like judges appointed to particular cities."[21] But in the *Summa Theologiae* he varied the imagery and wrote that each bishop was like a king in his own diocese.[22] In the *Summa contra Gentiles* Thomas wrote that the keys were promised to Peter alone at Matt. 16.19 "so that it might be shown that the power of the keys was to derive through him to the others."[23] But in the same work he repeated that Christ himself gave to the disciples the power to remit sins (without distinguishing between power of orders and power of jurisdiction); and here he added that "spiritual power" derived from all the disciples to others.[24]

One might hope to find a definitive solution in Thomas' own commentary on Matthew; but again the texts are ambiguous. Glossing Matt. 16.18, "Upon this rock I will build my church," Thomas observed that not only Peter but all the apostles were established as foundations of the church "by the concession of Christ and the authority given by Christ." But, on the words "Whatsoever thou shalt bind on earth it shall be bound in the heavens...," Thomas commented, "He gave this power immediately to Peter; the others received it from Peter."[25] Then, when he came to Matt. 18.18, where Christ repeated to all the apostles the words "Whatsoever you shall bind on earth...," Thomas wrote, "These words were said to Peter above; here however it is said to the whole church." Then he added (following Origen) that the power given to the apostles by Christ "is not universal but in a particular place, since he gave universal power to Peter."[26] This last view, that Christ gave a local power to the apostles, was quite consistent with the position of the thirteenth-century episcopalists.

Thus some of Thomas' texts would have been acceptable to the secular masters of theology at Paris who attacked the doctrine of pure, unmixed, papal monarchy. But other texts, if given a plain and literal interpretation, seem to assert a most extreme 'derivational' theory of papal power. Possibly the literal interpretation is too extreme to be true. Thomas affirmed at one point that both the key of orders and the key of jurisdiction descended from Peter (see above, n. 19). Yet the *communis opinio* of the time held that every priest received at least the power of orders directly from Christ at his consecration. Perhaps Thomas attached an unusual significance to the words 'descend' and 'derive.' If he meant only that communion with Peter was necessary for the licit exercise of spiritual power, his text was innocuous enough.

Evidently there is no simple solution to these problems. The difficulty is not only that Thomas himself never wrote a systematic treatise on Thomistic ecclesiology. No modern scholar has written one either (though there is an abundant specialist literature on particular points). On the matter that particularly concerns us, the modern scholars who have studied the texts most closely simply disagree. Ratzinger is content to observe that Thomas did not present a systematically developed doctrine of the primacy like Bonaventure. Heynck insists that, whenever Thomas refers to a derivation of power from Peter, he must always be understood to mean that only the use of such power is derived. Zuckermann objects with some asperity that this is to ignore the plain literal sense of Thomas' texts. Yves Congar, whose authority in these matters deserves the highest respect, approaches the subject with extreme caution. He praises Thomas for his "discreet" language, argues that Thomas did not 'necessarily' regard the pope as *fons et origo* of all power in the church, and suggests that "probably" he believed episcopal power to be derived directly from Christ.[27] If Congar is correct then we might discover a pleasing symmetry in Thomas' views on the ideal constitution of the state and the actual constitution of the church. In both spheres he would favor a pluralistic form of government rather than pure unmixed monarchy.

It may be, however, that in the end we shall have to acknowledge a certain irreducible incoherence in Thomas' various utterances. He simply never addressed head-on the problem of the source of episcopal jurisdiction. For us the important point is that Thomas certainly developed, on a scriptural basis, a doctrine of the mixed constitution that was in principle applicable to the church. Moreover the possibility of so applying it was not overlooked. In the next generation John of Paris took over Thomas' arguments and explicitly applied them to the government of the church. In considering the New Testament texts he leaned more overtly than Thomas to an episcopalist point of view. "All the apostles received the same power as Peter ..." he wrote, "(they) received honor and power in equal fellowship with him. It is not said from him."[28] Thomas had compared the bishop to a king in his own diocese. John took the analogy further. A king, he wrote, did not receive his power from the pope but from "God and the people." Likewise a prelate in the church did not receive his power through the pope but directly from God and from the people who elected him or consented to his election.[29] For John, therefore, the government of the church was at any rate not a pure papal monarchy as Bonaventure had defined it.

John's doctrine of a mixed constitution for the church was developed directly from the thought of Aquinas. John repeated almost word for word Thomas' description of the form of constitution established for Israel in the Old Testament and reached a similar conclusion, "Thus it was the best mixture because everyone had a place and share in the constitution." But then John went further than Thomas and added "It would certainly be the best constitution for the church if, under the one pope, many were chosen by and from each province so that all would participate in some way in the government of the church."[30]

The further development of Aquinas' ideas lies outside the scope of this paper. We may note, however, that John of Paris' teachings were taken up by fifteenth-century conciliarists and through them influenced subsequent traditions of ecclesiology and political theory. The theological development of the originally quite secular idea of a mixed constitution remains an interesting subject for further research. When such research is undertaken its inevitable starting point must be the work of Thomas Aquinas.

NOTES

[1] *Divi Thomae Aquinatis Opera Omnia* (Paris: L. Vives, 1889), *Summa Theologiae*, 1. 2ae. 105. 1 (*Opera* II, 674).

[2] *Summa Theologiae*, 2. 2ae. 183. 2 (*Opera* IV, 483-484).

[3] *Summa Theologiae*, 1. 2ae. 97. 3 (*Opera* II, 595-596).

[4] *Summa Theologiae*, 1. 2ae. 95. 4 (*Opera* II, 587).

[5] *Contra Gentiles*, 3. 81; 4. 76 (*Opera* XII, 358, 588).

[6] *De Regno*, 1. 2 (*Opera* XXVII, 339).

[7] C.H. McIlwain, *The Growth of Political Thought in the West* (New York: The Macmillan Company, 1932), p. 332.

[8] *Decretum Gratiani ... una cum glossis* (Venetiis: Apud Iuntas, 1600), *Glossa ordinaria ad Dist.* 19 c. 9. Hostiensis, *Lectura in Quinque Decretalium Gregorianarum Libros* (Venetiis: Apud Iuntas, 1581) ad 4. 17. 13.

[9] *Codicis Dn. Iustiniani Libri* (Venetiis: Apud Iuntas, 1608), *Glossa ordinaria ad* 1. 17. 1 (In Mommsen-Krueger, 1. 14. 1).

[10] Henry Bracton, *De Legibus et Consuetudinibus Angliae*, ed. G.E. Woodbine (New Haven: Yale University Press, 1915-1942), II, 33, 19.

[11] *Summa Theologiae*, 1. 2ae. 105. 1 (*Opera* II, 674-675). Thomas noted that Moses and his successors were designated by God. But this was exceptional, "because that people was ruled under the special care of God."

[12] E. Gilson, *The Christian Philosophy of St. Thomas Aquinas* (London: V. Gollancz, 1957), p. 330.

[13] *In Libros Politicorum*, 2. 7 (*Opera* XXVII, 165).

[14] *Contra Gentiles*, 4. 76 (*Opera* XII, 588). Thomas used the argument here, however, only to defend papal headship.

[15] *In Psalmos Davidis Expositio,* Ps XLV. 3 (*Opera* XVIII, 515).

[16] Yves Congar has provided an excellent guide to the whole controversy with extensive references to the medieval source material and to modern literature, "Aspects ecclésiologiques de la querelle entre mendiants et séculiers," *Archives d'histoire doctrinale et littéraire du moyen âge,* 36 (1961), 35-151

[17] Various modern interpretations of Thomas' position are discussed by C. Zuckerman, "Aquinas' Conception of the Papal Primacy in Ecclesiastical Government," *Archives d'histoire doctrinale et littéraire du moyen age,* 48 (1973), 97-134.

[18] *Commentum in Libros IV Sententiarum. In 2 Sent.* 44 exp. text. (*Opera* VIII, 593-594).

[19] *In 4 Sent.* 18. 2. 2. Also Thomas wrote "... although the power of binding and loosing was given to all the apostles in common, nevertheless to signify that there was some order in this power it was given first to Peter alone in order to show that this power ought to descend from him to others." (*In 4 Sent.* 24. 3. 2. *Opera* XI, 44).

[20] *In 4 Sent.* 19. 1. 1 (*Opera* X, p. 551). A further complication arose from the 'due matter' theory of jurisdiction. This held that, just as a priest at his consecration received full power to consecrate the Eucharist, but could exercise that power only over the due matter of the sacrament, bread and wine, so too he received at his consecration full power to remit sins but could exercise this power too only over a 'due matter,' in this case a congregation submitted to his jurisdiction. Hence a grant of jurisdiction did not confer a distinctly new power on a bishop or priest, but only defined the subjects over whom a pre-existing power could be exercised. Thomas used this argument in discussing penitential theology. But in other contexts he clearly used the word jurisdiction to mean an overt power of judging in the external forum. The intricacies of this point are lucidly discussed by Zuckerman, art. cit. (n. 17).

[21] *In 4 Sent.* 20. 1. 4 (*Opera* X, 579).

[22] *Summa Theologiae,* 2. 2ae. 184. 6 (*Opera* IV, 493).

[23] *Contra Gentiles,* 4. 76 (*Opera* XII, 588).

[24] *Contra Gentiles,* 4. 74 (*Opera* XII, 586).

[25] *In Matt. Evang. Exp.,* c. 16 lect. 2 (*Opera* XIX, 473-475).

[26] *In Matt. Evang. Exp.,* c. 18 lect. 2 (*Opera* XIX, 499). Origen observed that at Matt. 16.19 Christ used the plural form *(in caelis)* but at Matt. 18.18 the singular form *(in caelo).*

[27] J. Ratzinger, "Der Einfluss des Bettelordensstreits auf die Entwicklung der Lehre vom päpstlichen Universalprimat," ed. J. Auer and H. Volk, *Theologie in Geschichte und Gegenwart* (Munich: K. Zink, 1957); V. Heynck, "Der richterliche Character des Bussakraments nach Johannes Duns Scotus," *Franziskanische Studien,* 47 (1965), 339-414; Zuckerman (n. 17), 133-134; Congar (n. 16), 94, 95, 150.

[28] Ed. F. Bleienstein, *Johannes Quidort von Paris: Über königliche und päpstliche Gewalt* (Stuttgart: E. Klett, 1969), p. 109. John was here following a pseudo-Isidorian text included in Gratian's Decretum at *Dist.* 22 c. 1.

[29] Bleienstein, 113-114.

[30] Bleienstein, 175.

XIV

NATURAL *L*AW AND CANON LAW
IN OCKHAM'S *DIALOGUS*

An earlier approach to Ockham's theory of natural law, which still finds support in some modern scholarship, emphasized a supposed relationship between the great Franciscan's specific political doctrines and his general philosophical principles. More recently, several scholars have argued that Ockham's political theory can best be understood when it is related to the real-life controversies in which he became involved and to the arguments available to him in the commonly accepted ideas of his time, especially the ideas of the medieval canonists. In this essay, I want to argue that some further investigation of Ockham's canon-law sources can lead to a better understanding of his teaching on natural law.

Approaches to Ockham

The two approaches mentioned above need not be mutually exclusive – Jürgen Miethke combined both of them in his study of Ockham's intellectual development.[1] But it may still be useful to inquire which is the more helpful and informative approach in considering any particular aspect of Ockham's thought. The first approach is found in various older histories of natural law. Heinrich Rommen, for instance, wrote that 'an evolution set in which, in the doctrine of William of Occam on the natural moral law, would lead to pure moral positivism, indeed to nihilism.'[2] To such writers it seemed evident that Ockham's philosophical nominalism and voluntarism precluded the development of a coherent natural-law doctrine in his works. Earlier scholastic philosophers, above all Thomas Aquinas, had seen natural law as inherent in the very being of things, which in turn reflected the eternal reason of God. But Ockham's nominalism, it was argued, excluded a belief in universal immutable principles and his voluntarism reduced all natural morality to mere arbitrary command

4

– the command of an inscrutable God who could change at will any existing standards of good and evil. Such arguments lead to a paradoxical conclusion: Ockham certainly did present a doctrine of natural law in his political writings, but for him the natural law provided only a mutable, unstable, shifting standard for regulating human conduct.

There are obvious objections to this whole approach. Ockham hardly ever referred to his earlier philosophical doctrines in his later works on ecclesiology and political theory. Moreover, there were good reasons for this. Ockham was convinced that Pope John xxii had fallen into heresy, and he wanted to convince the whole Christian world of the pope's error. He could obviously do this more effectively by arguing from generally accepted principles than by relying on his own controversial and suspect innovations in philosophy. Moreover, his voluntarism, his view on the absolute power of God's will, was simply irrelevant to this dispute. Ockham had no interest in demonstrating that God could have created some other moral universe – a universe in which perhaps John xxii might have been right after all. He wanted only to prove that the pope was wrong in the world that actually existed then and there, and wrong to the point of heresy. Moreover, Ockham's nominalism did not in fact prevent him from asserting that, in the actual existing world, general principles of natural morality could be discerned by human reason. Finally, it has been doubted whether any necessary implication can exist between abstract metaphysics and specific political doctrines.[3]

The most sophisticated formulation of the first approach to Ockham was presented by Georges de Lagarde in his *La naissance de l'esprit laïque au déclin du moyen-âge*.[4] De Lagarde wrote more cautiously and sensibly than one might suppose from reading only his critics, but he did emphasize the destructive tendencies in Ockham's political thought and related them to his general philosophical positions. In the generation after de Lagarde's work appeared many scholars – among them Kölmel, Boehner, Morrall, Bayley, Junghans – criticized his central theses.[5] They all found Ockham's political ideas more conservative and constructive than de Lagarde had. Kölmel in particular addressed himself to Ockham's natural-law theory. He pointed out that Ockham's doctrine was not formulated as an integral part of his whole philosophy but as a response to the particular circumstances of his dispute with the Avignon papacy. This led to other disagreements with de Lagarde. Whereas de Lagarde emphasized the variety of natural laws in Ockham, Kölmel found a core of rational equity that gave a kind of unity to them all. De Lagarde emphasized Ockham's voluntarism, Kölmel his rationalism. De Lagarde emphasized rights, Kölmel norms. But in spite of all this Kölmel still

5 Natural law and canon law in Ockham's *Dialogus*

chided Ockham a little for departing from the beautiful simplicity of Aquinas' unified natural-law theory and seemed to regard this as a regrettable innovation.[6]

Recent authors more sympathetic to de Lagarde's general approach typically express that sympathy in a moderate and cautious fashion. They acknowledge that there is no relationship of strict logical entailment between Ockham's philosophy and his political theory – one could not deduce the latter from the former. But they still discern broad areas of congruence between the two departments of his thought, and think it important to explore these congruities when evaluating Ockham's political theory. A.S. McGrade, for instance, has discussed a parallel between Ockham's 'logical individualism' and the treatment of individual rights in his political works. Gordon Leff, emphasizing particularly the concepts of necessity and contingency, has maintained that, in discussing spiritual and temporal power, Ockham 'produced a devastating critique of the traditional assumptions about the nature of each' and that he did so 'largely by drawing upon his own wider philosophical and theological assumptions.'[7]

There seems to be no denying that resemblances exist between Ockham's philosophy and his political theory. One would expect this; after all we are not dealing with a schizophrenic. The problem for a historian of political thought is to decide whether the investigation of these resemblances has any explanatory force, whether it really advances in any significant way our understanding of Ockham's teaching. Such investigation could certainly do so if it showed that specific, unusual tenets of Ockham's philosophy were reflected in specific, unusual tenets of his political theory. But this never seems to be the case. Sometimes the philosophical positions attributed to Ockham are too vague to be significant. (The concepts of 'necessity' and 'contingency,' for instance, were by no means Ockhamist peculiarities.) And often the political views that are correlated with Ockham's philosophy were fourteenth-century commonplaces, held by many other thinkers who adhered to different philosophical positions.

When considering de Lagarde's treatment of individual rights, for instance, we have to remember that medieval law was saturated with concern for rights, a concern expressed in a crisp phrase of the *glossa ordinaria* to the *Decretum*: 'No one is to be deprived of his right except for a very grave offence.'[8] We may recall, too, that it was Ockham's adversary, John xxii, who insisted on an original, individual right of property inhering in Adam, and Ockham who, to dispute the pope's conclusion, invented a peculiar doctrine of Adam as a sort of corporation sole.[9]

Treating a related question, de Lagarde, and Leff following him, emphasized

6

that Ockham's legal theory recognized the existence of a kind of moral 'no man's land,' a great juridical terrain unregulated by rational moral law, a region where human will had free play, 'a zone of absolute human autonomy' as de Lagarde put it.[10] But here again we are dealing with a medieval platitude. Civil and canon lawyers and earlier scholastic philosophers all acknowledged the existence of a mass of legal rules that depended only on human choice. Roman and canon lawyers often recalled the maxim, 'What has pleased the Prince has the force of law' and the *glossa ordinaria* to the *Digest* declared simply, 'No reason can be given in matters of purely positive law ... '[11] The canonists also liked to quote a phrase of Juvenal in discussing papal legislative power – 'in eo est pro ratione voluntas.' The human choice on which positive law depended might be expressed simply through the will of a ruler or through the tacit agreement of a people embodied in custom. In either case the function of such law was to regulate matters that were morally indifferent but that needed to be regulated in an ordered society. Thomas Aquinas made the same point when he taught that some human laws were not deduced from natural law but merely determined matters that natural law left open.[12] Vague references to 'voluntarism' or 'necessity and contingency' just do not advance our understanding of Ockham's thought in this area. His teaching on positive law was entirely conventional; it has no significant connection with his philosophical presuppositions.

These observations suggest that an investigation of Ockham's sources might help us to understand the content of his work. Around 1328, when Ockham was residing at Avignon, the Franciscan minister-general, Michael of Cesena, ordered him to investigate the decretals of Pope John XXII, dealing with Franciscan poverty. Ockham, unhappily and reluctantly according to his own account, came to the conclusion that the pope's teaching was heretical. At this point he seems to have embarked on a concentrated study of the canon law relating to church property and to heresy.

Many modern authors have noticed the frequent quotations from canon law in Ockham's political writings. It is very hard, however, to characterize the extent of the canonistic learning that he acquired. Certainly he never achieved a professional grasp of the structure of the whole corpus of canon law; there were always odd gaps in his knowledge and understanding. For instance, Ockham inveighed against Innocent IV for denying that infidels could legitimately hold property or jurisdiction, apparently in happy ignorance of the fact that Innocent had presented a classical defence of infidel rights in his great commentary on the *Decretals*.[13] Again, when discussing the question whether a pope could define a new article of faith, Ockham cited an obscure commentary of Alanus on the *Compilatio prima*. (The text was transmitted

7 Natural law and canon law in Ockham's *Dialogus*

to fourteenth-century jurists in Guido de Baisio's *Rosarium*.) But Ockham could never see, or he would not admit, that his own understanding of the text was essentially the same as that of John xxii's curial canonists.[14] On another point, Ockham attacked John xxii for applying to the Franciscan Order the canonistic concept of a corporation as an 'imaginary person,' a 'persona ficta.'[15] Rather, Ockham maintained, the order was made up of real individuals. But the canonists' 'fiction theory' – developed especially by Innocent iv again – was intended to assert precisely this point. It was because only individuals had real personality that a group of individuals (a corporation) could be considered as one person only by a fiction of the law. Gierke maintained, as a central theme of his great work, *Das Deutsche Genossenschaftsrecht*, that Innocent iv's doctrine substituted an atomistic individualism for the 'properly medieval' doctrine of the real personality of the group.

There are evident limits, then, to Ockham's understanding of canonistic thought. However, his knowledge went beyond a mere surface acquaintanceship with a few scattered texts of the *Decretum* and *Decretals*. When he was writing the *Dialogus* at Munich, Ockham complained that he had no reference works available except the canon law and the Bible. But at least he had these texts in editions that included the ordinary glosses, for he quoted from them directly, especially from Johannes Teutonicus' gloss on the *Decretum*. But Ockham seems to have known more than this. In his earlier studies at Avignon he would have had all the books he needed and expert canonists (like Bonagratia of Bergamo) to guide his reading. Ockham's teaching on papal heresy has much in common with Huguccio's and I think he must have read Huguccio at some point. In the *Dialogus* he included a brief quotation from Hostiensis. It seems to me very probable that Ockham was also acquainted with the *Rosarium* of Guido de Baisio. (One passage of Ockham's *Breviloquium* seems a close verbal paraphrase of a text in the *Rosarium*.)[16] Guido's popular work, completed c 1300, presented a vast compendium of earlier, half-forgotten, commentaries on the texts of Gratian's *Decretum*. It could have provided a mine of information for Ockham. The substantial but little-noticed treatise on natural law at the beginning of the *Rosarium* is especially interesting because, in a quite unusual fashion for a thirteenth-century canonist, Guido wove together canonistic and philosophical texts – Huguccio and Johannes Faventinus and Hostiensis intermingled with Aristotle and Thomas Aquinas and Alexander of Hales. Ockham presumably did not have all these canonistic works available to him in Munich. The most probable hypothesis is that, while at Avignon, he acquired a rather extensive knowledge of canonistic commentaries on the limited number of canon-law texts that particularly interested him, and that, in his later writings, he worked from a dossier of notes or from memory. This would explain why one so often encounters echoes of canonistic teachings in Ockham without any specific quotation or direct reference to a legal source.

All this may be of interest in considering Ockham's intellectual formation. But evidently we need to raise here the same question that we asked earlier in considering Ockham's philosophical positions. Does an approach to Ockham's political theory through research on related topics of canon law really help us to understand his thought? Does it have any explanatory force? The answer is not obvious. Gordon Leff, for instance, was sceptical of such an approach. He began his book on Ockham with the words 'Ockham was an innovator' but then at once rejected the view that 'identification and assessment of an outlook begins with a thinker's antecedents, both intellectual and circumstantial.' On this one might observe that it is impossible to know whether a given thinker was an innovator or not, or where and how he was innovating, or how he was led to innovate unless we know the state of antecedent thought and something about the thinker's own circumstances. Many writers on Ockham's political theory – even Leff himself – mistakenly attribute to him radical novelties of thought when in fact he was restating familiar ideas of his own time.

However, this argument does not quite meet Leff's main point. He realizes that in addressing some questions – questions of biography and influence – a study of Ockham's antecedents and circumstances is relevant. But he denies that such study is necessary for investigating 'the nature of the thought itself.' Leff argues on logical grounds that we must understand a system of thought before we can explore its antecedents. But this ignores all the hermeneutical problems of text and context that are discussed in so many recent works on intellectual history. From Leff's point of view it is irrelevant to ask when or how Ockham learned canon law if we are really interested in the questions, 'What did Ockham think and what was the nature of his thought?'[17] I would suggest, on the contrary, that it is sometimes scarcely possible to know what Ockham did think – or even what he wrote – without some knowledge of his canonistic sources. Ignorance of them can lead to misunderstandings. For example, Leff himself misunderstands the concepts 'clavis scientie' and 'clavis potestatis' as used by Ockham and the Franciscan Spirituals because of his disinclination to consider the canonistic background of these terms.[18]

In the particular area of natural law, the canonists can help us to understand both where Ockham was innovative (if at all) and what he actually meant to say. The following notes on two crucial texts will serve to illustrate these points.

9 Natural law and canon law in Ockham's *Dialogus*

III Dialogus 2.3.6

This text has always seemed of central importance to students of Ockham's natural-law theory. Ockham suggests here that there are not one, but three kinds of natural law and that much of the content of natural law is mutable, sometimes it seems by the mere choice of those whom it affects. We will discuss each of the three types in turn, but in order to understand them, we first need to know a little about the context of the argument in which they occur. At this point of the *Dialogus*, the Master was concerned to argue that the Roman people possessed an enduring right to elect the pope, a right which could not be taken away from them without their consent but which they could assign to others by their own choice. The Disciple objected that such a claim could not be established either by divine law or human law. The Master replied that it could be justified by divine law if the term was used broadly to include all natural law.[19] This led him to an analysis of his three different types of natural law in search of one that would justify the right of the Roman people – and he eventually found it in the third type.[20]

In the past, interpretation of Ockham's thought in this passage was impeded by textual corruptions in the two printed editions. However H.S. Offler has recently provided an accurate version of the text. So the problem now is not so much to understand what Ockham wrote or what he meant as to decide whether his thought was in any way unorthodox or innovatory. Recourse to earlier canonistic writings is indispensable here since Ockham based his exposition explicitly on the texts of Gratian and much of his argument is a word-by-word commentary on a passage of Isidore of Seville that was included in the *Decretum*. It will be useful to quote this text at the outset: 'Natural law is common to all nations since it is held everywhere by instinct of nature, not by any statute; as for instance the joining of man and woman, the procreation and education of children, the common possession of all things, the one liberty of all, the acquisition of things taken by air, land, or sea. Also the return of a thing deposited or of money loaned. For this or anything like this is never unjust, but is naturally held to be equitable.'[21]

The mere quotation of the text clears up one point. It is evident that Isidore was using the term 'natural law' in several different senses; and the fact was as apparent to the first commentators on the *Decretum* as it was to Ockham. Indeed Ockham's threefold division of natural law will seem modestly restrained to anyone familiar with the more luxuriant imaginings of the early Decretists. Stephen of Tournai gave four meanings of the term 'ius naturale,' and then, adding 'and if you do not shudder at a fifth meaning' went on with

10

another. The author of the *Summa in nomine* found as many as seven meanings. Johannes Teutonicus, in the ordinary gloss to the *Decretum*, a work which was certainly available to Ockham when he wrote the *Dialogus*, limited himself to four basic meanings, two of which correspond closely to two of Ockham's definitions. Huguccio added a cautionary note: 'Not all the examples of natural law given here refer to the same meaning of natural law; therefore a prudent reader will be careful to discern which example refers to which meaning.'[22]

The mere multiplication of definitions is thus traditional. The problem is whether Ockham's specific categories conform to earlier ideas or whether they present, as Pierre d'Ailly wrote later, 'a new and very fine division of natural law.' Let us consider the three types in turn.

Natural Law I. This is defined thus: 'In one way natural law is called that which conforms with natural reason, which in no case fails, such as, "You shall not commit adultery," "You shall not lie," and things of this sort – in this first way natural law is immutable and invariable and indispensable as at *Dist. 5 ante* c.1 and *Dist. 6 post* c.3.'[23]

Later we shall need to consider in a little more detail Ockham's views on the relationship between natural law and reason as developed elsewhere in his work, but so far the doctrine put forward is entirely traditional. Gratian himself, in the texts cited by Ockham, identified natural law with the moral precepts of the Old and New Testaments, especially the Decalogue. 'There are in the (old) Law certain moral precepts like "You shall not kill." Moral mandates pertain to natural law and are shown to have never changed.' Gratian also wrote that this immutable natural law existed 'from the beginning of the rational creature'[24] and the Decretists commonly observed that reason enabled men to discern the basic principles of morality that were also set forth in Scripture. Guido de Baisio, in his *Rosarium*, quoted Huguccio on this: 'Natural law is divine law, namely what is contained in the Mosaic and evangelical law ... And this law is called natural ... because natural reason leads and impels us to the things contained in divine law.'[25] We can therefore agree with McGrade that this first definition of natural law 'is more significant as an acknowledgment of common ground with the previous tradition than as an original contribution.'[26]

Natural Law II. At first glance it may seem different from Ockham's second kind of natural law, for here he tells us that 'in one meaning of the term natural law is not immutable.' Ockham here took up the text of Isidore that we have already quoted, focusing on the words 'the common possession of all things, the one liberty of all.' But existing law recognized private property and servitude, Ockham noted. So common possession and universal liberty could not belong to the immutable natural law of the first definition. Accordingly Ockham put forward his second definition: 'In another sense natural law is that which is to be observed by those who use only natural equity without any human statute or custom. It is called natural because the contrary is against the state of nature as instituted and if men lived according to natural reason or divine law it (the contrary) would not be kept or observed.'[27] Thus this law existed before the Fall and it would have continued to exist if man had not sinned, if he had lived 'according to reason.' It indicated a good and equitable state of affairs, but it was not immutable like the moral precepts of Natural Law I. It had indeed been modified by the human laws introducing property and servitude.

The notion of a changeable natural law has seemed innovative, even subversive, to some modern critics. But in fact, from the time when major commentaries on the *Decretum* began to appear in the mid-twelfth century, the canonists showed themselves aware that some of Isidore's varieties of natural law could not be considered immutable. A decisive clarification was offered by Rufinus (c 1160). He argued that natural law consisted of 'commands and prohibitions' on the one hand and of 'indications' ('demonstrationes') on the other: 'It commands what is good like "You shall love the lord thy God," it prohibits what is harmful like "You shall not kill," it indicates what is fitting like "They shall have all things in common" or "The one liberty of all" ... ' Rufinus' doctrine came to be very widely accepted among the Decretists and they commonly explained that while the commands and prohibitions of natural law were immutable, the 'indications' could be changed by subsequent human law.[28] The argument was repeated in Guido de Baisio's *Rosarium*, again in a formulation from Huguccio. Sometimes, too, the canonists – like Ockham – specifically identified this kind of natural law with rational equity, as in this definition from the *glossa ordinaria* of Johannes Teutonicus: 'In a third way natural law is called an instinct of nature proceeding from reason and the law proceeding from such nature is called rational equity and all things are said to be common by this natural law, that is, they are to be shared in time of need.'[29]

The last phrase of Johannes Teutonicus may serve to remind us of another aspect of Ockham's doctrine. The relationship between natural law and property was especially important to Ockham because of his involvement in the dispute over Franciscan poverty which gave the original impetus to all his political writings, and he discussed the law that we have called Natural Law II in other works, especially the *Opus nonaginta dierum* (OND) though without developing there the threefold classification of the *Dialogus*.[30] In the OND he explained that, although the natural law favouring community of property could be modified by human law, it could not be totally abolished since in time of necessity all things were still regarded as common. Hence a person in extreme need had a right to use the goods of another. Here again Ockham was following a common canonistic doctrine. It was introduced into Decretist commentary by Huguccio and widely adopted in later works, including the *glossa ordinaria*, as we have seen. In view of the subsequent development of his argument about the third type of natural law (considered below) it is interesting that Ockham referred to this right of use derived from the second natural law as 'a right of nature that cannot be renounced.'[31] Self-preservation in some circumstances was not only a right but a duty.

There is one more significant point about the second type of natural law where the discussion in the OND augments that of the *Dialogus*. In the latter work Ockham declared that Natural Law II could be modified for reasonable cause. But in the OND he put the point more emphatically: The right to appropriate, he argued, derived from 'a dictate of natural reason,' given the 'corrupt nature' of fallen man. Kölmel saw a significant innovation here in that Ockham based two kinds of rational natural law on the two states of man, before and after the Fall. The doctrine, Kölmel observed, is not to be found in Duns Scotus or Thomas Aquinas. But it is to be found in Guido de Baisio, commenting on the same Isidorean text as Ockham, and referring here to Alexander of Hales as his authority: 'Natural law dictates differently as regards common and private property ... for in the state of nature as well instituted it dictated that all should be common; in the corrupted state of nature it dictated that some things should be private ... according to Alexander.'[32] Once more Ockham seems to be following faithfully in the footsteps of his predecessors.

Natural Law III. Ockham's third kind of natural law is the most complex and interesting one. His definition was based on the authority of Isidore's text at *Dist.* 1 c7, especially on the words 'restitution of money loaned' and 'repelling of force by force.' But the real purpose of the definition was to defend the right of the Roman people to elect the pope and their capacity to renounce that right – the starting point of this whole involved discussion of 'ius naturale.' The definition ran like this: 'In a third way natural law is called that which can be gathered by evident reason from the law of nations or other law or from some human or divine action, unless the contrary is established by consent of those whom the matter concerns. And this can be called natural law by supposition.'[33] 'Suppositio' is a technical term in Ockham's logic, but

13 Natural law and canon law in Ockham's *Dialogus*

he does not seem to be using the word in any specialized sense here. His 'ex suppositione' means simply 'on the supposition that' or 'on condition that.' Thus, supposing that private property has been introduced by human law, then it is evidently reasonable that debts should be paid; and, supposing that violence actually exists (though this is contrary to natural law in the first two senses), then it is evidently reasonable that force should be repelled with force – unless, in either case, the contrary has been agreed.

This last definition of Ockham may seem finally to support the view that he did invent a new kind of natural law, a shifting, changing, unstable 'ius naturale' dependent only on the will of the people concerned. But this argument can be misleading unless we understand the sense of 'ius naturale' that Ockham had in mind. So far I have been translating the term as 'natural law' but to continue to do so would be inaccurate. Ockham was really writing here about natural rights. It was the natural rights inherent in individuals or communities that they could freely renounce, not the natural laws that bound them. (A person with a right to receive payment could cancel the debt. A person under attack could waive his right of self-defence.) In this area there was a sort of progression running through the whole passage we have discussed. Ockham's first definition of 'ius naturale' dealt with moral precepts that were immutably binding, laws in a strict sense.[34] The second 'ius naturale' still dealt mainly with law, with principles of rational equity. Its provisions could be modified by human law but they gave rise to rights that were sometimes inalienable. Ockham's third 'ius naturale' was concerned much more with rights than with laws and with a class of rights that could be renounced by consent of their holders. The real interest of the text is that it raises, perhaps for the first time, the problem of the alienability of natural rights, which later became of great importance for natural-law theorists. Here, if anywhere, Ockham moved beyond the limits of earlier canonistic discourse.[35] And yet, even here, most of his definition was composed out of conventional elements. Ockham began by asserting that in the whole mass of human law and human conduct there were embedded principles of 'ius naturale,' discernible by reason. This of course was standard doctrine. According to the common teaching of Roman and canon lawyers, although human laws varied from place to place and time to time and sometimes might be merely arbitrary, often they exemplified principles of rational natural law. Defining the characteristics of human laws, Isidore wrote that they should be 'honorable, just, *according to nature* [italics mine] ... convenient to time and place, necessary, useful ... ' and on the words 'according to nature' the *glossa ordinaria* commented 'i.e. natural reason.'[36] Among the earlier canonists, Alanus provided a definition that closely approximates that of Ockham: 'Whatever is

14

naturally equitable, whether in the law of nations or civil law or canon law, is contained in natural law.'[37]

In this same gloss Alanus also offered a doctrine of 'relative' natural law essentially the same as Ockham's 'ius naturale ex suppositione.' Alanus used the technical terms 'ius simplex' and 'ius respectivum' to convey the same idea. For him, simple natural law showed what was equitable in itself, without regard to human laws; 'relative' natural law indicated what was equitable when preceding positive law was taken into account. Thus Alanus pointed out that some of Isidore's definitions of natural law could be accepted only on the presupposition that human law had already instituted private property.[38] This was the same point that Ockham would make later.

The final element in Ockham's definition asserted that the rights he was discussing could be renounced by consent. Specifically, he argued that the Roman people could renounce their natural right to elect the pope. As to the existence of the right, Ockham asserted that, supposing a ruler was to be appointed, then every community had a natural right to choose its own head. Hence, on the further supposition that Peter had established his chair at Rome, the Roman people had a natural right to elect the pope. But, just as the people transferred their jurisdiction to a ruler when they elected him, so they could transfer the right of election itself. And so the argument reached its conclusion. A suppositional right associated with the third kind of 'ius naturale' could be renounced by consent of the people concerned.[39]

As to the originality of all this: The idea that every people had a right to elect their own ruler was becoming common in fourteenth-century political thought, so its occurrence in Ockham is not surprising or particularly significant. Also, earlier canonists had discussed the renunciation of rights in great detail, usually concluding that some rights but not others could be alienated. However, their discussions dealt with rights held under human law, not specifically with natural rights. The underlying principle was that a person could freely renounce a right that was introduced solely for his own advantage but could not do so when some public good was involved. For this reason Hostiensis doubted that the cardinals could renounce their right to elect the pope in spite of the general principle which he cited: 'Anyone can renounce his own right.'[40]

Hostiensis was unusually interested in the specific problem that Ockham raised about the electoral role of the Roman people conceived of as a natural right. Discussing the election of an emperor he declared that the Roman people held this right: 'By the common right of every corporate body to elect a ruler for itself ... or from natural reason on which right is based.' Hostiensis also considered the residual rights the Roman people would possess in the election of a pope if the college of cardinals should become extinct during a papal

15 Natural law and canon law in Ockham's *Dialogus*

vacancy.[41] And he discussed in great detail whether the electors of the pope could renounce this right of election. But, as just noted, when he took up this point it was the role of the cardinals rather than that of the Roman people that he considered, and the cardinals held their right by positive canon law. So, here again, Hostiensis did not quite reach the point of discussing the renunciation of natural rights.

Ockham did then introduce a new element into natural law theory by overtly raising this issue. To that extent he was an innovator. But it follows from all the preceding discussion that Ockham's theory of 'ius naturale' was for the most part conservative and conventional. De Lagarde was right in emphasizing the concern with rights, but Kölmel was right in pointing out that this concern arose from the circumstances of Ockham's dispute with the papacy rather than from his philosophic voluntarism. Ockham's views on natural law most certainly did not lead him to what Rommen called 'pure moral positivism' indeed to nihilism.' He insisted rather that natural law was ascertainable by right reason and that its moral principles were immutable. His argument provides a typical example of the way in which political ideas often evolve. Ockham set out to use the conventional ideas of his time in a contemporary dispute; but in applying those ideas to his own particular circumstances he made a significant adaption of them. The adaptation has a certain interest for historians of political thought because, as it happens, it raised an issue that would become of great significance in the natural-rights theories of a later age.

I Dialogus 1.8

This passage poses a different question and we can deal with it more briefly. The problem here is one of textual corruption – to determine what Ockham actually wrote. At this point in the *Dialogus* Ockham's Master claimed to be describing the content of canon law. He asserted that, along with theological doctrines and purely positive laws, the canonistic works included many moral principles that could not be supported by any reason – 'moralia quae nulla possunt ratione muniri.' This is the one text of the *Dialogus* that seems overtly to support a 'voluntarist' doctrine of non-rational moral law. De Lagarde naturally made use of it. In spite of Ockham's statement about 'reason which in no case fails' at III *Dialogus* 2.3.6, de Lagarde wanted to maintain that Ockham's theory of natural law was founded on basically irrational principles. To be sure, Ockham called the permanent moral content of natural law (Natural Law I) a 'dictate of reason,' but in fact, de Lagarde argued, no rational justification for this dictate was presented and it had to be accepted as an indemonstrable postulate. De Lagarde was right up to a point. Ockham was not arguing that moral precepts could be educed by some chain of reasoning. Rather he asserted that reason could perceive them as first principles per se nota. Here Ockham was following a common scholastic usage.[42] Evidently the word 'reason' was being used in a special sense. Still it would seem perverse for de Lagarde to translate 'dictamen rationis' as 'impératif irrationel' ... except that he could appeal to this one text of Ockham – 'moralia quae nulla possunt ratione muniri' – to support his interpretation. Francis Oakley also quoted the same text in an article maintaining that Ockham formulated an essentially voluntarist theory of law.[43] Kölmel, who found the text inconsistent with his view that Ockham's natural-law theory was basically rational, could only suggest that we ought not to take it literally since it was inconsistent with other passages in Ockham's work. In fact our text stands out awkwardly as a major obstacle to any coherent, consistent interpretation of Ockham's natural-law theory.

Even in his earlier ethical writings, where he did not specifically develop a theory of natural law, Ockham often asserted that right reason was a guide to moral conduct.[44] In his political writings he frequently referred to a rational natural law, and in the Dialogus itself, in the passage already discussed, he found a rational basis for each of his three types of natural law. Such considerations led George Knysh, in an unpublished study,[45] to doubt the authenticity of the printed version of Ockham's words (and indeed the whole text of the Dialogus in Goldast is notoriously full of corruptions). It might still be argued that Ockham was not a wholly consistent thinker and that he might well have presented differing views in different, widely scattered parts of his work. We can carry the argument further, however. It is not difficult to show that, within the actual context of the discussion in which it occurs, the reading given in our printed texts is simply impossible. The text is corrupt: the problem is to determine how it can reasonably be amended.

The corruption becomes evident if we consider first the broader context of the discussion, then the specific setting of the critical words. At this point in the Dialogus Ockham was concerned to argue that theologians were better qualified than canonists to determine whether any given assertion was orthodox or contrary to faith. It could be argued on the other side that various definitions of faith were in fact contained in the books of canon law. Ockham responded to this with the rather audacious assertion that canonists were in general not the best exponents of canon law. As for texts of Roman law embedded in the canonistic collections, civilian jurists were more expert; as for nearly all else, theologians and philosophers could provide a more profound insight into the texts. It is at this point that our disputed passage occurs:

17 Natural law and canon law in Ockham's *Dialogus*

The books of the canonists are nothing but collections of authorities ... in which some purely theological matters are declared and expounded, as in those in which heresies are condemned ... Also certain purely moral principles are transmitted in them which can be defended by no reason [*moralia ... quae nulla possunt ratione muniri*] as is plain in many chapters of the Decretum and Decretals. And some things are commanded and prohibited in them which are merely positive, dependent on human will, and which can reasonably be changed or altogether abrogated, as appears at ... *di 9 Sicut quidem* ... As regards the moral principles which can be supported by no reason, if they are universal ... canonists can in no way excel those who are endowed with natural reason and learned in moral philosophy ...[46]

This passage raises several questions. The first one is: What has happened to the whole body of rational natural law which Ockham made so much of elsewhere? It has simply disappeared from this account of the content of church law. It is odd that the Disciple – who is usually full of objections – did not notice the omission, and all the more so since in the dialogue surrounding our passage both Disciple and Master referred, in quite conventional fashion, to a natural law known by reason as a part of canon law. At the outset of the discussion the Disciple acknowledged that theologians might have a better understanding of some aspects of canon law – 'especially those that are derived from theology or natural reason and that are not merely positive.' After hearing the whole passage quoted above, the Disciple again stated that the Master's argument sounded convincing as regards 'theological matters and imperial laws and those that are purely moral and natural.' But there was no 'moral and natural' law in the description that the Master had just given, if we follow the printed texts. Then the Master himself referred to 'natural law, which is not only found in the Law and the Gospel but also in true moral philosophy.' This is consistent with the view Ockham often expressed elsewhere that moral law was known by reason – hence it would be accessible to moral philosophers – but it seems inconsistent with the specific text we are discussing.

But the text is corrupt. The fact will be evident to a reader who approaches it with any elementary knowledge of the canonistic works that the Master claims to be describing. The disputed words – 'moralia quae nulla possunt ratione muniri' – occur twice in the passage quoted. At the first occurrence the Master referred to '*moralia* which can be supported by no reason, as is plain in many chapters of the *Decretum* and the *Decretals*.' But these 'many chapters' do not exist. Gratian and the canonists following him used the term 'moralia' in a quite different sense to designate those teachings of the Old Testament that belonged to natural law and were accessible to human reason.

18

(Ockham actually quoted the relevant text of Gratian making this point a little farther on in the present discussion.[47]) The canonists distinguished the 'moralia' of the Old Testament from its 'ceremonial' precepts precisely because, for these latter, 'no reason can be given.'[48] Elsewhere in the *Dialogus*, Ockham called attention to this distinction of the canonists, again quoting Gratian.[49]

At the second occurrence of our text, if Ockham actually intended to write 'moralia quae nulla possunt ratione muniri' then his argument makes no sense. Ockham asserted that, in expounding these 'moral principles which can be supported by no reason,' the canonists 'in no way excel those who are endowed with natural reason and learned in moral philosophy.' But if the 'moralia' under discussion had no rational basis then these moral philosophers would have had no special competence to discuss them. If we adhere to the printed text Ockham's argument is a simple non sequitur.

Clearly Ockham must have intended some different meaning. A final solution of this crux will require a critical study of all the manuscripts of the *Dialogus*. Meanwhile it is easy to think of various possible emendations. Perhaps the simplest solution, from a paleographical point of view, would be to suppose that Ockham wrote 'moralia quae naturali possunt ratione muniri.' That would make good sense in the context of the argument and abbreviations for 'naturali' and 'nulla' could be very similar in a fourteenth-century hand. But no manuscript evidence is available to support this reading. There are other solutions however, for which some preliminary manuscript evidence can be offered. Referring to the merely positive laws which were subject to variation, Ockham (according to Goldast) cited *Dist. 9, Sicut quidem*. But there is no chapter with the incipit *Sicut quidem* in *Dist. 9* or anywhere else in the *Decretum*. The closest parallel is *Dist. 14 c2 (Sicut quedam)*. There Pope Leo I wrote: 'Sicut quedam sunt que nulla possunt ratione *convelli* ita multa sunt que aut pro necessitate temporum aut pro consideratione etatum oportet temporari ... [italics mine].' This is the text Ockham had in mind. A Florence manuscript of the *Dialogus* gives the correct reference to *Dist. 14 c2* and the corresponding reading in Ockham's text, 'moralia que nulla possunt ratione convelli.' Ockham meant to assert here what he asserted so often elsewhere, that moral precepts were immutable, not that they were irrational.

It is still not easy to see how 'convelli' became changed to 'muniri' in the printed editions. But Knysh's suggestion of an intermediate form – 'mutari' – proves valuable here, for the Florence manuscript does in fact give 'mutari' at the second occurrence of the text.[50] The most likely sequence of events is this: Ockham originally wrote 'moralia quae nulla possunt ratione mutari' on both occasions, giving the sense of his canonistic text correctly, but slightly paraphrasing it as he often did with canonistic citations. Then, in one man-

19 Natural law and canon law in Ockham's *Dialogus*

uscript tradition, a creative scribe, noting the discrepancy between Ockham's words and the actual text of *Dist.* 14 c2, substituted the 'correct' word 'convelli' at the first occurrence of the text. And, in another manuscript tradition, a careless copyist mistranscribed 'mutari' as 'muniri' on both occasions. For a final version of the text we must await H.S. Offler's critical edition of the *Dialogus*. For the present it seems clear at least that we can abandon the reading 'moralia quae nulla possunt ratione muniri' and the interpretations of Ockham's thought that have been based on it.

Finally, given Ockham's well-known views on the relative merits of canonists and theologians, it is a pleasing irony that in this instance a little canonistic learning is needed in order to understand what Ockham, the theologian, was trying to convey to his readers.

APPENDIX

After this essay was completed, I was able to check several more manuscripts of the *Dialogus*. All of them give the readings 'convelli' and 'mutari' in place of the two occurrences of 'muniri' in the printed editions.

The reference to Distinctio 14 of the *Decretum* is given in various forms – as 14, xiv, xiiii, and (incorrectly) as ix. In medieval scripts an Arabic '14' can look very like a Roman 'ix.' It seems that at some stage of the transmission '14' was mistranscribed as 'ix,' the form that appears in the Lyon edition of 1494. Then this was reprinted as '9' in Goldast's edition.

The following transcript is from Vatican Vat lat 4097. Variant readings are given from the Goldast edition (G), the Lyon 1494 edition (L), and from the following manuscripts: Florence, Laurenziana Plut xxxvi dext 11 (F), Frankfurt, Staatsbibl lat quartt 4 (F1), Vatican, Vat lat 4001 (V1), Vat lat 4096 (V2), Vat lat 4098 (V3), Vat lat 7196 (V4), Reg lat 370 (V5).

Quedam vero pure moralia traduntur in eis que nulla	1
possunt ratione convelli sicut in capitulis decretorum	
et decretalium patet innumeris. Quedam autem precipiuntur	
in eis et prohibentur que sunt pure positiva ex humana	
dependentia voluntate que pro necessitate et utilitate	5
possunt rationabiliter variari seu penitus abrogari ut	
patet *extra, de consanguinitate et affinitate*, c. *Non*	
debet et di. 14 Sicut quedam ... Quantum vero ad pure	
moralia que nulla possunt ratione mutari si universalia	
sunt nec in memoria nec in intellectu possunt canoniste	10
naturali preditos ratione et in philosophia instructos morali	

20

et perfectos in scientia rationali excedere quoquomodo.

1 vero] etiam F1; pure] pura V2
2 possunt ratione] trp. V1; convelli] muniri G L; in capitulis decretorum et
decretalium patet innumeris] patet in multis capitulis decretorum et decretalium
F1 G L
4 in eis] om. V3; pure] mere F G L, pura V2
5 dependentia voluntate] trp. F1 G L; que] hec autem V1 V5, autem V2
6 seu] et F1 G L V1
8 di. 14] xiv di. c. F1, di. 9 G, di. ix L V2 V3, di. xiiii V1; quedam] quidem G L
V1, quidam V3; vero] om. F V1 V2 V5; pure] pura V2, om. G L
9 possunt ratione] trp. F1; mutari] muniri G L
10 in intellectu] om. in V2 V5
11 preditos ratione] trp. F1 G L; instructos morali] trp. F1 G L
12 perfectos in scientia rationali] in scientia rationali perfectos F1, in scientia
naturali perfectos G L, in scientia perfectos naturali V3, perfectos in scientia
naturali V1 V2 V5

NOTES

1 J. Miethke *Ockhams Weg zur Sozialphilosophie* (Berlin 1969). Miethke provides
a good bibliography of earlier work on Ockham.
2 H. Rommen *The Natural Law* (St Louis 1947) 58 (first published as *Die ewige
Wiederkehr des Naturrechts* in 1936)
3 C. Zuckermann 'The Relationship of Theories of Universals to Theories of
Church Government in the Middle Ages: A Critique of Previous Views' *Journal
of the History of Ideas* 36 (1975) 579–94
4 G. de Lagarde *La naissance de l'esprit laïque au déclin du moyen-âge* 1st ed, 6
vols (Paris 1934–6), 2nd ed, 5 vols (Paris–Louvain, 1956–63). A similar point
of view was presented in M.J. Wilks *The Problem of Sovereignty in the Later
Middle Ages* (Cambridge 1964).
5 W. Kölmel 'Die Naturrecht bei Wilhelm von Ockham' *Franziskanische Studien*
35 (1953) 39–85, and 'Wilhelm Ockham – der Mensch zwischen Ordnung
und Freiheit' in *Miscellanea mediaevalia*, ed P. Wilpert (Berlin 1964) 204–29;
P. Boehner 'Ockham's Political Ideas' *Review of Politics* 5 (1943) 462–87; J.B.
Morrall 'Some Notes on a Recent Interpretation of William of Ockham's Political
Philosophy' *Franciscan Studies* 9 (1949) 355–69; C.C. Bayley 'Pivotal Concepts in
the Political Philosophy of William of Ockham' *Journal of the History of Ideas*
10 (1949) 199–218; H. Junghans *Ockham im Lichte der neueren Forschung*
(Berlin–Hamburg 1968)

21 Natural law and canon law in Ockham's *Dialogus*

6 De Lagarde responded to Kölmel in the second edition of his *Naissance*. Kölmel reiterated his views in *Regimen Christianum* (Berlin 1970).

7 A.S. McGrade 'Ockham and the Birth of Individual Rights' in *Authority and Power: Studies on Medieval Law and Government Presented to Walter Ullmann*, ed, B. Tierney and P. Linehan (Cambridge 1980) 149–65; G. Leff *William of Ockham: The Metamorphosis of Scholastic Discourse* (Manchester 1975) 616. The problem of relating Ockham's philosophy to his political theory is complicated by the fact that the philosophical works themselves are undergoing major re-evaluations by modern scholars such as Boehner. For a more positive approach to Ockham see, for example, H.A. Oberman *The Harvest of Medieval Theology* (Cambridge Mass 1963).

8 *Decretum Gratiani ... una cum glossis* (Venice 1600) gloss *ad Dist.* 56 c6. The view that Ockham first introduced the concept of individual, subjective rights, advanced by Villey, is unpersuasive. See M. Villey *La formation de la pensée juridique moderne* (Paris 1962) 226–72.

9 *Breviloquium*, ed R. Scholz (Stuttgart 1944) 3.15, 138

10 De Lagarde *Naissance* VI (1946) 122; Leff *Ockham* 633

11 *Inst.* 1.2.6; *G1. ord. ad Dig.* 3.1.1.3. On positive law in general see G. Le Bras, Ch. Lefebvre, and J. Rambaud *L'âge classique 1140–1378: Sources et théorie du droit* (Paris 1965) 385–96.

12 *Summa theologiae* 1.2ae 95.2. (Guido de Baisio quoted this passage in his *Rosarium*.)

13 Innocent IV *Commentaria ad* x3.34.8; Ockham *Octo quaestiones* 1.11 in *Guillelmi de Ockham opera politica* I, ed H.S. Offler (Manchester 1974) 47. Compare *Breviloquium* 3.1 107–8.

14 On this text see my *Origins of Papal Infallibility* (Leiden 1972) 194–5, 226. Compare I *Dialogus* 1.14 in M. Goldast *Monarchia S. Romani imperii* II (Frankfurt 1614) 421.

15 *Opus nonaginta dierum* c6, *Opera politica* I 366

16 See 'Ockham, the Conciliar Theory, and the Canonists' *Journal of the History of Ideas* 15 (1954) 40–70 at 45.

17 Leff *Ockham* xv

18 Ibidem 642 and *Heresy in the Later Middle Ages* I (Manchester 1967) 241, 246, 249. See the comment in my *Infallibility* 188.

19 The identification of divine and natural law was very common in Decretist sources. See, for example, *Dist.* 1 c1, 'Omnes leges aut divinae sunt aut humanae. Divinae natura constant ... '

20 The argument has an obvious relevance to the actual circumstances of the times – the election of the antipope Nicholas V in Rome and the role of the emperor in the affair.

22

21 *Dist.* 1 c7

22 Many Decretist texts on natural law are printed in R. Weigand *Die Natur-rechtslehre der Legisten und Dekretisten von Irnerius bis Accursius und von Gratian bis Johannes Teutonicus* (Munich 1967). For the ones cited above see 148, 196, 219, 255.

23 Goldast *Monarchia* 932, 'Uno modo dicitur ius naturale illud, quod est conforme rationi naturali quae in nullo casu fallit, sicut est, non moechaberis, non mentieris, et huiusmodi ... ius naturale est immutabile primo modo et invariabile ac indispensabile, dist. 5 § nunc antem et dist. 6 § his ita respondetur ... ' Earlier (Goldast 812) Ockham had noted that God could make exceptions to natural law of this sort. But this was not due to any novel 'voluntarism.' Earlier writers often made the same point with reference to the same Old Testament examples that Ockham cited. For canonistic examples see Weigand *Die Natur-rechtslehre der Legisten* 407–43.

24 Gratian *Dist.* 5 *ante* c1, *Dist.* 6 *post* c3

25 Guido de Baisio *Rosarium decretorum* (Strasbourg 1473) np, *Dist.* 1 *ante* c1. For other texts see Weigand's index, sv 'Naturrecht; als (natürliche) Vernunft.'

26 A.S. McGrade *The Political Thought of William of Ockham* (Cambridge 1974) 178

27 See Goldast *Monarchia* 933. The text here is corrupt and we have used the corrected version presented by H.S. Offler in 'The Three Modes of Natural Law in Ockham: A Revision of the Text' *Franciscan Studies* 37 (1977) 207–17 at 212: 'Aliter dicitur ius naturale, quod servandum est ab illis. qui sola equitate naturali absque omni consuetudine et constitutione utuntur. Quod ideo dicitur naturale quia contraria est contra statum nature institute et, si homines viverent secundum rationem naturalem aut legem divinam, non esset servandum nec faciendum. Isto modo et non primo modo ex iure naturali omnia sunt communia ... ex quo concluditur quod ius naturale uno modo accepto vocabulo non est immutabile ... ' In using the awkward double-negative form 'contrarium est contra statum nature' Ockham perhaps had in mind the parallel phrase of Aquinas, 'natura non inducit contrarium' (*Summa theol* 1.2ae 94.5 *ad* 3).

28 Weigand *Die Naturrechtslehre der Legisten* 147, 388–94

29 G1. *ord. ad Dist.* 1 c7

30 See my *Medieval Poor Law* (Berkeley–Los Angeles 1959) 32–5, and for a more detailed treatment, G. Couvreur *Les pauvres ont-ils des droits?* (Rome 1961).

31 *Opus nonaginta dierum* c65, *Opera politica* II 577–8

32 *Rosarium ad Dist.* 1 c7. See *Summa Fratris Alexandri* IV (Quaracchi 1948) 348. The relevant text is usually attributed to John de la Rochelle.

33 Goldast *Monarchia* 933; Offler 'The Three Modes of Natural Law in Ockham' 213: 'Tertio modo dicitur ius naturale illud, quod ex iure gentium vel alio aut ex

23 Natural law and canon law in Ockham's *Dialogus*

aliquo facto divino vel humano evidenti ratione colligitur, nisi de consensu illorum, quorum interest, contrarium statuatur. Quod poterit vocari ius naturale ex suppositione ... '

34 Of course, in a broad sense, every natural law can be said to imply a right. A precept such as 'You shall not steal' implies that one's neighbour has a right to his property. Ockham understood this, as did the canonists, but he was not concerned with the point in the present discussion.

35 The whole problem of Ockham's contribution to the growth of natural-rights theories still awaits a definitive treatment. See the comments of R. Tuck *Natural Rights Theories: Their Origin and Development* (Cambridge 1979) 22–4.

36 *G1. ord. ad Dist.* 4 c2

37 Weigand *Die Naturrechtslehre der Legisten* 228

38 Weigand *Die Naturrechtslehre der Legisten* 228: 'Item sciendum [est] quod [et] est ius naturale simplex et respectiuum. Simplex quod sine precedenti positione juris positivi demonstrat aliquid equum esse quale est istud "deum diligere", "omnia esse communia". Respectiuum est quod demonstrat aliquid equum habito respectu ad precedens ius positiuum, quale est hoc: "adquisitio eorum que celo" etc.; nisi enim apponatur prius aliquem hominem habere proprium non erit istud equum "acquisito" etc.' Guido de Baisio quoted an analogous doctrine from Laurentius in his *Rosarium ad Dist.* 1 c2. Laurentius taught that some laws were 'bona et equa simpliciter,' others 'equa respectu alterius iuris quod est iniquum vel minus equum.'

39 This point does not seem to have been raised before in discussions on natural law, but in the background was a large body of medieval speculation on alienation of sovereignty. See P.N. Riesenberg *Inalienability of Sovereignty in Medieval Political Thought* (New York 1956).

40 Hostiensis *Commentaria ad Decretales* (Venice 1581). For a general discussion see *Com ad* x 3.31.16 112v, and for the cardinals in particular, *Com. ad* x 1.9.10 91v.

41 *Com ad* x 1.6.34 60r; *ad* x 1.6.6 38v

42 III *Dialogus* 2.1.15; Goldast *Monarchia* 884. Compare Thomas Aquinas 'The precepts of natural law are to practical reason what the first principles of demonstrations are to speculative reason' (*Summa theol.* 1.2ae 94.2.3).

43 De Lagarde, *Naissance* VI (1946) 144 n11; F. Oakley 'Medieval Theories of Natural Law: William of Ockham and the Significance of the Voluntarist Tradition' *Natural Law Forum* 6 (1961) 65–83 at 68; Kölmel 'Naturrecht' 54, n67

44 D.W. Clark 'William of Ockham on Right Reason' *Speculum* 48 (1973) 13–36; L. Urban 'William of Ockham's Theological Ethics' *Franciscan Studies* 33 (1973) 310–50; K. McDonnell 'Does William of Ockham Have a Theory of Natural Law?' *Franciscan Studies* 34 (1974) 383–92

24

45 G.D. Knysh 'Political Authority as Property and Trusteeship in the Works of William of Ockham' (PhD thesis, London University 1968). Knysh suggested that for 'muniri' we should read 'mutari.' On this see below.

46 Goldast *Monarchia* 405 (the *Dialogus* was also printed in an edition of Lyons 1494; but Goldast's version was reprinted from this text. Hence the two printed versions do not provide two independent witnesses): 'libri canonistarum non sunt nisi quaedam collationes ex auctoritatibus ... in quibus quaedam theologica pure explicantur et declarantur sicut in illis in quibus haereses damantur ... Quaedam vero pure moralia traduntur in eis, quae nulla possunt ratione muniri, sicut patet in multis capitulis decretorum et decretalium. Quaedam autem praecipiuntur in eis et prohibentur quae sunt mere positiva ex humana voluntate dependentia, quae pro necessitate et utilitate possunt rationabiliter variari et penitus abrogari ut patet ... *di 9 sicut quidem* ... Quantum vero ad moralia quae nulla possunt ratione muniri, si universalia sunt, nec in memoria nec in intellectu, possunt canonistae naturali ratione praeditos et in philosophia morali instructos et in scientia naturali perfectos excedere quoquo modo.'

47 Ibidem 406 l20, citing Gratian's comment at *Dist* 6 *post* c3

48 G1 *ord.* ad *Dist* 6 *post* c3

49 III *Dialogus* 2.2.15; Goldast *Monarchia* 915: 'moralia mandata ad naturale ius spectant atque nonnullam imitationem recepisse monstrantur.' But again the text is corrupt. For 'nonnullam imitationem' read 'nullam immutationem.'

50 Ms Florence, Laurenziana Plut xxxvi dext 11 f3ra. The same readings ('convelli' and 'mutari') occur in ms Frankfurt, Staatsbibl lat quart 4. I am grateful to Dr Rega Wood and Professor H.S. Offler for supplying transcripts from these two manuscripts.

XV

FROM THOMAS OF YORK
TO WILLIAM OF OCKHAM
THE FRANCISCANS AND THE PAPAL
SOLLICITUDO OMNIUM ECCLESIARUM
1250-1350

Modern students of Ockham's ecclesiology agree that the *venerabilis inceptor* was a very intransigent and very influential critic of the Avignon papacy. They disagree about almost everything else concerning his thought. Some historians see Ockham as a revolutionary figure, an "éveilleur du monde moderne," others present him as "an interpreter and defender of the achievements of the past." (1) Some call him a sceptic, others extoll his orthodoxy. Running through all these diverse interpretations one can discern two main lines of argument. Those

---

(1) G. DE LAGARDE, *La naissance de l'esprit laïque au déclin du moyen age*, V (Louvain-Paris, 1963), p. 337; J. B. MORRALL, *Some Notes on a Recent Interpretation of William of Ockham's Political Philosophy*, in *Franciscan Studies*, N.S. IX (1949), pp. 335-369 at p. 369. Good bibliographies are given by C. VASOLI, *Guglielmo d'Occam* (Firenze, 1953) and by W. KÖLMEL, *Wilhelm Ockham und seine kirchenpolitischen Schriften* (Essen, 1962). Various modern interpretations of Ockham's thought are discussed in stimulating fashion by de Lagarde whose work provides the best general treatment of Ockham's ecclesiology and political theory.

scholars who approach Ockham's ecclesiology by way of his nominalistic philosophy and find a close connection between the two spheres of thought usually regard him as a radical innovator. Those who seek to explain Ockham's theology of the church by seeking out sources for his ideas in earlier theological and juristic writings often succeed in persuading themselves of his essential conservatism. Our own position is different. We would maintain that Ockham was indeed a radical, even revolutionary critic of the structure of the medieval church; but we would also argue that his ecclesiology cannot be really understood unless it is seen as a logical — though unforeseen — culmination of a whole tradition of Franciscan thought concerning the pope's *sollicitudo omnium ecclesiarum.*

The ideas that we wish to explore can be traced through the works of the greatest Franciscan masters of the century before Ockham — Thomas of York, Bonaventura, Pietro Olivi (2), Duns Scotus, Alvarus Pelagius. At first glance it will seem paradoxical to associate Ockham, the implacable adversary of John XXII, with these great predecessors who are all known as ardent defenders of papal power.

---

(2) Pietro Olivi might seem an exception. Certainly the prophetic speculations in his commentary on the Apocalypse were interpreted by the Spiritual Franciscans of the next generation as anti-papal pronouncements. But, in Olivi's two *Quaestiones* that dealt clearly and explicitly with the role of the pope in the church of his own day, he showed himself a zealous defender both of papal power in general and of the legitimacy of Boniface VIII's position in particular. It is these two *Quaestiones* (*infra* n. 42, n. 46) that have been used in the following discussion.

The point is that the peculiar pressures of the controversies in which the Franciscans became involved led them, not only to exalt the papacy, but also to attack the episcopate. In the end the most extreme of them came to reject utterly the ancient doctrine that in modern times has come to be called " collegiality." And a concept of collegiality is precisely what Ockham's ecclesiology most conspicuously lacks.

We need not pursue in detail all the history of the disputes between friars and bishops in the Middle Ages (3). It will be recalled that the new mendicant orders, armed with papal privileges, were able to set up churches and undertake pastoral work without permission of the local bishop or even against his will; and, naturally, they attracted offerings and bequests that would normally have gone to the local clergy. The claims of the Franciscans were especially exasperating. They not only syphoned off diocesan resources for the support of their own order but, at the same time, claimed to be the only true practitioners of evangelical poverty in that they had renounced all possessions both

---

(3) On these controversies see above all YVES CONGAR, *Aspects ecclé-siologiques de la querelle entre mendiants et séculiers dans la seconde moitié du XIII² siècle et le début du XIV²*, in *Archives d'histoire doctrinale et litté-raire du moyen age*, XXXVI (1961), pp. 35-151. Fr. Congar gives a chronology of the various disputes, lists the editions and manuscripts of the polemical works that they inspired, and provides excellent bibliographies of modern work on the theologians involved. His magisterial article provides an indispensable starting point for all subsequent work in the field. We have not thought it necessary to reproduce in the subsequent notes all the bibliographical information that he provides.

individually and corporately. From about 1250 onward bishops and secular masters in the universities began to protest against papal policies favoring the friars. The spokesmen for the secular clergy always accepted the doctrine of the pope's primacy of jurisdiction and the principle of the papal *sollicitudo omnium ecclesiarum*. But they argued that bishops too possessed an inherent jurisdiction along with their pastoral responsibilities and that the pope could not simply centralize out of existence all the rights and duties that Christ Himself had assigned to the bishops as successors of the Apostles. The friars replied to these arguments by developing more and more extreme theories of papal sovereignty.

Neither side in the dispute can be wholly admired. The bishops were striving to defend the divinely-ordained structure of the church — as they understood it — but they were often actuated by motives of pride or even of sordidly pecuniary self-interest. They failed to see that the pastoral system based on parochial units which they defended so obdurately was itself a product of historical evolution, and they were determined to prevent the further necessary evolution represented by the work of the friars. The Franciscans were resolved that no fossilized institutional structures should impede them in their truly evangelical task of preaching the Gospel to the poor and simple throughout the world. But they aroused understandable resentment by making a boast of their very humility; and in their more polemical writings they showed little respect for the ancient traditions and law of the church. Moreover, the friars' natural desire that papal bulls favoring their cause should be regarded as unerring pronouncements drew the problem of papal infallibility into the arena of public debate for the first time in a fashion that rendered very difficult any cool-headed and lucid discussion of it.

One might expect that a dispute of this sort would give rise to a distorted tradition of ecclesiology. It was indeed such a tradition that Ockham inherited. We shall explore some of the ideas of his Franciscan predecessors and then try to show how the presuppositions that Ockham inherited from them help to explain the characteristic twists of his own thought.

Medieval argumentation about the roles of popes, bishops and friars in the church centered around three famous passages of the New Testament, Matthew 16:18-19, John 20:21-22 and John 21:15-18. In the first passage Christ promised to Peter the " keys of the kingdom of Heaven." In the second passage He apparently conferred on all the Apostles the same power of " binding and loosing " that he had first promised to Peter. In the third passage Christ re-affirmed Peter's pastoral responsibility for the whole church with the words *Pasce oves meas.* Also prominent in the discussions was a text of Gratian's Decretum, *Dist.* 21 c.1, which declared that all the Apostles received with Peter " an equal share of honor and power." The commentators on the Decretum discussed the structure of the church in far more detail than any other group of scholars before the middle of the thirteenth century and a sketch of their conclusions will provide a convenient introduction to the developments that occurred after 1250 (4).

In discussing *Dist.* 21 c.1 the Decretists commonly explained that the power of binding and loosing included both a power of orders and a power of jurisdiction. All the Apostles were equal in orders but Peter excelled " in dignity of prelacy, in administration, in jurisdiction. " (5) The essential difference between pope and bishops lay in the fact that the pope was *iudex ordinarius omnium*, while each bishop exercised jurisdiction only in a limited geographical area. " Plenary power," wrote Huguccio, " consists in command, necessity of obedience and universality. Each bishop has two of these in his own diocese, namely command and necessity of obedience. The supreme pontiff has all three... " (6) All bishops were dependent on the pope in that communion with the See of Peter was essential for the licit exercise of ecclesiastical jurisdiction. The pope, moreover, could define the geographical limits of a bishop's power by creating new dioceses or by dividing or uniting old ones. The Decretists did

---

(4) The summary of canonistic positions that follows is based on my *Foundations of the Conciliar Theory* (Cambridge, 1955) and *Pope and Council: Some New Decretist Texts*, in *Mediaeval Studies*, XIX (1957), pp. 197-218.

(5) Huguccio *ad Dist.* 21 ante c. 1 (*Foundations*, p. 33), « Petrus prefuit illis in dignitate prelationis, in administratione, in iurisdictione... ».

(6) Huguccio *ad Dist.* 11 c. 2 (*Foundations*, p. 146 n. 2), « Plena potestas consistit in precepto, necessitate observantie, generalitate. Quilibet episcopus duo istorum habet in sua diocesi, scil. preceptum et necessitatem observantie. Summus vero pontifex habet tres... ».

not, however, regard the pope as the actual source of episcopal jurisdiction. Episcopal authority, they held, was derived from election and consecration. A bishop did not indeed begin to exercise jurisdiction until his election was confirmed, but the confirmation was essentially a certification of the validity of the electoral process. It would not confer any new power for a well-known maxim of canon law laid down that, *Qui confirmat non donat.* Since the bishops shared in the divine power that Christ had bestowed on the church their authority could supplement that of the pope and the canonists therefore accorded greater authority to certain decrees promulgated by pope and bishops together in a General Council than to those of the pope acting alone. In particular they held that any pope was bound by the canons of preceding Councils in matters touching the faith and the "general state of the church." Individual popes might err, the Decretists held. Canons of General Councils provided a surer guide to the truths of faith because they were " established by universal consent." After some initial hesitations the canonists also came to teach that the fathers of a Council were competent to pass judgement on a pope accused of flagrant heresy.

Thomas of York, who wrote his *Manus qui contra omnipotentem* (7) in 1256 to defend the Franciscan Order against an attack by the secular masters of

---

(7) Ed. M. Bierbaum in *Bettelorden und Weltgeistlichkeit an der Universität Paris, Franziskanische Studien*, 2 Beiheft (Münster in West. 1920), pp. 37-168.

the University of Paris, incorporated much of this Decretist argumentation into his treatise. After a lengthy defense of Franciscan poverty he turned to a discussion of the pope's right to bestow preaching privileges on the friars. Thomas began by quoting Huguccio literally, " Plenary authority contains three things: command, universality and necessity of obedience "(8); and he continued by presenting a selection of texts from the Decretum that emphasized the headship and supreme authority of the pope in the church. Then, still closely following Gratian, he pointed out that the Apostolic See could grant particular dispensations against general decrees of Councils — provided that they were not contrary to justice or equity or opposed to truth or Holy Scripture (9). The argument concluded with a demonstration that the privileges granted to the friars were indeed not contrary to Scripture or to any divine ordinance but rather were justified by the crying needs of the people and the insufficiency of the priests. Any good prelate, Thomas maintained, would welcome additional preachers in his diocese. The bishops had no reason to fear that their own status would be undermined for the friars

---

(8) *Op. cit.*, p. 138, « Plena auctoritas secundum apparatum continet tria: preceptum, generalitatem, necessitatem observantie... ».

(9) *Op. cit.*, p. 140, « Ex hiis omnibus liquet auctoritas plena sedis apostolice vel mutandi vel condendi... dummodo mandata eius non sint iustitie et equitati dissona ... aut quibus ueritas non contradicit sicut habetur *Dist.* 12. c. *Scit sancta*, aut quibus scriptura sacra non est contraria, quia, qui contradicit scripture contradicit iuri naturali, sicut habetur *Dist.* 9 c. cum ergo...

were sent out to help them, not to prejudice their authority (10). So far the argument was conservative and persuasive and the author might well have ended his exposition at this point. (A little later on, in the 1280s, John Peckham and Richard of Middletown presented very convincing defenses of the Franciscan position based on essentially these same principles). Thomas of York had one final point to make, however, and it opened up a Pandora's box of new possibilities. Relying on the fashionable pseudo-Dionysian imagery, he not only maintained that the existing papal policy was in fact not prejudicial to episcopal power but also asserted that in principle no papal action could be called prejudicial to the rights of inferior prelates since all their authority was derived from the pope. "An inferior prelate has nothing except what he has from a superior, namely the supreme pontiff... and therefore whatever the superior does it is not prejudicial to him." (11) This assertion was not backed by cano-

---

(10) *Op. cit.*, p. 142, «... non est in bonorum prelatorum preiudicium, si in eorum adiutorium committatur inferioribus predicationis officium »; p. 148, «... manifeste sunt rationes, uidelicet populi indigentia et sacerdotum, ut pro pluribus eorum loquar, insufficientia ».

(11) *Op. cit.*, pp. 152-153, « Est igitur hierarcha unus, a quo est influentia potestatum et ordinationum in omnes personas hierarchicas et influentiarum distributio, prout maior uel minor fuerit hierarchie humane ad angelicam, immo ad diuinam assimilatio »: p. 154, « Ita nichil habet prelatus inferior nisi a superiore, uidelicet summo pontifice... et ideo quicquid faciat superior circa actionem inferioris ex ratione, non est in ei preiudicium... p. 155, « Et insuper non est in preiudicium inferioris concessio superioris, ubi et iurisdictio inferioris totaliter pendet ex ordinatione superioris ». A similar doctrine on the pope as source of all authority in the church

nical authorities as the earlier arguments had been
and it was not developed in great detail though
evidently the statement that a prelate had " nothing "
except what he received from the pope required some
further explanation.

A much more careful and mature exposition of
the same theme was provided by St. Bonaventura.
The Seraphic Doctor's general contribution to the
development of the doctrine of papal sovereignty
in the Middle Ages has been discussed by several
modern authors (12). We shall concentrate on two
particular aspects of his thought that are of special
relevance for our argument — Bonaventura's treatment of the pope as a supreme source of jurisdiction
in the church and as a supreme exponent of the
faith of the church.

---

was taught by Innocent III, again in theological rather than canonical
terms. See MIGNE, *Patrologia latina*, CCXV, col. 279, «... vocatis caeteris
in partem sollicitudinis hunc assumpsit in plenitudinem potestatis... quoniam in capite viget sensuum plenitudo, ad membra vero pars eorum aliqua
derivatur ». (On the earlier evolution of the formula *in partem sollicitudinis...
in plenitudinem potestatis* see J. RIVIERE, *In partem sollicitudinis... évolution
d'une formule pontificale*, in *Revue des sciences religieuses*, V (1925), pp. 210-
231). A similar view was expressed by Robert Grosseteste, the founder of
the Franciscan school at Oxford in his *Epistolae*, ed. H. R. LUARD (Rolls
Series, London, 1861), p. 389. But Grosseteste's whole career shows that,
in mid-thirteenth century, such an opinion could be held by a very vigorous defender of episcopal rights. See *Grosseteste and the Theory of Papal
Sovereignty*, in *Journal of Ecclesiastical History*, VI (1955), pp. 1-17. The
use of pseudo-Dyonisian imagery by both sides in the disputes between
friars and bishops was discussed by Y. CONGAR, *art. cit.*, pp. 114-145.

(12) See especially J. RATZINGER, *Der Einfluss des Bettelordensstreites
auf die Entwicklung der Lehre vom päpstlichen Universalprimat, unter beson-
derer Berücksichtingung des heiligen Bonaventura*, in *Theologie in Geschichte
und Gegenwart*, ed. J. AUER and H. VOLK (München, 1957), pp. 697-724.

XV

Bonaventura's description of the thereefold nature of the pope's plenary power differed significantly from that presented by the canonists and by Thomas of York. " Plenitude of power," he wrote, " is threefold, for the supreme pontiff alone has the whole plenitude of authority that Christ conferred on the church; and he has this authority everywhere in all the churches just as in his own particular Roman see; and from him all authority flows to all inferiors throughout the universal church in so far as it pertains to particular individuals to share in it, just as in Heaven all the glory of the saints flows from that fount of all good, Jesus Christ." (13) Bonaventura developed this theory that the pope was the source of all authority in the church — including episcopal authority — in considerable detail. He referred often to the power of binding and loosing as the characteristic form of ecclesiastical authority and insisted that this power came always from the pope whether it was exercised in the *forum externum* (in an act of excommunication) or in the *forum internum* (in an act of sacramental absolution). " This power of binding and loosing was granted

---

(13) *Quare fratres minores praedicent, Doctoris Seraphici S. Bonaventurae ... opera omnia*, 10 vols (Quaracchi, 1882-1902), VIII, p. 375, « Triplex est autem hujus potestatis plenitudo, scilicet quod ipse Summus Pontifex solus habet totam plenitudinem auctoritatis quam Christus Ecclesiae contulit, et quod ubique in omnibus ecclesiis habet illam sicut in sua speciali sede Romana, et quod ab ipso manat in omnes inferiores per universam Ecclesiam omnis auctoritas, prout singulis competit eam participari, sicut in coelo ab ipso fonte totius boni Christo Jesu fluit omnis gloria Sanctorum... ».

first to one supreme priest on whom was conferred universal power as a supreme head ... thence it descends first to bishops, then to priests from the one head." (14)

An obvious difficulty arises here. The sacerdotal power of the keys, the power of Holy Orders, which was exercised in "loosing" a sinner in the sacrament of penance, was received by every priest at his ordination. All the theologians of the thirteenth century, including Bonaventura, agreed that this power came directly from God and that it stamped on the priest an indelible "character" which could not be taken away by the pope or by any human power. How then could Bonaventura maintain that the authority to bind and loose came from the pope? His explanation was that two powers were needed for a priest to absolve a sinner, the sacerdotal power of the keys of course, but also, in addition to this, a power of jurisdiction. The power of the keys came to every priest from God at his ordination but jurisdiction came always from an ecclesiastical superior and hence, mediately or immediately, from the pope.

---

(14) *Breviloquium* VI, 10 (*Opera*, V, p. 276), « ... ipsa hierarchia ecclesiastica debeat esse secundum potestatem iudicariam ordinata; ideo haec potestas ligandi et solvendi concessa est, primo, uni primo et summo sacerdoti cui collata est tamquam summo capiti potestas universalis; et deinde secundum particulares ecclesias dividitur in partes, ita quod primo in episcopos, deinde in presbyteros descendit a capite uno ». Cf. *Breviloquium* VI, 12, p. 278, « ... Pontifex summus, Christi vicarius, fons et origo et regula cunctorum principatuum ecclesiasticorum a quo tanquam a summo derivata ordinata potestas usque ad infima Ecclesiae membra ... ».

Thomas Aquinas, about the same time, expressed a similar view in a particularly nuanced form and it is interesting to compare his view with Bonaventura's. Thomas pointed out that the sacerdotal character possessed by all priests included two capacities, a capacity to consecrate bread and wine in the sacrament of the Eucharist and a capacity to bind and loose in the sacrament of penance. One power concerned the real body of Christ, the other the mystical body of Christ, and each could be exercised only in relation to the proper material for which its use was destined. The act of consecration required wheaten bread as its subject; the act of binding and loosing required a penitent sinner subject to the priest's jurisdiction (15). Like Bonaventura, Thomas held that jurisdiction was received from an ecclesiastical superior but, in his view, the conferring of jurisdiction merely designated a group of persons over whom the priest's intrinsic authority was to be exercised. By a little straining of his texts one can argue that Thomas was still adhering to the older tradition of thought which saw the pope as a universal pastor who defined the limits within which each prelate's authority was to be exercised but not as the actual source of their authority. Certainly John of Paris succeeded in combining in one and the same treatise a statement of

---

(15) *In IV Semt.* Dist. 18 q. 1 q. 2 ad 1,2; Dist. 19 q.1 a.2 sol.3. The same doctrine was presented by Richard of Miccletown, *In IV Sent.* Dist. 24 a.5 a.1 ad 1.C f. CONGAR, *art. cit.* p. 89 n. 149, n. 150.

Thomas's doctrine with an assertion that the power of ecclesiastical prelates came, not from the pope, but from God immediately and from the people who elected them (16). And Fr. Congar has argued that Thomas himself might not have endorsed the proposition that the pope was *fons et origo* of all power in the church (17). However this may be, there is no ambiguity at all in the position of Bonaventura. For him jurisdiction was an actual positive power, derived from the pope, separable from the power of orders in theory and practice, an indispensable component of every priest's or bishop's authority over his flock (18).

---

(16) *De potestate regia et papali*, ed. J. LECLERCQ (Paris, 1942), pp. 199, 209-210.

(17) *Art. cit.*, p. 95. To me it seems that, although Thomas's teaching on the power of the keys was ambiguous, the other crucial passage in his commentary on the Sentences (*In II Sent*. Dist. 44 Expos. Text.) was quite explicit in asserting that the pope was the source of all ecclesiastical jurisdiction.

(18) L. HÖDL apparently misunderstood Bonaventura's position on this question. See his *Die Lehre des Petrus Johannis Olivi O.F.M. von der Universalgewalt des Papstes* (München, 1958), p. 10. Olivi attacked the view that a priest without jurisdiction lacked the power to absolve, not because of any defect in the priest's own authority, but solely on account of a defect in the *materia debita*. Hödl presents this as a sharp break with the doctrine of Bonaventura. But Bonaventura never defended the view that Olivi attacked. His position was essentially the same as Olivi's. He mentioned the *materia debita* theory but did not use it to deny that each priest needed a positive power of jurisdiction. Cf. Olivi, *Tractatus de sacramentis*, cit. HÖDL, p. 10 n. 26, « Praeterea plura canonica iura dicunt, quod nullus potest absolvi nisi a suo iudice. In quo expresse fatentur, quod praeter potestatem ordinis exigitur ad hoc iudiciaria iurdisdictio et potestas »; Bonaventura, *In IV Sent*. Dist. 19 a.2 q.2 (*Opera*, IV, p. 506), « Quod iterum requiratur jurisdictio, patet sic: sacerdos enim est mediator et ... arbiter et iudex... talis autem iudica-

This position was stated most clearly in Bonaventura's commentary on the Sentences. " One (ecclesiastical power) is founded principally on orders, the power of consecrating; another is founded principally on jurisdiction, the power of excommunicating; ... another is founded on orders and jurisdiction, the power of binding and loosing in the penitential forum. Since the sacerdotal character cannot be taken away the power that flows from charatcer cannot be taken away de dacto. But since jurisdiction descends from superior to inferior in due order, so that its plenitude is in the supreme pontiff, he can take it away together with the power that flows from it." (19) Such arguments had an obvious relevance in the disputes between mendicants and seculars. If it could be shown that dishops were mere agents of the pope (who alone possessed the totality of ecclesiastical

---

tio non est sine aliqua iurisdictione in eum qui iudicatur quia nemo potest aliquem iudicare nisi qui iudex eius constituitur ab eo qui potest ».

(19) *In IV Sent.* Dist. 24 a.1 q.3 (*Opera*, IV, p. 645), « Quaedam namque est fundata super ordinem principaliter, ut potestas conficiendi; quaedam super iurisdictionem canonicam principaliter ut potestas excommunicandi; quaedam super ordinem et eminentiam, ut potestas ordinandi; quaedam super ordinem et iurisdictionem ut potestas absolvendi et ligandi in foro poenitentiali. Et quoniam character auferri non potest, ideo potestas, quae consequitur characterem, de facto auferri non potest. Sed quoniam iurisdictio descendit ordinate a superiore ad inferius, ita quod plenitudo est in Summo Pontifice; ideo potest auferre eam et potestatem quae consequitur ipsam ». See also Dist. 18 p.2, a.1 q.3, p. 640 and *Quare fratres minores praedicent* (*Opera*, VIII, p. 376), « Primus et praecipuus est Summus Pontifex ... ita quod omnes inferiores Ecclesiae rectores curam et totam potestatem quam habent super subditos ab ipso accipiunt, mediate vel immediate ... ».

power) then no diminution of the bishops' power and no transfer of pastoral responsabilities to a different set of papal agents (the friars) could reasonably be regarded as a usurpation of divinely ordained rights of the episcopate.

However, a major difficulty had to be overcome before such a conception of the bishops' status could find general acceptance. Certain well-known texts of Scripture seemed to assert quite plainly that Christ conferred authority on all the Apostles, not on Peter alone; and a universal tradition of the church held that all bishops were successors of the Apostles. Given this situation there were two ways in which the continuing authority of bishops in the church could be impugned. One way was to argue that the power of the keys which Christ conferred on all the Apostles was merely a power of orders and that Peter alone received the jurisdiction which was required for any licit act of ecclesiastical authority. This argument had a major disadvantage in that a proponent of it could not logically use in defense of papal power the most famous of all Petrine texts — *Tibi dabo claves regni caelorum* — although the popes themselves, all down the centuries, had pointed to these words of Christ as the very foundation of their power (20). The second way of minimizing episcopal authority in the church was to argue that

---

(20) Bonaventura himself expressed uncertainty as to whether Christ conferred both jurisdiction and orders on Peter with the famous words, *Tibi dabo claves. In IV Sent.* Dist. 18 q. 2 a.1 q.3 (*Opera*, IV, p. 489), « Ad illud quod quaeritur quando data est haec potestas (excommunicandi)

the bishops' role as successors of the Apostles did not endow them with all the rights, duties and status of the original Twelve, that they were " successors " only in some distorted or diminished fashion. The obvious disadvantage of this argument was that it inevitably cast doubt on the status of the bishop of Rome as successor of St. Peter. Although the medieval friars were slow to grasp the fact it is indeed difficult to attack the Apostolic Succession without also attacking the papacy.

Bonaventura was much more charitable and reticent than some of his successors, and he never indulged in overt polemics against the episcopate as such. But he certainly provided a very adequate theological foundation for later writers who would be less discreet than himself. The first of the two arguments mentioned above, which was eventually adopted by Augustinus Triumphus, relied heavily on Bonaventura's teaching concerning orders and jurisdiction. But Bonaventura himself seems clearly to have acknowledged that Christ conferred on all the Apostles, and not only on Peter, a divinely

---

Petro? dici potest, quod simul data est utraque, quia data est potestas clavis in sua plenitudine. Vel potest dici quod non simul sed potestas clavium promissa fuit Matthaei decimo secto et data Ioannis vigesimo: *Accipite spiritum sanctum* etc; potestas vero excommunicandi insinuatur fuisse data Matthaei decimo octava ubi, postquam dictum est: *Si ecclesiam non audierit* etc. additum est *Amen dico vobis, quodcumque ligaveris* etc. ». In general Bonaventura was quite consistent in using the word *clavis* to mean the power of orders, not the power of jurisdiction. But here he used the term plenitude of the power of the keys to mean orders and jurisdiction combined. There is a similar usage in the immediately preceding paragraph.

ordained authority to rule the church. " The Lord
Jesus Christ, before he ascended into Heaven, committed his holy church to the Apostles, and principally to blessed Peter, to be ruled and expanded,"
wrote Bonaventura, and he went on to assert that it
was the Apostles who first divided the church into
" patriarchates ... bishoprics, parishes and other
canonical divisions." (21)   Elsewhere he called them
" the foundation of the church." (22)   Evidently
Bonaventura had no intention of belittling the role
of the Apostles in the early church. But, on the
other hand, he drew a sharp distinction between
those first Apostles and the bishops of his own day.
The Apostles, he wrote, had been both evangelical
preachers, dedicated to a life of perfection, and also
prelates set over Christian communities. Bishops
succeeded only to the role of prelacy (23).   Another

---

(21) *Quare fratres minores praedicent* (*Opera*, VIII, p. 375), « Dominus
Jesus Christus... sanctam Ecclesiam suam, ascensurus in coelum, Apostolis regendam et dilatandam commendavit, principaliter beato Petro
Apostolo... Sed ut ordinatius gubernaretur universalis Ecclesia distinxerunt
eam sancti Apostoli per patriarchatus, primatus, archiepiscopatus, paro-
chias et alias canonicas distinctiones... ». But Bonaventura went on in this
same passage to assert that the pope was the source of all authority in the
church (*supra* n. 13). See also *In IV Sent.* Dist. 18 p.2 a.1 q.3 (*Opera* IV,
p. 488), « Quod enim in Ecclesia aliquis habeat potestatem, hoc est ab ipso
Christo qui potestatem contulit Apostolis et praecipue ipsi Petro... ».

(22) *In III Sent.* Dist. 25 a.1 q.1 (*Opera*, III, p. 535), «(apostoli) qui
erant fundamentum universalis Ecclesiae constituti... ».

(23) *Expositio super regulam* 4, 13 (*Opera*, VIII, p. 416), « Praedicta
enim paupertatis districtio non fuit imposita Apostolis ut praelatis cum
nondum illo tempore praelati essent nec etiam sacerdotes sed tantum
authentici praedicatores missi toti mundo... Succedunt ergo episcopi Apostolis in culmine auctoritatis, in obligatione et debito virtutis et sancti-

distinction was implied by the fact that Bonaventura always referred to the bishops' power as coming from the pope (the successor of Peter) while never denying that the Apostles' power came from Christ Himself. Indeed he consistently wrote as though the pope stood in relation to the bishops, not as Peter to the Apostles, but as Christ to the Apostles. (24) But this was, in effect, to deny to the bishops any real authority at all in face of the pope. They became, in this view, not vicars of God but vicars of the pope; and Bonaventura actually described them as such (25).

If now we turn to Bonaventura's treatment of the teaching authority of the pope and the church we find the same dichotomy — a great reverence for the first Apostles combined with a marked reluctance to attribute to contemporary bishops the same role in the church as theirs. When defending his doctrine of evangelical poverty in the *De perfectione evangelica* and again in the *Apologia Pauperum*, Bonaventura pointed to three principal sources of Catholic truth (which we shall encounter again in Ockham) — the words of Scripture, the faith of the church and the judgements of the popes (26). Thus

---

tatis sed non in forma illius districtae disciplinae et paupertatis debito supradictae ».

(24) See especially *In Hexameron collatio XXII* (*Opera*, V. p. 439), « (episcopi) locum tenent Apostolorum. Super Apostolos autem est Christus, et post Petrus ».

(25) *Quare fratres minores praedicent* (*Opera*, VIII, p. 377), « ... ipsi plebani sint vicarii episcoporum in suis parochiis sicut episcopi Summi Pontificis in officiis sibi commissis ... ».

(26) *De perfectione evangelica* q.2 a.1 (*Opera*, V, p. 130), « ... omnimo

the teaching on poverty enshrined in the Rule of St. Francis could be held as a sure truth of faith because it was proclaimed in Scripture, accepted by the church and approved by the papacy. Bonaventura's frequent emphasis on the faith of the universal church as a guide to truth might seem at first glance to be a continuation of the thought of the canonists who held that dogmatic decrees of General Councils were to be revered like the Scriptures themselves because they were enacted with general consent. But in fact Bonaventura meant something quite different. He noted that the college of the Apostles was capable of making a corporate pronouncement in the Apostle's Creed (27), but he never acknowledged that any other ecclesiastical assembly was capable of expressing qith unerring truth the faith of the church. General Councils had no significant part to play in Bonaventura's ecclesiology; he mentioned them only to insist that the pope was not bound by their decrees (28); and this was per-

---

omnibus abrenuntiare pro Christo culpandum non est ... ad quam sufficientissime astruendam una sola auctoritas expressa ex ore Christi, consulentis dimmittere omnia esset sufficientissima, etiam si multa glossarum et expositorum et doctorum dicta viderentur esse contrarium »; q.2 a.2, »p. 153, « Concludendum est ergo secundum dictum huius hominis unius, quod universalis ecclesia tota erraverit et decepta fuit ... quod est horribilissimum et incredibilissimum, quod Deus permitteret sic errare universaliter populum sanctum suum ... Quod si hoc non est sapientia, sed potius temeritas sedem apostolicam velle iudicare, quae a solo Deo iudicatur et eius iudicium et sententiam reprobare ... procul ergo haec fiant a cordibus fidelibus et Christianis ». See also *Apologia Pauperum* (*Opera*, VIII, pp. 235, 305).

(27) *In III Sent.* Dist. 25 a.1 q.1 (*Opera*, III, p. 535).

(28) *Apologia pauperum* c. 11 (*Opera*, VIII, p. 313), « Nulla igitur possunt ad huius status impugnationem allegari iura civilia, nulla etiam

haps an inevitable result of his re-interpretation of the status of the bishops. When Bonaventura wrote of the unerring faith of the universal church he never had in mind a consensus formulated by an assembly representing the church. He meant rather — and Ockham would follow him in this — that practices and beliefs that were adhered to throughout the Catholic world could be taken as sure guides to the truths of faith (29).

Bonaventura never considered (as the canonists had done) the possibility that a particular decree of a pope might conflict with the generally accepted faith of the church; and, indeed, he interpreted the words, " I have prayed for thee Peter that thy faith shall not fail ... " as referring to the faith of

---

iura canonica. Nam *Extra, De electione* (X. 1.6.4), *Romanae ecclesiae legem nulla concilia praefigunt ... ».* See also *In I Sent.* Dist. 11 a.1 q.1 (*Opera,* I, p. 212), *In IV Sent.* Dist. 19 Dub. 6 (*Opera,* IV, p. 513).

(29) *In IV Sent.* Dist. 3 p.1 a.2 q.2 (*Opera,* IV, p. 70), (On the words used in baptism) « Quia hanc formam servat tota Ecclesia ... si Christus ipse non instituit, instituit Ecclesia instinctu Spiritus sancti, et hoc tantum est ac si ipse proprio ore dixisset »; Dist. 18 p. 2 a.1 q.5, p. 490, (On repeated excommunications) «... hoc habet usus Ecclesiae universalis, quam errare est impossibile ut videtur »; Dist. 45 a.2 q.1, p. 943, (On prayers for the dead) « Item, hoc ostenditur auctoritate Ecclesiae et usu, quae orat pro defunctis ... ». In another context Bonaventura discussed the indefectibility of the church, *In IV Sent.* Dist. 4 p.1 a.2 q.3 (*Opera,* IV, p. 105), « Sacramentum baptismi prodest parvulis merito fidei Ecclesiae militantis, quae, quamvis possit deficere in aliquibus personis specialiter, generaliter tamen nunquam deficit nec deficiet iuxta illud Matthaei ultimo, *Ecce ego vobiscum sum usque ad consummationem saeculi.* Unde sicut species semper salvatur in aliquo individuorum, sic fides in aliquo fidelium et hoc, divina providentia faciente. Nec unquam fuit, postquam incepit Ecclesia, quin semper esset aliquis, qui Deo placeret; sic nec unquam erit ».

the universal church (30). Theologians have often admired Bonaventura for his serene confidence that the faith of Peter and the faith of the church would always be one. It must be added that he had no reason not to be serene. He preferred to ignore the historical arguments concerning alleged errors of popes in the past which had so perplexed the Decretists, and he enjoyed the consistent support of the popes of his own day in the various controversies concerning Franciscan poverty in which he became involved. The real test of his convictions would have come if a pope had denounced as heretical the doctrine of evangelical poverty that Bonaventura held to be rooted in Scripture, approved by the unerring church and confirmed by the decrees of preceding pontiffs. That was the situation that Ockham had to face.

Of course nothing of the kind happened in Bonaventura's lifetime or in the years immediately after his death. On the contrary, in 1279 Pope Nicholas III defined the doctrine of the perfect poverty of Christ and the Apostles in language that closely followed Bonaventura's, and in 1281 Pope Martin V bestowed on the mendicant orders the most far-reaching of all the papal privileges granted to them in the thirteenth century. These two decrees, *Exiit qui seminat* and *Ad fructus uberes*, gave rise to a

---

(30) *In IV Sent.* Dist. 20 p.2 a.1 q.2 (*Opera*, IV, p. 532), « ... ita dictum est Petro lucae vigesimo secundo: *Ego pro te rogavi, Petre, ut non* deficiat fides tua; constat quod hoc dictum est Petro in persona Ecclesiae ... Et si hoc, Ecclesia universalis non decipitur, nec errat ».

new round of controversies. In the course of them two eminent Franciscan doctors took up certain arguments of Bonaventura and pressed them to conclusions much more extreme than those of the Seraphic Doctor himself. Duns Scotus (if he was indeed the author of the *De perfectione statuum*) (31) insisted on a radical discontinuity between apostolate and episcopate, while Pietro Olivi addressed himself more explicitly than Bonaventura had done to the problem of the pope's unerringness in faith.

The author of the *De perfectione statuum* began with an assertion that the intrinsic nature of the church made necessary the presence within it of two quite distinct states of life which corresponded to two separate classes of persons. The first state was that of the prelates. Their role was to rule the congregations entrusted to them, administer the sacraments routinely, enforce necessary acts of external observance. But the very existence of such duties implied that there must be another state of life whose followers would bring into existence the congregations of Christians that the prelates ruled over (32). The followers of this second way of life

---

(31) The manuscript evidence favors Duns Scotus's authorship; the content of the work gives rise to doubts. For a discussion of the question see G. J. KIRBY, *The Authenticity of the « De perfectione statuum » of Duns Scotus*, in *The New Scholasticism*, VII (1933), pp. 134-152.

(32) *De perfectione statuum* ed L. VIVES, *Joannis Duns Scoti ... opera omnia*, XXVI (Paris, 1895), p. 501, « Quod status praelatorum ecclesiasticorum praesupponit statum alium probatur, quia status praelatorum respectu subditorum est status secundum quid generantis patris ... »; p. 509, « Quia status patris generantis perfectior est et prior statu patris secundum quid generantis tantum, et curam de bona nutritione et conversatione

were the friars. Their responsibility was to preach, convert infidels, encourage Christians to inward contrition for their sins. This state of life, the author declared, was more arduous, more perfect, more essential to the existence and perfection of the church than the other one (33). The author had simply split into two separate halves the duty of pastoral care that, in former times, had been regarded as the sole responsibility of the bishop. He justified this manoeuver by asserting that the episcopal office was ill-suited to continue the work of Christ in the church. Infidels could be converted, Christians could be moved to true repentance, only by the example of a life of evangelical perfection, he argued. But bishops were not bound to such a life (34). On the contrary they could

---

habentis ... ». The argument was essentially the same as that of Bonaventura (*supra* n. 23) but it was developed in a quite different spirit.

(33) This was repeated over and over again. See e.g. p. 599, « ... quae vita (apostolica) sive qui status statu praelatorum ecclesiasticorum... est prior, mundo necessarior, difficilior et perfectior ad purgandum, illuminandum et perficiendum, in ecclesiastica hierarchia pars principalior, sine qua ecclesiastica nec fuisset nec perfecta esse posset ... Quandocumque duo status sic se habent quod unus per se et directe valet ad infidelium ad fidem conversionem, fidelium in fide confirmationem, peccatorum contritionem, excitat imperfectos ad perfectionem et omnes ad voluntariam bonam operationem; alius per se et directe solum est ad baptizandum in fide generatos et filios sibi subditorum fidelium ad Ecclesiam deportatos, poenitentes et confiteri volentes ad absolvendum, fideles inobedientes ad excommunicandum, et sic ad bonam fidelium operationem exterius compellit ad exercendum; quanto fides est mundo necessarior quam sacramentalis in aqua ablutio ... tanto unus status magis quam alius est in se perfectior et mundo simpliciter magis necessarius; sed status vitam apostolorum tenentium et status praelatorum sic se habent ».

(34) *Op. cit.*, p. 501, « Secundo probatur quod ... praelatus ratione

enjoy as great honors, riches and luxuries as the kings of men themselves — even infidel ones. They could labor, litigate and lead armies to acquire wealth and power. "Like the Stoics, who sought happiness in luxuries of taste and touch," (35) bishops could regale themselves with delicate food and drink or even take their pleasure with wives since this was not excluded by the intrinsic nature of their office. The author was not attacking contemporary abuses but the state of episcopacy as such — and he did not trouble to coneal his contempt for it.

Like other defenders of the friars, the author of the *De perfectione statuum* insisted strongly on the doctrine of papal sovereignty (36); but it was not

---

vitae quam debet de necessitatis salutis tenere, non potest ostendere se credere quae oportet de mundo et vita ista et futura aliis praedicare. Et quod hoc possunt soli illi qui vitam tenent apostolorum .. Et quod etiam tales et non alii status hab⁀nt secundum evangelium homines in fide generare ». Bonaventura, on the other hand, acknowledged that bishops could « generate » as well as rule the flock of Christians, *In IV Sent.* Dist. 20 p.2 a.1 q.3 (*Opera*, IV, p. 534), « ... episcopi qui sponsi sunt et habent vim generandi filios et filias ... ».

(35) *Op. cit.*, p. 509, « Non repugnat essentialiter statui praelatorum tot habere et tantos vel majores honores, divitias et delicias, potentiam et familiam tantam, sicut infideles, reges eorum et principes terrae, et sicut ipsi, sic isti post electionem pro praedictis obtinendis laborare, litigare, exercitum ducere ... Et quantum Stoici, qui felicitatem ponebant in voluptatibus gustus et tactus, in cibis et potibus delicatis, et cum uxoribus quibus ratione essentiali status non repugnat delectari ».

(36) *Op. cit.*, pp. 546-547. The author compared the grades of the ecclesiastical hierarchy to the sphere of the seven planets; the friars corresponded to the eighth sphere of the fixed stars; the pope to the ninth sphere which ruled and moved the others.

at all easy to fit the papacy into the peculiar picture of the church that he presented. The simplest way of doing so would have been to declare that the supreme pontiff, who stood above prelates and friars alike and directed all their activities, combined in himself the qualities of both orders. Duns Scotus (?) indeed recognized this as the ideal state of affairs. But he could not have been unaware that all his animadversions about the wealth and power of the bishops applied *a fortiori* to the papacy of Boniface VIII, and so he concluded that possession of supreme power over the church and profession of the perfect state of life were separable from one another and did not have to exist in the same person (37). Having acknowledged this the author devoted a lengthy argument to proving that the " state " of the papacy was intrinsically less perfect than the " state " of the friars — for the friar performed a more meritorious act in renouncing the world than the pope did in assuming the responsibility for ruling it. The pope's *sollicitudo* was not in fact a grievous burden at all according to our author. Rather it was *valde delectabilis!* (38) There

---

(37) *Op. cit.*, p. 547, « Decet enim principalem hierarcham et omnium gubernatorem et regulatorem summae esse perfectionis; sic enim fuit de Christo et consequenter de beato Petro, ejus perfecto et universali vicario ». p. 545, « ... dictat ergo ratio quod ipsam (perfectam vitam) praecipue debet tenere dominus Papa. Sed quia potestas regendi alia est a vita conversandi, et ab invicem possunt separari, potest potentia esse in uno, et vita in alio personaliter distincto ».

(38) *Op. cit.*, p. 549, « ... sollicitudo, quam habet Papa circa regimen universi, non est gravis et poenalis, sed valde delectabilis ».

is a tiresome note of envy and spite and strident vanity running through the whole treatise. It would be pleasant to think that some lesser figure than Duns Scotus was responsible for it. The fullest account of the pope's status came at the end of the work. Here the author explained in detail how pope, bishops and friars were related to Christ, Peter and the Apostles. In Christ, he argued, three states were embodied. As God, Christ was lord of all men. As the Redeemer, sent to win back erring sheep to the true fold, he typified the human state of evangelical perfection. As prelate and bishop, he ruled over the flock of Christians that his teaching and perfection of life had brought into existence. Peter, " the perfect and universal vicar of Christ," was heir to all three states. He was lord of all men, a follower of the life of evangelical perfection, and supreme prelate of the church. Subsequent popes possessed all the " power and dignity " of Peter. They succeeded, that is to say to the first and third states but, as we have seen, not to the second. The rest of the Apostles inherited the second and third of the states that Christ had held. They were both evangelical preachers and ecclesiastical prelates. Subsequently, however, the two functions were separated. Bishops succeeded only to the office of prelacy, friars to the far superior office of preaching (39).

---

(39) *Op. cit.*, p. 558, « Inter quos erat beatus Petrus tanquam Chritsi perfectus et universalis vicarius, et quantum ad hoc quod Christus totius mundi erat dominus, et respectu conversorum fidelium ecclesiasticus prae

The whole work is a strange piece of theological fantasy. It implied, among other absurdities, that the church had had to get along for twelve centuries (until the advent of St. Francis) without one of the elements most essential to its "existence and perfection." A blank disregard for historical reality is one of the more disconcerting characteristics of the polemical treatises written on behalf of the friars around 1300. Again, while the whole argument for the friars rested on the doctrine of papal supremacy, the author could fit the papacy into his theory of the church only by acknowledging that there was as marked a discontinuity between Peter and subsequent popes as between the Apostles and subsequent bishops, with the corollary that the friars were in a very real sense superior to the pope. No doubt John XXII was led in the end to condemn the extreme doctrine of Franciscan poverty because he saw that it implied a criticism of all existing ecclesiastical institutions, including the papacy. The author of the *De perfectione statuum* indeed not only maintained that the most important function of the supreme pontiff was to cherish Franciscans (40) but

---

latus, pastor et episcopus, cui succedit in potentia et dignitate Papa, Christi vicarius; aliis autem Apostolis succedunt alii episcopi, non inquantum erant apostoli ad conversionem populorum missi, sed inquantum super populum fidelem erant praelati ecclesiastici, pastores et episcopi ... Christo autem et Apostolis et discipulis specialiter et principaliter pro ovibus quae perierunt domus Israelis ... missis succedunt modo qui pro salute christianorum ... vitam perfectam et poenalem cum sana doctrina fidei et contemptu mundi tenent Christi et Apostolorum ... ».

(40) *Op. cit.*, pp. 559-561.

went so far as to assert that the pope's own continued status as pope depended on his faithful discharge of this duty. A pope could not compromise the doctrine of evangelical poverty by refusing to administer property donated to the Franciscans *and still remain pope*, he wrote (41). Ockham was to come to much the same conclusion.

We find a similar paradox in two *Quaestiones* of Olivi on the subject of papal power. Again the status of the papacy was exalted, but in such a fashion as to imply that any individual pontiff could quite easily divest himself of that status voluntarily or even involuntarily if he failed to discharge faithfully the high duties of his office. The first *Quaestio* was written in the 1270s, perhaps about the same time that Nicholas III promulgated the bull *Exiit qui seminat* with its explicit endorsement of the Franciscan theory of apostolic poverty. Olivi addressed himself to the question " Whether the Roman pontiff is to be obeyed by all Catholics in faith and morals as an unerring model " (42) — an important issue for the Franciscans who were at that time basking in the papal favor but still under attack from the secular clergy. Olivi set out quite fairly the traditional arguments against papal inerrancy — e.g. the doctrine was not contained in Scripture;

---

(41) *Op. cit.*, p. 533, « ... non potest Papa manens Papa tali potestati renuntiare ».

(42) Ed. M. MACCARRONE, *Una questione inedita dell'Olivi sull'infallibilità del Papa*, in *Rivista di storia della Chiesa in Italia*, III (1949), pp. 309-343.

Peter himself had erred in his judaizing policy and had been rebuked by Paul; Gratian's Decretum recorded that other popes, like Anastasius, had also erred in the past. But, in spite of such objections, Olivi concluded that his question had to be answered in the affirmative. God had established the pope as a supreme judge in matters of faith and it was unthinkable that he would permit his chosen judge to err (43).

Olivi then set out to buttress this conclusion with a threefold argument. First he demonstrated that the right ordering of the church required it to have a single head. Secondly he maintained that the church as a whole was unerring and proved this by citing the Old and New Testaments and the formula " I believe in the Holy Catholic Church " from the Apostles' creed. He also added at this point an argument from St. Anselm which, strictly speaking, dealt with indefectibility rather than inerrancy. The end of all creatures was to serve man, Olivi wrote, and the end of man was eternal salvation. It followed that, in every generation down to the end of time, there would always be some of the elect living on earth. If it were otherwise the whole end of natura would be frustrated (44). In

---

(43) *Art. cit.*, p. 327, « Item, impossibile est me a Deo adstringi sequi fixe et immobiliter regulam errabilem: sed omnes sumus adstricti certitudinaliter credere et sequi quod romanus papa tradit esse credendum et sequendum ... »; p. 331, « Ad primam questionem dicendum quod ab omnibus catholicis est romano pontifici in fide et moribus obediendum ».

(44) *Art. cit.*, p. 341, « Sed Deus fecit omnia propter usum hominum et maxime illorum de quibus superna civitas perficienda erat ... ergo,

the third stage of his argument Olivi undertook to explain how the inerrancy of the church was expressed in the decrees of its head. It was necessary, he wrote, to distinguish between personal errors and "magistral" errors, and necessary also to distinguish between a true pope and a man who merely bore the name and appearance of a pope. Certainly a pope could not err in a magistral pronouncement *and still remain a true pope*. The whole church was unerring and so it could not be united to an erring head. Such a one became rather, as a heretic, inferior to any Catholic (45).

Olivi's argument broke off rather tantalizingly at this point, but he returned to the problem of an erring pope in a later *Quaestio* written after the abdication of Pope Celestine in 1294 — *An papa possit renuntiare papatui* (46). Much of the *Quaestio* was devoted to an exposition of the pope's sovereign jurisdiction in ecclesiastical affairs. Such power

---

quacumque hora eis non servirent, sed solis reprobis, quodammodo suo fine in illa hora frustrarentur ».

(45) *Art. cit.*, pp. 342-343, « ... si dicatur ... quod papa existens verus papa et verum capud ecclesiae non potest errare ... de hac clarum est quod nec papa nec sedes romana potest in fide pertinaciter errare, saltem errore communi seu magistrali ... Papa autem sic errans, errore scilicet communi, cum habeat rationem capitis erronei, et non solum persone singulariter et quoad se erantis, impossibile est quod papa sic errans sit verus papa et verum capud ecclesie. Et ideo secundum iura nullus hereticus publicus seu in quantum hereticus, quod idem est in proposito, habet potestatem benedicendi et maledicendi in ecclesia, quia omnis fidelis est maior eo ».

(46) Ed. L. OLIGER, *Petri Iohannis Olivi de renuntiatione Papae Coelestini V quaestio et epistola*, in *Archivum Franciscanum Historicum*, XI (1918), pp. 309-373.

was needed in the church, Olivi held, in order to make possible the progressive explication of the truths of faith through all the ages (47). Accordingly the pope's judgement was to be accepted in all doubtful matters unless it was " openly contrary to the law and faith of Christ. " (48) The argument concluded that it was not contrary to the law of Christ for a pope to abdicate and that, therefore, Celestine's declaration of his own right to do so had to be accepted as a valid pronouncement.

In the second part of his *Quaestio* Olivi was concerned to refute the argument that papal power could be taken away by God alone. Here he relied on the time-honored distinction between orders and jurisdiction. The pope's power of orders, like that of any bishop, was indeed indelible, but his power of jurisdiction, like all jurisdictional power in the church, was transferable. At this point the problem of an involuntary forfeiture of jurisdiction

---

(47) *Art. cit.*, pp. 347-352. Later (p. 362) he wrote of the « nova explicatio sublimium veritatum fidei catholice ... magis et magis per successionem temporum in ecclesia Dei sancta, « then gave as an example the evangelical way of life proclaimed by St. Francis and its approval by the popes in his own century.

(48) *Art. cit.*, p. 351, « Constat enim ... quod papa potest novam legem condere de quocumque, quod non est contra Christi fidem et legem et quod in omni tali et etiam in omni sententiali et autentica expositione dubiorum christiane legis et fidei est sibi credendum et obediendum, nisi aperte esset contraria fidei Christi et legi ». Cf. OCKHAM, *Breviloquium*, ed. L. BAUDRY (Paris, 1937), pp. 134-135, « Ista tamen prerogativa potest attribui sibi pre aliis ut nemini, nisi qui ve veritate fuerit certus, liceat post determinacionem, diffinicionem vel assercionem pape publice dogmatizare ... Quantecumque enim auctoritatis fuerit papa, semper est sibi veritas preferenda precipue que ad jus divinum dinoscitur pertinere ».

by a supreme pontiff arose. Olivi had maintained that a pope could freely enact new laws provided that he did not contradict the Gospels, the Apostles and the church Fathers in matters in faith. But what if he did so contradict them? " All ecclesiastical jurisdiction is taken away by manifest heresy," Olivi replied (49). If such a case arose it was the duty of the cardinals to depose the pope and elect a new one; but the deposition was more a recognition of the fact that the pope had forfeited office throught his own behavior than a judicial sentence (50). For Olivi the pope was a sovereign lord of the church in the fullest sense so long as he retained his jurisdiction; but that jurisdiction itself was, to use Olivi's own expressive word, *mobilis*.

We are concerned primarily with the Franciscan tradition of thought but we way note in passing

---

(49) *Art. cit.*, p. 357, « Omnis autem iurisdictio ecclesiastica tollitur per heresim manifestam ... » Olivi also held (p. 356) that a prelate should be deprived of his jurisdiction if he became mad, or guilty of shameful conduct, or a waster of the goods of the church, or blind, or deaf and dumb.

(50) *Art. cit.*, pp. 356, 358-359, « Rursus ... cardinales gerunt vicem superioris in eligendo papam et in preceptorie cogendo ipsum consentire electioni et in ipsum consecrando et in eius renuntiationem acceptando. Si autem papam propter aliquid crimen deponerent, credo quod hec depositio potius modum renuntiationis haberet quam iudiciarie condempnationis ... » Fr. Oliger praised Olivi for avoiding the conciliarist implications that he finds in the treatises on papal abdication of John of Paris and Giles of Rome. It might be argued that the extreme curialism of Olivi was much more dangerous to the stability and good order of the church. His view that the cardinals alone could decide, for a variety of reasons and without any judicial process, that the occupant of the papal throne was not a true pope would have provided a complete justification for the behavior of the cardinals who precipitated the Great Scism in 1378.

that, by the early fourteenth century, leading masters of all four mendicant orders were writing extensively and sometimes extravagantly on the subject of papal power. John Baconthorpe, the English Carmelite, taught that a General Council was not competent to judge even a heretical pope (51). Augustinus Triumphus, the most eminent doctor of the Augustinian Hermits, held that Peter alone (and not the other Apostles) received jurisdiction from Christ. He also maintained that the pope was not only the source of all jurisdictional power in the church but also the source of all power of orders, and that the supreme pontiff could, if necessary, even abolish the episcopate (52). Hervaeus Natalis, the Dominican master-general, explained in more detail than his predecessors had done how jurisdiction was transmitted from the pope to inferior grades of the hierarchy. A bishop's jurisdiction, he wrote, was not derived from election but from confirmation " made by the pope or one on whom the pope confers the right of confirming." Moreover, according to Hervaeus Natalis, the status of the bishops in the church was not analagous to that of the barons of France or the princes of Germany in the secular sphere. Rather they stood to the pope

---

(51) B. SMALLEY, *John Baconthorpe's Postill on St. Matthew*, in *Mediaeval and Renaissance Studies*, IV (1958), pp. 91-145 at p. 138.

(52) J. M. WILKS, *The Problem of Sovereignty in the Later Middle Ages. The Papal Monarchy with Augustinus Triumphus and the Publicists* (Cambridge, 1963), pp. 383, 386, 531 (citing Augustinus Triumphus's *Summa de potestate ecclesiastica*).

in the same relationship as bailiffs or stewards to a secular king, as mere servants that is to say, appointable and dismissable at the will of the ruler. It followed that a General Council was in no way of greater authority than a pope (53). (A king with his servants has no more authority than a king alone). Hervaeus Natalis was perhaps conscious of the fact that he was going against the whole canonical tradition of the church for he concluded the treatise *De jurisdictione* (in which the above opinions were set out) by stating that he did not presume to discuss matters of positive law which pertained to the jurists, but had set out rather the conclusions that followed from divine law and reason. Ockham would appeal to the same authorities.

For a final consideration of the Franciscan tradition as it had developed by the time of Ockham himself we can glance at the work of Alvarus Pelagius. When Pope John XXII denounced the Franciscan doctrine of the absolute poverty of Christ, Alvarus stood at the same crossroads as Ockham, hesitated, and then took a different path. He too was dismayed at the pope's action and he incorporated much of Bonagratia of Bergamo's protest against it in his own *De planctu ecclesiae*. Alvarus, however, like most of the Franciscans, finally succeeded in convincing himself of John's orthodoxy and became an ardent defender of the pope. There is little

---

(53) L. Hödl, *De iurisdictione. Ein unveröffentlichter Traktat des Herveus Natalis* (München, 1959), pp. 28, 29, 34.

that is original in his ecclesiology. He borrowed extensively from the Dominican, James of Viterbo, and, for the rest, presented a mélange of the various views that we have already discussed. Like Bonaventura, Alvarus taught that the pope's jurisdiction came from God directly and was itself the source of all other jurisdiction in the church (54). Like Bonaventura again, he emphasized equally the unerringness of the whole church and the teaching authority of the pope. He took the words *Ego rogavi pro te Petre* ... as referring to the faith of the universal church rather than to the faith of Peter alone, but he also taught that papal pronouncements (whether expressed in conciliar canons or decretal letters) possessed the same authority as the Scripture themselves (55).

In spite of holding these views, Alvarus Pelagius acknowledged that, since the pope was after all a man, it was possible for him to err in faith, and indeed he showed an unusual grasp of the juridical problems that could arise from such a contingency (56). But the canonical solution of an

---

(54) N. Iung, *Un Franciscain théologien du pouvoir pontifical au XIV² siècle, Alvaro Pelayo.* (Paris, 1931), p. 100, « Quia omnis jurisdictio ab eo (papa), ipse (papa) autem immediate ipsam a Deo recipit ». (Citing *De statu et planctu ecclesiae*, I art. 17).

(55) *Op. cit.*, p. 175 (citing *De statu*, I art. 16); p. 176 (citing *Collyrium adversus hereses*, ed. R. Scholz, *Unbekannte kirchenpolitische Streitschriften aus der Zeit Ludwigs des Bayern*, II (Rome, 1914), p. 506).

(56) Alvarus Pelagius was a doctor of canon law before he became a friar and turned to the study of theology. Moreover his master, Guido de Baysio, was something of an antiquarian and was more familiar than any other canonist with the elaborate glosses that the Decretists had devoted

appeal to a council of bishops was inconsistent with the basic tenets of Alvarus' ecclesiology. He suggested at one point that there might be an appeal from a pope badly informed to a pope better informed; but this provided no way out of the impasse if a pope persisted in obdurate heresy. Alvarus agreed with Baconthorpe that a Council could not enact a juridical sentence against a heretical pope — for the fathers of the Council possessed no jurisdiction that was not held from the pope himself. His final solution was similar to Olivi's. A heretical pope deprived himself of his own office. In such a situation the church ought to take action to provide itself with a new head without awaiting any judicial sentence (57). These conclusions of Alvarus Pelagius have evident parallels in the thought of William of Ockham, to which we can now turn.

The controversies among modern scholars have at least made it clear that any final judgement on Ockham's thought ought to be based on what is most distinctive in his work. Like all scholastic

---

to this question a century earlier. Alvarus's own views follow rather closely those of the canonist Huguccio. There are parallels too between Huguccio's thought and Ockham's. See my *Ockham, the Conciliar Theory and the Canonists*, in *Journal of the History of Ideas*, XV (1954), pp. 40-70.

(57) N. IUNG, *op. cit.*, pp. 178-179, « Si ergo papa contra incorrigibiliter in heresi permaneret jam damnata notorie, nec renuntiare vellet papatui sicut posset, tunc cardinales possent et deberent ab eo recedere et alium eligere ... (*De statu*, I art. 34); « Si tamen papa est incorrigibilis in casu heresis notoriae vacat papatus et Ecclesia providebit sibi de papa ». (*Collyrium*, p. 507); « Et quod in casu etiam heresis judicem non habeat, etiam concilium generale ». (*De statu*, I art. 34).

writers, Ockham devoted many pages to restating the arguments of his predecessors (usually without acknowledgment). Often enough he influenced later thinkers more as a populariser of well-established earlier ideas than as an originator of novel doctrines. And, obviously, it is easy to present Ockham as a conservative if one concentrates on the least original aspects of his thought. All this is especially true of the lengthy passages in Ockham's works devoted to criticising the papal *plenitudo potestatis* understood as sheer arbitrary despotism. He had virtually nothing fresh to say on the subject. In spite of his railing against abuses of papal power he held an entirely conventional view on the primacy of the See of Peter itself, and this was implied by the very nature of the criticisms he presented. In the *Breviloquium*, for instance, where Ockham expressed his own views with unusual clarity, he developed three main arguments against papal absolutism. The pope, he pointed out, was given power only for the " edification " of the church; he could not arbitrarily regulate matters that God had left to the free judgement of man by imposing works of supererogation " without urgent necessity"; he could not exercise jurisdiction in purely temporal affairs (58). As to the first two assertions, surely no reputable medieval theologian ever denied them. Bonaventura himself, having written that Peter received every power that it was fitting for a man to have,

---

(58) *Breviloquium*, pp. 22-25, 48-51, 51-54.

added "and this for the edification of the church "; (59) and Olivi noted that the pope could not impose works of supererogation (60). These were matters of *communis opinio*. Ockham's third limitation on papal power was more controversial, but many of his predecessors who were ardent defenders of papal primacy in the church had held that the pope's jurisdiction was limited to spiritual affairs.

Moreover, we cannot agree with de Lagarde's view that Ockham broke new ground when he asserted that the only unerring *Romana ecclesia* was the whole *congregatio fidelium*. This opinion had been widely held among the canonists ever since the late twelfth century (61). What then was distinctive about Ockham's thought? All its unusual, characteristic features arose from the fact that Ockham was a vehement critic of the papacy without being in the least a conciliarist. " It is astonishing," J. B. Morrall writes, " that it should ever have been imagined that Ockham was a sponsor of belief in the supremacy and infallibility of the General Council." (62) Ockham in fact did not believe that a General Council was necessarily unerring in faith. He did not believe that the convocation of a General

---

(59) *In IV Dent.* Dist. 20 p.2 a.1 q.5 (*Opera*, IV, p. 539).

(60) L. HÖDL, *op. cit.* (*supra* n. 18), p. 20.

(61) *Foundations fo the Conciliar Theory*, pp. 41-46. Cf. de LAGARDE, *La Naissance...*, B, ʼp. 145.

(62) *Ockham and Ecclesiology*, in *Medieval Studies Presented to Aubrye Gwynn S. J.* ed. J. A. WATT, J. B. MORRALL and F. X. MARTIN (Dublin, 1961), pp. 481-491 at p. 481.

Council was necessary before a pope could be held guilty of heresy. He did not believe that a Council of any kind could perfectly represent the universal church. Many medieval dissidents had attacked the papacy; Ockham was the first of them to attack the General Council This was his personal contribution to medieval ecclesiology (63).

Ockham arrived at his conclusions by combining in a new and startling fasion two old doctrines that had been commonly taught by earlier theologians and canonists, but taught separately from one another — the doctrines that the universal church was infallible so that it could never err in faith, and that it was indefectible so that it could never fail to survive even if only in a few individual members. One can trace a clear development in this matter. Bonaventura presented the two doctrines quite separately; Olivi began to associate them with one another (64); Ockham fused them together into a single system of thought. His characteristic argument was that the *congregatio fidelium* whose unerring judgement provided a certain guide to the true faith might consist of a tiny group, or even one single individual, dissenting from the doctrine of the rest of the church (65). He was driven to adopt

---

(63) MORRALL, *art. cit.* has shown that the detailed but inconclusive criticism of the unerring authority of General Councils presented in the *Dialogus* is supported by more explicit statements in Ockham's other polemical works.

(64) *Supra*, n. 29, n. 44.

(65) This position was set out most clearly of all in the *Tractatus contra Ioannem, Guillelmi de Ockham opera politica*, ed. J. G. SIKES etc., 3 vols

this position precisely because he was determined to resist the pope without resting his case on an appeal to the Council. It is this that has to be explained if we are to understand the essential nature of his thought.

Some scholars have maintained that Ockham's basic conservatism and devotion to Catholic orthodoxy prevented him from embracing so radical a doctrine as Conciliarism. But this seems a perverse interpretation. The implications of Ockham's arguments were far more disruptive of all established ecclesiastical order than the mild Conciliarism of, say, a John of Paris. Other modern scholars, as we noted at the outset, have found a key to the understanding of Ockham's ecclesiology in certain pre-suppositions said to have been derived from his nominalistic philosophy. We may agree that there was no actual opposition between Ockham's theology and his philosophy; in studying his work it is one mind that we have ot deal with, not two. The difficulty is that other medieval nominalists,

_____

(Manchester, 1940-1956), III, p. 67, « Sed forte quaeret aliquis, quo modo potest universalis ecclesia quamcumque veritatem catholicam explicite approbare cum non possit insimul convenire ... veritates catholicae ab universali ecclesia approbantur quando praelati communiter et populi comprehendentes viros et mulieres, easdem veritates sub verbis apertis expressas tamquam catholicas expresse vel tacite confitentur, licet nequaquam simul conveniant ... et nullus invenitur catholicus qui tali assertioni resistat. Sicut enim, iuxta promissum Salvatoris, fides catholica est usque ad finem saeculi permansura: ita semper erit aliquis in ecclesia, clericus vel laicus, prelatus vel subditus qui cuicumque errori, qui umquam omnibus fidelibus populis per quoscumque vel quemcumque inculcabitur ut credendus, cum instantia forte resistet ».

such as Jean Gerson, upheld the supreme authority of the Council as representing the universal church, while the only two medieval thinkers of comparable stature to Ockham who denied the ultimate authority of the Council in matters of faith, Wycliff and Hus, stood at the opposite end of the philosophic spectrum. They were extreme realists. Given these facts it seems impossible to maintain convincingly that Ockham's philosophical views adequately account for his theology of the church.

Ockham evidently took for granted the doctrine of evangelical poverty formulated in the polemical treatises of the Franciscan theologians. When we understand that he also took for granted much of the ecclesiology embedded in those same treatises his whole position becomes comprehensible. There was not much regard for the General Council as an institution of church government in Ockham's works; there was not much regard for it in Bonaventura's works either. The Franciscan theology of the church, as it developed from Thomas of York to Alvarus Pelagius, tended more and more to eliminate all centers of ecclesiastical authority except the papacy. None of the Franciscans ever denied that papal leadership might fail, that the pope might conceivably fall into heresy. But they saw no other offices in the church, established by direct divine authority and qualified by their intrinsic nature to represent either God or the Christian people. There was only one supreme ruler and below him a mass of servants and subjects, " nought but a naked people under a naked crown." This way of thinking was compounded out of a strange mixture of absolutism and anarchy. Many previous theologians had explored the absolutist side of the doctrine; it was left for Ockham, because he really believed that the pope was a heretic, to exploit its anarchical implications.

Ockham's implicit acceptance of the system of thought whose development we have outlined was hinted at in the *Breviloquium*. There he developed at considerable length the argument that the pope's *plenitudo potestatis* was limited by the rights bestowed by God on on other men; but there was no mention of episcopal rights. In the same work Ockham observed that Peter's authority came directly from God while episcopal jurisdiction was derived from confirmation by an ecclesiastical superior (not from election) (66). The most detailed explanation of his position, however, is to be found in the *Dialogus*. In the lengthy section devoted to refuting the view that all the Apostles were equal to Peter, Ockham, for once in this enigmatic work, left the reader in no doubt as to his own opinions. He argued that Christ promised to Peter both the power fo the keys and primacy over the whole church in the words

_____

(66) *Breviloquium*, p. 109, « Aliqua enim jurisdiccio est a solo Deo ... Sic eciam beatus Petrus potestatem quam habuit per illa verba Christi: *Pasce oves meas*, a solo Deo recepit ... jurisdiccio episcopalis recipitur a sola confirmatione, non tamen absque elecctione previa per quam tamen eleccionem non confertur episcopalis jurisdiccio ». When distinguishing between the apostles and subsequent bishops in the *Opus nonaginta dierum*, *Opera politica*, II, p. 823, Ockham used the same argument as the author of the *De perfectione statuum* (*supra* n. 35) — the intrinsic nature of episcopacy did not exclude the possibility of marriage.

recorded at Matthew 16:18. Christ actually bestowed the keys, understood merely as a power of order, on Peter and the Apostles together, with the words *Accipite spiritum sanctum* (John 20:22). He conferred on Peter power over the other Apostles with the words *Pasce oves meas* (John 21:15) (67). Ockham conceded that Christ assigned certain specific tasks to the Apostles — teaching, baptizing, remitting sins — but he maintained that Peter alone received authority to *rule* the church and that this was conveyed in the words of John 21:15 (68). According to Ockham Peter was the only *pastor* established directly by Christ in His church. Whem, in the course of the Dialogus, the Disciple objected that, according to St. Paul, Christ established other pastors, the Master replied that they were established " throught the mediation and authority of Peter " and he added, *quod verum est* (69).

---

(67) *Dialogus*, ed. M. GOLDAST, *Monarchia S. Romani Imperii*, II (Francofordiae, 1614), p. 863, « Cum ergo dicitur, quod Christus potestatem clavium non videtur Petro tradidisse per haec verba: *Tu es Petrus* etc. Respondetur, quod tunc Christus non tradidit Petro potestatem clavium, sed promisit... potestatem clavium, quae competit ratione ordinis, accepit Petrus simul cum aliis apostolis per verba praescripta *Ioh.* 20; aliam tamen potestatem accepit super apostolos, cum Christus sibi dixit: *pasce oves meas* ».

(68) *Dialogus*, p. 855, « ... licet Christus dederit apostolis aliquam potestatem specialem, nunquam tamen concessit eis potestatem generalem vel aequalem potestati Petri. Verbo enim generaliori usus est in praeficiendo Petrum, scilicet verbo *pascendi*: quod communius est quam verbum docendi, vel baptizandi, aut aliud tale. Quibus verbis usus est in concedendo potestatem in aliis apostolis ».

(69) *Dialogus*, p. 856, « Christus, qui etiam nunc ecclesiam non desinit invisibiliter gubernare, secundum apostolum quosdam mediante Petro

Ockham was consistently hostile to all ideas of collegial authority. He showed no understanding of or sympathy toward the experiments in parliamentary government which, in the secular sphere, were so characteristic of his age. When he considered the possibility of a plurality of " popes " existing simultaneously he brushed aside as obviously absurd the notion of a collegiate headship of the universal church but explored, with apparent fascination, the idea of a church temporarily divided into separate provinces, each ruled by its own independent " pope " (70). In the section of the *Dialogus* that we have been considering he declared explicitly that Christ did not establish any collegial solidarity among the Apostles. " Christ did not set the Apostles over the other faithful as a college but as individual persons " (71).

Evidently enough no conciliar theory could have been built on theological foundations like these. Some canonists had suggested that the whole *congretatio fidelium* might be more perfectly represented in a Council where spokesmen for the laity met with the bishops than in an assembly of bishops alone (72);

---

constituit pastores. Nec apostolus dicit, quod Christus dedit absque ministerio Petri quosdam pastores; sed quod dedit pastores, quia dedit eos mediante ministerio et auctoritate Petri, quod verum est ».

(70) G. TABACCO, *Pluralità di papi ed unità di chiesa nel pensiero di Guglielmo di Occam* (Torino, 1949).

(71) *Dialogus*, p. 866, « Christus non praefecit apostolos aliis fidelibus tanquam collegium, sed tanquam singulares personas ... ».

(72) *Foundations of the Conciliar Theory*, p. 149. Ockham misquoted the canonistic text (*Dist.* 96 c. 4) in characteristic fashion. The Decretists

but no one had ever supposed that a Council could represent the church at all without the participation of bishops who would bring to it the collegial authority that they held as successors of the Apostles. Let us emphasize again that Conciliarism, the view that a pope could be deposed only after a General Council had sat in judgement on his case and condemned him, was not at the beginning of the fourteenth century a radical doctrine but a conservative one. It was the position generally adopted by the curialist canonists of the time whom Ockham attacked so vigorously, and it was indeed the doctrine best calculated to defend the papacy against attacks from cliques of malcontents supported by royal or imperial power (73). But such a position was rendered untenable by the theories of the friars which had transformed the bishops into mere servants of the popes. A lord is not judged by his lackeys. Ockham, therefore, like Olivi and Alvarus Pelagius, preferred to rely on the old argument that a heretical pope was "les than any Catholic," without, however, ever explaining satisfactorily how the actual fact of the pope's heresy was to be authoritatively established.

---

had held that a General Council could certainly decide a question of faith and that laymen ought to be summoned to the Council to make it as representative as possible. Ockham appealed to their authority to prove the quite different assertion that « secundum canonicas sanctiones ... quaestio fidei ... *non solum ad generale concilium* aut praelatos vel etiam clericos, verum etiam ad laicos et ad omnes omnino pertinet Christianos » - *Epistola ad fratres minores, Opera politica*, III, p. 10.

(73) *Foundations of the Conciliar Theory*, pp. 212-216.

There were two basic premises in Ockham's theology of the church. The first was that Peter alone received authority from Christ to rule the church. The second was that Peter's successor had become on obdurate heretic. Perhaps it is not possible to construct a coherent ecclesiology on the basis of such pre-suppositions. Certainly Ockham did not succeed in doing so. One has the impression that he is constantly on the brink of formulating conclusions that would be, if not orthodox, at least sensible. But the expectation is always disappointed. Each new argument leads on only to another level of paradox.

How can we know with certainty the truths of faith? From Scripture, Ockham tells us over and over again, Scripture rationally interpreted and understood primarily in its simple literal sense (74). Was Ockham then inviting his readers to eschew theological subtleties and become simple Bible Christians, following the plain words of the Scriptures and caring for nothing else? This might have been a becoming attitude for a son of St. Francis. But it was not Ockham's attitude at all. In the controversy over evangelical poverty he displayed the most

---

(74) *An princeps, Opera politica,* I, p. 254, «... prima regula et infallibilis in huiusmodi est scriptura sacra et ratio recta ... »; *Epistola, Opera politica,* III, p. 16; *Contra Ioannem, Opera politica,* III, p. 46; *Contra Benedictum, Opera politica,* III, p. 255; *Breviloquium,* pp. 130-131, «... sensus scripture misticus qui non est contrarius veritati ... licet ad edifficacionem et exhortationem possit adduci, tamen ad probandum et confirmandum disputabilia et dubia, de quibus inter Christianos est contencio, allegari non debet nec potest ».

tortuous and evasive subtelty in arguing that the words of Scripture could not possibly mean what they evidently seemed to say whenever the literal sense was not in accordance with his own position. Moreover, as he found more and more supposed heresies in John XXII's pronouncements, Ockham found it useful to emphasize the existence of a whole body of Catholic doctrine, not contained explicitly in Scripture and yet certainly true, and so authoritative that a man who denied any part of it could rightly be denounced as a heretic (75).

How could men know which doctrines possessed this special authority? Ockham gave his first answer in the *Opus nonaginta dierum*. " What the Roman pontiffs have once defined in faith and morals stands immutably " (76). Was Ockham then an early defender of the doctrine of papal infallibility? In a way he was, but not at all in the manner of the nineteenth century partisans of the doctrine. Ockham quite consistently maintained that unerring definitions of faith promulgated by a pope possessed

---

(75) *Contra Ioannem, Opera politica*, III, pp. 44-52. Like Olivi, Ockham thought it was the task of the church to carry on a progressive explication of the truths of faith from age to age. He went so far as to assert that he would adhere to the faith of the universal church even if a text of Scripture seemed to contradict it (*op. cit.*, p. 73). On this matter see especially Heiko A. Oberman, *The Harvest of Medieval Theology* (Cambridge, 1963), pp. 361-393.

(76) *Opus nonaginta dierum, Opera politica*, II, p. 833. Tne argument was first used by the Franciscan Chapter-General of Perugia (1321) in an attempt to establish the immutability of Nicholas III's decree, *Exiit qui seminat*. It was repeated in Michael of Cesena's appeal against John XXII. Ockham quoted it from there.

a unique authority in the church and were permanently binding on all Catholics; but he insisted with equal emphasis that not all papal definitions were unerring (77).
Where then could men find a criterion to distinguish true pronouncements from false ones? In the faith of the church, Ockham replied. All doctrines that the universal church accepted were unerring and hence immutable (78). As we have noted, the canonists, in apparently similar fashion, held that dogmatic decrees of General Councils were to be held as immutable because " they were established by universal consent." Was Ockham then a conciliarist after all? We have seen that indeed he was not. He emphasized over and over again that consensus was no certain guide to truth; unanimity alone would suffice (79). For him a Council was only " part of the church " and the true church consisted, not only of the Christians alive at any given time but of all the Catholic prelates and peo-

---

(77) *Opus nonaginta dierum, Opera politica*, II, p. 837, « Quia in diffinitione eorum, quae pertinent ad fidem et bonos mores, nichil debet potentia, nisi quod decernit scientia ... si papa per quamcunque potentiam diffiniret aliquid contra illud, quod scientia dictat diffiniendum in fide et bonis moribus, diffinitio sua nulla penitus esset, immo liceret cuilibet Christiano hoc scienti ipsam detestari, respuere et sicut haereticam reprobare ».

(78) *Contra Ioannem* (*cit.* supra, n. 65); *Opus Nonaginta dierum, Opera politica*, II, p. 851, « Qui scienter impugnat determinationem universalis ecclesiae vel doctrinam, est haereticus manifestus ... ».

(79) *Epistola, Opera politica*, III, p. 15; *Opus nonaginta dierum, Opera politica*, II, p. 383; *Contra Benedictum, Opera politica*, III, p. 261; *Breviloqium*, pp. 164-165.

ples who had succeeded one another down the course of the centuries (80). Was Ockham then essentially a traditionalist, finding certain truth in the consensus of past ages, " appealing to the universal church in time as against the universal church in space " (81). It is an attractive hypothesis but it will not hold water. Ockham's insistence on unanimity, his reiterated assertion that the faith of the church might live on in some small dissident group, destroys the possibility of an appeal to the consensus of the past as a sure guide to the truths of faith just as effectively as it destroys the possibility of an appeal to the consensus of the present. Indeed, it followed as a logical conclusion from Ockham's premises that the true faith in his own day might have been represented by the adherents of any of the historic heresies that had lingered on into the fourteenth century, by the Monophysites of Egypt or the Nestorians of Syria or, coming closer to home, by the Cathars of Provence. To maintain that the Catholic faith is what Catholics have always believed is a mere tautology. The problem is — how are we to identify the Catholics? Ockham can give us no clear answer.

There seems to be only one rational conclusion to this whole involved argument. If the only certain truths of religion are those that all Christians

---

(80) *Contra Ioannem, Opera politica*, III, p. 65, « Sed auctoritas ecclesiae quae etiam fideles non solum in hac vita simul degentes, sed sibimet succedentes praelatos et populos catholicos comprehendit, valet ad finem et certitudinem catholicae veritatis.

(81) J. B. MORRALL, *art. cit.* (n. 62), p. 488.

have always held unanimously then we are left with the barest essentials of the faith — that there is a God, that Christ is His son, that we should strive to obey His commands. It would seem then that a wide variety of opinions on all other theological issues could be tolerated within the church. On this theory it would be proper for each man to choose his own religious beliefs according to his judgment and conscience, the unlettered peasant relying on his simple hearsay knowledge of Scripture, the learned theologian calling on all the subtelties of his art to arrive at his chosen position. Ockham occasionally wrote as though this might conceivably have been his opinion. Was he then, at bottom, an apostle of religious liberty, an advocate of private judgement in matters of faith? Not in the least! He wanted to have all his adversaries condemned and punished as heretics. As Tabacco rightly observed, if by some twist of fate Ockham himself had ever become pope, theologians who centured to disagree with him would have trembled before the severity of his judgements (82).

Ockham's theory of the church is a kind of mirror image of traditional Franciscan ecclesiology or, one might say, a sort of precisely analogous yet eplosively destructive anti-amtter. The tangle of paradoxes that he presented cannot reasonably be regarded as an attempt by a brilliant logician to construct, on the basis of his philosophical insights,

---

(82) G. Tabacco, op. cit., p. 38.

a coherent system of ecclesiology, Ockham's polemical works reveal to us rather the subtlest thinker
of the fourteenth century engaged in exploring, with
an intricately Gothic elaboration of argument, all
the possible corollaries of an essentially flawed set
of theological premises concerning the pope's *sollicitudo omnium ecclesiarum.*

XVI

ORIGINS OF PAPAL INFALLIBILITY

PRECIS

The history of the doctrine of infallibility must be understood in order to understand the theology of infallibility. This history has unfortunately been badly misunderstood under the influence of modern theological biases. The modern doctrine, deriving from Vatican I, has led theologians into a *cul-de-sac* from which they find it impossible to emerge.

The historian detects several paradoxes: (1) how the attempt to enhance the sovereignty of the pope by attributing infallibility to him has in fact radically reduced his sovereignty by binding him to the decrees of his predecessors; (2) how the first advocates of papal infallibility in the middle ages were not extreme papalists but those anxious to restrict papal power.

Taking issue with Manning's attempt to prove infallibility by the argument from silence, and with Döllinger's interpretation of the canonical tradition of the medieval church, Tierney holds that the canonists of the twelfth and thirteenth centuries provide no foundation for a doctrine of papal infallibility, as is often alleged. It is an unfounded assumption that the doctrine was a generally received teaching of that era.

The real origin of the doctrine can be found in the enigmatic theologian Olivi writing during the late thirteenth century controversies over the meaning of Franciscan poverty. Tierney holds that Olivi's position, the first explicit espousal of papal infallibility, not only departs from the more traditional canonical doctrine on papal sovereignty but is a doctrine aimed at restricting the power of future popes. The popes of the time, Nicholas III and John XXII, wanted no part of the new doctrine and condemned it vigorously; it resurfaced only later when it could prove useful to the papacy against Protestantism and Gallicanism.

The historian finds it difficult to accept the modern theologian's assertion that infallibility slowly unfolded and emerged over the centuries in some type of development. Rather the historical evidence shows that the doctrine was not part of *depositum fidei*. It would seem that the papacy in adopting the doctrine for purely pragmatic reasons has done itself and the church more harm than good.

This paper[1] will present a purely historical discussion on papal infallibility. But, since the whole subject has recently become a

---

Brian Tierney (Roman Catholic) was born in England, studied at Pembroke College, Cambridge University, receiving his B.A. (First Class Honors) and Ph.D. He is presently Goldwin Smith Professor of Medieval History at Cornell University. A Councillor of the Medieval Academy of America, he is also Editor of *Studies in the History of Christian Tht.* He has written numerous books and articles on medieval law and Church history, including the seminal work, *Foundation of the Conciliar Theory*, 1955.

1 This article is based on excerpts from a forthcoming book, *Origins of Papal Infallibility, 1150-1350*, to be published shortly by E. J. Brill of Leiden. In this book the conclusions set out somewhat baldly in the text above are presented in a framework of supporting arguments and references and in the context of a more detailed investigation into the medieval concepts of infallibility, sovereignty and tradition.

matter of urgent theological debate, it would perhaps be disingenuous not to state at the outset my attitude to the substance of the doctrine which is to be considered. It seems to me then that, once the history of infallibility is properly understood, it becomes hardly possible—even allowing for all theories of development of dogma—to maintain that the doctrine of papal infallibility formed part of a *depositum fidei* handed down by Christ to the apostles. And, if the infallibility doctrine was not part of this "deposit," then of course it is not part of the Catholic faith.

However that may be, my purpose here is not to propound some new theology of infallibility but simply to point out that all the participants in the current theological controversy are basing their arguments in part on misunderstandings of history. The truth is that the doctrine of papal infallibility was first propounded in the years around 1300 by men who were desperately anxious to restrict the powers of the contemporary popes. Nearly all the first defenders of the doctrine were condemned as heretics. The first Roman pontiff who had to deal with the idea that popes might be infallible, John XXII (1316-1334), was inclined to dismiss the whole idea as "pernicious audacity." This is the tangled situation that has to be explored if we are to understand the origins of papal infallibility. First we must glance briefly at some aspects of the modern doctrine.

"*Infallibility* in the spiritual order and *sovereignty* in the temporal order are two perfectly synonymous words." This view of Joseph de Maistre was widely accepted as a self-evident truth—almost a platitude—by the various parties in the nineteenth century debates over papal infallibility. The most ardent Ultramontanes, the most reluctant inopportunists, and the most stalwart opponents of the dogma of 1870 were all agreed on the one point, that to declare the pope infallible would be to enhance his sovereign power as head of the Church. Louis Veuillot wrote, "We must affirm squarely the authority and omnipotence of the pope as the source of all authority, spiritual and temporal. The proclamation of the dogma of the infallibility of the pope has no other objective." At the other end of the spectrum, Döllinger called an early draft of the infallibility decree a "Magna Carta of ecclesiastical absolutism" and complained that the doctrine finally promulgated had reinforced the "sovereign caprice" of the pope. The dogmatic decree itself proclaimed the infallibility of the pope and his supreme jurisdiction over the church as two interrelated aspects of a single coherent doctrine.

ORIGINS OF PAPAL INFALLIBILITY

Yet de Maistre's dictum is not really a platitude. It is more of a paradox. The words "infallibility" and "sovereignty" do not have the same meaning. It would be more true to suggest that the ideas they express are intrinsically incompatible with one another. It is of the essence of sovereignty (as the concept was understood both in the nineteenth century and in the Middle Ages) that a sovereign ruler cannot be bound by the decisions of his predecessors. It is of the essence of infallibility (as the doctrine was formulated at Vatican Council I) that the infallible decrees of one pope are binding on all his successors since they are, by definition, irreformable.

This point is not presented as a mere verbal equivocation. Real issues of ecclesiastical power are involved. If the popes have always been infallible in any meaningful sense of the word—if their official pronouncements as heads of the church on matters of faith and morals have always been unerring and so irreformable—then all kinds of dubious consequences ensue. Most obviously, twentieth century popes would be bound by a whole array of past papal decrees reflecting the responses of the Roman church to the religious and moral problems of former ages. As Acton put it, "The responsibility for the acts of the buried and repented past would come back at once and for ever." To defend religious liberty would be "insane" and to persecute heretics commendable. Judicial torture would be licit and the taking of interest on loans a mortal sin. The pope would rule by divine right "not only the universal church but the whole world." Unbaptized babies would be punished in Hell for all eternity. Maybe the sun would still be going round the earth.

All this is impossible of course. No one understands the fact better than modern theologians of infallibility. If past popes have always been infallible—again, we must add, in any meaningful sense of the word—then present popes are hopelessly circumscribed in their approaches to all the really urgent moral problems of the twentieth century, problems involving war, sex, scientific progress, state power, social obligations, and individual liberties. The existence of this dilemma helps to explain the rather eccentric development of the doctrine of infallibility during the past century. Since Vatican Council I, Catholic theologians have felt obliged to defend some form of papal infallibility. Real infallibility has regrettable implications. In the years since 1870, therefore, theologians have devoted much ingenuity to devising a sort of pseudo-infallibility for the pope, a kind of Pickwickian infallibility.

They have achieved this in two ways. Some theologians have raised such endless, teasing, really unanswerable questions about the significance of the term *ex cathedra* as used in the decree of Vatican Council I that they find it possible to dismiss any papal definition they disagree with as "not infallible." Other theologians, more reprehensibly (from a historian's point of view), have devised hermeneutical principles so ingenious that the infallible definitions of the past can never embarrass them. By the application of such principles any doctrinal pronouncement, regardless of its actual wording, can be re-interpreted to mean whatever the contemporary theologian thinks that its framers ought to have meant. One is reminded of the Cheshire Cat in Alice-in-Wonderland. The body of a past pronouncement disappears but its grin of infallibility persists. The modern theology of infallibility—or pseudo-infallibility—has of course been elaborated in rich and impressive detail but its underlying principles can be formulated without undue distortion in two simple general rules (Tierney's Laws let us say). They are as follows: (1) All infallible pronouncements are certainly true but no pronouncements are certainly infallible. (2) All infallible pronouncements are irreformable until it becomes convenient to change them.

Fortunately, for the purposes of the present study we shall not need to pursue in more detail the intricacies of contemporary Catholic apologetics and hermeneutics. The theologians of papal infallibility have obviously worked themselves into a complicated cul-de-sac. But a historian cannot do the theologians' work for them; he cannot show them how to get out of their cul-de-sac; it is enough, perhaps, if he can show them how they got into it in the first place. We have begun by emphasizing the paradoxes of modern theology because it is impossible to understand the history of infallibility without some awareness of those paradoxes. The central point is that to attribute infallibility to a whole line of rulers is to curtail radically the sovereign power of each individual monarch (since each monarch is bound by the infallible decrees of his predecessors). Yet, perversely it may seem, modern enthusiasts for the doctrine of papal infallibility have always wanted to increase the power of the reigning pope—hence their paradoxes and evasions. Historians of infallibility have started out from the same mistaken assumptions as the theologians. They have always assumed that the first advocates of a doctrine of papal infallibility must necessarily have been ardent

XVI

defenders of absolute papal power. They are sometimes a little puzzled that they do not find infallibility proclaimed in the writings of the extreme papalists of the high Middle Ages—men like Giles of Rome, James of Viterbo, Augustinus Triumphus. In fact, the presuppositions that historians have commonly brought to the consideration of this question have made it impossible for them to frame a convincing account of how the doctrine first came to be formulated.

The history of the doctrine of papal infallibility has been rather neglected by recent scholars; but the subject received its fair share of attention in the controversies of 1870. Then two general lines of argument emerged which we can illustrate in their more extreme forms from the polemical writings of Manning and Döllinger.[2] Manning maintained that the doctrine of papal infallibility had been held by the church from its first foundation. Among scriptural texts he emphasized especially Luke 22.32. "I have prayed for you Peter that your faith shall not fail." And he insisted that the stability of the faith of the Roman see had been acknowledged by the Fathers from the time of Irenaeus onward. Manning conceded that none of the texts that he produced from the first fifteen centuries of the church's history actually asserted that the pope was infallible. What they proved, he maintained, was that the church had constantly acted on the assumption that this was the case. The doctrine of papal infallibility was "in possession" down to the time of the Council of Constance. It was never challenged before the fifteenth century. That is the reason, according to Manning, why we find the doctrine overtly stated and defended only from the fifteenth century onward. Manning was really relying on an argument from silence. "The thought that either the See or the Successor of Peter could fail in faith is not to be found in those thousand years (from the fifth century to the fifteenth century)," he wrote. For Manning, the fact that the doctrine of infallibility was not denied in the early church proved that it was universally accepted.

For Döllinger, on the other hand, the silence of the early Fathers and councils concerning papal infallibility established beyond doubt that the doctrine was utterly alien to the primitive church. "Up to the time of the Isidorian forgeries no serious attempt was made anywhere to introduce the neo-Roman theory of Infallibility. The popes did not dream of laying claim to such a privilege." Döllinger attri-

---

2 H. E. Manning, *The Oecumenical Council and the Infallibility of the Roman Pontiff* (London, 1969) ; J. J. I. von Döllinger (Janus), *The Pope and the Council* (Boston, 1870).

buted the subsequent growth of the doctrine to "forgeries and fictions." He emphasized especially a text of the pseudo-Isodorian forgeries on the mid-ninth century, "The Roman church remains to the end free from the stain of heresy." Misled by such forgeries, later popes and canonists propounded wildly exaggerated theories of papal power. Pope Gregory VII in particular "must have held the prerogative of Infallibility the most precious jewel of his crown." Döllinger traced the influence of the pseudo-Isodorian forgeries through the canonistic collections of Deusdedit, Anselm of Lucca and Burchard of Worms to the Decretum of Gratian (c. 1140). Gratian's book of canon law was a massive work of synthesis whose appearance marked the beginning of a new era in the history of ecclesiastical jurisprudence. Döllinger correctly observed that it "displaced all the older collections of canon law and became the manual and repertory, not for canonists only, but for the scholastic theologians." He seems to have regarded its influence as wholly baneful.

According to Döllinger, the doctrine of papal infallibility was firmly established in the canonical literature of the church by the mid-twelfth century. Down to the thirteenth century, however, dogmatic theology remained unaffected by the canonists' theory, for the theologians hardly ever wrote on problems of papal power in their technical treatises. It was Thomas Aquinas, according to Döllinger, who "made the doctrine of the pope a formal part of dogmatic theology." Seeking for arguments against the Greeks he turned to the forged texts of Gratian and to other, more recent forgeries. The effect of his work was to introduce "the doctrine of the Pope and his infallibility . . . into the dogmatic system of the Schola."

There would be little point in our retracing step by step all the weary arguments of the nineteenth century polemicists about the significance of the texts referring to papal authority in the early church. But it is necessary to note at the outset that neither of the two sharply opposed positions that we have presented—nor any subsequent variation of them—provides an acceptable account of the historical origins of papal infallibility. Manning's version of the argument from silence may seem as irrefutable as it is unconvincing. But, after all, the silence of the early church was not altogether unbroken. The scriptural text most commonly cited in favor of papal infallibility is Luke 22.32. There is no lack of patristic commentary on the text. None of the Fathers interpreted it as meaning that Peter's successors were infallible. No convincing argument has ever been put forward explaining why they should not have stated that the text implied a doctrine of papal infallibility if that is what they understood it to mean.

The fundamental objection to Döllinger's account is that it is based on a radical misunderstanding of the canonical tradition of the medieval church. Döllinger was anxious to prove that the doctrine of papal infallibility originated in ninth century forgeries. But this led him to apply a kind of double standard in his interpretation of canonical texts. When dealing with genuine patristic writings Döllinger always used the argument from silence in a negative sense. Since the doctrine of papal infallibility was not explicitly affirmed it was taken to be implicitly denied. But, when he dealt with forged texts, Döllinger was quite willing to see papal infallibility implied even though it was not explicitly asserted. And, in this interpretation, he was very probably wrong. It is by no means clear that any of the forgers, or the popes and canonists who accepted their texts, the men whom Döllinger regarded as the originators of the doctrine of papal infallibility, actually embraced any such doctrine.

A modern historian cannot exclude the possibility that some eccentric or prescient pope or canonist of the ninth, tenth or eleventh century may have secretly cherished in his heart the dogma of 1870. The point cannot be proved one way or the other. What can be proved is that no public teaching affirming the infallibility of the pope was transmitted to the canonists of the twelfth and thirteenth centuries in whose works, for the first time, abundant texts for the investigation of this whole question become available. The commentators on Gratian's Decretum knew all the most important texts —genuine and forged—relating to the authority of the pope and the indefectibility of the Roman church. They did not associate those texts with any doctrine of papal infallibility. They showed no awareness that any of their predecessors had ever associated them with such a doctrine. We would maintain that the theologians of the thirteenth century could not possibly have taken the doctrine of papal infallibility from the canonical tradition of the church because the doctrine simply did not exist in the writings of the canonists.

Nevertheless an investigation of the thought of the medieval canonists provides the necessary starting-point for a study on the origins of papal infallibility for, on one important point, Döllinger was entirely correct. Early scholastic theologians offered almost no discussions on the structure of the church. In the twelfth century the whole field of study that we call ecclesiology was regarded as a province of ecclesiastical jurisprudence. If, then, we are to understand the medieval church's conception of its own nature and structure in the century before the emergence of the doctrine of papal infallibility we must turn first to the writings of the Decretists and the Decretalists.[3]

It is no part of our argument to minimize the claims that the canonists put forward on behalf of the pope in the sphere of ecclesiastical jurisdiction during the period 1150-1250. They certainly insisted that the authority of the Roman see included a right to pronounce on disputed questions concerning matters of faith; and it is certainly true that this claim of the papacy provided an essential basis for later theories of papal infallibility. In the canonistic writings of the twelfth and thirteenth centuries, however, the idea of papal jurisdiction was sharply separated from the idea of the church's infallibility. So far as the medieval canonists are concerned, there can be no question of maintaining that they took the doctrine of papal infallibility for granted but never saw any need to articulate it because it had never been disputed. There is no "argument from silence" involved here. The canonists were not silent on this matter. They discussed over and over again the problem of maintaining the unerring faith of the church and invariably came to the conclusion that the pope alone could not provide an adequate guarantee for the stability of that faith. "It would be too dangerous to entrust our faith to the judgement of a single man," one of them wrote. The canonists did not argue that an infallible head was necessary to sustain the faith of the church. Rather they maintained that, however much the head might err, divine providence would always prevent the whole church from being led astray.

The canonists were led to adopt this attitude in part by the nature of the source material that formed the foundation of their science. In Gratian's great compendium of canonical texts, drawn from every age of the church's past, they found no assertion that individual popes were infallible but they did find several cases of particular pontiffs who were alleged to have sinned and erred in matters of faith. Also Gratian included in the Decretum a text asserting that the pope's immunity from human judgment did not

---

[3] The following discussion on the thought of the medieval canonists is based on texts published in my *Foundations of the Conciliar Theory* (Cambridge, 1955) and "Pope and Council: Some New Decretist Texts," *Mediaeval Studies*, 19 (1957), pp. 197-218.

extend to cases in which he was found straying from the faith. The particular case that attracted most attention from the Decretists concerned Pope Anastasius II (496-498). This Anastasius was a relatively blameless pontiff. He reigned at a time when the churches of Rome and Constantinople were divided by the Acacian schism, which had arisen out of a late variation of the monophysite heresy sponsored by the Greek patriarch, Acacius. Anastasius went so far in trying to reconcile the heretics that, according to his enemies, he became tainted with heresy himself. After the pope's death they recorded in the *Liber Pontificalis* that he had been "struck down by the divine will." Gratian incorporated this passage into the Decretum and it was widely accepted throughout the Middle Ages as historically accurate and canonically authoritative. The medieval canonists knew nothing of Pope Honorius (625-638) who really did blunder in handling the recondite details of the monothelite controversy and whose case gave rise to interminable discussions in the nineteenth century controversies over papal infallibility. In medieval debate Anastasius served as a sort of substitute Honorius. (Dante duly found a place for him in the Inferno.)

Although the medieval Decretists knew of cases of erring popes they also had before them the whole body of texts (genuine and forged) from which the later theory of papal infallibility would be constructed. The decree *Pastor aeternus* of 1870 started out from the primacy promised to Peter at Matt. 16.19 ("I will give you the keys of the Kingdom of Heaven") and then went on to argue that this primacy necessarily included an infallible magisterium by citing Luke 22.32 ("I have prayed for you Peter that your faith shall not fail"). Precisely the same juxtaposition of texts occurred in the Decretum at *Dist.* 21 *ante* c. 1. *Pastor aeternus* presented the formula of Pope Hormisdas—"In the apostolic see the Catholic religion has always been kept undefiled" as evidence that papal infallibility had always been taught by the church. Gratian included the same formula in the Decretum along with other texts asserting that the Roman church had never erred "from the path of apostolic tradition." To the Ultramontane theologians of the nineteenth century it seemed self-evident that a Catholic who accepted these scriptural and canonical texts must also accept the doctrine of papal infallibility. The medieval Decretists showed how a wholly different Catholic ecclesiology could be built on the foundation of these same passages.

The key to the understanding of this Decretist ecclesiology lies in the canonists' conservative, patristically-inspired exegesis of Luke 22.32. Theorists of papal infallibility from the late Middle Ages onward generally assumed that Christ's prayer for Peter was intended to guarantee the unfailing faith of Peter's successors in the papacy. The Decretists knew of no such interpretation. Huguccio's great *Summa* on the Decretum (c. 1190), which provided a synthesis of the preceding fifty years of Decretist scholarship, offers a typical comment:

> *That your faith shall not fail* is understood to mean finally and irrecoverably for, although it failed for a time, afterward he was made more faithful. Or in the person of Peter the church is understood, in the faith of Peter the faith of the universal church which has never failed as a whole nor shall fail down to the day of judgement.

For Huguccio and his contemporaries the words of Luke 22.32 did not confer any gift of infallibility on Peter himself, let alone on subsequent pontiffs. They often noted that Peter's faith had indeed "failed for a time," usually referring to his denial of Christ after the Last Supper. They also sometimes recalled that Peter had erred in his judaizing policy and that Paul had had to rebuke him in this matter. According to their interpretation, Christ did not promise to Peter immunity from error in his leadership of the church but rather the grace of final perseverance in the faith. Even if Luke 22.32 had been applied to Peter's successors in the papacy it could hardly have formed the basis of a theory of papal infallibility so long as it was understood in this sense.

But in fact Huguccio and his contemporaries did not apply the text to Peter's successors. They recognized that two interpretations were possible. Christ's words could be taken to refer to Peter alone or they could be given a wider interpretation. But in the latter case they referred, not to future popes, but to the faith of the universal church. This was the common doctrine of the Decretists. One encounters it over and over again in their works and it was included in the universally accepted *glossa ordinaria* of Johannes Teutonicus.

Moreover, when the Decretists wrote that the universal church, or the faith of the church would not "fail" they were not thinking of "infallibility" in the modern sense but more strictly of indefectibility. Christ's promise to Peter was taken to mean simply that the church would always survive; it meant that the true faith would always live on, at least in some tiny remnant even in an age of mass apostasy. This is brought out more clearly in another comment of Huguccio (on Matt. 16.18):

> The gates of Hell Vices and mortal sin . . . shall never prevail so that there are no good persons in the church, whence Christ said to Peter as a symbol of the church "I have prayed for you Peter that your faith shall not fail . . ." or "gates of hell" means heresies and schisms . . . which likewise shall never prevail against the church so that they totally pollute it.

Similarly Johannes Teutonicus wrote in his glossa ordinaria (ad Dist. 19 c. 7), "The church cannot be (reduced to) nothing for the Lord prayed for it that it should not fail."

The canonists' understanding of Luke 22.32 was decisive for their interpretation of the formula of Pope Hormisdas and other texts asserting that the Roman church had never erred. Typically they explained that phrases describing an unerring "apostolic see" or "Roman church" could make sense only if they were taken to refer, not to the pope alone, but to the whole congregation of the faithful. Huguccio commented on such a text (attributed by Gratian to a pope Eusebius):

> (The apostolic church) has never erred: There is an objection concerning Anastasius. But perhaps this (pope) came earlier. Or perhaps, and this is better, he speaks of the faith of the universal church which has never erred. For although the Roman pope has sometimes erred this does not mean that the Roman church has, which is understood to be not he alone but all the faithful, for the church is the aggregate of the faithful; if it does not exist at Rome it exists in the regions of Gaul or wherever the faithful are. The church can indeed cease to be but this will never happen for it was said to Peter, and in the person of Peter to the universal church, that his faith should not fail.

Elsewhere Huguccio wrote "Wherever there are good faithful Christians, there is the Roman church." Such views were commonly expressed by the Decretists. An anonymous French canonist observed that the unerring "Roman church" was the "universal church" and an anonymous English one that the church could not err simultaneously "in its whole body." Laurentius wrote, "Although the pope, who can be judged for heresy, has erred the Roman or Catholic church which is understood as the congregation of Catholics has not erred." Similarly Alanus, "Even though the pope erred the faith endured in the church which is the congregation of Catholics." One

Decretist found the proposition that the Roman church could not err so improbable that he suggested the relevant text might have been written by an anti-pope. (He fell back however, on the usual doctrine that, in such a context the term 'Roman church' had to be taken to mean the whole body of the faithful.) Finally we may quote a text of Johannes Teutonicus which brought together the two strands of thought we have been pursuing, the distinction between the erring pope and the unerring congregation of the faithful and the interpretation of Luke 22.32 as essentially a guarantee of the indefectibility of the universal church.

> I ask of what church is it said here that it cannot err? . . . It is certain that the pope can err as in *Dist.* 19 *Anastasius* and *Dist.* 40 *Si papa*. I answer: the congregation of the faithful itself is here called the church . . . and such a church cannot not be . . . for the Lord himself prayed for the church, *Dist.* 21 § 1 v. *"I have prayed for thee. . . ."*

Evidently the medieval canonists were moving in a climate of thought very different from that of the nineteenth century Ultramontane theologians. The canonists believed that popes could err and could err in their official capacity as supreme pontiffs (as in the case of Anastasius). Of course modern theology does not deny that a pope can err. But when modern Catholic theologians have to take note of errors promulgated by popes as heads of the chuch they discriminate between official infallible pronouncements and official non-infallible pronouncements. The medieval canonists knew nothing of such distinctions. They were content to distinguish between the pope who could err—and err in any of his pronouncements so far as they knew—and the universal church whose faith could never fail. Ideas akin to the modern doctrine of papal infallibility never occurred to them. The theologians of the time, in their much scantier comments, did not dissent from the teaching of the canonists. The twelfth-century church simply did not believe that the pope was "possessed of that infallibility with which the divine Redeemer wished that his church should be endowed."

The real origin of the doctrine of papal infallibility is a curious one. The idea that the pope was indeed "possessed of infallibility" first arose at the end of the thirteenth century in the course of a complex dispute concerning the Franciscan doctrine of evangelical poverty. The originator of the new theory was Pietro Olivi (c. 1248-1298), an important but enigmatic figure in the history of medieval thought. Throughout his career as a theology teacher Olivi was repeatedly accused of heresy and repeatedly professed himself to be a loyal and orthodox Catholic. Although he formulated the first argument in favor of papal infallibility he was posthumously condemned for having despised and rejected the authority of the Roman church. Some of his works are filled with wild apocalyptic speculations; others contain only conventional scholastic argumentation. After his death his followers identified him with the seventh angel of the Apocalypse; his enemies called him Antichrist. Modern scholars disagree as to his essential orthodoxy or heterodoxy.

Olivi propounded his new theory of papal infallibility in a *Quaestio*—probably written in 1280—which posed the problem "Whether the Roman pontiff is to be obeyed by all Catholics in faith and morals as an unerring standard (*tamquam regule inerrabili*)."[4] Olivi answered this question in the affirmative. It would be impossible, he wrote, for God to oblige us to obey the Roman pontiff and then permit the pontiff to err in faith. Here Olivi went beyond the modern doctrine of infallibility. Modern theologians teach that Catholics are indeed obliged by many authentic—but non-infallible, possibly erroneous—rulings of the Holy See. But Olivi was not unaware of the need for qualifications and refinements in defining the precise "mode of inerrancy" to be attributed to the pope. His *Quaestio* ends with a page of densely packed distinctions which are of the highest importance for understanding his theory of papal authority.

In the first place, wrote Olivi, it was necessary to distinguish between different kinds of error. An error could be merely personal or it could be "magisterial," i.e., it could be merely an individual opinion or it could be proposed as a public teaching which would affect the faith of others. Again, some errors were entirely incompatible with sincere faith while others concerned matters of human knowledge which had little relevance for the truths of religion. Finally a pope might be pertinacious in error or willing to accept correction.

In the second place, Olivi proposed a distinction concerning the Roman see and its bishop. An institution might be the Roman see only in name and appearance or it might be the Roman see in true fact. The same was true of the pope.

Last of all, Olivi considered the meaning of the term "inerrancy"

---

4 Ed., M. Maccarrone, "Una questione inedita dell' Olivi sull' infallibilità del papa," *Rivista di storia della chiesa in Italia*, 3 (1949), pp. 309-343.

itself. The pope or the Roman see could be called "unerring" either absolutely or only conditionally. For instance, one could add a condition by stating that the Pope could never err so long as he remained true pope and true head of the church (and the same could be said of the Roman see). Granted this condition it was quite clear that neither the pope nor the Roman see could err pertinaciously in a matter of faith, at any rate not by propounding an error "magisterially"; for the whole church could not err and so it could not be united to an erring head.

The novelty of Olivi's teaching on papal infallibility has been little recognized in modern scholarship. All the authors who have considered the question at all have been misled by the widespread but quite unfounded assumption that papal infallibility was a generally received doctrine of the church in the twelfth and thirteenth centuries. Even Michele Maccarrone, who first published Olivi's *Quaestio* on infallibility, claimed no great originality for its central thesis. In introducing Olivi's text, he observed that the doctrine of papal infallibility was being widely discussed in the 1270's and that the Greek emperor, Michael Paleologus, had professed his belief in the "infallible magisterium of the Roman Pontiff" in his confession of faith presented to the Council of Lyons. Moreover, according to Maccarrone, Thomas Aquinas and Bonaventure both adhered to this same teaching; and, finally, the doctrine of infallibility, which was "always maintained and pre-supposed" in the church, had been widely proclaimed in the canonical works of the preceding century. All these views are mistaken of course. Michael Paleologus' profession of faith contains no reference to any "infallible magisterium" of the pope. No such doctrine is to be found in the works of Thomas or Bonaventure. And the whole idea of papal infallibility was alien to the canonists' way of thinking. The real problem, then, for a historian of dogma is to explain why Olivi should ever have felt moved to formulate such a radical and novel theory in the first place.

Olivi's doctrine of papal authority was inextricably bound up with his attitudes to the teaching of St. Francis of Assisi on holy poverty and to the authentication of that teaching by the Roman church. To understand his thought, therefore, we need to consider briefly some problems of the Franciscan Order and especially some developments of Franciscan Joachimism in Olivi's lifetime. St. Francis had taught his followers to live in a state of evangelical poverty and Pope Gregory IX had provided a juridical definition of their way of

ORIGINS OF PAPAL INFALLIBILITY

life in 1231 when he declared that Franciscan poverty—in contra-
distinction to older forms of monastic poverty—required the abandonment of wordly goods "singly and in common." All the Franciscans accepted this formula as a true definition of the intentions of
St. Francis. But, in Olivi's time, the Order was dividing into two
mutually antagonistic groups. The party of the "Community" held
that the one really essential element in a vow of apostolic poverty was
the technical renunciation of property rights. The "Spirituals," led
by Olivi, argued vehemently that "poor use"—the practice of severe
frugality in day-to-day living—was just as important.

This might seem to be merely an internal dispute over a point of
discipline within the Franciscan Order. But, for Olivi (and for many
of his contemporaries), Francis of Assisi was not merely a great and
lovable saint. Rather he was an apocalyptic figure, sent by God to
complete his revelation to man and so to inaugurate a new era of
world history. Olivi set his interpretation of the eschatological role
of St. Francis in a framework of sacred history derived from the
Calabrian visionary, Joachim of Flora. In the time-scheme that Olivi
employed the whole history of the human race was divided into two
epochs corresponding roughly to the Old and New Testaments. Each
epoch was further divided into seven ages which were associated both
with the seven days of creation and with the seven angels of the
Apocalypse.[5] For Joachim the sixth angel had a special significance.
He believed that, with the opening of the sixth seal of the scroll of the
Lamb, the veil of the literal interpretation of Scripture would be torn
aside and, for the first time, the true spiritual meaning of the Gospel
would be revealed to man. Olivi gave a concrete significance to these
vague predictions by identifying Francis of Assisi with the angel of
the sixth seal and his teaching on holy poverty with the final revelation
of the spiritual meaning of Scripture.[6] Thus Francis' teaching on
poverty had a cosmic significance. The right understanding and
the right definition of that teaching was of the utmost theological importance. The general acceptance of the true teaching of St. Francis

---

[5] Joachim is better remembered for his trinitarian division of history into
an age of the Father, an age of the Son, and an age of the Holy Spirit. He also,
however, used the "double-seven" scheme described above. See, most recently,
M. Reeves, *The Influence of Prophecy in the Later Middle Ages* (Oxford,
1969).

[6] The Joachimite texts of Olivi discussed here are printed in J. J. I. von
Döllinger, *Beiträge zur Sektengeschichte des Mittelalters*, II (Munich, 1890).
The identification of Francis with the angel of the Apocalypse was based on
the fact that Francis was marked with the Stigmata while the angel of the
sixth seal was "signed with the sign of the living God."

would lead on to a new age of the church culminating in the second coming of Christ.

But, before this final consummation, the church had to undergo a climactic struggle between the true church, faithful to the teachings of St. Francis, and the forces of a "mystical Antichrist" served by a pseudo-pope, who would attack those teachings. A special feature of Olivi's Joachimism was his emphasis on the role of the coming pseudo-pope. This pontiff would "plot against the evangelical rule." False doctrine would be proclaimed from the papal throne. Almost the whole world would be deluded. But, in the end, the tiny remnant of the true church would triumph. Then at last the church would enter the final, seventh age, an age of peace and joyous tranquillity.

Modern scholars have found it hard to reconcile Olivi's Joachimite predictions of a coming pseudo-pope, who would deceive almost the whole church, with his frequent protestations of undying loyalty to the Roman see. Some have suggested simply that Olivi was schizophrenic. Livarius Oliger, for instance, observed that one half of Olivi's mind was "perspicacious, profound, and penetrating" while the other half was "mystical, abstruse, irreparably snared by Joachimism." Other scholars have argued that Olivi's attitude to the papacy changed radically in the last years of his life when he wrote the Joachimite *Lectura* on the Apocalypse. Such views are not only mistaken. They miss the central point of Olivi's whole system of ecclesiology. The truth is that Olivi's eccentric doctrine of papal infallibility was inspired by precisely the same idiosyncratic vision of sacred history that inspired his eccentric Joachimite fantasies.

The immediate occasion that stimulated Olivi to formulate his *Quaestio* on papal infallibility was the promulgation of the Bull, *Exiit*, by Pope Nicholas III in August, 1279. Olivi welcomed this Bull with the warmest approval for, in *Exiit*, Pope Nicholas not only approved the Franciscan way of life as his predecessors had done; he also affirmed as an official teaching of the Roman church the Franciscans' cherished belief that their way of practicing poverty was the very way of perfection which Christ had revealed to the first apostles. "We say that renunciation of property in all things in this fashion, not merely individually but in common . . . is meritorious and holy and that Christ, showing the way of perfection, taught this by word and confirmed it by example." *Exiit* also declared that the Franciscan Rule had been directly inspired by the Holy Spirit. Finally, in defining Franciscan poverty, the Bull did not neglect to mention the manner

ORIGINS OF PAPAL INFALLIBILITY

of using goods as well as the renunciation of property rights. (". . . They ought not to have the use of things in any superfluity or copiousness. . . .") Olivi regarded *Exiit* as a complete vindication of his own teachings. Son after it appeared, probably within a few months, he set down his novel doctrine of papal infallibility.

Olivi's enthusiasm for *Exiit* is easy to understand. But still, why infallibility? Why could Olivi not have been content to reaffirm the existing canonical and theological doctrine that the pope was an authoritative judge set over the church? After all, Bonaventure too had seen the need to exalt papal power in arguing that the decrees of the popes provided unimpeachable authentication for the doctrine of Franciscan poverty. But he had not found it necessary to elaborate a doctrine of papal infallibility. The difference in the thought of the two great Franciscans can be explained precisely by the peculiar tenets of Olivi's Joachimism. Bonaventure never envisaged the possibility that a Roman pontiff might seek to pervert the faith of the church. Olivi not only envisaged the possibility over and over again. He was obsessed with the fear that such a calamity was about to happen. From his point of view, therefore, it was essential that the papal decrees already enacted to define the faith—the decrees of true, orthodox popes—should be regarded as, not only authoritative for the present, but immutable, irreformable for all time to come.

For Olivi, of course, the doctrinal decisions that especially needed to be safeguarded were those concerning Franciscan poverty for, in his view, the coming reign of Antichrist and the pseudo-pope would be characterized by a rejection of those teachings. Indeed the pseudo-pope would be identifiable as such primarily because he would attack the doctrine of apostolic poverty. "The pseudo-pope will be pseudo because he will err in heretical fashion against the evangelical truth of poverty and perfection." The forces of Antichrist would rise up against precisely the doctrine that Nicholas III had proclaimed in the decretal *Exiit*.

Olivi was not alone in anticipating that a future pope might turn against the Franciscan doctrine of evangelical poverty. This fear was widespread among the more radical friars toward the end of the thirteenth century. As early as 1274 a rumor spread through Italy (a false rumor as it turned out) that Pope Gregory X was determined to impose the obligation of property-ownership on all the mendicant orders. His right to do so was vigorously challenged by a group of Spirituals from the March of Ancona (a group that later came under

Olivi's influence). Their leaders declared that such a decree would be

> ... not only inappropriate but damnable and leading to apostasy and not falling under his power and so impossible.

This was precisely Olivi's position. The final point we wish to make—and it is all-important for understanding Olivi's thought—is that this was not a position that could possibly have been sustained within the traditional framework of the canonical doctrine on papal sovereignty. In the canonists' theory no pope could be bound by the decree of his predecessor because, as their doctrine of sovereignty plainly stated, *par in parem non habet imperium* (an equal has no power over an equal). For them, it would have been impossible to recognize a pseudo-pope as "pseudo" simply because he chose to take a different line from his predecessors in dealing with the problem of Franciscan poverty. According to the canonists a future pope would have every right to do this. Even Bonaventure had cheerfully acknowledged that a pope could freely change the decision of his predecessor concerning the meaning of perfect poverty (though it never occurred to him that this papel power might one day be turned against the Franciscans). Olivi declared that each pope was bound "by the commands of God . . . and the authentic dogmas of the Catholic faith written in Sacred Scripture and held by the Catholic church. . . ." This was entirely conventional. The novelty in Olivi's position was that, from his standpoint, individual papal definitions (because they were infallible) could become parts of the "authentic dogma" of the church. And this in turn explains his account of the relationship between the popes and the Franciscan Rule. According to Olivi the Rule was authenticated by past decrees of the Roman see but it could not be changed by future decrees of the same authority. Viewed from the standpoint of the canonical theory of sovereignty such a position is simply nonsensical. Given the pre-supposition of papal infallibility it becomes entirely coherent and reasonable for, on that theory, the decrees of earlier pontiffs acknowledging that Francis' way of life was the way of Christ and the apostles could be seen as establishing an "authentic dogma" that was binding on future popes.

The significance of the distinctions that Olivi placed at the end of his *Quaestio* on infallibility will now be apparent. When Olivi wrote that the church could not be united to an erring head he did not mean that the pontiff occupying the Roman see could never err. He meant rather that a pontiff who was seen to err was not to be regarded as the rightful head of Christ's church. Thus the predictions of a coming pseudo-pope in Olivi's Joachimite writings dovetail precisely with the distinction presented in his *Quaestio* on infallibility between a man who was "pope only in name and appearance" and a true pope who was head of the true, unfailing church. The vigilant faithful could recognize a pseudo-pope from the fact that he rejected the teachings of his predecessors—since the teachings of genuine popes were infallibly true. Then they could overthrow him. Olivi wanted to diminish the capacity of future occupants of the Roman see to injure the people of God. That was why he insisted on the infallibility—and consequent irreformability—of doctrinal decisions already established by preceding popes. The new theory of papal infallibility was designed to restrict the power of future Roman pontiffs, not to loose them from all restraints. Naturally the popes of the time showed no inclination to embrace such an uncomfortable doctrine.

In the forty years after Pietro Olivi first formulated his theory of papal infallibility there was a sort of hiatus in the development of the doctrine. This is the more noteworthy in that a great new body of writing on papal power appeared at this time, stimulated by a new series of conflicts between the spiritual and temporal authorities in Christian society. The subject of ecclesiology as a separate branch of theology first emerged in the numerous treatises of the period bearing titles like *De potestate ecclesiastica* or *De potestate papae*. Yet the theologians of the time did not hasten to attack or defend Olivi's novel thesis. They seem to have been content to ignore it as a mere minor eccentricity of a writer who, soon after his death, came to be regarded as very eccentric indeed.

Then, unexpectedly, the whole issue burst into life again in the 1320s. Improbably, the situation that Olivi had envisaged actually arose. A pope came to power who was determined to condemn as heretical the Franciscan doctrine of the absolute poverty of Christ and the apostles. The Franciscan leaders responded by developing more and more refined theories of papal infallibility in order to demonstrate that Nicholas III's decree *Exiit* had established an irreformable dogma which a subsequent pope could not anull. The crisis began in 1322 when Pope John XXII invited a general theological debate on the subject of Christ's poverty. The Franciscans, assembled in general chapter at Perugia, indignantly declared that the doctrine of evangelical poverty had already been solemnly defined, that it formed a part of the intrinsic faith of the church, and so was not open to reconsideration. "If a pope revokes what one pope or several has determined concerning the faith . . . the church falters and there is doubt concerning the faith," one Franciscan spokesman declared. Pope John XXII later made it clear to the minister-general of the Franciscans that he regarded such protests as insolent in form and heretical in content.

To all the Franciscan arguments, which so plainly raised the question of the irreformability of papal dogmatic decrees, the pope replied with the cold language of juridical sovereignty in the Bull, *Ad Conditorem*:[7]

> There is no doubt that it pertains to the founder of the canons, when he perceives that statutes put forward by himself or his predecessors are disadvantageous rather than advantageous, to provide that they no longer be disadvantageous. . . .

At this point of the controversy John XXII seems to have viewed the issues involved in very simple terms. The idea that any decisions of his predecessors might be irreformable presented itself to the pope simply as a threat to his own sovereign authority. He was not entirely mistaken of course. The head of an ancient church may be an infallible teacher with the power to promulgate irreformable doctrines or he may be a sovereign ruler with the power to revoke the decisions of his predecessors. Perhaps, in a sensibly ordered church, the individual head would not be regarded as either sovereign or infallible. What is certain is that he cannot be sovereign and infallible at the same time. In so far as he perceived the dilemma at all, John XXII was evidently determined to opt for sovereignty.

In November, 1323, John exercised the power he had claimed for himself. In a solemn dogmatic decree (*Cum inter nonnullos*) he denounced as heretical the proposition "that Christ and the apostles did not have anything, singly or in common." This provoked an anonymous Franciscan at the court of the emperor Lewis the Bavarian to propound a new formulation of the doctrine of papal infallibility—intended of course to prove that, since John had contradicted an infallible decree of his predecessor, he had fallen into heresy. The distinctive feature of this new theory, which was presented in the emperor's Sachsenhausen Appeal of 1324, was that it based the doctrine of infallibility specifically on the nature of the "keys of the kingdom of heaven" that Christ had promised to Peter. An ancient tradition of the Church—going back to the Venerable Bede—held

---

[7] The various Bulls of John XXII quoted in the text above are to be found in *Corpus Iuris Canonici*, ed. E. Friedberg, II (Leipzig, 1879), cols. 1224-1236.

that Peter's keys were two-fold and consisted of a "key of knowledge" and a "key of power." In earlier writings, however, the term "key of knowledge" had been used only in discussions on the common sacerdotal power of "binding and loosing" that Peter shared with all priests. The anonymous Franciscan of the Sachsenhausen Appeal maintained, in a novel fashion, that Peter's "key of knowledge" conferred on the popes an ability to make unerring and irreformable pronouncements on matters of faith and morals.

> What the Roman pontiffs have once defined in faith and morals through the key of knowledge is immutable . . . it cannot be called into doubt by any successor . . . it is true for all eternity.[8]

This theory of the key of knowledge eventually crept into orthodox Catholic theology and it was warmly embraced by Cardinal Manning in the debates concerning the definition of 1870.[9] Pope John XXII on the other hand, in his Bull, *Quia quorundam*, condemned this early formulation of the doctrine of infallibility and irreformability as a work of the devil, "the father of lies." The Franciscan theory of the Key of Knowledge could find no support in the theological or canonical tradition of the church, the pope pointed out. Its proponents, he declared, were moved by "pernicious audacity" in putting forward such a "pestiferous doctrine."

In the years immediately after 1324 the theory of papal infallibility continued to be upheld mainly by Franciscan dissidents. The greatest of them by far was William of Ockham. He warmly defended the doctrine of the key of knowledge as set out in Sachsenhausen Appeal but also argued that the doctrine of papal infallibility could be given a much broader basis. The position he chose to defend was set out clearly in his first major polemical work:

> What the Roman pontiffs have once defined in faith and morals—whether through the key of knowledge or the key of power or through the papal authority or through any power whatsoever—stands so immutably that a successor cannot call it into question or affirm the contrary.[10]

---

8 J. Schwalm, *Die Appellation König Ludwigs des Baiern von 1324* (Weimar, 1906), p. 28.
9 *Op. cit.*, pp. 90, 147. "If I understand the doctrine which I suppose I must now call Ultramontane, but would rather call, as all the schools of Christendom do, Catholic, it is this—that the supreme and ultimate power, both in jurisdiction and in faith, or the *clavis jurisdictionis* and the *clavis scientiae*, was committed first and forever to Peter, and in him . . . to his successors."
10 *Opus nonaginta dierum* in *Guillelmi de Ockham opera politica*, II, ed. J. G. Sikes etc. (Manchester, 1963), p. 835.

Ockham played a major role in the development of the doctrine of papal infallibility. And if the fact has never been recognized in all the voluminous modern writing on his ecclesiology that is only another indication that the whole early history of papal infallibility has been persistently misunderstood under the influence of modern theological biases. Ockham's purpose of course was not to enhance the power of the pope. He persistently used the new theory of papal infallibility to undermine the old reality of papal sovereignty. The whole point of his argument was to prove that John XXII was a heretic, and so no true pope, because he had rejected an irreformable decree of a predecessor. Infallibility can be a corrosive concept in Catholic ecclesiology if all its implications are worked out both rigorously and audaciously. Ockham demonstrated this with exquisite ingenuity throughout the whole corpus of his ecclesiological writings. We cannot follow here all the convolutions of his thought. The details become very complex. But there is a beguiling simplicity about his central argument. It can easily be transposed into modern terms. If a Catholic theologian believes that a true pope is infallible (in any meaningful sense of the word)—and if he believes that the current occupant of the papal throne has erred in a solemn official pronouncement on faith or morals (as many believe that Paul VI erred in *Humanae vitae*)— then the theologian has no choice but to denounce the current occupant of the papal throne as a pseudo-pope. The logic is impeccable. Few modern theologians will be disturbed by it precisely because so few of them believe in any meaningful doctrine of papal infallibility.

The origins of the doctrine of papal infallibility have to be sought in the intricacies of Joachimite radicalism, in Franciscan aberrations concerning the theology of poverty, and in the whole ambivalent relationship between the Franciscan Order and the papacy. Given this background, it is understandable that the medieval popes wanted no part of such a doctrine. Eventually, pro-papal theologians found that the idea of papal infallibility could provide a useful weapon in their struggles against Gallicanism and Protestantism. But this was only in the sixteenth and seventeenth centuries when the origins of the doctrine had been forgotten.

We have said that a historian cannot do the theologians' work for them and we shall not attempt the task here. Theologians must bear in mind, however, that there is a whole historical dimension to the problem of infallibility. Vatican Council I did not simply decree that the pope was infallible. It declared that the dogma of infallibility

ORIGINS OF PAPAL INFALLIBILITY

belonged to "the ancient and constant faith of the church" and that, in promulgating it, the council was "adhering to the tradition received from the beginning of the Christian faith." Some theologians, moreover, are willing to acknowledge that theology itself is likely to "wither away in blind isolation" unless its conclusions can be endowed with some degree of historical credibility. So far as the doctrine of papal infallibility is concerned, this desirable state of affairs has not yet been achieved.

All the standard Catholic discussions of infallibility emphasize continuity rather than change in the church's teaching on this matter; at most the authors acknowledge that the doctrine is one that has "ripened" in the course of the ages. But it is very hard for a historian to see the emergence of the doctrine of papal infallibility as the slow unfolding of a truth that the church has always held. He sees instead the rather sudden creation—for reasons that are complex but historically intelligible—of a novel doctrine at the end of the thirteenth century. The doctrine did not emerge inevitably because it had always been pre-supposed. It was invented almost fortuitously because an unusual concatenation of historical circumstances arose which made such a doctrine useful to a particular group of Franciscan controversialists. The slow process of growth that followed was a growth in the understanding of the papacy that, in the circumstances of a new historical epoch, the advantages of the doctrine for polemical purposes on the whole slightly outweighed the disadvantages.

In reaching this decision the popes may well have been mistaken. Infallibility is a double-edged weapon. The originators of the doctrine had no intention of using it to increase the power of the popes. And modern theologians, who have tried to use the concept of infallibility to enhance papal authority, have had to intepret it in ways that verge on the ridiculous. Nowadays it is the *defenders* of the doctrine of papal infallibility who labor most diligently to render that doctrine meaningless. It is the *defenders* of the doctrine who tell us that the plain words "irreformable *ex sese*" really mean "all papal definitions are open to re-interpretation." With friends like this one might think that the doctrine of papal infallibility hardly needs enemies. Yet the theologians keep on insisting that the meaningless doctrine they have invented during the past century has always formed an intrinsic part of the Catholic faith and that to abandon it would compromise the whole structure of Catholic truth.

In reality there is no convincing evidence that papal infallibility formed any part of the theological or canonical tradition of the church before the thirteenth century. The doctrine was invented in the first place by a few dissident Franciscans because it suited their convenience to invent it. Eventually, after much initial reluctance, it was accepted by the papacy because it suited the convenience of the popes to accept it. The doctrine of papal infallibility no longer serves anyone's convenience—least of all the pope's. It gives scandal to Protestant and Orthodox Christians. The papacy adopted the doctrine out of weakness. Perhaps one day the church will feel strong enough to renounce it.

XVII

INFALLIBILITY IN MORALS: A RESPONSE

All Catholics agree that, all through the centuries, the Church has maintained its fidelity to the word of God. The current debates over infallibility are concerned with the problem of how we can best express this truth. Above all, they have raised the question of whether a continued adherence to the doctrinal definition promulgated at Vatican I is indispensable for a Catholic understanding of the Church's teaching authority. As these discussions proceed, it seems especially important that we avoid misunderstandings of one another's positions. I think that Gerard J. Hughes, in his recent very stimulating article on "Infallibility in Morals," has misunderstood Hans Küng.[1] More importantly, Hughes's argumentation illuminates in striking fashion a major issue involved in the recent debates which has so far evoked little explicit discussion. Since Hughes's argument deals with a problem that has a historical dimension—the difficulty of formulating moral propositions that are not liable to falsification through future experience—a historian may be permitted an attempt at further clarification.

Let me first explain what I take to be the neglected "major issue" of the modern debate. Everyone seems to agree on this point at least, that the concepts of infallibility and irreformability are very complex. Over and over again one reads that, if they are not to be rejected outright, such concepts need to be rethought, reunderstood, reinterpreted. Even before the controversy over Küng's book broke out, Karl Rahner was writing that there could be no exercise, in the future, of an infallible magisterium "as it was formerly conceived of."[2] Moreover, in the course of the recent debates, a surprising degree of consensus has emerged concerning the scope of the teaching authority that a pope can actually exercise in the modern world. It is apparently more limited than we used to suppose. The central issue at stake, therefore, is not whether the pope is infallible in some simple, old-fashioned sense of the word "infallible." It seems clear that he is not—at any rate, it seems clear that Rahner and Küng and their various supporters are agreed on this point. What is by no means clear is how far the newer ways of looking at papal authority are compatible with the doctrine of papal infallibility that was defined at Vatican I and reaffirmed at Vatican II. This is the issue that, I think, requires further discussion.

[1] Gerard J. Hughes, "Infallibility in Morals," THEOLOGICAL STUDIES 34 (1973) 415-28.
[2] "Zum Begriff der Unfehlbarkeit in der katholischen Theologie," in *Zum Problem Unfehlbarkeit* (Freiburg, 1971) pp. 9-26. The article was originally published in 1970.

508

Catholic scholars who argue that the doctrinal definition of 1870 is no longer defensible are always accused of naivety, of failing to understand the subtleties of modern theological discourse, of attacking simplicistic positions which modern proponents of papal infallibility are no longer interested in defending. Such scholars may reply—sometimes indignantly but usually with little effect—that the extremely subtle and fine-spun theories which modern proponents of papal infallibility are interested in defending bear little or no resemblance to the doctrine actually defined in 1870—which they continue to find unacceptable. More overt debate on this point might be useful. It might even help to clear the air. After all, a theologian ought not to condemn those who have explicitly attacked the doctrine of 1870 without considering how far he himself has implicitly abandoned it.

Hughes's article provides an excellent example of the point I am making. The author does not question the theology of infallibility underlying the definition of Vatican I. Nor does he reject the actual formula which declares that ex-cathedra definitions of the pope in faith and morals are irreformable. But he maintains that, in fact, the pope cannot promulgate irreformable definitions on moral questions. Küng, needless to say, is in entire agreement on this point. But Hughes is sharply critical of Küng. In the following note I want to argue two points: (1) that Hughes has misunderstood Küng, and (2) that Hughes's position is incompatible with the doctrinal definition of 1870.

HUGHES AND KÜNG

Hughes's criticism of Küng is directed against Küng's use of phrases like "infallible propositions," "infallible and immutable propositions of faith," and especially "propositions that are a priori infallible." Along with other recent critics, Hughes points out that only persons can be fallible or infallible; propositions are simply true or false. The point might seem fairly trivial. Küng, after all, was simply following a common usage of other writers on infallibility. But according to Hughes, Küng's language leads to a major confusion of thought, a confusion between infallibly defined propositions and necessarily true propositions. Hughes invites us to consider the following statements: (1) "If an infallible person teaches that p, then it necessarily follows that p is true." (2) "If an infallible person teaches that p, then p is a necessary truth." He then suggests that "Confusion between (1) and (2) is surely behind Küng's talk about 'infallible propositions' . . ." (p. 416).

It seems to me that this is not the case. Küng's meaning is indicated in one of his first uses of the term "a priori" (*von vornherein*). "The pope does not err, not merely in fact, in ex cathedra decisions; but in such decisions, in principle, a priori, he cannot err." [3] If this early usage of the term "a priori" is borne in mind, the meaning of all Küng's later references to a priori infallible propositions is plain enough. He is simply making the point that if such propositions existed, they would not merely be true; in addition, we *would know* a priori that they were true simply because they proceeded from an infallible teaching authority. Thus he writes: "By infallible propositions we mean—wholly in the sense of Vatican I—statements which must be considered as guaranteed a priori to be free from error . . . ." [4] Küng is intending to say only what Hughes has said in the statement "If an infallible person teaches that p, then it necessarily follows that p is true." Küng merely adds that we also know beforehand, *von vornherein*, that the teaching of the infallible person will be true. This is what he means by "a priori infallible propositions." [5]

Of course, Küng is really concerned to argue that there is no infallible teaching authority in the Church and that there are no propositions from which, a priori, the possibility of error must be excluded. His argument is always cast in a negative and somewhat elliptical form and it is perhaps not overclear in places. Küng believes, of course, that the Church affirms permanent truths, doctrines that always have been true and always will be true. His point is simply that we cannot know beforehand, a priori, that a given statement will enunciate such a truth simply because it proceeds from a particular organ of the Church's magisterium. In arguing this point, Küng suggests that because of the inherent imperfections of human language we cannot be certain a priori that any verbal statement will be wholly free from error. Readers may not find this argument and its applications convincing. But, at any rate, Küng's argument does not involve the particular error for which Hughes reproaches him. Küng states that "infallible propositions" (the teachings of an infallible authority) can be known a priori to be true; but he does not state that they enunciate "necessary truths." In one phrase that Hughes finds particularly obnoxious, Küng seems to be struggling to make precisely this distinction. He refers to "propositions that are not regarded as self evident in the philosophical sense, though theological infallibility is attributed to them." [6] Küng is indicating that, typically, the content of a supposedly "infallible proposition" will not be a "self evident" or a "necessary" truth. Nevertheless theologians will hold that the proposi-

---

[3] *Infallible? An Inquiry* (Garden City, N.Y., 1971) pp. 140–41.
[4] *Op. cit.*, p. 150.
[5] Küng has recently explained this in more detail; see *Fehlbar? Eine Bilanz* (Zurich, 1973) pp. 351 ff.
[6] I have given the translation used by Hughes. The wording is slightly different in the American edition of *Infallible?* (see p. 170).

tion is bound to be true in a different sense. It has to be true, they maintain, because it proceeds from an unerring authority.

The distinction between infallibly defined propositions and necessary truths is not of the greatest importance for Küng. But it is all-important for Hughes. Necessary truths are timeless truths, he points out. If, then, we confuse infallibly defined propositions with necessary truths, we are liable to take a "further downhill step" and suppose that infallibly defined propositions must always express "timeless truths" or "be true for all time." Hughes maintains that this is not the case. In particular, he holds that infallibly defined propositions regarding morals *cannot* be "timeless truths."

In introducing his discussion of this problem Hughes puts forward for analysis the following statements: (1) Murder is wrong; (2) There are three persons in God; (3) Britain is a member of the Common Market. The first statement is true, necessary, and timeless merely because it is tautologous. (The word "murder" implies the idea of wrongful killing.) The second statement is not tautologous but it is also true, necessary, and timeless. The third statement is true but it is neither necessarily true nor timelessly true, as the other two are. At one time Britain was not a member of the Common Market, and at some time in the future she may again not be a member. And yet there is still a sense, a "weak sense" Hughes calls it, in which any true statement is true for all time. Whatever happens to Britain in future, it will always be true that Britain was a member of the Common Market in 1973. The purpose of Hughes's argument is to prove that all moral principles—provided that they are stated rigorously "in normal form" so as to avoid tautology—can be timeless only in the "weak sense" of proposition 3 above. We can say only that if a moral statement was once true, it will always be the case that it was once true, even if at some future time it ceases to be true. But moral truths can be infallibly defined according to the definition of 1870. Theologians, therefore, should not confuse infallibly defined truths with "necessary truths." Nor should they suppose that infallibly defined truths are necessarily "true for all time."

Hughes arrives at this position by an argument that takes as its starting point the criticism of a supposed confusion in Küng's work. It should be noted, however, that when Küng writes of "infallible and immutable propositions," he is not differing from other Catholic theologians in his understanding of the nature of infallibly defined doctrines. (The difference is simply that Küng does not believe such doctrines exist.) It has been common ground in earlier discussions that if a doctrine has been infallibly defined, it must in principle remain immutably true. Thus on the central point at issue—whether an infallible authority can put forth irreformable doctrines in the area of moral teaching—the view that Hughes rejects is not a mere eccentricity of Küng. It is a view that hitherto has been held by nearly all Catholic theologians. As to the initial point about the proper use of the word "infallible," Hughes is right in principle, of course. Only a person (or an institution) can be infallible. Propositions and teachings can only be true or false. The problem has perhaps arisen because, when we are writing of infallibility, we usually have papal infallibility in mind, and the vast majority of the pope's definitions are not infallibly defined truths. When we want to refer to such truths, it is not enough, then, to write "papal definitions." We should have to write something like "papal definitions promulgated by the pope in his capacity as an infallible teacher and satisfying all the requirements for an infallible pronouncement." Phrases like "infallible definitions" and "infallible propositions" have been used by many writers (including myself) as useful pieces of verbal shorthand to avoid such circumlocutions. But they are not strictly accurate, and if they give rise to misunderstandings we ought to try to avoid them in the future. The difficulty of doing so is very clearly brought out by Hughes himself. On his first page he deplores the fact that "It has, unfortunately, become common practice to describe not merely persons as infallible, but also their teachings." On his last page he writes of "the infallible teaching of the Church."

HUGHES AND INFALLIBILITY

Like many recent writers on the problem of infallibility, Hughes is much concerned with the "time-bound" nature of moral principles. We can perhaps best illustrate his approach to the question by considering a familiar example of such a principle, one that the Church formerly upheld but that has not proved to be of permanent validity: "Of its intrinsic nature, all taking of interest on loans is wrong." Küng cited this principle and the general prohibition of usury in the Middle Ages that was based on it as an example of an error of the universal Church in the area of moral teaching. But in the agrarian world of the early Middle Ages the prevailing forms of usury were in fact socially harmful. The Church was probably wise to prohibit all usury in those circumstances. Küng's critics have naturally not failed to point this out. But so far as the problem of infallibility is concerned, this kind of criticism misses the whole point of the argument and of similar arguments about other changes in the moral teachings of the Church (e.g., in the matter of religious persecution). The point is that the Church was deceived by the circumstances of a particular time and place into supposing (and declaring) that a merely expedient principle of economic policy was an immutable truth of Christian morals; and an infallible Church ought not to be deceived in this way.

Medieval moralists did not argue simply that the prohibition of usury was an appropriate policy because of the observable ill-effects of usury in their own society. They maintained that all taking of interest was inherently wicked because it offended against immutable natural law and against the divine revelation of Scripture. And for centuries the Church proclaimed this moral doctrine with the full weight of its teaching authority. When a commercial civilization grew up, the Church's established teaching on usury gave rise to great difficulties. In the end the most complex casuistry failed to resolve all the difficulties while maintaining intact the underlying moral principle. If that principle had been enunciated infallibly by the Church, the situation would have been impossible. In fact, the Church eventually changed its teaching.

Consideration of cases like this has led some theologians (like Küng) and some historians (like myself) to doubt whether the Church does in fact enjoy the gift of infallibility in defining doctrine in matters of morals. Defenders of the definition of Vatican I will usually argue that, in the particular case under discussion, no strictly infallible definition was ever promulgated. But Hughes's position is quite different from either of these. He argues that all infallible definitions in matters of morals are precisely of the type represented by the statement "All taking of interest on loans is immoral." That is to say, they define rules of conduct that are roughly appropriate to the time and place of the definition but are necessarily liable to falsification in the light of subsequent experience. This, he argues, is not due to any lack of infallible teaching authority in the Church; it is due to the intrinsic nature of moral propositions themselves. "No moral proposition in normal form," Hughes argues, "can be either a timeless or a necessary truth" (p. 425). And he maintains that accordingly "the dogma of infallibility can be expected to have less far-reaching results in morals than it does in dogma" (p. 427).

Hughes's discussion proceeds from an argument asserting that all moral statements are necessarily inadequate to a conclusion maintaining that they are all necessarily reformable. Moral statements are necessarily inadequate, he argues, because in order for the statement to be adequate without being merely tautologous the subject would have to contain "nonmoral descriptions of a potentially infinite number of morally relevant circumstances" (p. 423). (The subject has to be nonmoral because if it implied a moral judgment, as in "Murder is wrong," the statement would be a tautology.) But, the author argues, it is inherently impossible to satisfy this requirement. To illustrate the point, he considers the statement "Lying is always wrong" as an example of the difficulties that arise when we attempt to formulate a moral principle adequately "in normal form." If we attach a moral significance to the word "lying," the proposition in tautologous. If we regard the word "lying" as morally neutral, the statement is untrue. We might reformulate it by defining "lying" as "not telling the truth when the person has a right to it." But here the word "right" implies a moral judgment and again we have a tautology. If we try to define more precisely the circumstances in which not telling the truth is wrong, "we can never come to the end of listing facts which could be material facts, which could make a difference ..." (p. 424). The author concludes that any moral statement can only be "true as far as it goes"; it can be valid in the sense of applying to the particular cases the moralist had in mind; it can provide a rough guide to right conduct in such cases; but it can never be "adequate" in the sense of applying to the whole range of actions and still less to the whole range of possible future actions that might fall within the scope of the original definition. "Moral principles are of their very nature time-bound; for some of the morally relevant considerations which would have to be included to make the principle more adequate will have to be described in terms which become available only at a later date" (p. 425).

If all this is true, it follows that "moral principles of their very nature cannot be completely irreformable" (p. 425). If a moral principle is inadequate, there must always be a possibility that it will be proved false by a subsequently emerging case. (If we find one single example in which the taking of interest is licit, then the general statement "All taking of interest is wrong" is not merely inadequate; it is false.) Hughes sees this clearly enough and insists on it. He maintains, therefore, that all moral principles must be reformable, and not only in language and in mode of expression. Also, "they will necessarily be reformable in regard to their content" (p. 426).

But what, then, are we to make of Vatican I's statement that ex-cathedra pronouncements on faith and morals are "irreformable of themselves"? Hughes replies that all true statements are timeless and irreformable in the "weak sense" of the words, just as the statement "England is a member or the Common Market" is (as we have described) timelessly true in a weak sense. "Irreformability in morals must therefore mean that if a moral principle ever was true, however inadequately, then it will at all times remain the case that it was true, however inadequately" (p. 426). To take the example we have already considered: if it was roughly true in the twelfth century that the taking of interest on loans was wrong, it will always be the case that it was roughly true in the twelfth century that the taking of interest on loans was wrong. Apparently Hughes takes this to be the real inner meaning of the doctrine enunciated at Vatican I about the inherent irreformability of infallibly defined moral teachings. He is not calling into question the validity of the Council's definition. On the contrary, he refers to it approvingly, writing of "the irreformability insisted upon—and quite rightly, in my view—by Vatican I." It is just that, when we are dealing with moral questions, an unusual connotation must be attached to the word "irreformable." The argument is not that the Church lacks the authority to define infallibly in matters of morals; it is rather that—because of the intrinsic nature of moral propositions—when the Church does define infallibly in this area, its definitions cannot be irreformable in the normal sense of the word.

I am reminded of a common medieval argument that was applied analogously to various modes of exercise of ecclesiastical authority. If a priest pronounced the words of consecration over oatcakes instead of over wheaten bread, the consecration would not produce an act of transubstantiation. This would not be due to any defect in the sacerdotal power of the priest; it would be due to the inherent nature of the material to which his sacerdotal power was applied. Hughes argues somewhat similarly. When the Church defines infallibly a truth of morals, the definition does not produce an irreformable doctrine. This is not due to any defect in the defining power of the Church; it is due to the inherent nature of the subject to which the defining power is applied.

This argument seems to me invalid. The most obvious, simple response to it on an elementary level might be to point out that the Church has, from the beginning, enunciated moral principles that have proved to be "timeless" in the strong sense of the word. Let us take the most obvious example: "To love all men is good." Following the strict logic of Hughes's argument, we should have to maintain that, although this principle has not yet been proved false by experience, there must always exist a possibility that this will happen in the future. ("No moral principle in normal form ... can be either a timeless or a necessary truth.") Perhaps one day, then, we shall discover some race of humankind that ought to be hated. Jesus gave us a good rough rule of conduct but, because of the intrinsic nature of moral principles, He could not be entirely adequate in this area.

Evidently, to a Christian, this is nonsense. Hughes would perhaps prefer to assert that the proposition "To love all men is good" is not expressed in normal form because it is tautologous. It does not seem to me that this is the case. Missionaries who have to convince non-Christian peoples that they should love their enemies could perhaps provide evidence on the point. But even if we agree that the statement is tautologous, uncomfortable consequences still follow from the argument. As Hughes points out, moral propositions are "unhelpful" when they are necessarily true simply because they are tautologous (p. 421). We are left with the unconsoling reflection that the most fundamental moral affirmations of the Christian Church are either tautologous, and so not helpful, or nontautologous, and so not timeless.

But the fact that Hughes's argument leads to uncomfortable conclusions does not in itself prove that the argument is invalid. To demonstrate this, we need to reflect for a few moments on the inherent nature of the infallible teaching authority that was claimed for the Church at Vatican I. Hughes maintains that, although the Church is infallible, it cannot promulgate doctrines in matters of morals that are irreformable in content. I would maintain that if the Church were infallible, then it most certainly could promulgate such doctrines, and that, accordingly, to deny that the Church can promulgate irreformable moral teachings is to deny that the Church is infallible in this area. This conclusion is not vitiated by Hughes's arguments about the intrinsic nature and necessary inadequacy of moral propositions. The reason is that Hughes's arguments (by their own intrinsic nature) cannot possibly apply to the pronouncements of an infallible Church.

Let us consider again our familiar statement "All taking of interest on loans is sinful." This statement has indeed turned out to be false or, at any rate, inadequate. But Hughes argues that all such statements, by their very nature, must necessarily be inadequate. And this does not seem to be the case. Let us suppose that the number of ways of taking interest on loans is indeed infinite. There is nothing in the linguistic or logical structure of our statement to exclude the possibility that it might apply to each and every instance of interest-taking. Hughes surely cannot be asserting that it is intrinsically impossible for a general rule to apply to an infinite number of instances. Why, then, should he assert that "No moral principle ... can be either a timeless or a necessary truth" and that "Moral principles of their very nature cannot be completely irreformable"?

Hughes does not fail to provide an answer to this question, and it is a very simple and commonsensical one. He offers much intricate and interesting argumentation about truth, necessity, and timelessness. But, at bottom, his assertion that all moral principles are reformable does not depend on this argumentation. His assertions are not justified by the arguments about the necessary structure of moral propositions; rather they are justified (if at all) by an argument about the necessary limits of human understanding. Hughes maintains that every principle a moralist can formulate must necessarily be inadequate because the moralist

516

cannot be aware of all the range of possible applications of his principle at the time when he formulates it. Still less can the human mind of the moralist foresee all the possible future applications of his principle. Therefore no moral principle can be irreformable. This is the essence of Hughes's argument. Fortunately he states it for us in very plain and unambiguous language. "The thesis depends simply on the fact (as I assume it is a fact) that our factual knowledge at any given time is incomplete..." (p. 426).

But such a thesis cannot possibly apply to a supposedly infallible, divinely guided Church. God's knowledge is not incomplete. No theologian has ever argued that the exercise of infallible teaching authority in the Church is an exercise of unaided human intellect. The underlying premise of every theory of ecclesial infallibility is a belief that in certain circumstances the Church enjoys divine assistance in promulgating doctrines on faith and morals. This was, of course, written into the dogmatic definition of 1870: "We teach and define that ... the Roman pontiff, when he speaks ex cathedra..., by the divine assistance promised to him in blessed Peter, is possessed of that infallibility with which the divine Redeemer willed that His Church should be endowed for defining doctrine regarding faith and morals, and that therefore such definitions of the Roman pontiff are irreformable of themselves...."

In referring to "divine assistance," we are not, of course, suggesting that infallibly defined doctrines proceed from direct divine inspiration. The argument can be better put in the more usual negative form. In an infallible Church, divine providence would prevent the magisterium from defining, as permanent truths, moral principles that could prove false in the light of subsequent experience. It does not follow from the definition of Vatican I that the Church can mechanically grind out an infallibly defined answer to each new moral problem that arises. But it does follow that when and if the Church feels able to define a doctrine with the full weight of its authority, that doctrine will be valid for all time. The whole point of claiming infallibility for the Church is that, in the case of an infallibly defined proposition, divine assistance prevents the errors that would normally arise from the necessary limits of human knowledge.

Once this central premise of the theology of infallibility is acknowledged—that the Church enjoys divine assistance when defining infallibly—then all Hughes's argumentation about the necessary "inadequacy" and "time-bound" nature of moral propositions disintegrates; or, at any rate, it can be seen to be irrelevant when we are discussing the teachings of an infallible Church. According to Hughes's own arguments, there is no reason why a Church guided by an omniscient God should not define moral principles that are both adequate and timeless—that is, irreforma-

XVII

INFALLIBILITY IN MORALS 517

ble in the strong sense of the word. When, therefore, Hughes maintains that all moral principles defined by the Church are "necessarily . . . reformable with regard to their content," he is not really making a statement about the intrinsic nature of moral propositions; he is denying the infallibility of the Church.

CONCLUSION

Hughes has analyzed with great clarity and perspicacity the difficulties inherent in the task of framing an irreformable moral principle. As we have indicated above, a historian, approaching this same problem from his different perspective, finds abundant evidence of these difficulties in the actual changes that have occurred in the Church's teachings on certain moral questions over the course of the centuries. It may be that Hughes is right in his central contention. It may be that the Church cannot define a moral doctrine in such a way as to guarantee in advance that the content of the doctrine will remain irreformable through the whole course of future time. But we ought not to suppose that one can maintain this point of view while still adhering to the doctrine of infallibility as it was defined at Vatican I.

JOHN PETER OLIVI AND PAPAL INERRANCY: ON A
RECENT INTERPRETATION OF OLIVI'S ECCLESIOLOGY

There are some areas of theology where an accurate knowledge of the history of a doctrine is especially helpful in understanding the nature of the doctrine itself. This seems most obviously true concerning papal infallibility—the doctrinal decree of 1870 specifically referred to "a tradition received from the beginning of the Christian faith." We can hardly provide an adequate theological interpretation of those words unless we know something, on the different level of historical understanding, about how the doctrine of infallibility first came to be articulated and how the ways of expressing it developed over the course of the centuries.[1]

In two recent books Ulrich Horst has made notable contributions to our understanding of this development.[2] But in the second one he offers a new interpretation of John Peter Olivi's teaching which seems to me unconvincing. Specifically, he denies that Olivi asserted any meaningful doctrine of papal infallibility. Since Horst's argument is presented as a critique of my own interpretation of Olivi, and since Olivi's texts are of really crucial importance for understanding the theology of infallibility in its early, formative phase, a response may help to advance our understanding in this difficult matter.

Probably writing around 1280, Olivi included in his treatise *De perfectione evangelica* a *quaestio* with the title "Whether the Roman pontiff is to be obeyed by all Catholics in faith and morals as an unerring rule (*tamquam regula inerrabilis*)."[3] In a book published in 1972, I treated Olivi's work as a major innovative step in the emergence of the doctrine of papal infallibility and related it to the Franciscan disputes of the 13th century in which Olivi was involved.[4] There are indeed scattered letters from the pontificates of earlier popes—Leo IX, Gregory VII, Innocent

---

[1] For a recent discussion on church history in relation to theological tradition, see James Hennesey, "Grasping the Tradition: Reflections of a Church Historian," *TS* 45 (1984) 153–63.

[2] Ulrich Horst, *Papst–Konzil–Unfehlbarkeit: Die Ekklesiologie der Summenkommentare von Cajetan bis Billuart* (Mainz: Matthias-Grünewald, 1978); *Unfehlbarkeit und Geschichte: Studien zur Unfehlbarkeitsdiskussion von Melchior Cano bis zum I. Vatikanischen Konzil* (Mainz: Matthias-Grünewald, 1982).

[3] The text is printed in M. Maccarrone, "Una questione inedita dell'Olivi sull'infallibilità del papa," *Rivista di storia della chiesa in Italia* 3 (1949) 309–43.

[4] *Origins of Papal Infallibility, 1150–1350: A Study on the Concepts of Infallibility, Sovereignty and Tradition in the Middle Ages* (Leiden: Brill, 1972).

III—which might have been used to support a doctrine of infallibility; but they were either not included in the standard canonistic collections or not so interpreted by the canonists. Nor did they attract the attention of theologians. Olivi was the first thinker, it seemed to me, who overtly proposed and defended a doctrine of papal inerrancy.

Horst disputes this conclusion. He asserts that Olivi did not teach a real doctrine of *papal* infallibility; rather, he attributed inerrancy to the universal Church and only a sort of derived, dependent authority to the pope. Such a teaching, Horst argues, "could never lead to the Vatican definition and in fact did not do so." Horst does not deny all trace of interest and originality in Olivi's discussion—that would perhaps have required superhuman hardihood—but he does conclude that Olivi was essentially a conservative thinker who did not advance significantly beyond the views of Aquinas and Bonaventure on the point at issue. We shall need to consider two questions, then: one about Olivi's originality, the other about the actual content of his teaching.

Horst's view about Olivi's relation to his predecessors is based in part on a re-evaluation of Aquinas' thought. He suggests that there was no substantial advance in Olivi's teaching about papal infallibility because, in any case, the major 13th-century development of doctrine in this area had already taken place a generation earlier, in the work of Aquinas. On this point, however, there was a significant change of emphasis in Horst's position between 1978 and 1982. To understand his argument, we need to digress briefly and consider some of the different ways in which a scholar can approach the history of a doctrine like that of papal infallibility.

We can ask questions about origins. Who first asserted and defended the doctrine? When? Why? What circumstances made the new teaching seem to its author acceptable? (Or true or useful or necessary?) This is the kind of question I tried to address in my book, and any detailed consideration of such issues does indeed lead to Peter Olivi as a figure of central importance. But we can also ask a quite different and equally legitimate kind of question. How was the doctrine defended in later centuries? What authorities, what arguments were used to sustain it? Horst's first book dealt essentially with this latter type of question: it discussed the commentaries on the *Summa theologiae* of Aquinas written by scholars of the 16th and 17th centuries. Horst was able to show persuasively how Thomas' texts were used to support a variety of emerging doctrines concerning papal infallibility. But of course this does not necessarily tell us anything about the personal standpoint of Thomas himself. A historian, especially one familiar with medieval exegesis, will not need any modern deconstructionist critic to persuade him that the texts he studies are polysemous. They take on different meanings in the

XVIII

minds of different persons, at different times, in different circumstances. This is, after all, a platitude of the historian's craft. We all know that the text of Magna Carta did not mean the same thing to 17th-century parliamentarians as to the barons of 1215. Historians of science often make the same point. As one of them has observed, "in using the seventeenth-century point of view one often positively misinterprets some of the fourteenth-century material."[5] So, too, the texts of Aquinas took on new meanings in the thought of his 17th-century commentators.

In 1978 Horst perceived all this and explained it clearly. He observed that, when Thomas wrote the crucial text of the *Summa* (2-2, q. 1, a. 10), "he did not anticipate what an echo this text would evoke." And again, "one cannot say that Thomas taught the infallibility of the pope in the sense of the later official definition." Aquinas did not think of the pope as exercising a personal privilege but as speaking "in the name of the faith of the universal Church." He never used the phrase that later became current, "The pope cannot err in matters of faith and morals." At this point Horst expressly agreed with my view that Aquinas remained generally within the bounds of 12th-century canonistic thought, where a doctrine of papal infallibility was certainly not asserted ("Darin ist B. Tierney zuzustimmen").[6]

In Horst's second book of 1982 the emphasis was rather different. He still acknowledged that Thomas did not overtly teach the doctrine of papal infallibility that later thinkers would derive from his texts, but he now saw a significant shift, a "turn" or "change" (*Wende*) in Thomas' thought, compared with previous doctrine. Thomas did not attribute to the pope a personal privilege of infallibility, but on the other hand he did not regard him as merely a spokesman for the faith of the universal Church.[7] He made "important steps in the direction of a personal privilege of the pope" and notable progress beyond the earlier views of the canonists.[8] This change of emphasis arises from a reappraisal of Thomas' well-known text at *Sum. theol.* 2-2, q. 1, a. 10. Horst chides me (not too gently) for neglecting this text ("Es ist mehr als erstaunlich und wohl auch bezeichnend dass B. Tierney ... dem Aquinaten lediglich eine Fussnote widmet, in der er nicht einmal auf *S th* II-II 1, 10 eingeht").[9]

---

[5] J. E. Murdoch and E. D. Sylla, *The Cultural Context of Medieval Learning* (Dordrecht/Boston: D. Reidel, 1975) 347.

[6] *Papst–Konzil–Unfehlbarkeit* 7, 22. Horst added that Thomas did not discuss the problems concerning a heretical pope and the relations between pope and council that arose in the works of the canonists.

[7] *Unfehlbarkeit und Geschichte* 218.

[8] Ibid. 219.

[9] Ibid. 219. Horst finds it "more than astonishing" that I devoted only a footnote to Aquinas and did not discuss 2-2, q. 1, a. 10. I find it mildly surprising that Horst did not trouble to read on in my book as far as p. 245, where he would have discovered another

To Horst it seems that my preoccupation with canonistic literature has prevented me from seeing the "turn" in Aquinas' thought; to me it seems that Horst's lack of familiarity with the earlier writings of the canonists makes it difficult for him to see how closely Aquinas adhered to their teachings.

At 2-2, q. 1, a. 10, Aquinas raised the question "whether it pertains to the supreme pontiff to formulate a creed (*symbolum fidei*)." He concluded: "The promulgation of a creed is made in a general council. But a council of this sort can be convoked only by authority of the supreme pontiff . . . therefore the promulgation of a creed pertains to the authority of the supreme pontiff." Horst emphasizes one of the supporting arguments: "The promulgation of a creed pertains to the authority of the one to whose authority it pertains to determine finally the things that are of faith, that they may be held by all with unshaken faith (*inconcussa fide*). But this pertains to the authority of the supreme pontiff. . . . " It is here that Horst finds the "turn" in Aquinas' thought, specifically in the use of the words *inconcussa fide*.

In fact, it is far from clear that Thomas intended to make any new claim for the pope at this point. His text is so ambiguous that it was quoted by both sides in the disputes of 1870. One obvious approach to the words emphasized by Horst would suggest that they were carrying on the thought of the previous argument. The meaning would then be that, when a creed had been agreed upon in a general council, it was promulgated by the pope to be held by all with unshaken faith. This seems confirmed later on, in Thomas' response *ad secundum*, where again he stated that new creeds were drawn up in general councils.[10]

If this is what Thomas meant, then of course his thought was quite traditional. We can certainly agree that he did not regard the pope as a mere "spokesman" for the Church, but it is hard to see why Horst regards this as an advance in doctrine. No major theologian or canonist of the time regarded the pope as simply a spokesman. They all considered him the divinely ordained head of the Church, to whom "greater and more

---

substantial footnote, devoted to this particular text. Horst might also have mentioned here my subsequent article which discussed in detail the canonistic background of 2-2, q. 1, a. 10, "A Scriptural Text in the Decretales and in St. Thomas: Canonistic Exegesis of Luke 22-32," *Studia Gratiana* 20 (1976) 363–77.

[10] In another work Aquinas noted that a pope could give judgment in a disputed matter of faith without summoning a general council—here again following earlier canonistic doctrine (*De potentia* 10, 4, ad 13). Since Horst lays such stress on the words *inconcussa fide*, we may note that Aquinas did not use this language when discussing the pope's authority specifically outside the context of general councils.

difficult matters" were to be referred, a supreme judge in matters of faith. But they did not regard his judgments as necessarily unerring.[11]

At the time when Thomas wrote, there already existed a large body of commentary on the canonistic and scriptural texts that he quoted in support of his arguments at 2-2, q. 1, a. 10. These texts had not hitherto been understood as implying a doctrine of papal infallibility. It seems to me unlikely that Thomas was intending to impose a new meaning on them without any further indication to his readers that he was doing so.[12] But in the end, we cannot know for certain whether Aquinas did actually consider the pope to be infallible in any sense. As Yves Congar has explained, "Perhaps it is possible to deduce that from his teaching, but the reasoning process must be supplied by us. For it is not certain that Thomas would have said it, or, if he did, he might well have added a condition to the conclusion."[13]

If Aquinas had really wanted to deduce a doctrine of papal infallibility from the existing doctrines concerning papal primacy and sovereignty, there were many obstacles inherent in earlier canonistic and theological tradition that he would have had to overcome—e.g., that a general council possessed a greater authority than a pope alone, that some popes had erred in faith, that Christ gave authority to all the apostles and not to Peter alone, that Paul rebuked Peter. Later defenders of papal infallibility, beginning with Peter Olivi, did raise such objections in order to refute them. Aquinas did not. Horst indeed emphasized Aquinas' lack of interest in possible limitations to papal power as an advance in his thought. But the point is that Aquinas never had occasion to raise the obvious objections, because he never chose to ask the relevant question: whether the pope was unerring in his pronouncements on faith and morals.[14] And

---

[11] This common teaching of the medieval canonists may seem paradoxical—that the pope could be supreme judge in matters of faith and yet liable to err. But if there is a paradox here, it has not been resolved by the modern doctrine of papal infallibility. Most decisions of modern pontiffs on emerging points of faith and morals are not regarded as exercises of the infallible magisterium; and yet they are definitive judgments, *letzverbindlich*, to use a favorite word of Horst, in the sense that there is no appeal to a higher church authority.

[12] This is discussed in "A Scriptural Text" (n. 9 above).

[13] Y. Congar, "Saint Thomas Aquinas and the Infallibility of the Papal Magisterium (Summa Theol., II-II, q. 1, a. 10)," *Thomist* 38 (1974) 102. Congar was inclined to see a latent doctrine of infallibility in Thomas' text, but he noted that the first "formal affirmations" of the doctrine came in the Franciscan poverty disputes (85).

[14] Horst is entirely right, of course, to insist that Thomas made very high claims for the papacy. But it still seems to me that the judgment expressed in my *Origins* (95, n. 3) was correct: "he claimed almost every conceivable power for the pope in church affairs—except infallibility."

of course the crucial advance in Olivi is that he did ask the question—and answered it.

In his *quaestio* Olivi not only moved beyond the thought of Aquinas but also beyond that of Bonaventure. Bonaventure wrote a treatise with the same title as Olivi's, *De perfectione evangelica*, and in it he included a *quaestio* on the same theme of papal authority. But Bonaventure asked simply whether it was fitting for all to obey one pope.[15] Olivi asked whether the Roman pontiff was to be obeyed by all "as an unerring rule." The difference is obvious.

In comparing Olivi's views with those of Bonaventure, Horst advances an argument—a mistaken one, I think—that influenced his whole interpretation of Olivi's teaching on inerrancy. Both of the Franciscan theologians, he points out, were interested in upholding the pope's supreme authority in order to safeguard the position of the Franciscan Order, which was dependent on papal approval. Olivi was particularly interested, Horst notes, to defend Nicholas III's decree *Exiit*, promulgated in 1279. But, the argument continues, there was no need for the Franciscans to attribute inerrancy to the pronouncements of individual popes in order to defend their position. The Franciscan Order had been approved by a series of popes and accepted by the universal Church—and this was all that either Bonaventure or Olivi needed to establish.[16]

But the decree *Exiit* did not simply approve the Franciscan rule. It advanced a new doctrine of evangelical poverty. *Exiit* asserted that the Franciscans had no ownership of property or "right of use" but only "simple use of fact," and that in this practice they were following a way of life instituted by Christ and the apostles. This doctrine was very precious to Olivi, but it was so far from commanding the general assent of the Church that Nicholas III forbade all discussion of it. When Pope John XXII revoked his predecessor's ban in 1321, widespread opposition was expressed. In 1323 John XXII promulgated a dogmatic decree declaring that "henceforth" it would be heretical to assert that Christ and the apostles had no right of use in the goods they had. Now Olivi, on the basis of his apocalyptic speculations, actually anticipated that in the near future a pseudopope would seek to revoke the doctrine of evangelical poverty asserted in *Exiit*. It was therefore of supreme importance for Olivi to assert that a true pope—and no one ever denied that Nicholas III was a true pope—was unerring in his pronouncements "on faith and morals." When the dissident Franciscans rebelled against John XXII in 1324, they did so precisely on this ground, asserting, in language

---

[15] "Utrum sit conveniens christianae religioni ut omnes obedient uni."

[16] *Unfehlbarkeit und Geschichte* 215, 230. Bonaventure's views on irreformability were more equivocal than Horst suggests; see my *Origins* 89–91.

reminiscent of Olivi's, that "what is once defined in faith and morals is true for all eternity and unchangeable. . . . "

This background will help us to understand the content of Olivi's *quaestio*, "Whether the Roman pontiff is to be obeyed by all Catholics in faith and morals *tamquam regula inerrabilis*." Olivi first posed a group of objections to this proposition, then a series of arguments in favor which relied heavily on canon-law citations. (The novelty here was that Olivi deployed the whole corpus of canonistic texts which earlier had been used to prove the pope's supreme jurisdiction in the Church to support a different claim concerning papal inerrancy.) Next, Olivi gave an affirmative answer to his question and proposed four further topics for discussion: the necessity for a single pontiff as head of the Church, the authority of the Roman see, the mode of inerrancy of both (i.e., pope and Roman see), and the obedience due from Catholics. Unfortunately, the *quaestio* as we have it is incomplete and breaks off in the middle of Olivi's discussion of the third topic. Thus we lack a detailed exposition of the whole of Olivi's thought; but we can still discern the major outlines of his position from the arguments in favor of inerrancy given in the first part of the *quaestio*. In discussing his third topic, Olivi wrote at some length about the infallibility and indefectibility of the universal Church. This we could be sure of, since it was defined as an article of faith: "I believe in one holy Catholic Church." Then Olivi introduced a series of distinctions designed to explain the manner in which inerrancy inhered in the pope and the Roman see. It is those distinctions in the last paragraph of the surviving text of the *quaestio* that led Horst astray in his interpretation of Olivi's teaching.

The distinctions suggested that the pope's unerring teaching authority could be exercised only in certain areas and under certain conditions. In the first one, Olivi distinguished between a pope's universal teachings and his personal assertions, and also between matters essential to the faith and other matters. Then he added that a man might be a true pope or a pope "only in name and appearance." Finally, he pointed out that inerrancy could inhere in someone "of himself or through another" (*per se aut per alterum*). Further, it could inhere without qualification (*simpliciter*) or only conditionally (*quoad quid*). For instance, Olivi continued, it was clear that a pope could not err on condition that he was indeed a true pope and true head of the Church. But it was conceivable that a "pope" might publicly teach heresy—then it would be clear that he was not in fact a true pope, for the Church could not be united with an erring head.[17] (In another work Olivi wrote: "All ecclesiastical jurisdiction is

---

[17] Ed. cit. 342–43: "hec enim impossibilitas [errandi] potest inesse aliquibus per se aut per alterum, et potest inesse simpliciter aut solum quoad quid; utpote si dicatur quod sedes romana existens sedes vera non potest errare, aut quod papa existens verus papa et verum

taken away by manifest heresy."[18]) Olivi's argument breaks off, tantalizingly, at this point. It would be fascinating to have his further reflections on the problem of a heretical pope, for Olivi was not only reviving an old theme of the canonists here but was raising an issue that would be discussed by many later defenders of papal infallibility from Cajetan onward. (Most of them acknowledged that a pope could indeed fall into heresy.) Olivi was evidently concerned in these last lines of the *quaestio* with his vision of a coming pseudopope who would seek to overthrow the teaching of *Exiit*—a teaching that could be regarded as infallibly defined and hence irreformable if (but only if) one accepted Olivi's teaching on papal inerrancy. His view was that a true pope could not err in his "magisterial" pronouncements on the faith; but a pontiff who showed himself a heretic by denying the truth already defined was a pope "only in name and appearance." [19] Horst seems to assume that this position is incompatible with the modern doctrine of infallibility; but in fact it is commonly asserted by contemporary supporters of the doctrine. As Karl Rahner put it, referring to the permanence of established dogmas, "A pope who neglected this and plainly repudiated it in a new definition would show himself to be a heretic who had lost his teaching authority."[20] To assert that a pseudopope may occupy the throne of Peter is one thing; to assert that a true pope can teach infallibly is another. Olivi, like many later defenders of infallibility, accepted both assertions.

In evaluating Olivi's doctrine, I wrote that "Olivi was, indeed, the first major medieval thinker who posed—and answered affirmatively—the question, 'Whether the Roman pontiff . . . is unerring in faith and morals.' "[21] Horst disagrees with this. Olivi's answer appears to me to be affirmative, he argues, only because I have ignored Olivi's "precise scholastic distinctions" and, above all, his view on the relationship between pope and Church.[22] According to Horst, Olivi actually presented the pope's inerrancy as dependent on that of the Church in a way that sharply differentiated his teaching from later theories of papal infallibil-

---

capud ecclesie non potest errare; et talis impossibilitas est secundum quid, et de hac clarum est quod nec papa nec sedes romana potest in fide pertinaciter errare, saltem errore communi seu magistrali. Cum enim ecclesia generalis errare non possit et sic per consequens nec capite erroneo seu falso veraciter coniungi et inniti possit. . . . Et ideo secundum iura nullus hereticus publicus . . . habet potestatem benedicendi et maledicendi in ecclesia, quia omnis fidelis maior est eo."

[18] See *Origins* 113, quoting Olivi's *De renuntiatione*.

[19] Ed cit. 342: "Est enim sedes secundum nomen seu secundum solam apparentiam. . . . Et idem potest dici de papa."

[20] *Zum Problem Unfehlbarkeit* (Freiburg: Herder, 1971) 23.

[21] *Origins* 91.

[22] *Unfehlbarkeit und Geschichte* 229.

ity. But in reaching this conclusion, Horst misinterpreted the relevant texts of Olivi and also presented a very idiosyncratic view of modern doctrine.

Horst refers to Olivi's distinctions (*simpliciter* or *quoad quid, per se* or *per alterum*) as of decisive importance; yet he misunderstands them. His argument runs like this. For Olivi, the quality of inerrancy belonged unconditionally and essentially only to God and the universal Church.[23] The Church had never experienced any wavering in the faith through the course of time. Horst finds it "astonishing" that Olivi, in a treatise devoted to the pope as *regula fidei*, did not say this of the Church's head.[24] For Olivi, the pope was actually an unerring *regula fidei* only so long as he was in accord with the universal Church.[25] The Church was an absolute standard (*absolute Grösse*); the pope possessed inerrancy only "in a certain manner" (*in gewisser Weise*); his inerrancy was only conditional (*secundum quid*) and only derivative (*per alterum*). Horst concludes: "This is obviously not infallibility in the modern sense, but at best the 'concretizing' of the general faith of the Church in an official teaching act of the papal magisterium."[26]

These last words are puzzling. They might be read as a precise description of the doctrine eventually defined at Vatican Council I. The actual words of the dogmatic decree of 1870 asserted that, when the pope spoke *ex cathedra*, he was "possessed of that infallibility with which the divine Redeemer willed that his Church should be endowed for defining doctrine regarding faith and morals."[27] Horst surely has a sophisticated understanding of modern doctrine, as is evident from his other writings. But at this point in his work, in his concern to distinguish sharply between Olivi's teaching and that of the later council, he himself seems to

[23] Ibid. 227.

[24] Ibid. 226. It would really have been astonishing if Olivi had written this. Medieval scholars, like modern ones, thought that some popes of the past had erred. (The case of Honorius was much discussed at Vatican Council I.) The problem then was to explain why the papal errors were not infallibly defined. The distinctions at the end of Olivi's *quaestio* point in the direction of modern solutions.

[25] Ibid. 228. In a sense this is true of course, both for medieval and modern theologians. Presumably no contemporary theologian is teaching that a pope speaks infallibly when his pronouncements are *not* in accord with the faith of the Church.

[26] Ibid. 227, 229.

[27] The translation is from C. Butler, *The Vatican Council* 2 (London: Longmans, Green, 1930) 295. Butler commented: "The infallibility of the Church is taken as the basic idea, the thing known and accepted by all Catholics as of Catholic faith. . . . Then it is said that the pope teaching *ex cathedra* is possessed of this same infallibility . . . another organ whereby the infallible teaching of the church is brought to authentic declaration." In fact, the argument at Vatican Council I moved in just the same way as the argument in Olivi's *quaestio*: from a generally accepted belief in the inerrancy of the Church to a consideration of how the Church's faith could be expressed unerringly in specific papal pronouncements.

distinguish between the faith of the universal Church and the personal infallibility of the pope in a way which is not consistent with the actual teaching of Vatican I. There is no incompatibility in insisting on the indefectible faith of the universal Church while affirming that this unfailing faith may—but only in certain circumstances—be defined infallibly by the pope. This was what Olivi asserted; this is what was asserted at Vatican Council I; and of course, like Olivi, the council held that the pope possessed infallibility only "in a certain manner," only *quoad quid*, to use Olivi's language, that is to say, only when certain conditions were fulfilled; and also *per alterum*, to use Olivi's words again, that is to say, not by his own intrinsic virtue but through another, through divine assistance.

According to Horst, Vatican I held that the pope was infallible "of himself" (*aus sich*).[28] But this is clearly an oversimplification. Horst had in mind the famous words *ex sese, non autem ex consensu ecclesiae*. But the council asserted here, not that the pope was infallible of himself, but only that certain pronouncements of the pope, made when certain conditions were fulfilled, with divine assistance, were irreformable of themselves (*ex sese*). It is hard to see why, for Horst, Olivi's failure to attribute an absolute infallibility to the pope makes his teaching alien to that of Vatican I. A few lines from Bishop Gasser's famous allocution of July 11, 1870 will illustrate how strongly he emphasized the infallibility of the universal Church and how little inclined he was to attribute an absolute, unconditional infallibility to the pope—and Gasser presented this allocution as spokesman for the deputation *de fide*.

All Catholic theologians agree that the Church is infallible in proposing and defining such truths, so that to deny this infallibility would be a very grievous error....

It is asked in what sense the infallibility of the Roman pontiff is absolute. I answer and frankly declare: papal infallibility is in no sense absolute, for absolute infallibility belongs only to God. All other infallibility, inasmuch as it is communicated for a certain end, has its limits and its conditions. This applies to the infallibility of the Roman pontiff. This, too, is restricted by certain limits and conditions....

We do not speak of personal infallibility, although we claim it for the person of the Roman pontiff—but not insofar as he is a single person but insofar as he is the person of the Roman pontiff or a public person, that is, head of the church in his relationship to the Church universal....[29]

---

[28] Ibid. 230.
[29] Mansi, *Sacrorum conciliorum . . . collectio* 52 (Arnhem/Leipzig: H. Welter, 1877) 1226, 1214, 1213.

Olivi could have agreed heartily with each of these declarations. They match his own formulations with extraordinary precision. There is certainly nothing so far that separates Olivi's teaching from that of the modern council. But we have not yet reached the heart of Horst's argument. When he states that, for Olivi, the pope's inerrancy was only "derivative," "mediated," "dependent," he apparently means that it was derivative in the sense of being conferred by the Church. This is how he understands the words *per alterum*. He suggests that the Church was set over the pope (*übergeordnete*), that the Church—not God directly— conferred a conditional inerrancy on the pope and could take it away.[30] If this interpretation were correct, Olivi would indeed have taught a doctrine different from that of Vatican I. But when Olivi presented his arguments for inerrancy, he set out a quite different position.

Horst suggests that, according to Olivi, the pope's inerrancy was derived from the Church. Olivi argues, plainly and simply, that it was conferred by God: "It is impossible for God to give to anyone full authority to define doubtful matters of faith ... with this also, that he would permit him to err.... But God gave this authority to the Roman pontiff."[31]

Again, in Horst's argument, the pope's inerrancy depended on that of the Church in such a way as to subordinate the pope to the Church. But Olivi argued in precisely the opposite sense, that papal power was "indefectible" because it was not dependent on any other power in the church. "Every cause and rule is more indefectible the more it is superior and higher than others and less dependent on them; but, of all the powers of the Church, the power of the Roman pope is of this sort. ..."[32]

It is hard to see how, in the face of such texts, Horst could argue that "From the beginning Olivi moved on a track that could never lead directly to the Vatican definition and in fact did not do so." In considering Olivi and Vatican I, we have to avoid crude anachronism. Self-evidently, Olivi could not have anticipated the whole future course of the doctrinal development that he was initiating. But, this being the case, it is rather remarkable how many elements of later doctrine found a place in this first attempt to expound a theology of papal infallibility. To describe the object of infallibility, Olivi used the same words that would recur in the

---

[30] Ibid. 227–29.

[31] Ed. cit. 328: "Item impossibile est Deum dare alicui plenam auctoritatem diffiniendi de dubiis fidei et divine legis cum hoc, quod permitteret eum errare.... Sed romano pontifici dedit Deus hanc actoritatem."

[32] Ed. cit. 326: "Omnis causa et regula quanto est aliis superior et principalior et minus ab eis dependens, tanto est indefectibilior: sed potestas pape romani omnium potestatum ecclesie est huius..."

definition of 1870, *in fide et moribus.* He seems to have been the first to refer to "magisterial" pronouncements of a pope in the modern sense of the word *magisterium.* He distinguished between the solemn definitions and private assertions of a pope; also between definitions in matters essential to the faith and in matters of merely human knowledge. Above all, Olivi was close to later ways of thought precisely on the issue where Horst raises objections: in his insistence "on a necessary link between the indefectible faith of the Church and the inerrancy of doctrinal pronouncements made by its head."[33]

There seems, then, no doubt that Olivi's arguments *could* have led to a theology of infallibility like that of Vatican I. The other question raised by Horst remains to be considered: *Did* they in fact do so? Did Olivi's views influence the later growth of the doctrine of infallibility or were they just a historical curiosity, a forgotten aberration? We need to bear in mind here the starting point of our discussion. To ask who first formulated a doctrine is not the same as asking how the doctrine was subsequently defended. Later theologians did not quote Olivi when discussing infallibility; they preferred to quote Aquinas, as Horst has shown abundantly. (Perhaps it is his familiarity with the later arguments that makes him so disinclined to acknowledge a Franciscan origin for the doctrine of papal infallibility.) The situation seems paradoxical. Olivi did articulate a doctrine of papal infallibility and Aquinas did not; but Aquinas, not Olivi, became a standard authority for later supporters of the doctrine. Still, the paradox is not too hard to explain. Thomas was a saint and an acknowledged great master of theology. Olivi was a controversial figure during his lifetime and he became a focus of bitter discord in the Franciscan Order after his death. In 1319 his writings were condemned by a general chapter of the Order and in 1326 Pope John XXII censured a number of propositions taken from his work. Olivi's tomb at Narbonne, which had become the center of a popular cult, was destroyed and his remains dispersed—either burned or thrown into the River Rhone, according to contemporary accounts. It is understandable that later, respectable theologians did not want to cite the work of such a suspect figure in defending their views on infallibility.[34]

But proof of citation is not the same as proof of influence. The point can be illustrated from the history of another quite different doctrine of Olivi. In one of his writings on the nature of property, he developed a theory of "subjective utility" which has seemed of the highest importance

---

[33] I used these words in *Origins* 121.

[34] On the other hand, Gallican adversaries of infallibility, including Bossuet, sometimes recalled the origin of the doctrine among the radical Franciscans, though without specific reference to Olivi. See Bossuet's *Gallia orthodoxa* in *Oeuvres complètes* 10 (Paris: Gaume Frères, 1846) 33.

to modern economic historians. One of them called it "a jewel of economic thought." And yet this theory aroused no interest or comment among Olivi's immediate contemporaries, so far as we know, and it was ignored after his death. Olivi's doctrine became well known in the later Middle Ages only because it was quoted by San Bernardino—but Bernardino quoted it without any reference to his source. Modern historians have discovered only quite recently that Peter Olivi, not Bernardino, was the real originator of the doctrine.[35]

The same kind of thing happened with Olivi's theory of papal infallibility, except that in this case it did not take a century for his influential, though unacknowledged teaching to enter the mainstream of theological thought. In 1323 a major dispute broke out between Pope John XXII and the Franciscan Order. In the course of the ensuing debates, theologians on both sides began to develop theories of papal infallibility that carried on Olivi's thought, though always without any specific mention of his quaestio. (The motives of the two sides were different of course. The Franciscans wanted to prove that a pope could not revoke the decision of a previous pope "in faith and morals," having in mind specifically Nicholas III's decree Exiit. The propapal theologians were mainly concerned to refute the argument that a pope was subject to a general council in matters of faith.)

It would be hard to imagine that theologians in either camp were ignorant of the views of Olivi; his writings had been a focus of intense debate and investigation ever since his death. It is easy, on the other hand, to see why neither side chose to quote him as an authority. The propapal writers would naturally not appeal to an author whose views the pope had condemned. But the leader of the dissident Franciscans, Michael of Cesena, had also been an adversary of Olivi and, as minister-general of the Order, had secured the condemnation of his works in 1319.

From this point onward the theory of papal inerrancy put forward by Olivi was always present in late medieval ecclesiology, though the new doctrine was slow to win adherents. The ecclesiological issues involved in the Franciscan disputes were taken up again by the writers of the conciliar epoch, along with additional ones raised by the crisis of the Great Schism. Horst has rightly emphasized the late conciliar period as an important era in the development of thought about papal infallibility. But the issues discussed in great works of ecclesiology like those of Johannes de Turrecremata did not all arise from the immediate crises of the age. Johannes and his contemporaries asked questions like these: Is

[35] For an introduction to this question, see J. Kirshner, "Les travaux de Raymond de Roover sur la pensée économique des scholastiques," Annales: Economie, sociétés, civilisations, 1975, 318–38.

inerrancy in the faith something separable from supreme ecclesiastical jurisdiction? Should we not follow the teaching of a single individual who is faithful to Scripture rather than any church institution? Does a pope's private heresy deprive him of jurisdiction? Does the Holy Spirit prevent him from erring in his public pronouncements? Such questions had deep roots in earlier canon law and theology, but they were first drawn into public prominence during the Franciscan disputes of the early-14th century. They continued to echo in the works of the Counter Reformation theologians that Horst has studied so well.

Horst is inclined to see the ecclesiology of the Franciscan disputes as only a prelude (*ein Praeludium, ein Vorspiel*) to the real development of the doctrine of papal infallibility that came later.[36] But the distinction does not seem very meaningful. (I suppose every formulation of infallibility doctrine before Vatican I could be called a prelude to the actual definition of 1870.) It is more fitting to see Olivi as the initiator of a process of development that would continue on through the centuries in response to the changing needs and pressures of the times and the changing perceptions of theologians. We do not yet have a full and adequate account of the development of the doctrine of papal infallibility. But we know enough already to be sure of one thing at least: if the whole story is ever written, Peter John Olivi will play a major part in it.

[36] *Unfehlbarkeit und Geschichte* 231–34.

GENERAL INDEX

Abbas Antiquus: Vlll 53
Abelard Peter: I 170; II 626; IV 24
absolutism
  royal: I 164,167–8, 174–5
  theocratic: I 167–8; II 626; III 556; IV 23;
    see also popes, authority of
Acacius, Greek patriarch: XVI 849
Accursius: X 408; XIII 3
Acontius: IV 37
Acosta, José de: V 305–6
Acton, John Emerich Edward Albert, Lord:
    IV 33; XVI 843
Adam (Old Testament): XIV 5
Adams, John: XII 647
Aegidius Romanus: VI 174
Africa: IV 44
  north: IV 20–1
Alanus Anglicus: II 629 n.60, 635, 641;
    VIII 48, 51–2; IX 490 n.19; XIV 6,
    13–14; XVI 851
Alberigo, Giuseppe: VII 54; X 408 n.22
Albigensian Crusade: IV 30–1
Alexander III, (1105–81), pope (Rolando
    Bandinelli): VIII 57
Alexander of Hales: VII 52; XIV 7, 12
alms: II 639, 642–3
Alvarus Pelagius: VII 52; XV 608, 641–2,
    648, 652
Ambrose, St., (c339–97) bishop of Milan:
    II 643
America: V 303, 317; XII 646–7, 650–1;
    XIII 1
American Indians: IV 29; V passim
Anabaptists: IV 35
Anastasius II, pope: XVI 849, 851–2
Ancona, March of (Italy): XVI 857
Andreae, Johannes: see Johannes Andreae
André-Vincent, Philippe: V 297–8, 300–3
Anglicus, Ricardus: see Ricardus Anglicus
Annals of Dunstable Priory: I 173
Anselm, St. (1033–1109), abbot of Bec,
    archbishop of Canterbury: XV 636
anthropology: see ethnography
Antonino, St. (1389–1459): VII 64
Apocalypse, angels of: XVI 855

apostles: X 401–2; XV passim
Aquinas, Thomas St. (c1226–1274): II 616,
    617–8 n.11, 621–2, 638, 643; III 549–52,
    553 n.14, 554, 557; IV 24–5, 32–3, 38; V
    passim; VI 169 n.6, 170–1, 174–6, 181;
    VII 50, 52; X 408 n.22, 409; XII 646–8,
    650; XIII 1–11; XIV 3, 6, 7, 12, 23 n.42;
    XV 619–20; XVI 846, 854; XVIII
    316–18, 326
Aries, Philip: VII 66
aristocracies: see constitutions, forms of
Aristotle (384–322 B.C.): III 549–51, 558;
    V passim; VI 182; XI 27; XIII 1–11;
    XIV 7
  language of: II 616
Arles, archbishop of: VIII1 48
Armenians: V 310
Asia: IV 44
Augustine, St. (354–430), bishop of Hippo:
    I 167; III 558 n.30; IV 20–1, 38; VII 55;
    XI 26–7
AugustinusTriumphus:VII 52; XI 26; XV 623,
    640; XVI 845
Austin, J L: VII 68
authority: VI 167–8, 174; see also popes,
    authority of
autocracy: see absolutism, royal
Avignon: XIV 4, 6, 7

Baconthorpe, John: VII 52; XV 640, 643
Baisio, Guido de: II 625; III 557–8; VII 52;
    XIV 7, 10–12; XV 642 n.56
Baldus: VII 57
Bandinelli, Rolandus: see Alexander III, pope
Baptists: IV 35, 36, 39
Bartholomaeus Brixiensis: IX 484
Basle, Council of: VII 52, 54, 56–7; XI 28–9
Bates, M. Searle: IV 42
Baxter, Richard (1615–91): IV 36
Bayle, Pierre (1647–1706): IV 37–8, 42
Baysio, Guido de: see Baisio, Guido de
Beccaria, Cesare, Marese di (1738–94):
    VI 168
Becker, Carl: V 295
Beer, Samuel: XII 646–8, 650